SUFFERING, POLITICS, POWER

SUFFERING, POLITICS, POWER

A Genealogy in
Modern Political Theory

Cynthia Halpern

STATE UNIVERSITY OF NEW YORK PRESS

Contents

Introduction

When we are in pain, when we suffer, we ask why. We ask why me, and not someone else? Why my child, who lies desperately ill, and not another? Why this illness, this death, this loss, defeat, lack, terror—what have I done to deserve this? What could I have done differently? Does it mean that I am unworthy? Does it mean that I am guilty? Is it a punishment for something I did wrong? One way of putting this whole set of questions is to say that it is a moral dilemma. Suffering raises the problem of good and evil, guilt and innocence, of the success, worth, or failure and lack of the self or the community in which it happens. Suffering is a moral experience, one that raises the question of the real and how it is justified. It is also, I argue in this book, necessarily also a political question. Insofar as we have come in the modern age to see suffering as something that has causes that can be known and remedies that can be devised, we have come to see suffering as both personal and political, both public and private, both subjective and objective, as something that we as human individuals and we as a human community must concern ourselves with.

The question of suffering is an ancient one. In ancient or traditional societies, suffering has always been seen as ubiquitous and inevitable, directly connected to and in the provenance of the gods, or the laws of the One God. Suffering is explained by the actions and reactions of supernatural divine beings who are beyond our ken and our control, but who can sometimes be propitiated. Suffering can also be understood as karmic, part of a grand cycle of the transmigration of souls in time, such that one's spiritual sins or moral disorders necessitate present sufferings as punishments and lessons, as retribution in this life for one's ill will or proscribed actions in some previous life.

In the modern age suffering is not only experienced differently, in contrast to past ages; perhaps even more important, it is rather that the selves that are experiencing it, the mechanics and techniques of its propagation, production, and circulation, and the logistics of its accountability, are at heart

1

fundamentally different. On the one hand, the *dimensions of the reality of suffering* have changed and continue to change and deepen so radically that we have arrived at a point where we now continually reconstitute a new world, one structured by suffering itself as an originary dimension of human experience and of time. On the other hand, modern selves in modern societies tend to see themselves as the ones responsible for the world and its history—not individually, perhaps, or even collectively, but generically. Human beings are the agents of history, the actors relevant to social and technological change. Suffering is thus, as I argue in this book, capable of being understood, and necessarily so, as a *political* question, that is, as one that opens up a public moral space for decision-making and that demands a public response through the exercise of power.

It will be my job in this book to examine how we came to develop particular models of suffering, and the notions of agency, power, causation, blame and responsibility that go with them from the early modern era to the present. Without understanding the historical context, without a genealogy of suffering in the modern age, contemporary theorizing—to say nothing of acting and responding to an economy of suffering whose growth appears exponential—we will remain confronted with a seemingly impossible knot of questions and violent urgencies. In choosing to examine the work of Luther, Hobbes, Rousseau, and Nietzsche, it is vital to emphasize that it is not my intention in this book to provide the reader with an encyclopedic exploration of the topic of suffering in modern political thought, nor am I looking to examine exclusively theorists who are themselves self-identified as concerned with the topic of suffering, or theorists who theorize about suffering as such in their works. Were this the case, I might find other theorists as relevant as the ones I have chosen here, or ones even more relevant; not Kant, perhaps, but certainly Marx, Pascal, or Kierkegaard. Nor, with a different intention, would Hobbes appear a particularly apt choice, given that he notoriously eschews both sentiment and morality, while Nietzsche excoriates both and is emphatically not concerned with the suffering of the innocent, of which he thinks there are none. The question of the value of suffering is what is at stake for these theorists.

What I will argue for here is the construction of a *problematic of suffering*, a genealogy of its theoretical and political development in several stages from the time of the Reformation. This problematic of suffering, while observable as a series of stages or a trajectory, involves, as genealogies do, several different perspectives that do not agree with each other, although they may depend on a necessary opposite stage, position or meaning for their own articulation. These perspectives involve basic fundamental issues such as the perspective of the sufferer and the perspectives of the agent and the knower, as well as the perspectives of the spectator, the persecutor, and the benefactor, and finally what has been called the aesthetic perspective, but which I argue is better understood or distinguished as the perspective of the creator. It is both the opposition and inclusion of all these perspectives that allows for the delineation of the problematic of the politics of suffering.

Suffering in our time is something we witness on a grand scale and often at a distance. When we witness on television or read in the newspapers about Azerbaijani refugee children dying by the thousands for lack of medications, or about Somali children dying from starvation by the tens of thousands, or of the millions of children in Africa dying or orphaned by AIDS, we imagine above all their innocence. They have done nothing wrong to deserve this. They are children, they are innocent of all wrongdoing, and so it is, to us, manifestly unfair, unjust, wrong that innocent children should suffer through no fault of their own. We want to ask whose fault it is that this is happening. Who made the decisions that led to these conditions, these outcomes? Who can be held responsible? What can be done? How can aid be mustered, transported, administered? To whom, of all the starving millions, should aid be given? It isn't fair, in some primordial way that we cannot fully understand, that one child is born into plenty and health and another into poverty, violence, and an early death. The question of justice, of fairness, haunts all instances of suffering that we cannot understand and this brings the question of morality, the question of justice, necessarily into any consideration of suffering and the actions it demands.

These are not the only ways to think and feel about suffering. In fact, it is not the way people for most of human history in most countries and cultures ever thought about suffering. This is a particular cultural construct, a Western response, and a modern response. In our own earlier traditions or in traditional societies, suffering is normally seen as natural and inevitable, inherent in human finitude, mortality and vulnerability, and directly connected to the providence of God. Suffering is traditionally referred to religion.

There are a multitude of different cultural and historical responses to suffering, but by far the vast majority invoke moral and religious forces to explain the meaning of suffering, especially that which seems most inexplicable: the suffering of the innocent for no reason. This is one reason for the development of such concepts as original sin and karma—that there are then no innocents. We all must bear with us from birth the taint of previous sinful existences, within us or among us, and thus we must deserve what happens to us, what we suffer whether we will or no. There must be a reason for it, a fault that goes back to the beginnings of time.

Our concept of the innocence of children, for instance, is a very particular cultural conception and certainly one that arose late in the West in the modern age.[1] Our conception that the suffering of the innocent should be acted on and remedied is also a modern notion. It depends on related notions of agency, of rationality, of scientific knowledge, and of taking responsibility that didn't exist in the premodern world. It depends on being able to delineate the conditions for accountability, for causation, and for assigning blame that are central aspects of the selves the modern age has produced: selves as knowers and doers as well as sufferers and sinners. In this book I explore how such selves came into being in the modern age; how sufferers and sinners became, in addition, knowers and agents, and then witnesses and spectators, persecutors and benefactors, and the unwitting producers of suffering; how those divisions and categories got made and how they function now to entail or curtail action, or constitute agency itself. It makes a difference how we categorize suffering.

Modern selves in modern societies tend to understand themselves, as no ancient people could, as living in a man-made world, a world in which human knowledge and ingenuity has decisively altered and established the conditions of all human and natural life. We are responsible. Human beings are the agents of history, the rational actors accountable for social and technological change. Modern selves act as citizens and agents of change, as subjects of language and thought, who create the world and continue to investigate it and to invent new remedies for its ills and new ways of getting around in it, or moving it out of our way. We present it and represent it, interpret it and destroy it, and sometimes remedy it.

Suffering is the most ancient question and the one that most urgently and intimately calls into question our moral or religious beliefs that there is justice and justification, innocence and guilt, fault and compensation, perhaps even redemption in life. It is the point of this book to trace genealogically the emergence of this modern sensibility and perspective, and the concomitant perspectives that are part of it; to show how these questions came to be the ones we tend to ask when we experience suffering, our own or that of others at a distance.

Suffering, because it is technologically present in our lives in a way that was not possible until this century (in terms of either the technologies that produce and manufacture new kinds of suffering or the techniques developed to shape, represent, and communicate it), is also the newest question, and one that is becoming more and more complicated, growing exponentially more complicated, every day.

Whereas we once needed to be concerned only with the distresses and losses of our family, our village, our tribe, our people on this side of the mountain or the sea, we now have before our eyes and minds the suffering of millions of unknown people from all over the world. And we have as well photographs of our world, taken from space or from the moon, and so we can see, with our own eyes, that we share one planet and that we are one world, interdependent, interrelated, all together in one boat. What happens to those unknown people affects us too, however much we incessantly pretend that they are "other" and of no concern to us. The events we watch are all manifestly connected, even though we cannot reliably trace the connections, and no one seems to be in charge or in control, no one has the power to act to stop these things happening, the resonating horrors of war, massacres, starvation, plague. Some people are more in charge than others, of course, some occupy positions of authority, power or decision-making such that we can point to their actions or their organizations as causally implicated in events as we witness them. But really, we have only theories about how these actions and decisions result in these events or produce these effects, and the theories have become pretty attenuated. We cannot trace direct linkages. We cannot delineate lines of responsibility or areas of moral clarity, except in the most isolated and rare instances.

Otherwise, a complete lack of moral clarity, or any other kind of clarity, seems to be the norm as far as suffering is concerned. But it is moral clarity that is at stake, for us, in the face of suffering, and that is the purpose of my writing, to show how problematical that kind of clarity is and why it is so. Moral clarity seems to be not only absent from our stage, but apparently even impossible in itself, self-contradictory and nonsensical, especially now in relation to public and private suffering. The forces that are at work to produce it on the scale we are witnessing seem to be accelerating out of control. The suffering we have witnessed in this past century is beyond belief, beyond credence, beyond comprehension. The Holocaust. The 60 million dead in the Stalinist gulag. Hiroshima. The mountains of skulls of the Khmer Rouge. The Cultural Revolution. The endless slaughters in Rwanda and the Congo. Kosovo. The list goes on and on. We cannot even imagine a way to give an account of all this. That's where we are.

Furthermore, we see suffering everywhere through a dozen different lenses, reflected in a myriad of different media. We read untold conflicting accounts of it, we trace uncertain histories, we peer at terrifying images, we produce, reproduce, simulate, replicate, reiterate, watch, create and suffer even more terrifying images, sometimes for the pleasure of it. We have become enmeshed in the production of hyperrealities, virtual realities, simulated realities—violence that is only a moment of anticipation in fantasy of what technology will make available for production in real time a year from now.

There seem to be no limits to what the mind of man can invent either for good or for evil and in its latest productions the two are inextricably mixed and meant to be so. We cannot reliably identify good or evil from a single stable perspective, much less from a universal one. We are caught in devolutions, deconstructions, deviations we cannot name or fathom, in processes that don't even have names yet, and yet processes in which suffering and its evaluation plays an integral part.

I am speaking of suffering in this book in the most generic way possible. Of course there are myriad forms of suffering, some much worse, deeper, more pervasive, more destructive or more traumatic than others. I am not differentiating them by rank, by severity, by publicity or numbers of people affected or by immutability or any number of other registers by which suffering might be measured. I am making a political decision not to rank suffering. The thorough theorizing of such differentiations will be made in my next book. On the whole I want to center this inquiry on suffering as a fundamental human experience, as yet undifferentiated, which relates to agency, to knowledge, to power and to time, all of which also remain to be differentiated and interpreted in this text. These are the most general dimensions of human life and death, and I am counting suffering as one of them. It is my intention to place suffering as such in the center of the crucial concerns of political theory, and to insist for the purposes of this project that ways of measuring the reality, the depth, the meaning, the purchase or significance of suffering change so greatly in history and in the modern age that what we take to be the most obvious of distinctions about suffering are very much the products of the historical forces analyzed here, the genealogy I am tracing in this book.

This is not to deny differences in who suffers or how badly, nor to deny differences in the importance, to one person or to world-historical change, of particular instances or various types of suffering. We tend to privilege certain forms of suffering over others, to count them as greater, harder or more demanding, or more compelling of response than others. I want to show how and why these sorts of interpretations, evaluations and privileging came to be seen as natural or necessary, and to suggest not only that this was not always the case or that it is not the case in other parts of the world or in other traditions, but moreover that how we interpret, evaluate and privilege suffering very much defines us. It will take another book to analyze how we in the West actually do characterize and characterize suffering in contemporary society, and therefore how we understand our responsibility to respond to it, or not.

If we tend to see mass killing as entailing the worst sort of suffering, as I think we do, it nevertheless makes a difference whether we see mass killing under the auspices of the Inquisition, as the Plague, or as a massacre based on nothing at all except personal tyranny. It depends on who is doing the looking. That is the point.

In this book I talk about how we came to develop modern models of suffering, and ideas of self, nature, history, and responsibility that go with them, from the early modern era to the present. In this introduction, I want to try to differentiate various kinds of suffering and to theorize the questions that suffering, in its various incarnations, raises both philosophically and politically. Suffering calls into question some of the most basic ideas of reality, value, and action that we use, and this is one reason it is a topic that stands at the center of ethical and political thought today. It is a necessary question of the nature of the real, which is maximally problematized in theory and practice today. Perhaps even more important, I want to provide an historical context here for contemporary theoretical analyses of suffering. The problems of identifying and acting to respond to suffering that seem to be growing incomparably complicated in the contemporary world come out of a heritage of religion, philosophy, morality, science, and politics that has formed our responses in crucial ways. Without understanding the historical context, the genealogy of suffering in the modern age, we cannot begin to unravel the threads or dimensions of what confronts us as an intractible knot of moral problems and violent political urgencies. The difficulties of this analysis make it plain not only how basic the issues at stake are, but also the paradoxes inherent in acting ethically or politically, in taking responsibility for suffering. The very idea that it could be our responsibility, not as sinful wretches but as masters, is prototypically modern.

The problems of suffering in our time have become more diverse and complicated than at any time in the past, the uncertainties associated with its identification, diagnosis, and responses made more incomprehensible by distance, by the conflict of widely differing values and cultures, and by technologies that both represent and produce suffering from innumerable sources, bringing them close to hand even as they make them more alienated.[2]

The impossibility of even identifying what constitutes genuine suffering is further encumbered by the multiplicity and the uncertainty of numerous conflicting cultural standards and moral beliefs. Even traditional moral and ideological schema for connecting victims and persecutors and rendering judgment are called into question by competing histories and traditions, and by the lack of clear causal links that can render such schemas operative. More fundamentally, questions about the existential reality of suffering and its authenticity, as we see it pictured around us, continue to multiply. The realities of suffering, of violence and deprivation and death, seem to demand a response, but not one we know how to make.

The experience of suffering in any one individual self is both unmistakable and ineffable, exceeding all expression and communication. Suffering is an experience, akin to Georgio Agemben's notion of infancy, that is prior to language, perhaps prior even to subjectivity, but "prior" in a way that denotes neither chronological order nor remote origin nor some mute substance that exists "before" language. The originality of suffering denotes not an origin in time or history, but an origin that lies at the juncture of the synchronic and the diachronic, a present origin that historicizes, the perpetually present origin of language and history itself, where subjects and objects begin. Suffering, like infancy, is experience itself. "Experience is the simple difference between the human and the linguistic. . . . For the very fact that infancy exists as such—that it is, in other words, experience as the transcendental limit of language—rules out language as being in itself totality and truth."[3] I look at this kind of origination and at the transcendental elements of suffering in this introduction, using the work of Agemben and Emmanuel Levinas, and ultimately in this book the work of Luther, Hobbes, Rousseau, and Nietzsche.

Suffering today blurs all the obvious modern boundary markers. It collapses public and private, art and technology, originality and reproduction, the witness and the cause, the sufferer and the production of suffering. It is enigmatic in ways we find both confusing and perverse. Take this example from the *New York Times Magazine* of June 11, 2000, an article entitled "Better Art Through Circuitry." A "technoartist" at NYU's Center for Advanced Technology, named Natalie Jeremijenko, "discusses the interface between technology and art," describing "one of her pieces, called Suicide Box":

> The Suicide Box is a motion-detection video system that was situated for a hundred days in the vicinity of the Golden Gate Bridge. It watched the bridge constantly when there was vertical motion, and it captured that on video. *It captured vertical motion—I think you're saying it recorded people leaping to their deaths. But it— you—didn't intervene?* I'm just the engineer, but yes, it did intervene, by generating information about a tragic social phenomenon that is otherwise not seen. The mechanics of having the sensor go off and release some big arm to catch these people is beyond my ability to implement. *Were the bridge authorities aware of the box?* Oh yes, I spoke to them repeatedly. *And did they ever ask to see your findings?* No, never. And when the video was shown at the Whitney Biennial, the most common audience reaction was, "Look, it's a Sony." . . . *What are you working on now?* "Bang-Bang," a set of low-power automated video cameras triggered by ammunition fire. Whenever there's an explosive event, it collects two seconds of video. They're being deployed in places where one would anticipate ammunition activity: East Timor, Kosovo, L.A.[4]

Thomas Keenan, in a talk he and David Gelber, a producer for "Sixty Minutes," gave about Kosovo at Swarthmore in the spring of 1999, elaborated on this aspect of the problem—technojournalism and its relation to the production of the violence it reports. During the fighting in Kosovo, a news team set up a camera at a certain urban intersection because a sniper was known to have killed passersby there. Once it became known that a camera was installed there, the sniper intensified his activities for the camera. In effect, the journalists were producing the killings they were representing. In one instance, shown to us on film, the journalists refused to help drag a wounded victim out of harm's way, despite the frantic cries for help of both helpers and the victim.[5]

Who is to blame in these technoart and technojournalist events? What are we doing when we photograph suffering and put it on our museum walls? What happens when recording it makes it recur? Is this pleasure? Edification? Is blame either to the point or ridiculous? What is the value of our knowledge of suffering, especially if it nullifies agency? Suffering as art and commodity, the politics of suffering for mass consumption and for pleasure as well as the problems of agency are some of the most intractable elements of suffering that require analysis and are part of what makes this book significant. It is only in the context of the history of modern science as well as of modern morality that these phenomena can begin to be mapped. Our technology and our blaming both converge in these conundrums. Our interests, our profits, and our voyeurism as well as our aesthetics and our responsibility are at stake in unraveling these convergences.

SUFFERING: WHAT IT CALLS INTO QUESTION

Suffering calls into question what is real and what is not, and how we count the real. In the modern tradition, the real takes place in the convergence of subject and object, in the correspondence of the material world and the consciousness that apprehends it and acts on it. Philosophically, pain, however, is what is quintessentially, axiomatically, beyond knowing. We cannot feel another's pain, nor can we adequately describe our own, or even identify the consciousness that suffers as our own. It is profoundly subjective and also the ownmost of our selves, experienced nevertheless as an otherness that cannot be encapsulated or sufficiently communicated. We can see it in the other, face to face, but we are unsure what to call this facility or this awareness.

Suffering is a presence to us as we experience it, an invisible presence, a demanding presence that endures and that has endurance, temporality, as its most essential dimension. Suffering is temporal presence in its most compelling force, and as such it demands presence in return, a response to something beyond language, apprehended but not known and certainly not appropriable by direction or intention or discourse. Emmanuel Levinas, in "Time and the Other," insists on the "*sui generis* implication that constitutes its essence. In suffering there is an absence of all refuge. It is the fact of being directly exposed to being. It is made up of the impossibility of fleeing or retreating. The whole acuity of suffering lies in this impossibility of retreat. It is the fact of being backed up against life and being. In this sense suffering is the impossibility of nothingness."[6]

Levinas says he emphasizes "the pain lightly called physical, for in it engagement in existence is without any equivocation." He thinks that in moral pain one can still "preserve an attitude of dignity and compunction, and consequently already be free; physical suffering in all its degrees entails the impossibility of detaching oneself from the instant of existence."[7] I argue, however, that his distinction is spurious. It is not possible to properly differentiate moral from physical pain, nor is it the physicality of pain that makes it feel as if it inheres in us. It is trauma that makes suffering intractible and inescapable, and trauma is always more than physical. In this sense, trauma is what is at stake here. Physical pain, like childbirth, can certainly be inescapable, but it need not be traumatic, and its suffering is temporary only. It can certainly preserve both dignity and freedom. Suffering willingly undergone for a purpose is different from meaningless suffering, as Nietzsche will convincingly demonstrate. Moral or psychological pain, pain that leads to suicide or to murder, nihilistic violence, pointless pain, or terror need not be physical but it is as fully inescapable. The relation between suffering and nothingness remains to be explored in this study. Because suffering runs directly up against nothingness and death, it calls into question the real at its most inescapable level.

Suffering is presence that is inescapable. It is this inescapableness that leads Levinas to connect suffering with the proximity of death. "But in suffering there is, at the same time as the call to an impossible nothingness, the proximity of death." It is not only that suffering calls to death as its end, but even that it opens up the dimension of death, as an event, an unknown that is "refractory to the intimacy of the self with the ego to which all our experiences return. . . . This way death has of announcing itself in suffering, outside all light, is an experience of the passivity of the subject."[8] Levinas stresses "this reversal of the subject's activity into passivity" in suffering.

Suffering, then, also calls into question both action and agency. Suffering is the passive voice of acting, as it were. It is the hidden opposite of agency. We suffer what we cannot act, or because we cannot act. Suffering means not being able to act. It is the dark side, the passive, negative otherness of acting and reacting. Suffering is what cannot be acted on, but only suffered. It is patience as opposed to agency. The patient is the one who suffers rather than the one who acts. What can we do is the primal question that arises from the experience of suffering, either in ourselves or in relation to what we see at a distance. Politics sits squarely in the middle of that void between active and passive, patient and agent, sufferer and deliverer. Insofar as we are the relevant sufferers in the world, we are also the relevant actors. Politics and political theory are consituted and reconstituted around the problematics of agency as these have changed over time. This is the genealogy of suffering, and thus necessarily also of agency, that is traced in this book.

Power and will, knowledge and representation, self and other, subject and object, public and private, language and world, all revolve, from this perspective, around the necessity to act and the reasons for or courses of action, that is, around suffering, the primeval, originary reason for acting. We suffer what we cannot change. What we cannot change has changed a great deal over the past several centuries, in the modern age. We have been able to change many things that the ancients and all previous peoples thought could not be changed, that were regarded as permanent physical features of the world. We are in the process of changing the genetics of human life itself, so what we can change is at the core of what political processes identify as their proper domain. Insofar as we can act, we bring politics to bear. Politics depends on and is a face of human agency. When we invent things we could never do before, we invent new political domains. What we can do necessarily involves policy, sooner or later.

On the other hand, we have not been able to change certain features of the landscape that seemed, once, transformable. While political tyranny proved amenable in some ways and in some cases to democratic revolution, reason and the social contract, certain forms of oppression and inequality that once seemed, even with violence, capable of being overcome, seem more intractible now. But the will has changed as well, and that too is part of the genealogy to be told here. Certain forms of suffering seem to be generic, endemic, or eternally recurring. Not necessarily those given by nature, as it turns out. But perhaps those given by history, which we once thought amenable to reform or revolution, seem somehow to belong to us as inherent in our very historicity and our finitude. Our relation to time cuts to the crux of the basis for action as it does to the basis of suffering, and that is what politics in our day is about. Time and its relation to suffering as constitutive requires theorizing.

In the uncertainties we face in responding to suffering in the contemporary world, several major issues recur. How real is suffering, how do we distinguish a "genuine" or "authentic" from a manufactured, artificial, virtual, or manipulated image, or does that difference matter any longer? Why does it matter? What action can we take? How realistic is it to identify certain causal chains connecting people, groups, or systems to those suffering? These questions lead us to even more recondite ones. Who suffers? Who is the subject of suffering, if the subject is no longer a viable unity or hypothesis of consciousness? Who fits the category of the victim, the masses, the oppressed? Which victims matter or count, and who gets to decide this? Who watches and does nothing? Who is the spectator, the mediator, the persecutor, the benefactor, the creator? Many different perspectives play a role in delineating the way the politics of suffering functions in our time. And these questions in turn call into question the very nature of politics as we have fashioned it in the modern age.

In this book, I begin with the perspective of the sufferer, especially as that
is represented in the work of Martin Luther. Luther is one of the first thinkers
to speak to us of the subjectivities of the modern subject and his anxieties.
He experienced himself as an afflicted and tormented soul, delivered into the
hands of a remote and unfathomable God, whose mercy and justification
had no cause except his freely given and unmerited grace. Man faced the
world as a helpless sufferer with no recourse to action or to works that could
alleviate his guilt or his doubt. Suffering was his lot and salvation lay beyond
his control. In the religious context, suffering is not only the natural condition of man but also the deserved state of his sinful soul; it is merited punishment for ineradicable moral waywardness and imperfection. Suffering
and the faith that relieves it is the sole property of man worth thinking
about. Suffering is the original primary human perspective.

But the religious context of suffering fails to survive the shattering of
Christianity in the Reformation and the glorious inventions of science and
the opening up of the geographical world that characterized the public space
of the Renaissance and the early modern age. Thomas Hobbes is one of the
first political theorists to rethink the politics of the world anew from the perspective of the man of knowledge, the scientist, and the perspective of the man
of action, the agent who can enter into rational contracts and establish order.
It is on the basis of these foundations that modern politics is established, and
this founding is indispensable to establishing the liberal political framework
within which all further elaborations of the question of suffering develop.
Knowledge and agency are fundamental categories of modernity itself.

As discussions and theoretical and ideological elaborations of suffering
become more complicated as the modern age comes into its own, even more
difficult matters are called into question by the realities of suffering. With the
politics of pity that evolves in the eighteenth century, epitomized in Rousseau's
work, the motives and emotions of the spectators of suffering, of the persecutors and the benefactors of the oppressed, are called into question and
judgments of morality are brought to bear on determining the guilty parties
and the appropriate punishment, even unto revolution. The authenticity of
the emotions of the spectator, of the intentions of the liberator, of the purity
of motivations of the accuser, or the decadence or depravity of the voyeur of,
or panderer to, suffering are all called into question in a way that was not
imaginable before this time. The creation of a kind of public space that did
not exist before modern times figures powerfully in the dilemmas that the
occupants of this public space face in regard to suffering.

Finally, the aesthetics of suffering comes to be a question in itself, and this
brings us to Nietzsche, to the evisceration of the moral point of view and
the uncovering of the inverted, sado-masochistic motivations of philosophy,
morality, and the ascetic ideal. In Nietzsche the modern liberal public con-

sensus breaks down, and its polarities are deployed against themselves to call into question the real, the actor, and the act of interpretation. The perspectives of the suffering and of the agent, of the spectator and the philosopher all come under renewed attack and together require a new, more encompassing perspective, the perspective of the creator. In the consummations of creativity and time, new dimensions of life are opened up, which include suffering as a necessary ingredient and interrogate the very intelligibility of strategies that seek to eliminate it. Suffering in the contemporary world raises the question of responsibility to its highest level, asking us to reformulate our notions of what suffering, action, and response look like, and what an ethics and politics of responsibility might entail, including the elements of memory and promising, of history and will, of the *pathos* of power in time and of the relation between self and other, as other, in face-to-face relations and at a distance. Levinas asserts: "Consequently only a being whose solitude has reached a crispation through suffering, and in relation to death, takes its place on a ground where the relationship with the other becomes possible."[9] What does it take for a being to reach a "crispation" of suffering?

GENEALOGY, DESCENT, AND THE BODY

Michel Foucault, in his famous gloss on Nietzsche's genealogy and history, stresses that Nietzsche, in developing his critical genealogy of morals, challenged the pursuit of the origins (*Ursprung*) of morality, or of philosophy, or of anything else, as a deceptive artifice, one that implies unities and essence in linear progression from a source, one that implies subjects and objects and stable frontiers as defenses against chaos, while in contrast things in history develop out of disruptions and irruptions, out of war and conflicts and the will to dominate, out of the discontinuities of passion and the will, and the clash of opposing theories and regimes of truth. The origin is not a site of truth from which truth may be deduced, but a site of loss and "the ancient proliferation of errors."[10]

Foucault stresses instead *Herkurft*, the notion of descent: "Where the soul pretends unification or the self fabricates a coherent identity, the genealogist sets out to study the beginning—numberless beginnings, whose faint traces and hints of color are readily seen by the historical eye." He emphasizes the "dissociations of the self" and the instability and heterogeneity of factors and fragments that all contribute to what the genealogist carefully assembles and accounts for.[11]

He also adds that descent attaches itself to the body, as we trace the genealogy of ancestors, "because the body maintains in life and in death, through its strengths or weaknesses, the sanction of every truth and error, as it sustains, in an inverse manner, the origin, the descent." In this he echoes

Nietzsche and we will trace this emergence of the centrality of the body, in suffering and in genealogy, in Nietzsche's work. Foucault reiterates that "Genealogy . . . is situated within the articulation of the body in history. Its task is to expose a body totally imprinted by history and the process of history's destruction of the body."[12]

It is in and through the body that life and death, suffering and time, solitude, mortality, and responsibility all have their being and location, their home. Ultimately, as Nietzsche brings home to us with violent recognition, suffering itself, human and temporal, may be paraphrased as "history's destruction of the body." Time itself is the "It was" against which Zarathustra rails and against which the will breaks. Suffering is what happens to us, whether we will or no, for or against our will, what cannot be changed. Time is a one-way arrow for human bodies, the inevitability of our being destroyed by history, by time. It is the basis for our suffering as well as the instinct, inverted, for our creation of history, religion, philosophy, morality, and politics.

Foucault also emphasizes the idea of "emergence" in the notion of genealogy, the various systems of subjection and domination, the struggle of forces against each other and of winners and losers out of which the constructions of history arise. They result from "substitutions, displacements, disguised conquests and systematic reversals." In this he ends up with a particularly Nietzschean perspective: "knowledge is not made for understanding, it is made for cutting."[13] The genealogy I am assembling in this book is made for understanding, but most of all it is made for cutting through the knots of the multiple relations to suffering that entangle and strangle us now. Genealogy, as both Nietzsche and Foucault affirm, is knowledge as perspective, and in order to create this genealogy, I have to use in turn several contrasting perspectives.

The genealogy of the politics of suffering brings into doubt some of the most basic understandings and some of the most taken-for-granted perspectives of modern life and thought. This genealogy is made out of the dissociations of the self, of conflicting views and theories, of reversals of meaning and intention, of discontinuities and denunciations, of struggles to the death and cutting to the bone. It is constructed out of several opposing perspectives that neither coincide nor cohere, but rather contradict each other, but which, in their opposition and succession, contribute to the historical and philosophical emergence of new perspectives, and a new, terrible kind of knowledge "made for cutting."

It is also a genealogy that adheres to and grows out of the body and its instinctual resources, for although I disagree with Levinas that physical suffering is somehow purer or more privileged than mental or moral suffering, the two are inextricable, and suffering is experienced by selves through bodies and souls, an effect of living together in time, which founds ethical and political life in part as an effort organized to respond to and change suffering. This effort reconstructs the nature of body and mind, subject and object, nature and history, power and responsibility, and world and theory, in order to do so.

There are several crucial perspectives at stake in this genealogy that are necessary to its construction. I have not simply chosen an interesting topic, suffering, and checked with some of the usual suspects in the history of political thought in order to hear what they had to say about it. In order to show the "substitutions, displacements, disguised conquests and systematic reversals" that constitute this genealogy of suffering, I have need of several critical perspectives—and these in particular and no others.

I start with the most basic, *the perspective of the sufferer*, of the afflicted. Martin Luther supplies the material of this anguish, the beating heart of the suffering body and soul, seemingly helpless and powerless in a remorseless world in the face of an unknowable God. From Luther I take a beginning in the vitals of the sufferer, the perspective of the one afflicted, and moreover, one who can hope for no surcease and no remedy in this world, except for faith in the unmerited grace of an inscrutable God. It is this helplessness that opens the way for a secular politics.

In the modern age, the perspective of the sufferer is only a beginning, and one that is replaced because it is without effective agency. The perspective of the sufferer is overlaid and in fact reversed by two related, opposing perspectives, the most fundamental characteristic perspectives of the modern age, *the perspective of the knower* and *the perspective of the agent*. The first represents the scientist and philosopher, who can investigate and discover the causes of suffering; the second represents the actor, the doer, the one who can act, who can use reason, method, and power to devise remedies, both scientific and political, for the natural causes of suffering in men and the world. This is the perspective of Thomas Hobbes, who lays the foundation for all of modern politics. His perspective is thus indispensable for all that follows.

Hobbes begins to found the establishment of a modern political and public space, the space of the social contract, where the wills of free and independent agents can devise protections for themselves and invent ingenious rules of law for their own self-preservation and eventually their flourishing. The perspectives of the agent and of the knower, the scientist, are crucial to the genealogy of the politics of suffering, and thus Hobbes is necessary to this construction.

It is true that Hobbes exhibits neither pity for nor moral anguish about suffering, nor does he indulge in indignation, accusation, or denunciation of those who generate it, and thus he is not an obvious choice, on a superficial level, as a theorist concerned with suffering. We have learned to expect, even demand, those kinds of responses to suffering; and it is to be hoped that in this book it will become clear why we have learned to expect those kinds of responses as well as how unhelpful they have become. But the fact that Hobbes does not concern himself unduly with the emotions we typically associate with suffering does not mean that he is not vitally interested in the subject or critical for developing its politics.

Hobbes does not mourn suffering, first, because he sees human suffering (misery as he calls it) as natural, inevitable, and perhaps even necessary. He sees it as inherent in human desire, displayed in human vanity and competition, and resulting in a salutary fear of violent death in humans congregated together. He identifies it as inexorably implicated in human subjectivity, in language and value, and thus as constitutive of the human self and society itself. Hobbes does not waste sympathy on suffering. Because he is both an agent and a knower, he analyzes it and tries to design a solution, the social contract and the rights it establishes and enforces for individual and communal self-preservation. He argues for the naturalness of such rights and of the consent that gives power to the sovereign to keep order. Hobbes associates suffering with violence (as indeed he does desire), and he sees no remedy for such violence except the setting of limits by power and reason. He does not seek to eliminate our inevitable suffering, nor does he condemn it. He acts to remedy it.

Human agency, method, and power can enable the founding of a commonwealth that can and will alleviate the rigors of natural violence and mitigate the causes of human suffering, even that of subjectivity itself. This move is indispensable to all further moves and proves a necessary, though contrasting, position to those that come to be encompassed under what Hannah Arendt, following Nietzsche, came to call "the politics of pity." These opposing positions eventually lead to the paradoxes of suffering we confront today. Hobbes does take suffering as his necessary starting point and it motivates the political agency he both depicts and deploys. This deployment is essential to the construction of the man-made political world that followed historically.

In this book I am not interested in exploring the topic of suffering in modern political theory and therefore I am not interested in theorists who are themselves self-identified as concerned with suffering or theorists who theorize about suffering as such in their work. From such a perspctive, Hobbes would not be an obvious choice. It is possible to see why Luther, Rousseau, or Nietzsche might be included in such a project, but Hobbes notoriously eschews both sentiment and morality, and he is emphatically *not* concerned with the suffering of the innocent, of which he does not seem to think there are any. But as I am not interested in such a project, but in showing something quite otherwise, Hobbes is indispensable.

I am arguing for the construction of a problematic of suffering as this was staged genealogically in consecutive, contradicting theoretical stages over several centuries from the time of the Reformation. The problematic of suffering involves several perspectives that do not agree with one another or cohere in a larger whole, including the perspectives of the sufferer, the perspectives of the agent and of the knower, and, as is worth repeating, the perspectives of the spectator, the persecutor, the benefactor, and finally including what has been called, misleadingly I believe, the aesthetic perspective, but which might be better understood as *the perspective of the creator*. All of these are necessary to cutting through and thereby knowing the politics of suffering.

Luc Boltanski's book, *Distant Suffering*, is the best analytical treatment of contemporary questions about the sociology of suffering I have found, and it has been a great help in sorting out, thinking through, and theorizing suffering.[14] Boltanski begins, however, with the politics of pity in Rousseau and Adam Smith in the eighteenth century, thereby missing the larger context of the modern age as a whole as it emerges in the sixteenth and seventeenth centuries and as these contexts condition the politics of pity that emerges in the eighteenth. The politics of pity arises because the problem of human suffering develops out of and in some senses in opposition to both the religious and scientific interpretations of suffering that preceded it. The politics of pity borrows the moral indignation of the religious framework, without in fact being able to assure itself of analogous grounds or criteria of judgment, and that's a part of the story that Boltanski leaves out. The politics of pity also enters decisively into debate, not to say war, with the scientific or natural-causal interpretation of suffering that forms the underlying foundation for modern political solutions of the problem. Boltanski usefully discusses what he calls the "aesthetic response" to suffering in Nietzsche, Baudelaire, Sade, and Bataille, although, as I hope to show, he mistakes and misidentifies the issues at stake in this response and leaves the analysis largely incomplete. The "aesthetic" response requires further differentiation.

But let's start with a summary of the politics of pity as this is exemplified in Rousseau, in contrast to Hobbes and Nietzsche. Boltanski acutely recognizes that the perspective that rules the politics of pity is *the perspective of the spectator*. He understands that this is a new perspective, although not quite I think why it is so important that this is the ruling perspective of this moral framework. The spectator does not participate in the suffering he observes. Boltanski argues that the perspective of the spectator is associated with two other perspectives, that of the persecutor and that of the benefactor, and he carefully delineates the problems of truth and blame that these perspectives bring into play. The spectator spawns a moralizing ideology of the real.

It is Hobbes's science that enables him to conceptualize the movement of mankind out of nature and into a man-made world in which human decision and will, human reason and language enable us to act so as to establish order, meaning, rules, and the conditions of social coexistence that can facilitate our productivity, our safety, and our lives. Hobbes does not have to worry about whether suffering is just or unjustified, because it is to him inherent in nature and life, and is amenable, at least in terms of minimal basic conditions, to human effort and power. Suffering is something that we can do something about. Human beings can found compacts, form commonwealths and associations that allow for the amelioration of the causes of the most basic forms of human suffering. Human beings can establish the conditions for constituting a man-made world in which they need not be afraid for their lives, which is the chief cause of their suffering. Hobbes can just begin to envision the rudiments of a man-made public space in which human decisions will hold firm, and in which human will can create the institutions that assure the fundamentals of human well-being. Knowledge sets the stage for the actions that can make life better.

Jean-Jacques Rousseau starts from a completely opposite, unspoken but pervasive premise—that human suffering is not justified—in distinct contrast to both Luther and Hobbes. He can come to this conclusion because he inhabits a world that he understands, dimly and confusedly and yet accurately, as a man-made world, a world crafted by human hands and constructed by human volitions, a world that has been built, historically; out of nature, surely, but in terms of human values and conceits, human needs and vanities, human failings and greed, human qualities and considerations that are not, or no longer, entirely natural. In order to make his profound accusation—that human suffering is unjust, and that it is caused by historical injustices that have been perpetrated by the powerful against the weak for the purposes of domination and enslavement—Rousseau must reconfigure how he conceives the way men moved "out of nature" and into history, and likewise, how they changed from being good, natural and free animals to being base, degenerate and wicked human beings.

Rousseau is a moralist as well as a sentimentalist. In the public spaces created by the architectures and technologies of the enlightened modern world, he is a spectator, who judges that the suffering he observes in the majority of men around him, in the masses, the poor, the oppressed, is not legitimate. The governments, the rulers who dominate society, the wealthy who control the resources and the values that prevail in modern culture, are not legitimate and their authority is not legitimate. Rousseau is looking at a world of suffering through the question of legitimacy—who rules and in the name of what ideals—and he judges that man's suffering is not justified because it is brought about by historical forces that have deformed the natural good nature of men and led them into wickedness and decadence. He confounds the problem of the relation between nature and history and that of the relation of the individual and the society with the question of morality and legitimacy. But he comprehends that it is in the movement from nature to history, whatever that means (which he cannot entirely solve, however much he tries), where the question of the justification of suffering changes. If suffering is simply natural, then there is nothing to be done. But if suffering is man-made, as the world of society is man-made, and as it has developed through human historical choices and decisions, then we can judge it according to the ideals given us "by nature" and we can call it to account. We can bear witness and we can judge, we can theoretically connect the persecutors with their victims and call violent retribution on them—then we can act. From the perspective of the public man, we can look on our works and judge them and then change them.

Rousseau concludes that it is necessary to begin again. It is necessary to start anew, with the free affirmations of free men, who will consent all together to be bound by the general will, which is the common will of them all as a collectivity, which transcends not only their separate individual wills but even their separate individual natures to found a new, collective nature, a new collective will, which will bind them only in their freedom and bring them justice, equality, and peace.

It is important that it is only from the perspective of the public spectator and the public spaces he surveys that the politics of pity, of denunciation and benefaction, can emerge. That public space and the possibility of the caring but disinterested spectator can only be founded upon the knowledge and the autonomous agency that is established in the modern age by science and reason, that is, in the modern polity. That is to say, on the foundations that Hobbes sets forth. Hobbes is not a spectator. He is a man of knowledge and an agent; his perspective is that of the doer, the builder, or of the physician, who diagnoses the problem and designs a solution. He does not doubt that a man-made artifice, the great Leviathan, can provide the order, stability, and foundations of common meaning that allow for public peace. He even discerns that such a public space can change the nature of men and make them see reason.

Rousseau lives a hundred years later and the public spaces and the public itself, the learned, literate and self-conscious public of modern politics is already making itself known. From the position of the spectator of what public man has made, of the kind of public life that has been constructed, Rousseau can begin to trace the process by means of which this space and this society came into being. He knows that he lives in a man-made, historical world, and he can try to determine what is needed to rectify the injustices he sees as integrated into but perhaps not necessarily integral to this world as it has been built in history. He can begin to trace the connections that we will come to know so well, the social constructions of identity, of class, of gender, of race, culture, and position that allow for the oppression, exploitation, and domination of the great masses of men and women. Rousseau begins to talk about labor in history, about the way men construct their world, and about who has a say in how it is built and who suffers the consequences of such decisions. Then, he can dream of a world, out of time, out of history, in some ideal future position, that will always be fresh and always be free, where a perfect equilibrium can be established. The social contract will create a perfect man-made world, away from the history we have known, in which equal justice and freedom are realizable.

So when we add the perspectives of the sufferer, the knower and the agent, to those of spectator, denouncer and benefactor, we come to a concatenation of perspectives on suffering that enable the proposition that suffering is unjustified and can be eliminated from the world, violently if necessary, but for the sake of the good.

Nietzsche is the thinker who brings this whole house crashing down, and it seems that he does so by the simplest means—he ridicules the notion that there is any way we can judge the "legitimacy" of nature or history or of suffering itself. We are part of the whole and we can never step outside it somehow, in order to see it whole and establish its value. Life is beyond our powers of estimation or evaluation. It is chaos and a wild dance, a dismembered god, a music we can only sometimes hear or play. There are no criteria, certainly no rational or philosophical criteria, which we could find that are not partial, perspectival, forged from the will to power. There is no judgment that we make that is not of us and part of our struggle to prevail. We invent moralities, philosophies, and interpretations in order to prevail—how else?

Nietzsche, like Hobbes to the fourth power, demolishes the conceit that we can remake the world without the parts we don't like. He does not deny in the least that we make the world. He denies that there is in nature, or in history, or in religion, or in philosophy, or in metaphysics, or in politics as well any possibility of any morality whatsoever that is inherent in the world. Any moral judgments made are made by us, for us, against us, and while we may devise formulas and ideas, languages and fetishes, institutions and commodities in order to establish positions of power that endure for a time and provide some measure of security or the illusion of control, illusion is all it is. From the perspective of suffering, which is preeminently the tragic nature of the real for Nietzsche, all our constructions, all our edifices, values and ideals, our ideas of redemption and resolution, of truth and revolution, only ultimately make it worse. We misunderstand the efficacy, even the necessity, the indispensability of suffering to the formation of great spirits and the world. Suffering has played a crucial part in the formation of the history of ideals with which we in the West operate on the world.

Nietzsche's genealogy of morals relentlessly attacks the origins of our religious, metaphysical, and moral impulses. He finds the origins of the highest ideals in the lowest instincts, the deformations of aggression, the *ressentiment* of slavery and domination, the craven weakness of the self-pitying masses and the priests who increase their torment with the notion of everlasting salvation or damnation. Pity is always debt and superiority, a manifestation of the will to power that is the driving force of life itself. The will to power is what has driven the history of this man-made world, ever more man-made at every moment, it seems, and thus denuded, shown for what it is—a transient world. God is dead and in that death comes the death of belief, the death of faith in all the transcendent ideals and values of truth that have come from the traditions we have inherited.

Everything passes away, and thus everything deserves to pass away, and we most of all, as bare, forked beings with split natures and the *pathos* of believing we can find the truth. If we find that the truth is that there is no truth except what we manufacture for our own purposes, and that we are served as well or better by a lie most of the time, or that we can't tell the difference, then what will serve for a limit to the will to power? The will to power turns to the will to truth, which under some conditions reveals itself as the will to nothingness, the will, pure and simple. This gives rise to the *perspective of the creator*, and Nietzsche uses that to sum up, encompass and surpass all the previous perspectives on suffering that have led us to this place. Our task, as creators, is to remake the world in our image; that is, after all, what we are. But that could turn out to be quite a dangerous and unholy task. How shall we choose which image?

Nietzsche diagnoses nihilism as the disease of our time. It is a disease of time itself, in fact. Without God and the "true world" by which we might measure and redeem this poor, real, imperfect one, we have only this world now, only this transient, impermanent finitude, the limit of what is, what was, and what cannot be changed, of what we are and what we have become. We are in time, and in the moment of time that is the present, we can come to realize ourselves and our suffering and to take responsibility for the history of the whole and for the suffering of all times and places. If we could will that, the eternal recurrence of the same, of what has been and will be again, Nietzsche argues, well, we might then continue the process of creating new values that affirm our lives, including our suffering as well as our joy.

But we would have to give up both revenge and blame. We could no longer pity suffering and simply denounce the oppressors and fancy ourselves the benefactors. We could no longer afford simply to try to eliminate suffering—we would have to try to discern what was useful or needed for the long-term health and sickness of the species. We would have to affirm all that we have all suffered—that in itself is an unimaginable task. We would have to acknowledge the interconnectedness of all things and move from "mass" to "species." We would have to see with the eyes of one disciplined by the rigors of suffering and of joy to become high spirits, and low ones too. We would have to become more and more all-encompassing. We would have to become larger, wider, deeper, more good, and more evil than ever, and not always be afraid. We would have to embrace the *pathos* of our will to power in time, which always passes away.

There is of course no definitive interpretation of Nietzsche, or of Luther, Hobbes, or Rousseau either. But the excursion through the genealogy of suffering in the politics of the modern age allows us to ask the question of suffering anew and to recognize the difficulties it presents in ways that would have been impossible without this history. That in turn forms the basis for theorizing suffering in the context of the present, which is more diverse and complicated than ever, and becoming more so every moment. That task of analysis still awaits us.

1

Suffering in the Context of Religion

THE DEATH OF GOD

At the end of the modern age, Friedrich Nietzsche famously announced that God is dead, and from the perspective of this event, the death of God, Nietzsche described the basic condition of modern life as one of nihilism, a condition of meaninglessness and the collapse of all hitherto believed Western values, a vacuum of emptiness and pointless violence, which he saw as the deepest context in which all modern thought, science, art, and politics takes place.

I want to begin this rather brief look at the religious construction of and response to suffering at the very beginning of the modern age with this end-time pronouncement by Nietzsche, because it is central to the argument of this book and to its culminating Nietzschean perspective: that behind the intricate, strange maneuverings of the advocates of new religious, scientific, and political viewpoints in the texts we are about to study, there is a large world-historical event looming, an event that takes centuries to ripen and to fully arrive, an event that is not yet finished, but which Nietzsche calls, correctly but ambiguously, the death of God. In order to understand what such an event might mean, we have to first get some idea of what kind of a story Nietzsche means to tell, and then we must look to the incipient voices of new early modern religion, in particular, that of Martin Luther, who gave us a new religion and a new perspective on suffering, which ushered in what we have come to know as the modern age.

When he looks to the modern age, Nietzsche finds not culture, which he understands as a true, organic unity, such as he discerned in ancient Greek tragedy, but rather the absence or disintegration of culture. It is important for the argument of this book that Nietzsche saw life and the health of culture in ancient Greek theater, especially the capacity of Greek tragic drama to come to terms with suffering in the context of both religion and spectacle that allows for art's self-overcoming of suffering. In our day, the spectacle of distant and mediated suffering constitutes one of its most deadly conundrums—a symbol and symptom of the destruction and disintegration of encompassing culture. According to Nietzsche, this disintegration, decay, or degeneration of modern European culture both portends and symbolizes the great danger from which he says the modern age suffers, the danger of nihilism. He understands the goal of his work, therefore, to be the necessity for "an unprecedented *knowledge of the preconditions of culture*,"[1] in order that culture may somehow be rebuilt and the disastrous conditions of modern nihilism not averted but perhaps in some instances overcome.

Nihilism for Nietzsche represented not only the outcome of the twisted foundational logic of European history, but a critical, pathological, but inevitable underlying historical condition of Western man, come to fruition in the modern age through the triumph of the unconditional will to power as will to truth. To know what is needed to oppose nihilism is a very large task, a task even of the will to truth, and it is no wonder that Nietzsche believed himself to be heroically overburdened. He thought he bore the responsibility for changing human history. As we will see, he made a beginning.

The grounding, or what might serve as one, for Nietzsche's investigations into the forces that formed and then destroyed civilization in the West was the ultimate context of present-day nihilism, which he characterized in terms of the death of God. Nietzsche first told the story of the death of God in a famous passage in *The Gay Science*, called *The Madman*:

> Have you not heard of that madman who lit a lantern in the bright morning hours ran to the market place, and cried incessantly: "I seek God! I seek God!"—As many of those who did not believe in God were standing around just then, he provoked much laughter. Has he got lost? asked one. Did he lose his way like a child? asked another. Or is he hiding? Is he afraid of us? Has he gone on a voyage? emigrated?—Thus they yelled and laughed. The madman jumped into their midst and pierced them with his eyes. "Whither is God?" he cried. "I will tell you. *We have killed him*—you and I. All of us are his murderers. But how did we do this? How could we drink up the sea? Who gave us the sponge to wipe away the entire horizon? What were we doing when we unchained this earth from its sun? Whither is it moving now? Whither are we moving? Are we not plunging continually? Backward, sideward, forward, in all directions? Is there any up or down? Are we not straying as through an infinite nothing? Do we not feel the breath of empty space? Has it not become colder? Is not night continually closing in on us? Do we not need to light lanterns in the morning? Do we hear nothing as yet of the

noise of the gravediggers who are burying God? Do we smell nothing as yet of the divine decomposition? Gods, too, decompose. God
is dead. God remains dead. And we have killed him.[2]

Finally, the madman, looking at the astonishment of his listeners, says, "I have
come too early, . . . my time is not yet. This tremendous event is still on its
way, still wandering: it has not yet reached the ears of men. . . . This deed is
still more distant from them than the most distant stars—*and yet they have
done it themselves.*" In the opening paragraph of Book Three of *The Gay
Science*, Nietzsche cautions us that even though God is dead, "there may still
be caves for thousands of years in which his shadow will be shown.—And
we—we still have to vanquish his shadow, too."[3]

The death of God is not merely a matter of seeing through and putting
aside previous religious beliefs. It is not just a matter of now knowing that
something is false that once we took to be true, namely, God's existence. God's
existence has served as the foundational framework for Western culture for
millennia, and the death of God that Nietzsche announces is an event. An
event is neither false nor true, it just is. This event, a long time coming and a
long time passing through us, into us, and around us, changes everything. As
Nietzsche explains it, it is a fate, what has been done and cannot be undone
in the modern age. What Nietzsche means by fate will be made clearer as we
proceed. But what Nietzsche means by history is important to even this pre-
liminary part of the inquiry. History is not what is contingent or accidental,
it is not about numerous chance possibilities, rather the opposite; it is about
what out of all those numerous possibilities actually happened, fatally happened, happened and cannot be changed. It is about the actual throw that came
up on the dice as they were cast, in fact, and not anything else. In this sense,
our history is our fate.

The death of God is our history and our fate; it encompasses a history
of our values and these values are fateful for us, a fateful inheritance. What
is the meaning of the death of God? How do events have meaning, and for
whom do they have meaning? What meaning does a death have for us? It
depends, as in all things, on our relationship to the deceased. This is part of
what Nietzsche will recover in *On the Genealogy of Morals*. He wants to
expose to us the underside of our long relationship with God, especially now
that he is dead, and we, he says, have killed him. It is also important for our
story that Nietzsche sometimes says that God was strangled by or because of
his pity.[4]

Nietzsche shows that our relationship with God was largely uncon-
scious, although its conscious, concrete elements were vast and conspicuous.
It has been the most significant relationship in the history of Western peoples.
Even after this death, the relationship goes on, as it does with the deaths of

fathers and mothers. The shadow of God stays on the wall of the cave for centuries; the shadow of God falls on us, and his memory, engraved in ritual pain on our bodies and rites, still determines many actions and events. The customs we have accrued from our relationship to God have a very long half-life. And they are, in a sense, radioactive too. That is to say, Nietzsche argues, they burn with a malignant force, a vengeful cruelty of suffering that lingers in the bone. The death of God is surely as significant as the birth of God, which is an event still quite alive in our memories and practices. The living God is different from the dead God, but we have to be able to trace the effects of his life to begin to fathom his death. Do we merely believe that God is dead, or do we know it, or practice it? How do we practice the death of God—that is Nietzsche's striking question. In the parable, men cannot yet hear the news that God is dead. The event is still coming from afar. Its repercussions are still reaching us, as the premonitions of an earthquake.

PROLEGOMENA TO AN ANALYSIS OF SUFFERING IN THE AGE OF TIME ABANDONED

In Nietzsche's *Zarathustra*, it is the ugliest man who kills God, out of revenge and hatred of God's pity as witness to man's suffering, because God was able to see into his most guilty and shameful hidden corners. He kills God because such a witness was intolerable. The ugliest man says: "But he had to die: he saw with eyes that saw everything; he saw man's depths and ultimate grounds, all his concealed disgrace and ugliness. His pity knew no shame: he crawled into my dirtiest nooks. This most curious, overobtrusive, overpitying one had to die. He always saw me: on such a witness I wanted to have revenge or not live myself. The god who saw everything, even man—this god had to die! Man cannot bear it that such a witness should live."[5] Nietzsche's parable can be read in one way as a symbolic statement about the ugliest man in each of us. He is identifying our hidden shame and affliction as motivations for our killing God, who, in some versions of the story, is strangled by pity for us. Nietzsche does assure us that this God was "a strange one." But he affirms, "whether it be god's pity or man's pity, it offends the sense of shame."[6] The politics of pity is in contention in this book, especially pity as a response to suffering. Rousseau and Nietzsche present opposing valuations of the politics of pity as it arose in the eighteenth century. But the context for this political struggle began much earlier.

When Martin Luther began to study the Psalms for his first series of lectures in Wittenberg, at about the age of thirty, in late 1513, he could not have been further from any idea that the God he was addressing, in whose presence he habitually experienced an overwhelming shame, but whose honor he believed he was in every way defending, was in any sense about to be murdered. It would have been inconceivable to him that any man, however many centuries later, in Saxony, could ever have come to the conclusion that he, Martin Luther, had in any way contributed to this death. And yet Nietzsche does not hesitate to name him thus. Evaluating such a scandalous claim is one of the things into which we are inquiring.

While in no sense is Luther the ugliest man of Nietzsche's fable, he was in fact a most afflicted, shamed, and tormented man, one who thought his shame and hidden affliction were literally bottomless and unforgivable, and moreover that they were seen, witnessed, known, and judged by God. Luther's God was also a "strange one," an unstable amalgamation of Augustinian divine righteousness, absolute judgment, humanist self-estrangement, and thundering wrath, reminiscent of Luther's own father but in a much higher key, known through struggle with his own *conscientia cauterisata*, his cauterizing conscience. Luther said:

> When I first read and sang in the Psalms *in iustitia tua libera me*, I was horror-stricken and felt deep hostility toward those words, God's righteousness, God's judgment, God's work. For I knew only that *iustitia dei* meant a harsh judgment. Well, was he supposed to save me by judging me harshly? If so, I was lost forever. But *gottlob*, when I then understood the matter and knew that *iustitia dei* meant the righteousness by which He justifies us through the free gift of Christ's justice, then I understood the *grammatica*, and I truly tasted Psalms.[7]

Luther made a very long journey from the torment of his guilt and shame to the illumination of his faith, his famous interpretation of Romans 1:17— "For therein is the righteousness of God revealed from faith to faith, as it is written 'The just shall live by faith.'" His revelation was of God's freely given and flowing grace, in this world of time and in the hereafter, by faith alone. The miraculous answer Luther eventually found to the question that tormented him all his life, the question of his own justification and of God's fateful judgment, came to him as he first began to struggle with the theology of mercy and suffering in these early lectures on the Psalms and later on Romans. "Faith is a living, daring confidence in God's grace, so sure and certain that a man would stake his life on it a thousand times. . . . Hence a man is ready and glad, without compulsion, to do good to everyone, to serve everyone, to suffer everything, in love and praise of God, who has shown him this grace."[8]

When Luther first began to be a monk, he could find no way out of his shame at his own unworthiness and sin and God's knowledge of it. His epiphany was an experience of God's overwhelming anger, and then of his mercy; an experience of gratuitous grace poured out over the secret sinfulness and anguish of the sinner, out of God's sheer goodness, his pity, as it were. Not as a response to any human merit, but only as an outflowing of God's pity. Out of Luther's sense of the impossibility of spiritual justification, and his wrath and guilt over this impossibility, a new personal and poignant, but also a newly inaccessible and more absolutely transcendent God was conceived.

It is possible to make the argument that this distance and the ultimate inaccessibility of God, as he was eventually conceived by Luther and other Protestant Reformers, helped lead to his ultimate demise. This is a complicated and delicate argument, one that can only be made from the perspective of the further history we have inherited. Luther's reformulation of the relation between faith and salvation was just one variation on a theme circulating at the time of the northern Renaissance, which was a time of extreme changes on all fronts. The new religion he initiated and passionately defended was most certainly a religion, which is part of what Nietzsche taxes him with. But the unity that was the Roman Catholic and Imperial Church was cracked open by it, and the faith of the faithful rent with it.

Luther's faith did ultimately issue in, although clearly it did not cause, a world from which God's active intervention was absent—a world ever more unsure of its foundations and the grounds of its moral judgments. What remained, as God was removed from public consensus and active intervention, was the private suffering of human beings, which inner, hidden religious faith consoled, justified, and made meaningful. Whether a man's faith was justified was unknowable by men, according to Luther; it was known only to God and had been predestined from the beginning of time by God's foreknowledge. A man's debt is settled only in the secret recesses of the hidden individual soul in its intimate relations to its redeemer. The debt could perhaps be bought off, but not by gold, only by God's pity, and only in the secret recesses of the heart and the soul. That is what Luther strives to make clear.

The basic meaning, doctrine, dogma, and rites of Christian suffering were derived from foundations set down in the Hebrew Bible, especially the faith articulated by the great prophets, Jeremiah, Ezekiel, and Isaiah. In both Jewish and Christian doctrines and practices, human suffering comes from God and takes its meaning from the moral laws of the domain of God. Human suffering is conceived in Christianity, from the Fall to the Resurrection, as deserved and justified punishment for human sin, the original sin of primordial disobedience, and the will to disobedience of Eve and Adam as this conception is developed in the theology of the Fall by Paul and Augustine, the greatest masters of Christian theology.

Suffering is understood as inherent in humanity, in its deformed will, but it serves a purpose that is above all redemptive. Suffering, God's suffering and his pity for man's sin and the agonies of his wrongdoing and guilt, is incarnated in Jesus as Christ. God became suffering and crucified flesh, the divine servant whose suffering and death did always already redeem, Luther insists, the sins of the faithful. Suffering is thus, paradoxically, supremely valued in Christianity; it is the highest, most elevated, and sublime value. However much pain, in natural or ordinary language, has always been described as undesireable by people, it began to have a place of peculiar and unique value very early in Western religion, bridging the gap between the human and the divine. Suffering was seen as a mark of the significance of man's relation to God, a sign of his guilt, his sin before God, which justified God's wrath and his punishment. The place of suffering in God's redemptive schema gave it supreme value. Suffering is central to Christianity, the apotheosis of its theology, worked out over centuries in the doctrines and rituals and practices of worship in the powerful institutions of the great and imperial Catholic Church and the Protestant Reformation churches. In the places and times that made up the history of reigning Christianity, religion and the Church occupied the entire social space and set the terms for all human interactions, on earth and in heaven.

At the beginning of the early modern age, which I am going to specify, somewhat arbitrarily, as starting from the early sixteenth century, we are still in a world where religion and the weight of the past, mythical and allegorical, ritual and cultural, dominated every sphere of human life. But the power of change was already in motion, and the overarching unity of the medieval Christian world and the Church that represented this unity came to be shattered beyond repair by the manifold, explosive unfolding of many diverse and new sacred and secular movements: the revivals and inventions, the technologies, visions, and navigations that constituted the Italian and then the northern Renaissance, and more important, the new religious revelations and intractible spiritual, dogmatic, and political conflicts that came to be known as the Protestant Reformation.

It is my central thesis in this chapter and this book that the way human suffering is conceptualized, comprehended, and constructed is one of the great, if sometimes hidden, constituent elements in any totalizing, overarching metaphysical framework or grand narrative by which human life is conceived and practiced. In this book I look at the politics of suffering from four separate but interconnected viewpoints—the viewpoint of the afflicted or sufferer as that is rendered by religion; the viewpoint of the agent and knower, as he reconstructs the causes and effects of suffering and devises scientific and political remedies for it; the viewpoint of the spectator and revolutionary, for whom the politics of pity for the masses as sufferers becomes a systematic indictment of history itself; and finally a viewpoint that combines all these previous views and transvalues all the elements at stake in these previous kinds of politics. Suffering is key to the study of these successive and contradictory ways of understanding and justifying politics. Considering these grand metaphysical systems in contrast to one another ultimately transforms the meaning of politics itself.

In this chapter I show suffering to be a profound basis for the most decisive and important series of changes that we count as having created modern Western history—the changeover, simultaneously abrupt and gradual, hidden, explosive, violent, and discontinuous, geographically as well as symbolically significant, from a religious to a secular world. Suffering marks one of the most powerful and determinative forces by means of which this changeover took place. A decisive symbolic inversion of meanings and values was effected by this change—the reversal from an especially high, centrally privileged, and elaborately cultivated meaning for suffering as sanctified, as the very essence of Christian sainthood, which represented the highest type of human being for both the educated and the uneducated classes in Europe, to an absolute rejection of the value of human suffering, now seen as physical and physiological as well as psychological, and completely of this world. Suffering understood as natural, lodged in the body, could perhaps be somewhat ameliorated by the careful attentions of physicians and scientists, inventors and technological manufacturers, and even eventually psychiatrists. Martin Luther anguished over the imprisonment of the suffering soul in the imperfect and sinful body. It is perhaps crucially important to realize that another theorist, Michel Foucault, four hundred years later, expressed comparable anguish over the imprisonment of the suffering and abused body in the suffocating disciplines of the modern soul. The meanings of "body" and "soul" have decisively changed, but more important, their values have been reversed, as has the locus of freedom. This is part of what it means to be modern.

One measure of the sheer dimensions of the change I am trying to sketch out in this small book has to do with the nature of time itself. Time turns out to be the most essential dimension or component of suffering, which lies at the root of all its forms. The theorizing of suffering, therefore, takes us from the transtemporal realm of Luther's God to the insistently, incessantly temporal world of contemporary existences—extemporaneous, mediated, virtual, simultaneous and fully historicized in a thousand different realms.

Suffering in a religious world is both temporal and timeless—it is endured now as well as redeemed above. Suffering in this world awaits the consolations, or condemnations, of the next. The temporal world of horizontal social relations is infused with the exigencies of the timeless, vertical transcendental world. The world beyond gives an anchor and a purpose for the horrors and indignities of this world; it shadows this life with the requirements of the next. The time of religious culture is the time of teleology, the movement of all beings toward God, toward the culmination of world history in apocalyptic judgment. Time is taken as a qualitative *progressus*, and man's life on earth as a vale of tears, ending not in death only, but in judgment beyond death.

All outcomes are unknowable, either redemption or irreversible damnation in the ultimate coming of the kingdom of God in final eschatological judgment.

Modern time, on the other hand, is secular time, worldly time, time set loose from God's immediate governance. It is a representation of motion itself, a mathmatical, measureable, linear continuum. It is abstract and perfectly exact, regularized time, the context of mathematically delineable movements of bodies in space. This time is divided into equal, and increasingly shorter, intervals, and counted off by clocks. The modern world runs temporally on the basis of fixed divisions of time of invariable weight. It can be said that the modern world is produced by the possibility and actualization of such invariable time. Souls in the old-fashioned sense are not germane to this kind of measure. Modern physical time is in one sense imaginary time, idealized and rational, but it is an ideal fit to man's measure, as the humanists of the Renaissance affirmed. It is time as counted out by means of man's counting instruments, clocks and metronomes, open to human invention and intervention, and in fact defined by that very capacity to be rationalized, regularized, devised as equivalences, and weighed by means of minutely calibrated debits or compensations.

Our relation to this measurable world and the possibilities of our knowledge of it become central human preoccupations in the ever-more encompassing void of the *Deus Absconditus*. We, as human beings, that is, as mental and linguistic, social and historical persons, are problematical in nature in this kind of a world. While "nature" can be directly conceptualized in terms of matter and motion, humans continue to defy being reduced to these terms. Human suffering, especially, defies this approach. No longer referenced to divine laws and the failures, defects, or guilt of men as measured by them, human suffering still cannot be easily measured in purely material categories, which becomes, in itself, a new problem of knowledge. Politically, human suffering, its causes and conditions, its weight and distributions, comes to constitute a new and grave cause for investigation and collective action. Natural causation becomes the intense focus of human knowledge. God is no longer the overt, publicly represented Supreme Good, directing all things morally, but rather the Great Unmoved Mover, the First Cause, the Eternal Clockmaker who sets the mechanical and temporal world in motion and then leaves it be. The forces that move and change the world are revealed in the motions of matter itself. Moral knowledge turns into an ongoing, escalating crisis. The clock does not reveal good and evil, but only measure itself, or so it is said.

Religiously interpreted suffering was always already contained in a spiritual and moral matrix, a world moving as a whole toward a moral end, a cosmos of potentialities and qualities, of sin and doubt, building toward the ultimate time of judgment and salvation. The relation of suffering to redemption was anything but accidental. It was spelled out in a religious meta-physics, where the eschatological end, the spiritual and moral culmination of time and the world, is the whole point. Suffering is always to be endured as, by definition, *temporary*, as the temporal world is our temporary habitation, a prelude to an eternal habitation, containing the consolations of heaven or the endless terrors of damnation. Suffering in this world is a test of the right-eous to be redeemed by virtue after death, and for all eternal souls ultimately to be judged in the messianic fulfillment of history. Suffering by human beings in this world, then, however severe, was morally and spiritually valued, even treasured, because of its meaning for God and for its contribution to the ulti-mate end, the eschatological redemption of the righteous and God's revenge on the unrighteous. Human life and its miseries was always part of lived time, God's time, part of a larger movement and narrative of progression through the sins of this world to the glorified fruition or vengeance of the next, perfect one. Even in its later or even Marxist and secular guises, there was always a thread linking the victims of this world to the saved and justified ones of the next.

Modern suffering, as we begin to see it in Luther and then as it became naturalized by Hobbes, Rousseau, and other modern thinkers, bears no rela-tion to redemption. In history, the meaning of suffering changed. For believers, human suffering remains part of God's unfathomable and irremediable will, inscrutable and unknowable. It is not that religion and spiritual suffering, however private and unknowable, did not continue to play a crucial role in creating human subjects and their self-understandings. It was, rather, that as the modern age progressed the unknowability and hence lack of public meas-ure and public consensus on the meaning of suffering rendered its value increas-ingly invisible, and thus decisively changed the way it was experienced. Over the course of the innumerable changes wrought by what we call modernity in the centuries following Luther, suffering came less and less to be experienced as spiritually valuable, privileged, and meaningful in relation to an otherworldly eternity. Modern skeptics came to doubt that our pains were watched over by an attentive (or punishing) divine presence; they came to doubt that suffering had this meaning and hence that it conferred value on or testified to human worthiness for salvation. So what meaning, then, could suffering have?

Even so, it might be argued that there was a great modern compensation for this loss of religious meaning, however incalculable it was as a loss. Suf-fering, as understood and explained in modern science, is actually *caused*, that is, it is brought about by certain actual, physical, material, bodily, factual, and historical conditions. These conditions are in ever-more-inventive ways visible and measurable, hence open to the manipulations of human ingenuity and power. In exchange for a divine guarantor of moral worth (or unworthiness), men could perhaps gain less actual suffering. As God's exclusive and exhaus-tive responsibility for our condition faded into a kind of spiritual technicality, our condition became ever more our own responsibility, open to our own technologies. Human responsibility for acting to end human suffering began to move to center stage.

Causation, as it comes to be conceptualized in early modern science, resolves itself, slowly and with interesting elaborations, into the necessary and sufficient conditions that bring something about—and many of those elements can be changed. So instead of redemption in the indefinite future, we have causation in the reasonably specifiable past and the immediate present, which can be addressed, studied, measured, and even fixed, at least ameliorated, sometimes cured, at any rate changed by human will, decision, and determination in the present. Moderns seem to have judged this a good enough bargain, perhaps even an improvement over the experience of eternally meaningful but incurable suffering that religion had previously fostered. Human suffering, as naturally caused, could be naturally bettered; it might even be entirely eliminated, as the most optimistic Enlightenment thinkers proposed. The elimination of human suffering became a conscious goal of modern thought and politics. (Part of Nietzsche's scathing, ironic scorn is directed to this "idiotic" misunderstanding of the situation on the part of modern idealists.)

The medical model of suffering came to be one of the most important for both public and private "diseases," as we see in Hobbes and, upside down, in Nietzsche. Both were, to begin with, great philologists; they diagnosed the causes of human suffering quite differently, but both saw science and the will to truth it embodies as the only course of action, and both understood as intrinsic and natural the abyss of meaninglessness that the world presents to men of knowledge. Hobbes, and later his contentious confrère Rousseau, are greatly optimistic about the possibilities for doing something, for quite opposite reasons. Nietzsche is not. But the diagnosis of the causes and effects of human passions, actions, and wills for human suffering became determinative for all of them in different ways.

To understand the modern construction of suffering, it is necessary to start with the way suffering in relation to the divine will changed in the architectural dimensions of the Protestant Reformation. This religious dimension of change both directly and indirectly precipitated and accompanied the myriad other changes, including scientific and technological as well as political ones that came eventually to establish what we call the modern age.

It might be wise to note here some qualifications of my use of the term "modernity" and its implied counterpart "postmodernity." There are in circulation at present a plethora of both temporal and substantive usages for the term "modernity" and related alternatives. Often historical and substantive conceptions are confused, and theorists end up attributing substantive content to what turn out to be temporal descriptions, or disguising one with the other. It is not altogether clear even how to differentiate temporal from substantive claims about modernity, which will become clearer as a problem as we delineate the ways history came to be differentiated from both nature and philosophy in modern political thought. History came to be thought of as a distinct discipline of knowledge, as well as the events that make up the past itself. As a discipline, it was often cast as directly opposed to both science and philosophy; it had with its own rules and originating assumptions, still highly contested. Time came to be "modern," in contrast to what came "before," according to some assigned date of demarcation. "Modern" is what's new, or now, relative to some past date. It can mean some new kind of thing, in relation to some old kind of thing. "In 1550 the new age was called 'modern' by Georgio Vasari in his Lives of the Painters, Sculptors, and Architects, because it revived the 'antique' style."[9] The revival aspect of history got radically recirculated later. But "modern" was a modern term.

I am working with both temporal and substantive claims about modernity. The temporal frame is according to ordinary usage in political theory; the substantive claims are part of what this work is about. Its point is to explore some of the substantive contents of both modernist thought and time, in relation to the question of suffering, and consequently what "postmodern" thought and times might be about in comparison. These are all metaphors of presence, signifiers of containers and divisions of contents, which only have reference in relation to a question, in this case, the question of suffering in time in modern political theory.

The substantive claims of political theory change as the basic configurations of its central terms of discourse change—in this case, suffering in relation to time, nature, will and power, self and community, knowledge and history. The dimensions of theory I am specifically looking at include action and agency, public spectatorship and pity, justification and denunciation, and time itself as a necessary limit of life, of human will, and of suffering in relation to human responsibility. The context of the modern is created by the questions asked in relation to the texts studied. Although it would probably be preferable to be able to enumerate all specific instances actually encompassed by a term like "modern political thought," they are innumerable, and what would it help? A certain indulgence is inescapably called for, then, in allowing generalizations that always exceed their mark. No book that culminates in four chapters on Nietzsche could possibly afford to be unaware of the perspectival, partial, and relative purchase of its terms or its insights. No language that I know has yet been devised to escape its own self-reflexive paradoxes.

SUFFERING FROM THE PERSPECTIVE OF THE AFFLICTED: MARTIN LUTHER

We start from the early days of the Protestant Reformation in the sixteenth and seventeenth centuries, when the distance between the human world and the world of the wholly Other, the Transcendent God, finally became so great that the connections between the two worlds began to crack, and the two major existing institutional mediators between them, Church and king, came under relentless and multiple attacks. The public division between God and man in the centuries leading up to the Renaissance and the Reformation had widened until the two realms were able to be broken apart, leaving a fearful hiatus, a radical cesura, an insecurity in human belonging in the world that would never again be closed. This radical separation of the temporal from the sacred realm not only evacuated God from everyday intervention in human affairs; it also opened up a public space in this world for more fully independent human action. As God became more and more perfect, unfathomable, and inaccessible, the anxiety of his dematerialization and that of the path to human salvation (begun in the twistings and turnings of ancient monotheism) became so overwhelming that men despaired of their ability to take any action in that direction at all, and turned their energies inward to the private soul, and also outward, onto the public matters of this world.

On the very first page of the second volume of his exemplary work, *The Foundations of Modern Political Thought*,[10] which will serve as my principal guide to this time period, Quentin Skinner presents a Martin Luther who, he says, is "obsessed by the idea of man's complete unworthiness . . . in which the sufferer comes to have a total mistrust in the value of his own existence." Luther wrote *The Bondage of the Will* in 1525, specifically as a response to Erasmus's discourse *On the Freedom of the Will* (1524).[11]

The question of the bondage or freedom of the will became a central philosophical obsession of the modern age. It had to do, in the first place, with whether man had the wherewithal to save himself, or the freedom to act justly. These are not exactly the same, but they were, as it were, the inner and outer, or private and public faces of one question, as modern philosophers were to divide it. Erasmus, having initially refused to put himself in between the Church and Luther, was finally pushed to a defense of traditional Catholic doctrine asserting the moral necessity of the freedom of the will, as Augustine had done centuries before. Luther thundered back against the humanist "equivocator" that our wills remain in total bondage to sin. "We can do nothing but averse and evil things . . . we are all under sin and damnation [and are left with] no capacity to do anything but sin and be damned."[12] The problem of the freedom of the will grew into the conundrum of freedom itself, the central value of the modern age. The question of man's freedom to choose, what it means, and how it is to be achieved, forms an insoluble problem in modern philosophical and political discourse. In *The Bondage of the Will*, Luther writes "we have all 'fallen from God and been deserted by God,' so that we are all completely 'bound, wretched, captive, sick, and dead.'"[13] If we are in bondage and have no free will, we are left to the desolations of an evil fate in a fallen world.

"Bound, wretched, captive, sick, and dead" could serve as a description of the believer's unrelieved state of suffering. It can be argued that the modern age, in both its religious and secular forms, begins with suffering. "Bound, wretched, captive, sick, and dead" is not so completely different, after all, from Hobbes's secular formulation of our natural condition as "solitary, poor, nasty, brutish, and short." The former sounds worse. The misery of man is the starting point for both of these, the most spiritual and the most secular, of analysts. The suffering of human beings is taken, virtually unilaterally, as the starting point of all further discussion.[14]

The reality of human suffering is the ground upon which the construction of the modern world, both spiritual and temporal, public and private, stands.[15] "Deserted by God" marks the distance between God and man. Luther's God is utterly inscrutable, a "hidden God, the *Deus Absconditus*, whose 'immutable, eternal and infallible will' is incapable of being comprehended by men at all. . . . The will of the hidden God is omnipotent . . . but it is also beyond our understanding."[16]

Martin Luther struggled all his life with the problem of God's wrath, and of his own wrath toward God. He was a monk, a preacher, a professor, a rebel, and a reformer, who in his struggle to come to terms with God's righteousness had to come to terms with man's sinfulness, his helplessness, his affliction. For Luther, God exhibited not only a vast distance from man, but also an absoluteness that made him unable to be in any way measured, accounted for, or counted on for a response. Luther came after Thomas Aquinas, who had set the rational world and the natural world into the divine plan of the entire order of being. Luther lived in the days of William of Occam's ascendency into the sanctum of the Church and the academy. A form of Occamism was dominant in the Augustinian monastery at Erfurt, where Luther became a monk; it was the reigning philosophical discourse of his education. It's impossible to imagine Luther without Occam, who changed the meaning of "realism" in religion and introduced a form of skepticism and empiricism into theology. Luther was later able to use Occam's realism to pry God from the Church. Occam severed the metaphysical connections between spirit, the invisible world, and the visible matters accessible to mind and human logic in the here and now.

> God has no ascertainable attributes and does not underlie any generalities which we can "think." We cannot know His intentions or His obligations: his *potentia* is *absoluta*. He has *infinita latitudo*, and there is no way of obliging or coercing Him by developing the right disposition, be it ever so saintly. All we can hope is that when

the judgment comes we will prove acceptable to Him, and that He will grant us an *extenuatio legis*.[17]

Occam's famous principle, *Non est ponenda pluralitas sine necesessitate*, not to multiply explanatory principles beyond what is necessary, served to separate what can be known from what cannot, and served notice that God was not to be bought or sold on earth. He was absolutely different, and earthly things are of no benefit in relation to God's absolute being. This was of crucial importance for Luther, who used it as a lever and pushed into implacable opposition the indestructible inner voice of the individual's conscience, his surrender to his own cross, to grace and faith in the Word, and the corrupt and exploitative Church, extracting coins from the poor and bribes from the wealthy, trafficking in the most forbidden substance of all, God's justice.

For Luther, "free choice avails for nothing but sinning." The experience of an absolutely unknowable God, "who foreknows all things . . . necessarily and immutably," leads to "a doctrine of double predestination—the contention that some men must already be predestined to be saved while others are predestined to be damned."[18] So there opens up an "unbridgeable gulf between God and man," and God appears "terrifyingly inexorable," while man is left "completely helpless."

The gulf, Skinner affirms, creates problems with God's righteousness. For Luther, the problem is not with historical injustice but rather with God's anger, which is presented in the context of his unfathomable difference, his complete inaccessibility. God demands that we follow his laws, which we are *by our nature* incapable of following. The despair this knowledge produced in Luther led him to his well-known "tower experience," sometime in the year 1513, in which he experienced God's righteousness as God's inexplicable, undeserved, incomprehensible, but very real mercy for his own unworthiness.

In explaining his experience, Luther said that he "hated the righteous God who punishes sinners, and secretly, if not blasphemously . . . I was angry with God and said, 'As if, indeed, it is not enough, that miserable sinners, eternally lost through original sin, are crushed by every kind of calamity . . . without having God add pain to pain . . . by the gospel threatening us with his righteousness and wrath!'"[19] (This is not so far from Nietzsche's blasting accusation centuries later that adding God's judgment to human suffering adds insult to injury and perversely makes injury worse. Luther certainly apprehended the problem, howevermuch he would not have approved of Nietzsche's use of it.)

But, at last, Luther said, "by the mercy of God, meditating day and night, I gave heed to the context of the words, namely, 'In it the righteousness of God is revealed,' as it is written, 'He who through faith is righteous shall live.'" He understood then that the righteousness of God is a gift of God, faith, "the passive righteousness with which merciful God justifies us by faith. . . . Here I felt that I was altogether born again and had entered paradise itself through open gates."[20]

> The core of Luther's new theology is constituted by his doctrine of justification *sola fide*, "by faith alone." He continues to stress that no one can ever hope to be justified—that is, granted salvation—by virtue of his own works. But now he argues that it must be open to anyone to perceive God's *gratia*—the 'saving grace' which He must already have granted as a totally unmerited favour to those whom He has predestined to be saved. . . . Righteousness of the believer is never *domestica*—never achieved by himself, and still less deserved. It can only be *extranea*—an "alien righteousness, instilled in us without our works by grace alone.[21]

What is important for our purposes is that Luther concludes that the Christian believer inhabits two separate worlds—a spiritual world, internal and private, the spiritual sufferings of which constitute his most powerful reality and through which he is connected to God's unmerited grace by faith, and an external, sinful, material, political world, abandoned by God, but presided over by powerful rulers, appointed by God, who command lawful obedience. Since the things of this world cannot affect one's salvation, total obedience is required.

Luther importantly included the family in his conception of the private world, as the place where the private individual finds a home and comfort. "For Luther the Christian family was the epicenter of human social existence. The family was an arena of compassion, concern, kindness, and emotion, but Luther also located learning obedience to authority in the family."[22] Jean Elshtain argues that Luther "tied the *nature, structure,* and *purpose* of secular order to that of the family."[23] This is perhaps an overstatement. Secular rulers figured crucially for Luther as the ordained repositories of God's power and will on earth. It is true that Luther saw the family as the heart of earthly human existence and that he held very modern views on the value of conjugal equality and the naturalness of sexual desire, even female sexual desire. But Luther stressed obedience, in the family and to the state. Because he held the natural, temporal world in so little regard and saw it as irremediably fallen and degenerate, he allowed only private relations and values to count toward earthly happiness and discouraged all interest in and participation in secular life and public political institutions. The private realm was profoundly real to him, as Erikson makes plain in his classic biography; the public one was much more obscure and threatening to him. In neither realm is human agency efficacious for what counts.

And there is certainly a sense in which Elshtain's claim about the social centrality of the family, structurally and historically, is quite correct. When the Church ceased to be the major public and private institutional power in society, the family became the modern institution in which the central relations of Christian life were experienced and empowered. By extension all spiritual and moral life, all life that inevitably centers around the emotionally charged occasions and judgments of sin, punishment, suffering, and redemption, all life that centers around psychic and bodily identity, all these most spiritually and morally charged issues of life, came to be lodged in the family. The family became, in a certain sense, the substitute for the whole lost unity of the Christian world. Only the modern state could count as having eventually displaced it.

From the perspective of the question of suffering, Luther's domestic realm marks the beginning of the extreme privatization of certain kinds of suffering that comes to characterize the early modern age. The Protestant *ecclesia* was a community of families, separated finally by legal barriers from the establishments of the modern state. All the consolations for suffering that had centered in the great medieval establishment of the Church were then forced into retreat to the redoubt of family and conscience, without a publicly certified vertical anchor in the public world. Suffering changes when it is no longer public, just as when it is no longer penance. In the first case, it is no longer an object of political action; in the second, it is no longer unambiguously moral.

TWO REALMS DIVIDED WITHIN AND WITHOUT

Political theorists have always identified the beginning of modern politics with the division of the world into spiritual and temporal jurisdictions, the *regnum* and the *sacerdotum*, a division that predates the modern age, but which historically generates the basic form of the public-private distinction. It is in terms of the public-private distinction that modern representative political authority is founded and delineated. It is important to follow at least some of the ins and outs of this separating out of the public-political from the private sphere, because the new forms of social and political life that identify the new age take their shape and structural power from the original tension inherent in the split, the difference between the invisible and the visible, the spiritual and the temporal, as this tension was experienced by both individual believers and communities of believers, in conflict and at war.

Christians who followed Luther and other Protestant Reformers, who created a myriad of different versions of the new faith, lived in a tense interplay between obligations—the obligation to this world's authority and the simultaneous obligation of righteous refusal to participate in its ways, especially in its violence. Marcel Gauchet argues that there was a "complementary relationship between inside and outside, both on the individual and collective levels. At the private level, it placed the unworldly deep within the self, while requiring external respect for the way of the world; publicly, it separated the righteous who renounce the world from the sinners who surrender to it." He also emphasizes "the potential for deep antagonism between the personal and social selves."[24] Individual liberty, what Luther first called Christian liberty, involves, even requires, a deep interiorization and subjectification of the self. The split in the soul came about in relation to the split in the world, which mirrored and made more potent the split in the individual. The self is divided as the world is divided. The privatization of faith also privatized suffering; even in the outer, fallen world, nothing could be done except obey.

What Luther and the "saints" who made a revolution alongside and after him felt was the energy that churned out of this profound inner split, which pitted conscience against the demands and obligations of this world, both requiring obedience. While Luther could go so far as to defy obedience to the Church, he could not countenance disobedience to temporal rulers. He spoke of "*Die zwo Personen oder zweierlei ampt*," two personalities and two callings, which a Christian must maintain on this earth.[25] The two regnums would be drawn differently historically, in different contexts and theories by different people for different purposes, as history gathered force from these energies, but the split subjectivity and the split in the world it reflects and doubles and is reiterated by is repeated over and over again in the modern age. Modernity itself may be characterized substantively by its production of polarizing constitutive oppositions. This is an era of mutually defining dualisms that repeat, obsessively, identities through exclusions.

Christian liberty, according to Luther, consists of inner freedom but outer obedience. His eventual violent and reactionary turn against the Peasants Rebellion in 1525, which was conducted in his name, made him a scandal to his friends. "The secular sword must be red and bloody, for the world will and must be evil."[26] Good above and evil below; the public realm is the evil realm, and what should we expect of it but suffering for man.

In Luther we see the emergence of the new modern subject. Suffering is an inextricable part of his modern subjectivity. It was on the "inner frontier," in Erikson's words, the frontier of consciousness and subjectivity, of guilt and conscience, that a profound facet of the modern self is forged in Luther. Luther knew himself to be a sinner: "*Tibi Soli Peccavi*, To you alone I have sinned," he said to God. Luther embraced suffering; he moved toward the willing affirmation of suffering, the willed surrender to the cross. It is from the perspective of the sufferer that he speaks.

In his *Heidelberg Disposition* of 1518, Luther denounced Aristotelian metaphysics and affirmed instead, "But he is a theologian who understands by observing visible things and the 'back parts of God' through sufferings and the cross."[27] For Luther, "we preach Christ crucified." The suffering, of man and God, is the touchstone of reality. "The more Christian a man is, the more evils, sufferings and death he must endure," he wrote in "The Freedom of a Christian."[28] It was Luther's willed acceptance of his suffering that allowed him finally to experience the relief of unmerited and predetermined grace. But it was only on the condition of man's sinfulness, undeservedness, and powerlessness that he could believe that faith and the Word would save him. The inner man remains in mortal conflict, and only through introspection finds his absolute condition. "Whatever is in your disposition, that the word of God will be unto you."[29] It is the most personal and inner disposition of the individual soul that inclines God toward mercy or condemnation. In this way, Luther both individualized and privatized the profound subjectivity of the self. "Luther's point of order shrunk to the thinnest thread, a tensile strand he hoped would hold tight in the shipwrecked social world of his age. Clinging to the anchor of the Self, the Christian subject, male or female, dramatically turned inward, for there, Luther said, the Kingdom of God was truly to be found. No matter what winds blew about in the storm, the free Christian could live in the midst of saints or satyrs, criminals or citizens, decay or delight for his 'true transformation . . . is entirely internal.'"[30]

The earliest Protestant Reformers began with the assertion of the necessity for Christians to obey unconditionally their lawful princes, who were ordained by God. But as the political consequences of the new faith began to be felt, and violent massacres were carried out for and against its adherents in what ended up becoming more than a hundred years of violent warfare, rebellion, insurrection, revolution, and counter-Reformation terror, the leaders of the Protestant forces, both religious and secular, ended up endorsing the right of a righteous people to resist ungodly rulers. This was a long and critical journey, made almost against their will by Luther and the more conservative Reformers. It proved indispensable for the formation of modern politics.

Luther wanted to save "the people of God living from the word of God" for God; he also wanted to attack the visible, and visibly corrupt, Catholic Church. He did so in part by insisting that "the true Church becomes nothing more than an invisible *congregatio fidelium*, congregation of the faithful, gathered together in God's name."[31] The true Church has no real existence except in the hearts of its faithful members. No mediators, either spiritual or temporal, are necessary, to get between the soul and God. No "pope, bishop, priests and monks, or princes, lords, artisans and farmers," Luther said in his 1520 address "To The Christian Nobility of the German Nation."[32] The result is that all law is given over to princes. The true Christian Church is "purely inward," a "government of the soul." In his important political tract of 1523, on *Temporal Authority: to what extent it should be obeyed*, Luther argues that "all Christians live simultaneously in two kingdoms, that of Christ and that of the world." The powers of the Church are

> entirely spiritual, since there is by definition no need for true Christians to be coerced. The realm of temporal authority is equally

claimed to be ordained by God, but is seen as wholly separate, since the sword is granted to secular rulers simply in order to ensure that civil peace is maintained among sinful men. All coercive powers are treated as temporal by definition. . . . Since the temporal power is ordained of God to punish the wicked and protect the good, it should be left free to perform its office in the whole body of Christendom without restriction and without respect to persons, whether it affects Pope, bishops, nuns, or anyone else.[33]

Skinner calls the result "an unparalleled extension of the range of secular powers."

There was a radical equalizing potential inherent in Luther's new faith. If all that matters takes place in the recesses of the individual soul, then it follows that all souls are the same and equal, and indeed Luther advocated a radical equality for human beings, to go along with their radical insecurity. "Religious experience was located around an intensely personal communication between the individual and God; the authenticity of the experience depended upon the uninhibited directness of the relationship. . . . everything that stood between God and man had to be eliminated; the only true mediators were Christ and Scripture."[34]

Luther advocated the "priesthood of all believers," a radical equality in the spiritual community that was subversive of hierarchy and authority. "There is no superior among Christians, but Christ Himself and Christ alone. And what kind of authority can there be where all are equal and have the same right, power, possession, and honor, and no one desires to be the other's superior, but each other's inferior?"[35] Luther's followers, especially his English followers, like Robert Barnes and William Tyndale, also asserted the necessity and significance of the invisible versus the visible Church. Barnes speaks of "the very true church" which is "invisible from carnal eyes," because it consists of nothing more than "the congregation of faithful men wherever they are in the world, and neither the Pope nor yet his cardinals are more this Church or of the Church than the poorest man on earth."[36] This conception contributes to a radical leveling of all men, despite rank and office. No intermediaries, no priests, are necessary for communion or salvation. No authorities can bind conscience. If each soul faces God alone, it naturally followed that lesser authorities might also be faced and brought to a halt by conscience.

But absolute obedience to God entails as well the necessity to submit to suffering. Luther tells the believer to "thank God that you are worthy to suffer for the sake of the divine word. . . . [Tyranny] is not to be resisted but endured." The people must be prepared to "suffer everything that can happen, rather than fight against your lord and tyrant," he wrote in direct response to the Peasants Revolt of 1525 in a tract he published the next year called *Whether Soldiers Too can be Saved.*[37] The Reformers also reiterated the ancient biblical injunction that the people suffer as a punishment for their sins. This is God's will. Tyndale says: "therefore, I say, is a Christian called to suffer even the bitter death for his hope's sake, and because he will do no evil. . . . evil rulers are simply a sign that God is angry and wroth with us."[38] The people's suffering is God's will, which he may exercise over us through tyrants to punish us for our sins. The experience of such a sufferer is guilt, anguish, and affliction, the deep sinfulness that gives meaning to suffering. However much such guilt deepens suffering, it also places it in the context of a spiritual life that gives it meaning and value. It asks that suffering be redeemed, eventually, if not in this world, then in the next. No man can know his ultimate fate. God's response to his suffering is unfathomable.

The true Church is invisible and it operates inwardly, in the deepening interior of the soul of the saint. The saints come together as *ecclesia*, but this means merely congregation, a purely spiritual body. The Church is not a jurisdiction. It has "nothing to do with the external justice and righteousness of the world, and therefore it has no power to make law or statutes to order the world, but only to preach faithfully and truly and to minister the word of God."[39] Here sanctity is invisible. Grace is invisible; it resides within the believer and within the community. This is in direct and absolute contrast to the highly visible edifice of the Catholic Church, which declares its visibility and its worldly jurisdiction. But by asserting the interiority and hiddenness, the invisibility of the new Church, Luther and the Reformers assigned all worldly jurisdiction to secular powers. For them, by contrast, the visible world and its chaos falls under worldly jurisdiction. And worldly matters are no business of the faithful. The invisible soul follows inner conscience, suffers endlessly, may not resist authority, and even dies in silence to testify to faith. Luther was never silent, of course, and the noise of his new faith, the uproar it engendered, was not in the end silenced. But what the uproar made clear, finally, was that faith cannot be coerced by any authority, religious or secular. No magistrate can rule over the private consciences of persons or congregations, as John Locke was to argue most eloquently.

The argument that ensued historically in the sixteenth century between the Reformers, who asserted the invisibility of the Church, and the defenders of the traditional visible and political Church is important for the overall argument of this book. One traditional mark of God's existence, even his materialization and his reliable connection to mankind, lay in his divinely given laws and ordinances, the proper forms of worship. God's invisibility was remedied, in a way, by the visibility, the materiality, the bodilyness of the suffering he was capable of inflicting on his people for their sins, and by the concrete ministrations of those he ordained. Or perhaps to put it a better way, the people's suffering was explained and justified in terms of God's need to be materialized in his laws and practices of worship, even though these were never transparent or unproblematical. What constitutes proper practices of worship in any religion has always been open to doubt, and its definition changes over time.

How faith is to be materialized, how conscience is to be expressed, how suffering is to be understood and addressed, by God and by princes, came to open warfare in the sixteenth century. The people suffered over the proper forms of God's materialization. At the Council of Trent in 1546, and in innumerable other battles, both dogmatic and political, God's materialization was in question in terms of the visibility or invisibility of his Church. The Church was still the locus of the remedy for suffering, but was it a visible place or an invisible state of mind? Was there a remedy in human action, however mediated, or none?

How is this now ever more immaterial, ever more elusive, silent, spiritual, inscrutable, and invisible God to be known and worshiped? The previous traditional solution, stretching back for two millennia, had been the institutionalization of the Incarnation—Christ and the Apostles embodied, materialized, made solid and visible in stone and glass, vestments and orders, laws and rituals, sacrifices and martyrdoms, in the world as the Church. They were a direct, dominating translation of God's justice, presence, and love impressed into hierarchies of worship and power to rule this world. Positively, the Church was empowered to minister to human suffering with time-honored and sanctioned remedies. It could be argued that the Reformation and the various breakthroughs to the modern age it represented constituted a final crisis of God's invisibility, a problematization of his materialization that could ultimately not be solved. It could be argued that this forms a large part of what Nietzsche was later to call the death of God. It could even be argued that what began as a crisis of God's materialization turned into a crisis of our own materialization by the time of the uncanny "end" of the modern era. When Nietzsche announced the death of God and the collapse of all the values that depended on him, directly and indirectly, he identified as the instrument of destruction the will to power as will to truth, which ultimately shattered all idols, not only those of religion but those of philosophy, morality and politics as well. This shattering left us unsure not only of God, as Luther was, but even more frighteningly, unsure of ourselves, of our own materiality, of our own substance. This comes to the fore in the problematics of postmodernism.

The argument begins with Luther, who begins with suffering, his own, and who then generalizes to the unworthiness and misery of human affliction and sin in a fallen world. From this misery and affliction he grasps God's always already given saving grace, his gratuitous mercy. By asserting God's irreducible invisibility, and the consequent invisibility of the faith of his elect, the true believers, those gratuitously saved and chosen through no merit or actions or works of their own, Luther dispenses with the problem of God's materialization altogether.

God is not material. He is not made manifest except as he came into time in Christ and in the Word. God is not materialized on earth at all, except insofar as nature, the world itself, and we in it, are his creations. But God remains invisible, transcendent, unintelligible, and unknowable, wholly Other, only to be approached in the secret hearts and souls of his own. There is no material church, no material spirit in the world, neither in law nor in rulers nor anywhere else. Spirit is immaterial. No physical certainty about it is possible. The world is thus cut loose, set free, revealed for itself alone as open to human reason and action. It follows, then, that human suffering, as spiritual affliction, cannot be remedied institutionally. Justice or right practices, sanctioned by God for the people and embodied in laws and princes, become subjective, perhaps finally meaningless, ephemeral at best. This was what the opponents of the Reformation understood to be the root of the heresy. Justice becomes merely a matter of positive laws given by kings and parliaments. As Hobbes insists, "There is no right reason in nature." God may not yet be dead, but he is certainly missing.

Historically, the concept of natural law lingered for many centuries as a ghostly reflection of what law in the Divine Imperium had been. But without an active, intervening God and a material, mediating Church, and without a divinely appointed ruler to embody and administer divine will, God's will becomes an abstraction, and, eventually, a mere location, a position, a signifier. As an abstraction, divine will has some staying power. But an abstract will, even in so powerful a guise as Kantian Reason, is rather too easily, even self-evidently, overrun by the passions, the interests, the will to power that always accompanies and directs it. Hobbes prophetically demonstrates this at the very beginning of the modern age and Nietzsche passionately insists upon it at the end. What Nietzsche scorns as Kant's "faculty" of moral reason begins to suffer from dematerialization almost immediately.

Historically, modern justice is an abstraction, as the social contract. What justice could mean without divine right to back it up necessarily became an object of doubt and conjecture, even an obsession, for modern political theorists. Without God to give it unity, universality, and will, and a certain absolute claim about the nature of reality, justice becomes friable, brittle, fractured, linguistic and conventional, a casualty of righteous and unrighteous contention, until it was positivized into what merely is said. As will become clear in later chapters, justice as the social contract, and even as the mystical body of the People, does not prove to have the holding power as an institution, or the compelling power as a bond, that divine justice as an institutionalized Incarnation did.

The modern state performs a somewhat similar function of holding, unifying, and universalizing power in the place of the Transcendent Signifier, exercising its symbolic and coercive powers over vast distances. But it doesn't quite have the moral authority which had been mustered for faith. Not that fewer men have died for nationalism than they have for faith. But the nature of moral authority changes under this onslaught, and it is moral authority that is demanded to account for and respond to suffering.

This is all to say that the argument about whether the Church, the mediator between the invisible and visible realms, the institution responsible for salvation and cosmic justice and the remedy of sin and suffering, whether the Church is visible or invisible, lies at the very crux of the issue that is posed by suffering and politics. Suffering is of its essence presence. If its remedy lacks presence, the justification for suffering falters. If the answering moral authority is visible, it physically unites the two worlds; it represents the unrepresentable. If it is not visible, it leaves us only this world of human bodies, human minds, and human needs, not in eternity, but in nature and history. The presence of human suffering is no less, even if its answer disappears. The question of justice emerges as the political face of this problem.

The People and the Revolution become by the eighteenth century alternative embodiments of justice and legitimate authority in historical time, after a short period of absolute monarchy that is necessarily transitional. But how the people are to embody justice, how their individual wills can be forged into the unity of the General Will, remained practically and theoretically unresolvable. How to make the General Will visible is another version of the same question, which Rousseau poses and tries to answer from the perspective of the spectator to the suffering of the masses, one who tries to devise a secular redemption.

By withdrawing faith into the secret recesses of conscience, Luther and the Reformers left the temporal powers to rule the world. "Our rulers must be obeyed in all things—and not merely out of fear, but (as St. Paul decrees) for conscience's sake. . . . It can never be justifiable in any circumstances for a subject to resist a ruler's commands."[40] Sheldon Wolin argues that "the emphasis on secular power should be viewed as the outgrowth of the deepening antipolitical radicalism of his [Luther's] religious convictions, which, by assigning exclusive rights over the 'political' to temporal governors and by minimizing the political character and ecclesiastical power of the Church, opened the way for a temporal monopoly on all kinds of power."[41] In this temporal space, a newly formed public realm, the argument began in earnest as to how sovereignty was truly to be founded and in what parties it was to be invested.

POPULAR SOVEREIGNTY AND
THE AUTONOMY OF PUBLIC AUTHORITY

The secular rulers of Europe were quick to take up the new faith as a potent weapon in their struggles against the Catholic Church. It is of historical importance that the princes of the many principalities of Germany and the kings and princes of England and Scotland, Sweden, Denmark, and the Netherlands all used the argument that the true Church is and must be an invisible congregation of the faithful in order to justify taking control over the "fiscal privileges and landed wealth of the Church within their territories . . . . these aims . . . provided the main motive in every country for the official acceptance of the Lutheran faith."[42] In Germany and the Low Countries, the Reformation was truly popular in many places and its acceptance less utilitarian than this commentary suggests, but even in Germany "these ambitions often supplied the dominant motive for the behavior of the secular authorities."

In the period that followed the spread of Reformation doctrines and the outbreak of violent hostilities in numerous localities all over Western and Central Europe, warfare between rival religious and political groups escalated over the next century. Three important and transforming accomplishments were achieved: first, the establishment of an autonomous, secular public realm and jurisdiction, presided over by political authorities who did not derive their legitimacy from God or the spiritual realm; second, the establishment and legitimation of popular sovereignty as the ultimate authority, conferring legitimacy on this autonomous public realm (which did not occur without a fight); and three, the opening up of the question of knowledge as the central philosophical obsession of thought in the modern age, especially as this question of knowledge, as science, was to be applied to natural law, moral knowledge, and justice, as demanded by the suffering. This is a long and complicated story, which has been told many times. I will only pick out certain moments in these developments for the purpose of pinpointing suffering in the private and public spheres in relation to the new religious and secular conceptions taking hold.

One of the most important changes occurred with the emergence of new forms of knowledge in the Renaissance, on the Continent and in England. Skinner traces the most decisive early influence to the work of Jean Bodin (1520–96), "the greatest French philosopher of the age," whose last work, the *Colloquium*, was completed in 1588. In this work, Bodin renews a form of high monotheism as the common ground on which all different types of believers might agree. "The most important point . . . is that God is the parent of all gods . . . the common Author and Parent of all nature, so that He may lead us into a knowledge of the true religion."[43] (It might be added that it is not a huge step from this Parent of all gods to Robespierre's Festival of the Supreme Being, 20 Prairial, Year II of the Revolution [June 8, 1794], inspired, it has been argued, by Rousseau. It should be noted that the Terror, however, was not conducted in the name of this Supreme Being, but in the name of the Sublime People, that mystical element which had become an earthly embodiment of sacredness, holding the position of ultimate or absolute righteousness on behalf of the Supreme Being.)

Bodin's even more radical argument for religious liberty, however, had to do with what Skinner calls the "unavoidable uncertainty at the heart of our religious beliefs." Costellio, a follower of Bodin, argues that the violent disputes of the time about religious matters can "arise solely from ignorance of the truth." He summarizes: "All religious persecutions are based in effect on a presumption of certainty about a range of questions over which no certainty can ever be attained." Bodin also finds no "indubitable foundations for any religious creed," which are all based on "faith and belief only."[44]

The question of knowledge moves to the center stage of proof for religious and political debate, and increasingly, the lack of knowledge or certainty about God's purposes and man's lack of access to or understanding of them comes to stand in place of knowledge itself as justification for action. Luther asserted our lack of knowledge concerning God's purposes and our own salvation. The philosophers assert that the evidence of our violent disagreements shows what we don't know. What begins to be an indispensable element in the religious debates of the next two centuries is the "unavoidable uncertainty," irrevocable, permanent, and pervasive uncertainty, a lack of knowledge about matters pertaining to God's worship. This lack of knowledge becomes finally the most important reason for setting these questions aside, bracketing them, placing them deliberately and legally in the private realm of conscience, and allowing public space to be open only for the resolution of public matters that can be decided on the basis of demonstrable public knowledge. The development of a new kind of demonstrable public knowledge, science, helped greatly in this displacement. The public realm was the realm of human agency, and Hobbes was the thinker who first addressed the question of such agency. While spiritual suffering was not something we could do something about publicly, there were some kinds of suffering that were open to human action.

As John Locke argued later in *A Letter Concerning Toleration*, what we don't know, what we cannot know, is beyond legislation, beyond the power of magistrates to decide.[45] What we can and cannot know effectively became the working criteria for explaining and justifying human action, and therefore, human suffering as well. Only true knowledge, said the philosophers and legislators, could justify coercion in the name of the commonwealth. We can have no such true knowledge, neither self-evident, nor demonstrable, nor agreed on by all rational men, on which to base religious prescriptions. The corollary, for politics, seemed to be that we can control and act as a body of people only on what we can know. The criteria of knowledge were changing.

The argument of the constitutionalists was that we can know whether magistrates are ruling for our welfare and the common good, and this knowledge and its deployments became the basis for the development of the people's right of resistance to tyranny. Since the people are the authors of sovereignty, as first Hobbes and later Locke and Rousseau all demonstrate, the "democratical gentlemen" will argue that the people, or their designated propertied representatives on their behalf, may dissolve and reconstitute such public authorities as they see fit. In contrast, people are not the authors of what God intends, and therefore, these matters must be left to the discretion of the individual subject.

That is to say, certain kinds of suffering must remain subjective, private, negotiated only with one's conscience and God, while certain other kinds of suffering, especially those deriving from the depradations of tyrannical and unjust rulers, are public and temporal and subject to the will and decisions of the people, the body of whom form the commonwealth. The people give legitimacy, or remove it, from rulers. This was not self-evident to some rulers (and still isn't), but the logic and power of this reasoning spread with ever-accelerating enthusiasm through the public places and discourses of Europe and then the New World in the next century. It eventually brought about a new kind of order everywhere it was carried.

The concept of knowledge changed radically in these years, and its importance increased to unprecedented proportions. The powers of knowledge became simultaneously more focused, more rigorous, and more powerful than ever, ruling on what was real and what was not. The division between the invisible and the visible became the division between the knowable and the unknowable. The kind of suffering that the soul undergoes is known only to God; it is not otherwise knowable and must be left to God. The suffering of the people, on the other hand, of the body politic, is visible and knowable, and finally, remediable, through rational knowledge and action. This is the force of the modern democratic revolution that defines the modern age.

Skinner argues that "there is no doubt that the main influence of Lutheran political theory in early modern Europe lay in the direction of encouraging and legitimating the emergence of unified and absolutist monarchies."[46] This is perhaps true in the short run, but not in the long run. The main consequence of Lutheranism was the separation of the private realm from the public realm, the establishment of a powerful interior individual conscience in relation to a unified secular space, a new public space, from which spiritual activity was eventually evacuated. It is the case that the original inheritors, profiteers if you like, of this breaking away of an autonomous public, secular realm were the natural rulers, the princes and kings in place in the various nationalizing territories, and that the theory and practice of the divine right of kings, of absolute monarchy, quickly moved to fill the vacuum left by departing divine authority. But this movement was only a way-station, a transitory form on the road to revolutionary change and the imposition of the rule of popular sovereignty through representative assemblies. At least that's how it looks to us, from the vantage point of later history. This is the verdict of the victorious knowledges that prevailed to found political power in the democratic political institutions of the age to come.

The rule of the Divine King and the rule of the Sublime People are mirror images of each other. Luther's radically equalizing doctrine of the "priesthood of all believers," and the democratic leveling brought about within the more radical sects, both religious and political, in the next century, made the transition to popular sovereignty as the standard value of the modern age seem almost inevitable. Kings, after all, had been the mediators between the divine and earthly realms long before Christianity, and they were the obvious heirs to the dethronement of the Church. But once divine grace and conscience, with all its torments, rested in every individual, the logic of the autonomy of the individual, seeking knowledge of God's will and then of the natural world, would seem if not necessarily, then perhaps inevitably, to generalize itself to the social collectivity. It seems to be part of the ontological split between subject and object, or nature and reason, part of the logic of the structural separation of spiritual and secular realms and public and private jurisdictions, that the individual and the commmunity would come to constitute themselves as self-sufficient entities and self-identifying elements.

Absolute monarchy constitutes power in this world as fully legitimate, and this expresses both the ontological independence of the political in itself, and the domain of metaphysical freedom. It is a "mirror" of the symbolic structure of the self-sufficient people, of "democratic power." Gauchet argues:

> The monarch gradually evolved from incarnating sacral dissimularity into realizing the collective body's internal self-congruence. He slowly changed from being a symbol of dependence on the organizing other into a legal representative and coercive force for bringing the political community (of the nation) into line with its autonomous reason for its existence and its own principle. The development of the political in the modern age was the practical deployment of this symbolic turnaround, along two major lines. One was the deployment of a type of State oriented toward taking complete control of collective organization; the other was a form of legitimacy based on the convergence of power and society, as well as the coincidence of action applied to the society and the expression of the society.[47]

The corollary of the campaign against the power and jurisdiction of the Church was the proclamation of the power and divine jurisdiction of the King, "effecting a transfer to the crown of all the jurisdictional powers which the church had previously exercised."[48] Skinner locates the "revolutionary" change at the moment when the "Church in England begins to mutate into the Church of England," and argues that here "a distinctively modern concept of political obligation begins to emerge: it was at this point, but not before, that it became possible for the secular authorities to legitimate the claim that they should be regarded as the sole jurisdictional power within their own territories, and thus they should be recognised as the sole appropriate object of a subject's political allegiance."[49] Here the impetus toward popular sovereignty that was to culminate in the seventeenth and eighteenth centuries really began.

In the seventeenth century, according to the early constitutionalists and contract theorists, public officials were made to be held accountable to lesser magistrates and then to representative assemblies. But they were held accountable in terms of political legitimacy, justice, and law. The newly forming public realm was the arena for the struggle over the nature of political injustice and for the settling of political rights and freedoms. Suffering, for individuals, was defined as private, through many varying historical permutations of the private realm. Suffering for the individual remained a matter of individual conscience, of private and family morality and Christian charity, of personal fortitude and the deep vicissitudes of the self. Private suffering was disallowed, until our own time, as a political claim upon the responsibility of public authority. Public suffering, however, became the modern object of politics, par excellence, as I show in the following chapters. The division between public and private suffering, however, remained unstable throughout the modern period. The fence between the two was constantly being moved for strategic purposes.

A crucial corollary implication of Luther's belief in the centrality of the individual and the family for all matters of faith was the conviction that the natural temporal world, the one wholly given over to the rule of kings and magistrates, was an unregenerate world, one from which the otherworldly saints, especially those of the more radical sects and wilder denominations of the Reformation, could and should utterly withdraw. The basic creed of the Anabaptists, for instance, was that "although the sword is ordained of God, it is outside the perfection of Christ."

> The secular authorities form no part of the regenerate world; they merely exist because of the unfortunate necessity for sinful men to be coerced. This leads to the conclusion that, even if the apparatus of secular power may be needed to keep the peace amongst the unregenerate, they themselves have no need of it, since they have all been released from their sins by the illumination of the Holy Spirit, and have thereby become an elect community within the unregenerate world. It was thus entirely logical for them to insist on what they unceremoniously called 'a separation from the abomination.' . . . They refused to bear arms or to make use of any 'unchristian, devilish weapons of force'; they declared that 'it is not appropriate for a Christian to serve as magistrate,' and accordingly refused to use

the lawcourts or to 'pass judgment between brother and brother'; and they declined to pay war-taxes, to recognize existing laws of property or to take part in civic or political affairs.[50]

True Christians are "sheep for the slaughter," they must be "baptised in anguish, tribulation, persecution, suffering, and death." The Quakers completely agreed. The dominant Puritan vision of the natural world as bleak and sinful, grim, gruesome, and unforgiving was to be carried over as foundational and axiomatic in its secular versions a century later. The early modern political theorists accepted the consequences of the view that the need for secular commonwealths originally arose in consequence of the Fall. That is to say, that it was a fallen world that needed to be governed by force by the now greatly extended powers of public authority.[51]

Perhaps the most important and long-lasting "consequence" of the Lutheran Reformation was what the theorists of the Thomist revival and the churchmen of the Counter-Reformation specified as the "greatest" or "root" heresy of the new faith and its justifiers—the denial of the efficacy of God's natural law in human law, and hence the denial of the existence of justice inherent in nature, in men's minds, and in their natural communities. Luther's insistence on the utterly fallen nature of man, the absolute inwardness and hiddenness of the single soul's struggle for justification, and that soul's ultimate dependence on faith, on grace alone, necessarily entailed that men could not in any way find, produce, or reproduce any reflection of God's justice in their own social arrangements. There was no natural justice on earth.

The Thomists understood that they needed to be able to show, "in the words of the *Decree concerning Justification*," issued at the Council of Trent, "that while men are doubtless full of moral weakness and are 'servants of sin,' the Lutherans must nevertheless be in error in denying men any element of "indwelling grace."[52] In the latter part of the sixteenth century,

> Bellarmine acknowledges in his treatise *Concerning Justification* that the main heresy which needs to be resisted is the widespread and dangerous belief (which he cites from Luther's discussion of Galatians) that "faith alone justifies" and that "there cannot be any inherent justice in the soul of man" (VI, 172, 178) And Suarez similarly recognizes, at the start of his account of man's subjection to law, that the error which needs above all to be extirpated is "the blasphemous suggestion of Luther" that "it is impossible even for a just man to follow the law of God."[53]

DeSoto and Suarez judge that this denial of man's inherent justice is the root and basis of all other heresies. "The early Jesuit theorists clearly recognized the pivotal point at which the political theories of Luther and

Machiavelli may be said to converge: both of them were equally concerned, for their own very different reasons, to reject the idea of the law of nature as an appropriate moral basis for political life. It is in consequence in the works of the early Jesuits that we first encounter the familiar coupling of Luther and Machiavelli as the two founding fathers of the impious modern state."[54]

Why was this the most important heresy of Luther and the Reformers? Why did it have such far-reaching implications for politics? What the early opponents of the new faith understood and what early modern political theorists had to grapple with as fundmental for everything else was the fact that denuding the world of all natural justice leaves everything up for grabs. A fallen world (where justice inheres only in vague and unemployable natural moral laws that are not agreed on and cannot specify ethical conduct or solve conflicts regarding the most basic issues of faith and responsibility) becomes a world where the mighty devise the rules and rights that serve them and secure them dominion, which they justify by calling themselves, for instance, "divine kings," or later, "the rational and industrious" (Locke). Men defend "by right" what they want and what they own against the encroachments of other men and against public authorities. If there is no justice in nature, then there is no natural rule of morality either, which can readily distinguish the victims from the perpetrators of injustice, or the righteous from the fallen. The political justice that is then given into the preserve of the state is carefully differentiated from the private rights of private individuals, which the state is devised to secure. Justice in its deepest nature becomes private when rights become private. This is the argument to which we turn next, in the works of Thomas Hobbes.

THE RELIGIOUS SOLUTION TO THE PROBLEM OF SUFFERING

In summary then, the religious construction of suffering is from the perspective of the sufferer, unrelieved in relation to an unknown God. It is the inevitable result of the human will, sinful, passionate, disobedient, perverse, and tormented, which is necessarily and deservedly punished by a righteous and unknowable God. Human suffering comes from fault, the guilt of human beings, whose selfishness, willfulness, and egotism lead to their affliction and wretchedness. This wretchedness can only be assuaged by God's absolute and predetermined judgment and the individual's willed submission to the goodness and grace of the Father. In the late medieval world, at the beginnings of the upheavals begun by the Renaissance humanists, who were trying to open up the cosmos to human curiosity, artistic creativity, classical learning and scientific invention, by alchemical magic and the printed word, a gloomy and prodigious monk, Martin Luther, both affirmed the power of the unleashed avenging individual conscience and split the world into warring camps. He also split the individual into nature and spirit, into dual obediences to the world of external authorities and to the desires and sufferings of the cauterizing conscience. Tormented and afflicted, sometimes feeling saved and sometimes feeling damned, he nevertheless attacked mercilessly the earthly home of the spirit on earth, its corrupt foundations and distorted fabrications.

Religion constructed suffering as justified, as deserved punishment, and as the overriding concern of the individual soul in relation to his world. The new religion's response to suffering, in contrast to the traditions of centuries, was not to provide a hierarchy of material and practical means to assuage guilt, alleviate suffering, and apportion eternity, but rather to focus the full intensity of guilt and responsibility on the individual conscience. The effect of Luther's faith was to withdraw from the soul its earthly compensations and ordinances and to vastly intensify both its torments and its consciousness of them, without offering apparent remedies. Total responsibility rested with the individual. Sin was original and predestined, salvation far off and uncertain at best. Suffering, in other words, became an unrelievable burden, a problem and an unresolved inheritance, the anxieties of which fueled the energies of those who manufactured the new discourses and political devices of the modern age. Unrelieved and unexplained, human suffering became an inheritance that they would have to address and for which they would have to find new solutions.

2

A Science of Suffering Bodies

Luther bequeathed to the men of science and philosophy who followed him historically a problem of suffering that proved intractible in terms of both their knowledge and their institutions. Religion had provided a meaning and a justification for suffering, which, while it was difficult and even unfathomable, did provide a moral code, sanctioned by God, for determining good and evil, virtue and vice, and which inserted suffering into that code as an index or marker of human morality, at least in God's eyes. When Christianity ceased to be one single overarching religion with a single unified Church, which could prescribe the requisite gradations of the meaning of suffering and promote the faith and sanctions to endure it, suffering threatened to become pointless, or worse, mistaken. The great Church split into warring factions, dogmas, and unsanctioned rulers, who sought to attain the victory for their faiths by armed violence. The moral authority of Christianity as well as its ritual capacity to ameliorate suffering were severely damaged. The new science, on the other hand, recently invented out of a combination of new cosmological theories, empirical and technological data, and developing mathematics, especially geometry, opened the way to entirely new realms of knowledge and to human claims of certainty and demonstrability, which religious knowledge at the time palpably lacked.

While religion had for centuries supplied a public rationale and purpose for human suffering (albeit one with heavy costs in guilt and pain for the sufferer), the new privacy of subjective faith and the manifest uncertainty of religious salvation, as proclaimed by Protestant doctrines of predestination, served to render human suffering institutionally unprotected and insufficiently justified by well-established doctrines. Human suffering, as a newly naked existential problem for all people, aggravated by the carnage of religious wars and the incessant fighting of political factions, moved to the center of human deliberations about nature, life, and knowledge. Modern scientific knowledge gave men new power over what they came to see as the natural conditions that caused suffering, but that knowledge was specifically not moral knowledge for the guidance of human conduct, either public or private. The problem of moral knowledge came to be an enduring, unresolved preoccupation of the modern age, precisely because science could not address it in its old guises and therefore transformed it into new ones. Because suffering continued to be understood as a moral problem, the question of the kind of knowledge that could respond to it only grew in intensity. This question of knowledge will be one of the main foci of the following chapters.

The modern age grew out of insurmountable religious differences among men. (I continue to use "men" in these pages because the theorists we are studying were in fact talking about men.) It had generally been the case up until this point in history, in Western societies, that men and women had understood justice to be, in one way or another, sacred or God-given, and accessible to the people, through law, knowledge, reason, or revelation. This was as fundamental an assumption of the Greek philosophers as it was of the Hebrew prophets in the Western traditions. It had been axiomatic for twenty centuries in one form or another that God was the ruler of the universe, that men suffered for their sins, and that eventually the faithful would find redemption for their suffering in heaven, however that was envisioned. Spiritual, moral, and political unity existed as one fully integrated and interrelated cosmic system, on earth as it is in heaven. The nature of the system was debated, of course, and its specific rules and theological precepts often violently contested. But the existence and inherent morality of the religious worldview generated out of the Hebrew and Christian traditions was not itself widely doubted in the European countries that made the earliest shift into the modern era.

An incalculable moral shattering occurred when men began to understand, experience, and finally kill for the sake of different beliefs, dogmas, and religious practices within what was considered not only the same religion, that is, Christianity, but the only true religion. Men had been killing people in other religions for all time. But what was other about this new religion? Unity no longer existed, men no longer agreed on the most basic Christian moral and religious truths, the moral law no longer moved them in one large (Catholic) direction, but rather in two (Catholic and Protestant) murderously opposed ones, and then in perhaps a thousand, sectarian, violently contradictory ones.

The incomprehensibility of this shattering is virtually impossible for us to imagine, living as we have been for several hundred years with its innumerable consequences. Nietzsche finally came to call it the death of God, and it is in that context the context of that death and what it means, that the most fundamental questions of this inquiry into suffering are formed.

Natural law, the truth of universal reason, was asserted in theory and practice as a working substitute for God's rule and overt protection, but since men couldn't agree on what natural law was or exactly what it told them to do, and it did not provide either the certainty or the security for doing it, justice had to be invented. And invented justice, as is all too clear to us by now, is not the same thing as God-given justice. It is partial. It is artificial and contrived. It is man-made. And, not surprisingly, it reflects the interests and the blindnesses of the men who invented it. It also has to be continually reinvented—it is not timeless.

It was not only the breakdown of the religious world that issued in the modern age, but also and nearly simultaneously, the invention and discovery of an entirely new dimension of human understanding, the birth of natural science out of new mathematics and new technologies, especially optics. The rediscovery of the classical world by the humanists of the Renaissance went hand in hand with new approaches to human knowledge, to the human body and the physical world, which led to the opening up of new realms of perception, calculation, and invention. The breakdown of religious certainty, accompanied by the revelation of new possibilities of scientific certainty, meant that the problem of suffering, which had been at the root of religious explanations of the world, now required a more scientific approach.[1] The perspectives of the knower and of the agent were called for—both humanist perspectives.

In this chapter and the several that follow, I examine in particular the work of Thomas Hobbes, as the first modern humanist theorist to apply the new scientific conception of mathematics and causation to politics. I will discuss other early modern theorists, especially Galileo, Descartes, Machiavelli, and Locke only a little, in relation to specific aspects of the worldview contested and at stake in this period. But "Hobbes set the foundation for the politics and theory that followed."[2]

Hobbes was able to develop a radically new argument about the nature of human suffering and consequently about the nature of human agency and human politics as a response to the problem of suffering. Hobbes started from the naturalness of human suffering as the central fact of his political theory. He saw human beings as bodies in motion, driven by fear and vanity, exercising the passion of their wills against one another in a "war of all against all." Hobbes clearly abstracted his logical argument from the miseries he saw around him that had resulted from the breakdown of political order in his time. His science sought to make sense of the history he experienced, although he clearly distinguished scientific from historical knowledge and gave the former precedence. He looked, with the clarity of a new will to knowledge, for the essential causes and effects that would allow the systematic thinker, among men entrapped in historical wars, to analyze their situation and come up with a rational solution for establishing order. He was seeking a method for a science of politics.

In contrast to the religious thinkers who preceded him, Hobbes interpreted suffering as entirely natural, taking place in a nature unencumbered by divine limits or priestly commandments. He interpreted men's conflict-ridden and miserable existence together as caused by clearly delineable natural drives and forces, a condition that could be conceptualized by means of abstract, universal, and demonstrable scientific propositions.

Hobbes and his successors found novel, exciting new images and metaphorical constructions, especially the notions of the "state of nature" and "the social contract," by which they could graphically depict the ways men could come to be able to live with and communicate with each other peacably. They developed concepts to explain how social relations developed in nature. Hobbes was the first to develop this metaphysical model, a diachronic structure of "conditional and hypothetical reasoning," which could be used to represent the real, underlying configurations of men's relations in nature, which could then be used to explain how these relations could be modified by human will, action, and rational agreement.

Hobbes and the modern theorists who came after him saw suffering as something natural to men living in the world, something inherent in their nature as men, and they developed an enduring structural analysis of how this kind of suffering could be changed. There was a profound optimism in this undertaking, even though the picture of the reality of the war of all against all was quite grim. Hobbes saw individuals as material bodies, with passions and wills that moved them toward pleasure and away from pain, but most important, into conflict with each other. He also posited the human capacity for reason—men had the rational ability to calculate their way out of their conflicts and the suffering it caused them and find a solution. Modern theorists began to theorize the development of modern selves— the creation of subjects as agents, and eventually as citizens, responsible actors who could be forged out of dangerous and unstable mélanges of passion, will, language, and power. As theorists they struggled from the beginning with conceptualizing the relationship between nature and time, or the place of history in the formation and achievement of human agency and political identity.

Hobbes and his contemporaries were often classicists as well as scientists. They had ancient secular progenitors to whom they could look for a non-supernatural approach to human nature. And they had the breakthrough conceptualizations of the new mathematics and optics and mechanics in order to start afresh, with a perspective on nature that posited bodies in motion (not necessarily souls), but bodies with desires, drives and passions that led necessarily, and logically, to both conflict and dread. The evidence was overwhelming that the interactions of such passionate and intelligent bodies could be fierce.

Thomas Hobbes approached the tumultuous events of his time as a renowned translator of Thucydides, as a rather imperious follower of Galileo, and as an intellectual rival of Descartes and Mersennes. He also approached the wrenching problem of the political violence of his day and of the previous century with an eye for the suffering it had caused. But he approached this violence armed with a Baconian optimism that the new philosophy, if followed rigorously, could forge a way out of men's confusion and fear.

Looking at Hobbes from the perspective of suffering involves a somewhat different take on Hobbes than the usual one, but it is one that amply repays serious study. The question of suffering gives Hobbes's picture of the state of nature a renewed depth and urgency. The domination he includes in his conception of the social contract can be powerfully illuminated by comparing it with a similarly coercive conception of contract found in Nietzsche's genealogy of morals. The foundation in violence that Hobbes sees in both the state of nature and the social contract sets him in sharp contrast to the conception of a mild and sociable state of nature and similarly rational social contract, which Locke so quickly thereafter devised, displacing natural violence onto property relations and normalizing the contract as a natural outcome of rational inequalities. This much less grim, rationalized conception, which prevailed in liberal thought for most of the modern age, represses and renders invisible the force, fraud, fear, debt, and cruelty, as Nietzsche would later characterize it, that archaic and originary contracts do indeed rely on. Comparing Hobbes's and Nietzsche's accounts, which I will do, helps to restore the balance, adding the irrational and coercive bases of social action and order to the rational and cooperative ones; it returns the repressed to critical consciousness.

In subsequent chapters, I also argue that language and the reconceptualization of the role of language that Hobbes presciently deploys play a crucial role in the struggles of modern theorists to differentiate kinds of meaning and knowledge, and to connect these with instinct, will, agency, and responsibility. Hobbes's understanding of language in particular reveals the subjectivity and relativity of linguistic meaning, especially moral meaning, which allows for a productive analysis of the problem of moral knowledge and of morality itself for later theorists of modernity and even postmodernity.

Hobbes can be interpreted as an early precursor of Nietzsche's analysis of the will to power, which operates thoughout the production processes of language, interpretation, representation, and moral evaluation. I also argue that the political model Hobbes develops—the state of nature and the social contract—constitutes a metaphorical, diachronc representation both of causes/processes of man's *pathos* in time, of human sociality, and, in embryo, of human historicity. This raises the question, addressed throughout this book, of the relation between philosophical and metaphorical language in political theory. Finally, Hobbes's representation of politics as the man-made, coerced, and social production of common meaning and justice through the social contract places human knowledge and power at the point of public response to human suffering.

THOMAS HOBBES AND THE NEW SCIENCE

Thomas Hobbes was the first political theorist (except perhaps for Machiavelli) to begin to grapple systematically with the implications of the disappearance of religious consensus, the breakdown of social order in religious and political wars, and the sudden nakedness of human suffering for politics. Like Luther, Hobbes writes of the human condition as one of unprecedented misery and unrelieved suffering, although he does not understand it in the way his religious predecessor did, nor call it by the name Luther gave it, namely, sin. Nor is he unduly sumpathetic toward it. He seems to write, rather, out of a kind of refined, precise rage. Hobbes wrote his greatest book *Leviathan* in 1651 in the midst of the English civil war, during which time the English beheaded their king, Charles I, in the name of liberty and the sovereignty of Parliament (in 1649), and Oliver Cromwell, head of the New Model Army, took charge of the government. This first modern democratic revolution "failed" in 1660, and the monarchy, greatly changed, was restored.[3]

Hobbes, a monarchist, a classicist and philologist, and a new philosopher, experienced with his countrymen widespread civil war and unpredictable, violent, rapidly changing political circumstances. He also wrote at a time when the whole of Europe had already suffered over one hundred years of social unrest, religious conflict, and violent warfare over religious values and the embattled jurisdictions of Church and state. It is not surprising that Hobbes starts from the premise of the utter total wretchedness of men, by *nature*. As a scientist, nature is his only concern. "Nature" is the operative term here, and the decisive one for Hobbes's argument, as well as for the mainstream of early modern and Enlightenment political philosophy over the next two centuries.

For moderns, it is in nature that suffering arises and it is by means of a knowledge of nature that a remedy for human suffering is to be found. But "nature," as I hope to show in this book, is not a concept that can simply be defined. Unlike mathematical definitions, philosophical concepts take their meaning from the contexts in which they are used and these contexts change historically. "Nature" was in Hobbes's time a particularly central and elastic term, one whose meaning was undergoing rapid change. The concept of "nature" was one of the foundational concepts of modern thought and a primary concept by means of which reality was interpreted and reinterpreted. While "nature" as a concept might have seemed simple enough, intuitively, as what was left behind when God was translated into an inaccessible transcendent realm, it turned out to be nothing of the kind.

The modern age as a whole can be seen as one long, extended, and tangled meditation on the meaning of "nature." Early modern scientists intended to streamline the term, using it to refer only to the most pared down geometrical conceptions of time, space, and motion. But however much "nature" was merely what was left over by God's removal elsewhere, as a concept it still retained the rich nuances of classical conceptions, and it was rapidly picking up new ones from technological operations—astronomy, anatomy, and mapmaking, for instance. Furthermore, "nature" retained complicated leftover shadows and ghostly dimensions of a moral and political kind that needed somehow to be accounted for. Suffering was one of those experiences of human existence which, when translated into purely natural terms, still presented insurmountable problems for scientific understanding. In fact, I am arguing that suffering is precisely the sort of test case that stretched the meaning of "nature" over and over again until it burst into "history." Human nature turned out to be "unnatural," as Rousseau argued later.

In the early modern theorists studied here, the concept of nature, particularly as symbolized by the "state of nature," reflects like a dark mirror the epistemological problems and moral predicaments of the time. A brief genealogy of nature, as it developed in early modern science, will give us an opening perspective on a genealogy of suffering, as that includes knowledge and agency and much else in the early modern age.

The question of knowledge lies at the core of modern thought, and nature is the general object of knowledge. Even as thinkers were beginning to argue that true knowledge of the will of God and of paths to salvation were not open or available to men, or at least that certainty about such matters could not be demonstrated, a powerfully different criterion of truth was becoming the norm. A new kind of knowledge was emerging, taking hold in the minds of the learned, establishing that norm. This knowledge claimed a new kind of truth, certainty, precision, and demonstrability that had never arisen before—modern science, sometimes also then called the new philosophy.

Thomas Hobbes was a humanist scholar, educated in the humanist traditions, and he was also a classical philologist, like Nietzsche, a great Latinist and Greek translator. His attention to language and to the importance of definitions throughout his work is exemplary and evidence of his philologist's passion for precise diagnosis. His first published work was a translation of Thucydides into English; he later translated Aristotle's *Art of Rhetoric* into English, and even wrote an epic poem in classical style, although not a very good one.[4] But the most important and far-reaching influences on Hobbes's intellectual and political development are elegantly described in Tom Sorrell's opening paragraph to his book *Hobbes*:

> Thomas Hobbes's philosophical ideas were formed by two great upheavals of the seventeenth century. One was local, political, dangerous, and as Hobbes believed, deeply irrational. This was the English Civil War. The other was largely Continental, benefited people in obvious ways, showed what reason could accomplish when properly guided and applied. This was the upheaval in scientific ideas that Hobbes thought had been started by Galileo. Mainly on the strength of writings occasioned by the first upheaval Hobbes claimed to have contributed something important to the second.[5]

Hobbes actually did contribute something important to the second, however much his contribution to the first won him true immortality.

Hobbes did not intend a career in either the Church or the university, so as a typical humanist would do, he took employment with William Cavendish as tutor to his son, and spent his life for the most part in the employ of the Cavendish family, tutoring three generations of Cavendish heirs, as well as, later, the future Charles II.[6] Of special importance for my purposes here was Hobbes's acquaintance through Cavendish with Francis Bacon in the early 1620s. Bacon was seeking to translate his Essays into Latin, and Aubrey tells us that Hobbes was his assistant for this translation. Aubrey says that "The Lord Chancellour Bacon loved to converse with Hobbes," that Hobbes "assisted his lordship in translating severall of his Essayes into Latin," that he became a favorite of Bacon, and that Hobbes was also used by Cavendish as a go-between in his dealings with Bacon.[7]

Although Noel Malcolm argues that "despite all these personal contacts, it is hard to find any evidence of a strong or direct Baconian influence on the substance of Hobbes's later philosophy," he acknowledges that the "tendency toward naturalism" and the "attack on false entities created by language" in Bacon's works, as well as "the general project of replacing scholasticism with a new but equally all-encompassing system of knowledge was also common to both writers."[8] He rightly asserts that none of these projects was peculiar to Bacon, and that other continental scientists, especially Galileo, were more important to Hobbes's development.

Nonetheless, Bacon stood for the new science and the new philosophy, especially for its English version and its intimate association with politics. Bacon personally embodied and personified these forces to the men of his generation and those coming after them. Bacon's conception of what the new science entailed politically gives us access to the largest dimensions of the new knowledge and its effects on social life. His works were undoubtedly known and studied by Hobbes.[9]

Francis Bacon lived his whole life near the center of power. He was Lord Chancellor under James the First. Bacon's importance to Hobbes was that he was a social as well as a scientific thinker. "He saw that something new was happening, in society as well as in science: he defined what this was, showing how it could be consciously utilized for the relief of man's estate."[10] Bacon stressed the importance for practical affairs of the invention of printing, gunpowder, and the compass, and "the opening of the world by navigation and commerce." He stressed experimental knowledge that could be gained by planned and directed investigation. He "wrote philosophy like a Lord Chancellor," that is to say, he brought system and coherence and "dignity" to scientific inquiry. "The true and lawful goal of the sciences is none other than this, that human life be endowed with new inventions and powers."[11]

What Bacon made plain was the connection between knowledge and power, the power of knowledge to change the human condition, to transform it for the better. This was a profound hope and determination of the modern age, and it remains a relationship that continues to occupy us. The relation between knowledge and power and the importance of that connection for conceptualizing and responding to human suffering was key for these Renaissance thinkers, as it is in this inquiry. Bacon had a utopian vision of what the new learning could accomplish for the betterment of human welfare; he went so far as to see in it the possibility of restoring man to his pristine and perfect condition before the Fall. He contrasted the brightness of hope for the future that the new science brought with the despair generated by the schoolmen, that is, medieval scholastics taking their philosophical premises from classical sources, especially Aristotle. Bacon said, "The destiny of the human race will supply the issue. . . . For what is at stake is not merely a contemplative happiness but the very reality of man's well-being and all man's powers of action. Man is the helper and interpreter of Nature. . . . Nature cannot be conquered but by obeying her. Accordingly, these twin goods, human knowledge and human power, come in the end to be one. To be ignorant of causes is to be frustrated in action."[12] Here the connection between causation and action could not be plainer. Action requires a knowledge of the causes of what one wants to change. That is why agency can be called into question when causation itself grows ambiguous, or changes its meaning contextually.

It is essential for the history we are reconstructing here that we understand the conjunction that did in fact arise in the early modern era between human knowledge and human power. It was a relation mapped out in philosophical discourses and activated in modern political reforms and revolutions to transform human social institutions. The knowledge of empirical causes created an entirely different conception of the universe than that which had previously existed. The new knowledge of causes made a new world of human action possible. The new science led in fact to an incalculable increase in human power in the world. Knowledge of nature, of the causes of all actions, of motions, from the orbits of the planets to the sufferings of the human heart, was at the very core of the new philosophy, profoundly changing the way men looked at the world and inevitably their ability to operate within it.

While Bacon articulated the force, the power of the new mathematics as part of a vision of a transformed world, Hobbes was one of the great thinkers to work out the systematic consequences of that vision. Bacon saw the new science as a way ultimately to end human suffering—a hope that proved perhaps somewhat too optimistic. But Hobbes was the first to address specifically and concretely how, and why, something like that might be accomplished. He hoped at a minimum for order, if not for the elimination of human suffering per se. The public causes of suffering were amenable to reasoned response.

Bacon contrasted his hopes for the new science with the despair of the schoolmen. He hoped for "a restitution and reinvigoration (in great part) of man to the sovereignty and power . . . which he had in his first state of creation. . . . We may hand over to men their fortunes, the understanding having been emancipated—having come, so to speak, of age. Hence there must necessarily ensue an improvement in man's estate and an increase of his power over nature," which could be "subdued to the uses of human life." As for the teachings of Aristotle and the schoolmen, "Such teachings . . . [constitute] a wicked effort to curtail human power over nature and to produce a deliberate and artificial despair. This despair in its turn confounds the promptings of hope, cuts the springs and sinews of industry, and makes men unwilling to put anything to the hazard of trial."[13]

Hobbes came to share Bacon's contempt for Aristotle and the schoolmen as he himself became absorbed in mathematics and the new science. The most important influence and model for these new ideas and methods for him was, of course, Galileo. It is reported that Hobbes visited Galileo at Arcetri in 1635 or 1636, on his third visit to the Continent, and that they even discussed the application of geometrical method to ethics, walking the grounds of the grand-ducal summer residence of Poggio Imperiale.[14] Hobbes understood himself to be applying Galilean methods and thinking to the problems of morality and politics. He explicitly sought to translate the new knowledge of mathematics and motion into a science applicable to human affairs.

Hobbes publicly acknowledged the importance of Galileo's achievement, describing his own work as exemplifying a similar kind of effort, in the Epistle Dedicatory of the *Elements of Philosophy*. In his critique of White's *De Mundo*, he called Galileo "the greatest philosopher of not merely our own but any age."[15]

Why was Galileo of such consummate importance for Hobbes and for the new science in general? We can consider at least five reasons. First, Galileo understood nature as a completely ordered system, mathematically linear and measurable, precise, and necessary. He was able to replace the once completely ordered system of religious certainty, which had fractured into warring fragments, with a new completely ordered system of mathematical certainty, which would form the basis of a new world, scientifically known and governed. Galileo contrasts science with scholastic law and the humanities, arguing that in the natural sciences, the conclusions of knowledge are absolutely true; "nature acts only through immutable laws which she never transgresses," caring "nothing whether her reasons and methods of operating be or be not understandable by men."[16] Nature's rigorous necessity results from "her" mathematical character:

> Philosophy is written in that great book which ever lies before our eyes—I mean the universe—but we cannot understand it if we do not first learn the language and grasp the symbols, in which it is written. This book is written in the mathematical language, and the symbols are triangles, circles, and other geometrical figures, without whose help it is impossible to comprehend a single word of it; without which one wanders in vain through a dark labyrinth.[17]

Second, although he accords priority to the mathematical structure of the universe and therefore to the a priori nature of knowledge, he also combines this confidence in the independence of mathematics with an insistence that "our disputes are about the sensible world, and not one of paper." So, however much general principles and the discovery of causes lead to understanding, we must "come to the particular demonstrations, observations and experiments," by means of the confirmation of the senses, that is, if we truly wish to explain something.[18] He was fortunate to have the earlier empirical conceptualizations of Johannes Kepler, his contemporary, and the prodigious labors of Tycho Brahe, "the greatest giant of observational astronomy since Hipparchus, . . . whose vastly more extensive and incomparably more precise set of data" helped to demonstrate empirically the truth of Galileo's general principles.[19]

Third, Galileo's mathematical metaphysics led him, as it had led Kepler, to the doctrine of primary and secondary qualities.[20] "Galileo makes the clear distinction between that in the world which is absolute, objective, immutable, and mathematical; and that which is relative, subjective, fluctuating, and sensible. The former is the realm of knowledge, divine and human; the latter is the realm of opinion and illusion."[21] This constitutes a new kind of Neo-Platonism, with far-reaching consequences. The real and primary qualities of objects are number, figure, magnitude, position, and motion, which are inseparable from bodies; all other qualities, like taste, odor, and color, are subjective, that is, deceptive, mediated to us through our senses and at best imperfectly known. Galileo explicates this radical notion in his explanation of heat as caused by bodies in motion. He enlarges this doctrine in the atomic theory of matter, that matter is resoluble into "infinitely small indivisible atoms," bodies in motion.[22] Hobbes began his analysis of human nature and justice from the methodological premise of bodies in motion, disagreeing with Descartes about the practical consequences of the subjective nature of secondary qualities.

Fourth, it is important to understand Galileo's contibution to the modern conception of time, as this was to have perhaps the most far-reaching effect of all. Previous to the modern age, the meaning of motion was understood in qualitative and substantive terms, seeking the end of motion in the teleology of the universe. For Galileo, it is the how of motion that becomes the object of analysis, and that by the method of exact mathematics:

> Physical space was assumed to be identical with the realm of geometry and physical motion was acquiring the character of a pure mathematical concept. Hence in the metaphysics of Galileo, space (or distance) and time become fundamental categories. *The real world is the world of bodies in mathematically reducible motions, and this means that the real world is a world of bodies moving in space and time.* In place of the teleological categories into which scholasticism had analysed change and movement, we now have two formerly insignificant entities given new meanings as absolute mathematical notions. The real world, to repeat, is a world of mathematically measurable motions in space and time.[23]

The basis of the real is space-time itself. In this conception, the real world, the material world that is visible to the human eye, comes to be replaced, or at least redescribed, by the conceptual, abstract world of ideal mathematical relationships. Space and time as understood mathematically are not perceptual, which is why secondary characteristics become uncertain in relation to the knowledge of time and motion, which is ideal, perfect, and completely demonstrable. It is an intellectual understanding of reality, rather than a naturalistic, qualitative, or moral one.

This new world of abstract space, time, and motion, of mathematical ideals and sensory perceptions, is so habitual to us that it is hard to imagine how very new it was to the men of the seventeenth century. The real world of space and time was infinite instead of finite and open instead of closed. Lived time, time as heretofore experienced by humans as endowed with moral qualities, spiritual potentialities, tragic fatalities, and exalted destinies, more or less disappears, and all time is technically the same, a linear becoming;

the present moment is all that is actually real. This amounts to a new conception of the real. The movement of time passes from the past into the future in even increments, with the present as the gateway to linear infinities on either side.[24]

Memory and imagination become enduringly significant metaphysical and moral problems in terms of this scientific conception of time and space, as we will see. Human historicity had no obvious or readily imaginable place in this physical and metaphysical model of the universe in the seventeenth century. Hobbes, Rousseau, and Nietzsche all grapple, in contradictory ways and with strongly clashing views, with the problem of connecting the meaning of human sociality and historicity, in which human suffering is constrained, to this scientific conception of reality.

Finally, Galileo replaced the rejected teleology of the scholastics with a new positive conception of *causality*. He was concerned with explaining not formal motion, but accelerated motions, and these necessarily presupposed some force or forces as cause. "Hence the cause of every motion which is not simple and uniform must be expressed in terms of force."[25] As Galileo and Descartes courageously define this motion, God ceases to be the cause of the substantive or moral motions of the world in any operative sense. He is the First Cause or Creator of the great machine, the force that sets the whole universe in motion. But, clearly, he is no longer the Supreme Good, actively intervening morally and spiritually in the actions of men. Descartes posits him as the necessary Guarantor of the truth of subjective impressions, without whom there would be no such guarantee. History disappears into a mere succession of events, too gross to be rendered mathematically, and therefore too general to be counted as an object of true knowledge. For Hobbes, this constituted an urgent problem that required solution.

It was during this same visit to the Continent in the mid-1630s that Hobbes became involved in debates taking place in the scientific circles surrounding the mathematician Marin Mersenne in Paris, and came to know Descartes and Gassendi. Richard Tuck, a foremost scholar of the period, says they didn't actually meet until much later. Hobbes became engaged in what Tuck characterizes as a kind of intellectual race concerning who first developed, although without publishing, the philosophical implications of the problem of perception. In his article, "Hobbes and Descartes," Tuck claims that "What was at stake here was nothing less than the invention of modern philosophy."[26]

The race between Descartes and Hobbes to define the parameters and implications of the new knowledge through the defining lens of perception was of ultimate importance in determining whether human suffering, or any moral or political response to it, could be constructed in the external, empirical world and therefore be open to rational remedy, or only construed as internal, referring only to an interiorized subjectivity. In fact, suffering came over time to be seen as both objective and subjective, until finally, the distinction itself began to be challenged. But Hobbes's line of thought proved to be the most conducive to analytical as well as political remedies. If Tuck is correct and Hobbes had already drafted all three *sectiones* of his universal philosophy, known as *De Corpore, De Homine*, and *De Cive* by 1640, as he claimed in the preface to *De Cive*, which was published far earlier than the others, then it seems that Hobbes developed his natural philosophy "as the next move in a game where Descartes was the previous player."[27]

The problem that Descartes, Gassendi, and Hobbes were all struggling with was the problem of perception. "They accepted the sceptical arguments against Aristotelianism (in all its forms)," as put forth by Montaigne and Pierre Charon and others. They were seeking a "post-sceptical science," that is, one that could affirm true knowledge, even though they accepted the argument that the data given us by our senses was "irremediably faulty," and that different perceptions of the same thing ruled out any true knowledge of the external world.[28]

Descartes, Hobbes, and Gassendi all wanted to affirm true knowledge of the world, but they devised very different solutions to what that might mean. They began with something completely new, the idea "that one could have true knowledge of an internal world, of one's perceptions *themselves*."[29] Gassendi published first, arguing that science depends on a knowledge of signs, that is, that sense perceptions are the signs of real natural events, which *cause* them. Tuck emphasizes that this attack on the representational theory of perception was common to Mersenne, Descartes, Hobbes, and Gassendi.[30]

The problem of perception led Descartes into what has been called "hyperbolical doubt"—"If our sense-impressions merely *signify* an external world, and are *caused* in some inscrutable way by it, how can we know anything at all about its properties: How, indeed, do we even know that it exists?"[31] Descartes was led thus to his profoundly enduring and influential position of metaphysical dualism, arguing that there are two kinds of things in the world, *res extensa* and *res cogitans*, material things and thinking things, and that without the help of a great trust in the goodness and honesty of God, we have no way of knowing anything, for the two kinds of substances never meet. "After 1637, the sceptical challenge to the new philosophy was not Montaigne or Charron but the hyperbolical doubt."[32]

It was a formidable challenge that remained intractable for the whole modern age—the challenge of skepticism came to inform the core questions of the possibility of knowledge for modern philosophy.[33] The position of radical skepticism, in its many variations, continually reconfigured the nature of knowledge, and thus of power, as these changed from sacred to secular conceptions. The challenge of skepticism and the numerous philosophical and political responses to it that were attempted eventually restructured radically the way suffering would be understood in a scientific age. The immorality of suffering came more and more to the fore, even as foundations for a moral response to it grew more elusive. This dilemma became central for Rousseau, as we will see.

Hobbes was the first philosopher to have an important and robust response to the challenge of Cartesian hyperbolic doubt, even as he formulated his own version of skepticism. He separated science/knowledge (also called philosophy—the three were not yet differentiated at this period) into two kinds, the kind that arises from definitions: "They are first truths; every definition is a true and primary proposition because we make it true ourselves by defining, that is, by agreement about the meaning of the words." His paradigmatic example was geometry. There is another kind as well: "But in the explanation of natural phenomena, another kind of procedure must be followed, which is termed Hypothesis, or supposition."[34]

In the *Elements of Law*, Hobbes says that "whatsoever accidents or qualities our senses make us think there be in the world, they are not there, but are seemings and apparitions only. The things that really are in the world without us, are those motions by which these seemings are caused." Our perception functions because of motion; "change is only conceivable as caused by the action of one material body moving against another."[35] So it is Hobbes's contention that all our perceptions, and ultimately our conceptions, arise in us insofar as we are bodies and because we are affected by the impact of other bodies on our own through the senses. Change as we understand it is only discernible because of motion, the most fundamental factor in the material universe. And for Hobbes, there is no other universe than a material universe. "There are no incorporeal spirits."

Hobbes emphatically denies the existence of "incorporeal spirits" and does not require God to guarantee the soundness of our perceptions. He was untroubled by Cartesian doubt, because, as Tuck puts it, "he stuck in a clear-headed fashion to the argument that whatever we experience, whether in sleep or waking, or at the hands of a malicious demon, has been caused by some material object or objects impinging upon us. We cannot know what that object is really like, but the Cartesian doubt does not matter: our inability to conceive of change without cause and cause without moving material objects is sufficient to establish the real existence of *something*. . . . Hobbes thus seemed (at least to himself) to have put forward the only convincing post-sceptical metaphysics."[36]

Hobbes not only gave us a thoroughly materialist reading of the world, but he understood that the nature of our understanding, which by means of language involves causation and sensation, subjects and objects, gives us "good enough" knowledge, upon which we can act, choose, and build. Tuck is correct, I think, to conclude that this materialist metaphysics came finally to be seen as and remains more convincing to many modern readers than Descartes's metaphysical dualism. But a fully materialist world was such a deep departure from previous religious accounts that it was furiously denounced by Hobbes's many critics and he was permanently stigmatized as an infamous atheist.

THE IDEA OF A SCIENCE OF POLITICS

The idea of a science of politics was the modern theorist's response to the collapse of Christian religious unity and certainty and to the descent of the body politic into chaos and civil war. Hobbes absorbed the new mathematics coming from Europe and the new sciences of his day—optics, astronomy, navigation, printing, chemistry—and turned this emergent expertise and precision to the study of ethics and politics. Hobbes began as a translator of Thucydides, and he himself wrote a history of the civil wars in England, but he contrasted the kind of knowledge that could be learned from history with the kind that could be learned from science, and found the latter to be far more accurate and powerful. While history deals always in particulars, science is based on propositional reasoning. While "experience concludeth nothing universally," science was capable of generating true and universal knowledge. (Thus suffering is always experienced in the particular, as historical, but its causes may be conditions that can be examined through abstract reasoning, that is, scientifically.)

Even as he developed his idea of a science, Hobbes came to reconceptualize the purposes for which one would develop a science of politics. While his science must involve the powerful (and often long and tedious) carefully crafted logical chains of propositions linked into a deductive system, it also had to be able to persuade and convince the newly arising common people, the public, now more literate and agitated than ever, about the truths of scientific political reasoning. The conclusions Hobbes sought to prove were both political and scientific—that rational men fear death and obey their sovereigns. His purposes in writing were political, and he judged the truth and the power of his theory not by how well it corresponded or conformed to reality as "given to us by the senses," but rather by how well it could effect changes in reality. "Theory, for Hobbes, was the measure of reality, not the reverse. The aim of political philosophy should be to change the world, not merely to explain it."[37] Hobbes had practical achievements to accomplish. But what did these achievements have to do with suffering?

Hobbes is in some ways the least convincing case for the thesis that political theory is written in response to human suffering, and he is therefore a good test case for that thesis. Hobbes is usually seen as the quintessential abstract philosopher, a purist, the political theorist most known for his concern to construct an absolutely tight logical case, a system of linked deductive propositions, a strictly rational materialist philosophy. *Leviathan* is positively a monument to the powers of human reason to systematize and organize diverse data of a psychological, historical, cultural, linguistic, and political nature into one flowing and logical coherent, complete argument. Of course, there are flaws in the argument, and a serious confusion obtains about how its abstractions connect to the "evidence of the senses" or to the reality they purport to describe. This is not a confusion that has ever been satisfactorily resolved, although the elements of the problem are quite differently understood now. A great deal more was at stake than the early moderns imagined. But the crux of the problem lay in language, as Hobbes was the first to recognize and to theorize.

My argument here is that this connection for Hobbes was not logical or representational or empirical, but in fact practical and political, and that the point of Hobbes's politics was to bring about a change toward the rational in the real political world around him, because he saw that world torn apart by strife and confusion, deception and ambition, delusion, violence and superstition, unreason and vainglory and war, and he was appalled at the folly, suffering and destruction so caused. He analyzed such suffering in the most rigorous scientific terms of which he was capable, which were considerable. But his was not a disinterested search for truth, a purely scientific intellectual project, however highly intellectual it was in its carrying out.[38]

Leviathan was not only designed to demonstrate the truth of Hobbes's political theory; it was designed to convince a large and obstreperous public, newly hatched into furious political activity, to think clearly about their essential condition and to act rationally, that is, to fear death and to submit to their rulers, for their own good and the good of the commonwealth. He did not make this as a moral argument or one derived from the perspective of the sufferer or the pitier of suffering. He made his argument as a rational and political one, from the perspective of the knower and of the agent. What he saw around him was the hardship and terror, suffering and chaos that a lack of attention to rational principles, and to what came to be called "enlightened self-interest," necessarily implied. Hobbes's answer to the question of knowledge, like his response to suffering, was political. The answer lies in the power of both fear and reason to move men to act, as thoughtful agents, to bring into being a working rather than a conflictual social conjunction.

Hobbes sought to bring about a more rational and practical culture to restore the social contract he believed could bring peace. He did not turn out to be entirely wrong. As the heirs of the age of reason that he helped instantiate, we have experienced both the benefits of this kind of rational culture and its necessary and hidden underside, the limits of reason and the inability of human beings to eliminate either suffering or irrationality from human life. It's not clear that Hobbes ever thought they could be eliminated. He did think a rational culture would be a marked improvement over the lawless aggressions and superstitious terrors of his own age.

Political knowledge, no matter how scientific or philosophical, is never merely epistemological. It is always actively interventionist, interested, propelled by power, desire and design, rhetorically compelling and urgent. It is politics by theoretical means, a proven historical force to be reckoned with. Hobbes's theory was the first real demonstration of the power of theory, as theory and as science, to create and destroy institutions—to practice politics.

We might also take note of some crucial questions left hanging here: (1) a scientific framework that begins with the premise of bodies in motion has only a rudimentary notion of time, something like a flowing succession of moments passing; a space-time continuum is not yet a real history; (2) causation is suspended in questions of will and power, although Hobbes and his successors labored mightily to bridge the gap between motion and will. From will comes decision and choice and all the moral and cultural consequences that flow from those—but how any of this is "caused" or necessitated never gets resolved, and it requires continuous reinterpretation and finally becomes entangled inextricably in the permutations of time itself. The *pathos* of power in time becomes, I argue, the clearest statement of what is at stake in this question.

Finally, (3) Hobbes knows history; he was the translator of Thucydides. He cannot account for history scientifically and considers historical knowledge inferior, because "experience concludeth nothing universally." Nevertheless, Hobbes conceptualizes time, and historical succession, in his most powerful theoretical construction—the movement from "the state of nature" to "the social contract."

The status of this kind of "origin" is still being widely debated.[39] Historicity in modern theory begins here, in the constructing of a beginning and an ending, two moments that always imply and accompany each other. The state of nature and the social contract, and the movement between them which is the founding event of political history, is simultaneously diachronic and synchronic. The movement is a structure that is an event, an originary event, always prior, always present, always original. It has always already happened—we are born into the middle of it. In this historicity is our suffering, a limit endemic to the human condition. It can only be exposed metaphorically and configured abstractly, but that is sufficient for action, as Hobbes concluded.

The stage for action, in fact, as Hobbes established, is set by the conditions that constitute the causes of this movement from nature to society. Hobbes gives us the basic and most fundamental framework for politics, as well as the primary consideration in any question of suffering. He presents the world of the agent who acts in relation to causal and rational knowledge in order to make decisions and in order to found communities. This is what modern politics is based on. It is the generic model. Agents who have the knowledge and means to act do not need to look upon the suffering with pity, or at least pity is not the operative response. They can act. It is this model that Hobbes contributes to the argument about the politics of suffering I am constructing here.

3

For the Lack of Moral Knowledge

The years leading up to and encompassing the English civil wars were some of the most violent, heterogeneous, confused, and chaotic in all of English history; they were years of continuous war, ideological ferocity, and passionate philosophical debate, of inflamed partisan conflict, and of jarring cultural and political change. The conflicts that raged between countrymen were both religious and political, and there was no clear line of distinction between these two realms. Where and how to draw the line was fiercely contested. The locus and nature of political authority was thrown into question, and the very meaning of membership in political community, in the body politic, was at stake in the violent struggles of the time. "Hobbes believed he was living in a time of virtually unprecedented ferment and cultural transition—a view that is hardly surprising, given the extraordinarily millenarian atmosphere that had enveloped the English imagination by the time of his writing."[1]

Hobbes understood himself to be writing not only a completely new kind of philosophy, a scientific philosophy, based on the indubitable foundations of mathematics and logical reasoning, but also that his science of politics had to reach an unprecedently new audience, a new public and a new public opinion, one not only avid for radically new ideas about politics, but one also dangerously susceptible to credulity and superstition, and to the ambitions of powerful men who preyed on men's fears and their irrationality to lead them away from rational decision-making.

It is not too much to say that Hobbes's entire theory and program of political reform was waged against religious fanaticism, superstitious beliefs, and downright ignorance, which was nurtured and garnered for war by ambitious men for their own purposes. There was, he wrote, a "Kingdom of Darkness . . . , *a Confederacy of Deceivers, that to obtain dominion over men in this present world, endeavor by dark and erroneaous Doctrines, to extinguish in them the Light, both of Nature, and of the Gospel; and so to disprepare them*

75

for the kingdom of God to come."[2] It was against this kingdom of darkness that Hobbes endeavored to gain ground.

Hobbes was denounced as an atheist in his time, and certainly his defenses of religious doctrine were circuitous, ironic, and suspect to the pious, as he subjected all religious and spiritual knowledge to the test of a materialist metaphysics. Nevertheless, Hobbes did not deny God, but only magical powers and their magisterial representatives. He did not ignore the power of Scripture over the men of his time, and he devoted by far the largest portion of *Leviathan* to discussing the interpretation of Scripture and its consequences for political reasoning. Nonetheless, it was in his theory itself, in the arguments he made in philosophical terms, and especially in his discussion of the nature of knowledge, that Hobbes made the most profound contribution to the modern understanding of the relations between language, culture, and politics.

THE SELF AS KNOWER AND AS AGENT OF CHANGE

It was natural in the sixteenth and even the seventeenth centuries for political writers to understand themselves primarily as counselors and educators to princes and to the ruling elite and their sons. Machiavelli's *The Prince* is the most obvious example of this genre, but Hobbes too was a tutor to princes, and the early versions of his theory were written in Latin and circulated to a small number of highly educated readers, political leaders, and elite thinkers. Nevertheless, by the time Hobbes wrote *Leviathan* in 1651, he had a larger audience in mind and a larger political purpose than just making a contribution to the knowledge of the learned of his day. A new political public was emerging in Hobbes's time; a new political space was being opened.

Political life had been blown wide open in many ways by the middle decades of the seventeenth century, not only by the impact of numerous wars and uprisings, but also by more peaceful and revolutionary technologies, like the printing press, first brought by William Caxton to Westminster in 1476. The growth of printed works and newspapers was exponential, and the swelling ranks of the literate and politically engaged public in the sixteenth and seventeeth centuries was one of the most important sociological changes of the time, which enabled new audiences to be addressed by the authors of new ideas.[3] English printers produced religious and devotional works, romances, and political tracts for an ever-more-receptive and avid reading and listening public. The conditions under which the transmission of knowledge was being accomplished were being fundamentally transformed. "By the early seventeenth century basic literacy had become very common even among the poor. The education of women, while continuing to lag well behind that of men, was also becoming socially respectable. . . . by the 1630s, perhaps as many of one-half of adult males, and one-third of all adults in England, could read."[4]

By that time as well, the *coranto*, "a printed compendium of news from many places, usually covering a period of about a week," later called a newspaper, had generated many competitors, and they were coming out weekly. The political importance of this new source of information can be inferred from the fact that "the crown banned them altogether in 1632, and only allowed publication to resume six years later under conditions of very strict censorship, as well as by the flood of newspapers that poured forth after the Long Parliament abolished all restrictions in 1640."[5]

There is good evidence that Hobbes changed his opinion about the nature and power of public opinion between the time that he wrote *The Elements of Law* and the time when he wrote *Leviathan*. David Johnston argues convincingly that in that first work, Hobbes stressed objective conditions of oppression as the most important causes of sedition: "Discontent was the first and most fundamental of these causes. It was, for him, a product of objective conditions, including deprivation, fear of want and bodily harm, and—more insidiously in his view—lack of power." By the time he wrote *Leviathan*, however, "seditious opinions" had become the most important factor in his account of the causes of rebellion, opinions that constitute "such Diseases of a Commonwealth as are of the greatest and most present danger."[6]

It is significant, of course, that Hobbes is looking for the causes of sedition or civil unrest and the harm and misery they bring. He is thinking like a scientist and from the perspective of the knower, of knowledge, seeking to identify the conditions for action. This, in and of itself, becomes the framework of the modern.

In fact, after arguing that the chief defects in commonwealths, which "resemble diseases of a natural body," come from insufficient claims to power by sovereigns, Hobbes cites as the next most important cause of the dissolution of commonwealths "the poison of seditious doctrines, whereof one is *That every private man is judge of good and evil actions*."[7] This, he says, is the case "under the condition of nature." Like a doctor, he is seeking the causes of the diseased civil body. "Insufficient claims" and "seditious doctrines" are the kinds of causes of the disease he identifies. It is clear that there is a difficulty in accounting for the exact nature of the relation between causes and doctrines, and some question of how doctrines can be causes of disease. The medical metaphor must do some difficult work here. Nevertheless, diseases can be cured by good doctors. It is precisely Hobbes's purpose in writing Leviathan to show how the most difficult and profound evil of men's natural condition can be remedied by the instition of the social contract and the authorization of the sovereign, establishing a commonwealth. This is precisely the cure Hobbes wants to effect. And it is also clear to him that the problem of private language goes to the heart of the issue.

Why is it so important how men judge good and evil actions, and whether they do so as "private men" or as "public men"? This question cuts to the core not only of Hobbes's theory, but also to the core of the problem of suffering and the kind of knowledge that is necessary to address it. It is a question that ultimately informs and finally also transforms the nature of political knowledge, as Hobbes shows. Hobbes is not looking for sin or guilt or punishment, that is, for moral and religious conceptions to characterize the defects in men's relations or in commonwealths. He is looking not to moral language, but to diagnostic, medical language: the defects of commonwealths "resemble diseases of a natural body." For Hobbes it is crucial that doctors do not morally condemn diseases, they cure them. The stance is in a sense disinterested; it is the stance of the agent of change and not the moralist judge. Hobbes starts with bodies in motion, and he means not only individual bodies, but also the bodies that are formed when commonwealths are formed. He is at pains to contrast natural bodies with the "artificial" character of the body, Leviathan—the state as a giant bodily artifact. It is the commonwealth as artifact that identifies it as something men construct by reason and method, and by their will to submit to authority by promising. Men can make what nature cannot: peace.

The medical model became one of the most important, potent, and influential of scientific discourses about natural bodies in the modern age.[8] It can be used to identify "fault" without connoting "moral fault," and thus naturalizes the whole discussion of bodies and diseases, their proper or improper functioning, without imputing either guilt or blame. And a defect can be repaired. There is a kind of objectivity imputed to the diagnosis that bypasses mere sentiment.

This is a significant step in the modern attempt to de-moralize political theory, something that has not always been seen as an improvement, as Rousseau makes clear in his passionate remoralizing of these same themes. Of course it is not the case that no values are contained in the medical model. Implicit in these discourses are norms that have their own disciplinary force. As Michel Foucault has so trenchantly demonstrated, medical norms carry the weight and power of their purported objectivity, which can constrict and condemn every bit as violently as any religious code. The model of science and medicine comes to have a force of legitimacy that religious belief seems utterly to lack in the modern age. It may be that the rise and fall of these ideals are commensurate and related, as Nietzsche will argue.

Nevertheless, the accent changes in science from moral condemnation to normalization and regularization, and this in turn changes the nature of suffering itself, subtly but irreversibly, from a matter of guilt and punishment to one of health and proper functioning. That is not small change. Blame, of course, reenters the piecure, but it is human blame, not divine. None of these terms or values are simple, straightforward, self-evident, or unproblematical. It took many centuries before they came to seem so. A good part of what the argument about suffering has been about has to do with what is lost and what is gained by this kind of change or exchange.

The danger Hobbes is consumed with in writing *Leviathan* is the danger of "seditious opinions" undermining the authority of sovereigns and leading superstitious and credulous men to sedition and to the dissolution of the commonwealth. But typically, Hobbes breaks this question down into its most basic constitutive parts. He recognizes the need to characterize and distinguish the relationship between men's bodies and their thoughts, their thoughts and their language, their ability to name things "right" and "wrong," and their ability to reason correctly about such public matters. His belief that there is a correct way to reason about these things makes him a scientist and a philosopher. His skepticism as to whether man can and will find that right way makes him a modern man, and in his time it also made him an authoritarian. He also seems, at least sometimes, to recognize that proof pertains only to geometry, and that correct reasoning in moral and political matters involves will, decision, and choice, not proof. He does argue that good proofs can and should influence choices. That makes him a pragmatist and a rhetoretician, as well as a politician.

The relationship between bodies and thoughts is at the heart of Hobbes's theory, and he seeks to make them the firm foundation on which he can build his conceptions of the state of nature and the social contract. Hobbes sees language as the key to men's understanding as well as their misunderstandings. The problem of language exemplifies the problem of men in nature, and it thus demonstrates and represents in essence how they suffer in this state of nature. They suffer from a lack of common meanings for the words they use, and most especially for the moral and political words they use. Even their suffering does not have a useful, common, and agreed-on name. The correct analysis of this problem, Hobbes contends, will take us a long way toward solving it.

It is perhaps worth emphasizing here a point that Nietzsche will insist on much later: that it is the meaninglessness of suffering, not just suffering itself, that torments and bedevils men and leads the human will to devise laws and truths and deceptive ideal worlds beyond this one, in order to give meaning to human suffering. Meaninglessness, in the sense of linguistic and existential chaos, the relativity and subjectivity of all moral and political ideas, and the inevitable finitude of human life, all of which generate human suffering, is the basis of the problem Hobbes exposes at the very beginning of the modern era. He also describes the deceptive nature of the doctrines of men of power, promoted as promises of an end (even a supernatural end) to suffering. Such doctrines lead men astray in a characteristic way and destroy their ability to see their way to a real and effective political solution to their problems. But I am getting ahead of myself here. We need to look at Hobbes's theory of language to apprehend the full import of this theory and its relation to his politics.

HOW LANGUAGE MEDIATES SUFFERING AND ACTION

In the first chapter of Part I of *Leviathan*, Hobbes begins with "the thoughts of man," which are, "every one a *representation* or *appearance* of some quality, or other accident of a body without us, which is commonly called an *object*."[9] Thoughts, that is, are the representations of the impacts of objects on our bodies. Thoughts are caused by the movement of bodies external to our bodies, their sensory impact on us, and the images or appearances we conceive to represent them. It should be clear by now what a radically new point of departure this is for a book of civil philosophy. It is both materialist and mechanical. It is also linguistic. How bodies can cause thoughts never really does become clear, even to the present. That they do, however, is a new point of departure.

Hobbes gets to language from two directions, but they reinforce each other. First, he understands language from the perspective of knowledge through the senses. As he says in the opening paragraphs of *Leviathan*, "the thoughts of man" are representations of the motions of objects on our bodies and senses. He says, "For besides sense, and thoughts, and the train of thoughts, the mind of man has no other motion; though by the help of speech, and method, the same faculties may be improved to such a height, as to distinguish men from all other living creatures." By speech, by naming, by language, "we turn the reckoning of the consequences of things imagined in the mind, into a reckoning of the consequences of appellations. . . . For words are wise men's counters, they do but reckon by them."[10]

But language does not just fall into our laps, and meaning is never unambiguous. Hobbes begins his understanding of the politics of language, as it were, from the problem of *inconstant* signification:

> When we conceive the same things differently, we can hardly avoid different naming of them. For though the nature of that we conceive, be the same; yet the diversity of our reception of it, in respect of different constitutions of body, and prejudices of opinion, gives every thing a tincture of our different passions. And therefore in reasoning a man must take heed of words; which besides the signification of what we imagine of their nature, have a signification also of the nature, disposition, and interest of the speaker; such as are the names of virtues and vices; for one man calleth *wisdom*, what another called *fear*; and one called *cruelty*, what another *jus-*

tice . . . . And therefore such names can never be true grounds of any ratiocination.[11]

Hobbes has a strikingly contemporary understanding of language: "For *true* and *false* are attributes of speech, not of things. And where speech is not, there is neither *truth* nor *falsehood* ."[12] Moreover, he insists that speech is always located in a speaker, who has passions and a body and his own "nature, disposition, and interests." There is no neutral or objective place outside of one's own social position and personal passions from which to speak. "Men give different names, to one and the same thing, from the difference of their own passions: as they that approve a private opinion, call it opinion; but they that mislike it, heresy: and yet heresy signifies no more than private opinion."[13] When there are only private opinions, how shall a public justice prevail?

When Hobbes complains that an existing commonwealth is dissolved when "every private man is judge of good and evil actions," he is contrasting this defect of an existing commonwealth with the state of nature, where there is no commonwealth, where there are only private opinions, and there can be no public justice or common agreed-on definitions of good and evil or just and unjust, because there is no agreement of men on anything, and each defines good and evil according to his likes and dislikes, for his benefit or to correct his deficit, naturally. In nature, there is no good and evil. There are only good and evil in language as it is used by men. How these terms are used by men is the great political question.

There is another way Hobbes comes to his understanding of language. In contrast to "arithmetic," where "the reason itself is always right reason, as well as arithmetic is a certain and infallible art," in nature, there is no "right reason":

> But no one man's reason, nor the reason of any one number of men, makes the certainty; no more than an account is therefore well cast up, because a great many men have unanimously approved it. And therefore, as when there is a controversy in an account, the parties must by their own accord, set up, for right reason, the reason of some arbitrator, or judge, to whose sentence they will both stand, or their controversy must come to blows, or be undecided, for want of a right reason constituted by nature; so it is in all debates of what kind soever.[14]

For Hobbes, the absence of right reason in nature and the conflicts of men over names carries a huge weight of political consequences—consequences involving violence and corruption, isolation and fear, death and destruction, and the uncertainty of all opinions, and therefore the necessity of political submission for the sake of self-preservation. The inability of men to agree on even the simplest meanings of terms, and especially moral terms, leads to the inescapable dangers of the political situation for men in a state of nature. In a state of meaninglessness and conflicting passions, they require reason backed by power to come to common definitions and to order. This analysis of language grounds Hobbes's political theory.

Human bodies in motion are driven by passion, by desire, by appetites and aversions, and these passions rule. In asserting this, Hobbes was writing in deliberate and marked contrast to the great majority of philosophers who preceded him and to many who followed him, all of whom distinguished the faculty of reason as the ruling component of human nature. But Hobbes, in *Leviathan*, sees reason as something painfully acquired only by great effort and education, something learned and trained, something artificial that has to be striven for, and which can fail when it is not learned or when it is led astray by vain imagination and superstition. "By this it appears that reason is not, as sense and memory, born with us; nor gotten by experience only, as prudence is; but attained by industry, first in apt imposing of names; and second by getting a good and orderly method . . . til we come to a knowledge of all the consequences of names appertaining to the subject in hand; and that is it, men call Science."[15] Science means something quite new in the world, if a true method can be established.

Hobbes sets people squarely in their desires, their appetites, and their aversions and what they imagine to be their advantage. In this he is fully consonant with both Rousseau and Nietzsche, although Rousseau divides desires into naturally moral and naturally immoral ones, while Nietzsche not only denies the existence of any moral differences in nature, but also denounces the imposition of the distinction in philosophy. There are no moral or immoral facts, only men to call them so. In this, he reiterates Hobbes's case. Nietzsche's genealogy of morals is designed, not unlike Hobbes's, to diagnose the psychological needs and motivations that lead theorists to read their own desires and interests into nature, and to analyze those needs. Nietzsche, like Hobbes, insists that passion motivates morality, a will to power that is often imperious and cruel, and which is always deceiving by insisting on its transcendent universality and impartiality. Although Hobbes explicitly connected knowledge and power, Nietzsche names passion the will to power, which motivates knowledge, indeed science, and he is far more aware than Hobbes could ever have been of the power of the constructions of which science proved capable.

Hobbes, at the very inception of modernity, wishes for the power of science to transform human nature, to bring a reasoned self-interest in men to bear on the construction of commonwealths. He is moved to fight "the Outworks of the Enemy," "the Dark Doctrine" that the souls of sinners are consigned to a place of "Eternal Torments" after their death.[16]

Nietzsche is also obsessed with the destruction and suffering caused by the "ascetic priests" of religion and their doctrines of guilt and sin, eternal punishment or eternal reward. Furthermore, Nietzsche, at the terrifying, ragged end of modernity, sees only too well what the success of the construction of a modern, rational scientific mentality and the modern state can do to create a new human nature, and new human selves, and he is begining to count the cost. We will get to this later. Here the point is only to remark that it is Hobbes who is the first to call the problem by its right names: the first who sees the problematical unmooring of passion and will, language and desire from any grounding either within or beyond nature, and their radical indeterminacy. He is the first modern, who by his analysis of the relation between desire and knowledge, sets the stage for Rousseau and for Nietzsche, for Freud's psychoanalytic theory and Foucault's poststructuralist theory. Hobbes is the first to analyze the modern subject and his world in terms of drives and desire, imagination and fantasy, and the linguistic, discursive, and conceptual symbolizations that help to create him as a subject and citizen in a body politic.

Hobbes shows an intimate understanding of the central place of subjective imagination and fantasy in social and political life. Hobbesian men in nature are not only bodies in motion, but egos in competition, and they compete through the distortions of their fantasies of their own worth and that of others, which is always comparative. "Virtue consisteth in comparison." Men's vanity and their need for power and glory contribute to the violence of natural social life. In nature the causes of quarrels are "competition, diffidence, and glory. The first, maketh men invade for gain; the second, for safety; and the third, for reputation."[17]

MORAL KNOWLEDGE—ITS ABSENCE

Hobbes is often understood, misleadingly, as merely an egoist, because he locates the nexus of human morality and reality in what we later come to call the ego. He situates the source of all value in the ego, but not in the ego alone; value and knowledge both come from the ego's entanglement in language, which is necessarily social. The question of where value comes from, once it does not self-evidently come from God, becomes one of the most important questions of the modern age, and one that remains violently disputed. Whether value, or morality, inheres in nature or is "only" created by man is crucially at stake in determining both the nature of human suffering and the value of human responses to it in subsequent political theories and in political practice as well. Hobbes rests securely in his attribution of the value-making power to human beings alone. Men use language to express their passionate wills, to gain power, and to establish institutions. Rousseau, as we will see in subsequent chapters, reinscribes morality in nature (and immorality in history, a problematical differentiation). Nietzsche reaffirms Hobbes's position with a vengeance.

Hobbes is clear: value comes from human imagination and fantasy and from the language humans create to designate the objects of their desires. Hobbes's list of vices and virtues in chapter 6 of *Leviathan* shows a rich appreciation of the power of fantasy, which was especially important to his attack on the delusions and deceptions of religion: "Fear of power invisible, feigned by the mind, or imagined from tales publicly allowed, Religion; not allowed, Superstition. And when the power imagined, is truly such as we imagine, True Religion."[18] Hobbes doesn't deny the existence of true religion, but he denies any supernatural or immaterial grounds for it.

More important, Hobbes understands that all moral terms, the ones that carry the greatest power and emotion, those terms which persuade men to act and which carry the most potent rhetorical power, likewise depend on men's passions and private opinions—they have no independent or objective moral reference.

> And because the constitution of a man's body is in continual muta-
> tion, it is impossible that all the same things should always cause in
> him the same appetites and aversions: much less can all men con-
> sent, in the desire of almost any one and the same object. But
> whatsoever is the object of any man's appetite or desire, that it is
> which he for his part calleth *good*: and the object of his hate and
> aversion, *evil*; and of his contempt, *vile* and *inconsiderable*. For these
> words of good, evil, and contemptible are ever used with relation
> to the person that useth them: there being nothing simply and abso-
> lutely so; nor any common rule of good and evil, to be taken from
> the nature of the objects themselves; but from the person of the
> man, where there is no commonwealth; or, in a commonwealth,
> from the person that representeth it; or from an arbitrator or judge,
> whom men disagreeing shall by consent set up, and make his sen-
> tence the rule thereof.[19]

Setting up a public authority or judge, a sovereign who will declare common meanings and establish laws, is the only way, Hobbes will argue, that common ground can ever be founded, that is to say, such ground is not discovered, but always created. This is the most basic foundation for *Leviathan*. Because each man defines his terms relative to his own desires and interests, each man sees his life through his own preferences and projections. Language does not establish a stable, unified, or uncontested context, through which, transparently, the real, the good, or the other can be directly apprehended. There are no references that hold good, or the same, across differences in people, stations, and circumstances. There is no "right reason" in nature at all. "But no one man's reason, nor the reason of any one number of men, makes the certainty; . . . And therefore, as when there is a controversy in an account, the parties must by their own accord, set up, for right reason, the reason of some arbitrator or judge, to whose sentence they will both stand, or their controversy must either come to blows, or be undecided, for want of a right reason constituted by nature; so it is in all debates of what kind soever."[20]

This is the heresy that the Counter-Reformation understood to lie at the root of all the others—there is no *right reason* in nature at all. There is no good and evil, no just and unjust, but only the things men call by those names, and they don't agree about what those names signify. This is still a controversial assertion. If God cannot guarantee that justice means justice, and manifestly he cannot, then men have to invent a mechanical god, Leviathan, to assign and enforce common meanings. In a way it doesn't even matter, Hobbes says, what meanings he enforces, as long as there are common meanings and established rules. The very ability to establish meaning at all is what is at stake. Hobbes is describing a world where the basis of any connection between people, between minds, is uncertain at best, impossible at worst. This is a world of individuals so private that even the meanings of their words are private, idiosyncratic, unreliable, and biased. It is a world where men need a judge to arbitrate between them in order to give order to their very language. It is a world of chaos and conflict, and hence of the most intense suffering imaginable, "in nature," as Hobbes makes plain.

Having shown that there is "no right reason in nature," Hobbes goes on to assert what was, by 1651, obvious to all—that "there is no such *finis ultimas*, utmost aim, nor *summum bonum*, greatest good, as is spoken of in the books of the old moral philosophers . . . [concerning] these qualities of mankind that concern their living together in peace and unity."

> Men do not live together in peace and unity: I put for a general inclination of all mankind, a perpetual and restless desire of power after power, that ceaseth only in death. And the cause of this, is not always that a man hopes for a more intensive delight, than that he has already attained to; or that he cannot be content with a moderate power: but because he cannot assure the power and means to live well, which he hath present, without the acquisition of more. . . . Competition of riches, honour, or other power, inclineth to contention, enmity, and war: because the way of one competitor, to the attaining of his desire, is to kill, subdue, supplant, or repel the other.[21]

Men in the state of nature fear other men, with good reason. They share no common meanings, opinions, or values, and they value themselves inordinately, passionately, and extravagantly, in relation to how they are valued by others. Moreover, Hobbes asserts, "virtue consisteth in comparison":

the *value* or worth of a man, is as of all other things, his price; that is to say, so much as would be given for the use of his power: and therefore is not absolute; but a thing dependent on the need and judgment of another. . . . Again, men have no pleasure, but on the contrary a great deal of grief, in keeping company, where there is no power above to over-awe them all. For every man looketh that his companion should value him, at the same rate he sets upon himself. . . . So that in the nature of man, we find three principal causes of quarrel. First, competition; secondly, diffidence; thirdly, glory. The first maketh men invade for gain; the second, for safety; and the third, for reputation.[22]

It is not merely that there is no natural standard of value in the world, but even more, that men's estimations of value are thoroughly self-laden, structured and saturated by fantasy, wrought by debt and by compensation, displacement and idealization, by radically subjective depreciations of others' worth in comparison to their own self-appreciation. This absence of any clear or natural standard of value means that "in the nature of man" we find competition, diffidence, and glory, and the motivations of men to act are for gain, safety, and reputation.[23]

All the causes of suffering are here, and men seek power to satisfy their desires and to secure their safety and liberty in the face of others of their kind doing likewise. There is no value in their suffering; it cannot be redeemed. Without God's interdictions and promise of final judgment and redemption, suffering comes to have no intrinsic value and no payoff. This represents an historical inversion of the first order, one that uniquely characterizes the modern age. Nietzsche became obsessed with precisely this question. How can we judge the value of value? How can we value our suffering if it has no redeeming value?

Hobbes is not seeking to redeem our suffering. He is seeking to naturalize and to humanize it, to make it subject to the actions of human power and will and to human decisions to change the conditions that cause it. Suffering cannot be redeemed, but it can be relieved and regulated, both by the common imposition of authoritative meanings and by the construction of a common power to keep the peace. Stability is a necessary condition for relieving misery. It is a necessary and sufficient condition for achieving peace.

HOW SCIENCE AND MORALITY ARE IN TRUTH A POLITICS

Hobbes's understanding of language and of the relativity of the meaning of words, especially moral words, radically changes the nature of the problem of morality for men. If moral meaning does not inhere in the nature of things, but is ascribed to various conditions by men in their subjective uses of language, uses which are and remain profoundly contested, then how we come to decide on moral meanings, like the moral meaning or value of suffering, becomes, as Hobbes demonstrates, a matter exactly and explicitly for politics. Hobbes's theory of language presciently foreshadows and anticipates contemporary arguments concerning the politics of language and signification in late modern and postmodern philosophy. Hobbes shows that politics is intimately and necessarily connected to all social uses of language. (He is not yet entirely clear that science is also a social use of language.) The model of politics he develops—the move from the state of nature to the social contract and their relationship to each other—is dynamic, a metaphorical, diachronic representation of both the causes and processes of man's achievement of constructive sociality and, in embryo, of human historicity. It is a structure that is constituted by an event, an event that is temporal, if not exactly one that takes place in time. The relation of such an event to time remains at issue in all the theories here considered.

By means of this theoretical construction, Hobbes also addressed, and helped to effect, a fundamental division in the modern world between the private and the public spheres, which was different from any classical version of that distinction. Privacy was not merely a legal category for Hobbes, but is, as it was for Luther, a profoundly subjective and objective primary reality, something that men could and necessarily would fall into that would undo all the effects of order and authority and would return civil society to a condition of chaos and meaninglessness. Hobbes not only addressed a newly emergent historical public in writing his theory; he also mapped the way from the private to the public in both the intellectual and political spheres. He argued that the public comes into being out of the fears and fantasies of private men, who together must come to reason their way to a common public life. By identifying the sociality inherent in men's relations, even in their inner estimations of worth, however, he also pointed to the way public values come to constitute the private man. The construction of the division simultaneously and reciprocally defines the two realms. Inner and outer are always mutually conditioning and arise co-dependently. They are only conceivable in relation to each other and are thus necessary to each other.

In mapping this division, Hobbes ends up assigning to the private realm most of the kinds of suffering we usually perceive as personal suffering—personal crises of conscience or of faith, family dysfunction, misfortune, despair, illness, and madness—all these troubles are both in theory and in practice relegated to the private realm, under the general oversight of the public authority, the sovereign, but outside his specifically delimited jurisdiction. The public realm itself, however, is the specific remedy for the kind of suffering that inheres in our social nature as such, as humans and collective beings. This suffering derives from the defects and injuries of our natural condition. (This reconstitution of the concept of "nature" denaturalizes some things, like community, and naturalizes others, like conflict.)

The most inescapable suffering is violence, fear, and early death at the hands of our fellows, which Hobbes designates as natural, inevitable, and demonstrable. This violence, and the coercive submission to social contract that he sees as its minimal remedy, is the most basic and primary kind of human suffering, the primal insecurity and chaos of the disordered "multitude," which Hobbes most famously characterized as the natural life of man: "Solitary, poor, nasty, brutish, and short." Hobbes says such a life is the natural expectation of any creature caught in a naturally lawless world. This most fundamental suffering, the cause of a host of other social injuries and illnesses, Hobbes seeks to redress by means of the "forced choice" of submission to the social contract. In this way, he reconstitutes fundamentally the nature of politics and also simultaneously the politics of nature. Politics is taking action in a disordered world to bring about order. Nature is the object of man's political action.

Hobbes sought a political remedy for the ills of the state of nature by creating a new scientific theory of politics, and it seemed self-evidently clear to the theorists of the modern age that that would help. Part of my task in this book is to make it clear how the idea of a science of politics came about, and how the idea of a science of politics, and in particular this science of politics, did in fact end up changing the politics of the modern age and did in fact lead to the creation of the modern state, based, precisely as Hobbes had hoped, on the balances and deficiencies of enlightened self-interest. Hobbes believed in theory, and in the power of theory to change human consciousness. Partly he believed in theory because he understood that he had hold of an entirely new species of theory, scientific theory, and that scientific theory, because it was true and demonstrable, must in the end prevail. It would change reality in conformity to its directions, even as much as it would in the end be changed by the constructions it effected in history. Science, as Nietzsche in particular feels compelled to demonstrate, has the power to become a "second nature" for us; a part of our very instincts, what in the end we bring to everything we see and touch, our will to truth. The will to truth, Nietzsche argues, is the most refined form of the will to power. I think Hobbes would not disagree.

There is a question in the scholarly literature about how "scientific" Hobbes's system of politics really was, and even of how Hobbes could have understood it to be scientific. He did understand it to be scientific, and not merely in connection to the natural sciences, but independently, as a knowledge based on language and experience. That is to say, he thought a science of politics to be both necessary, to address the reality of human existential suffering, and possible, because of the nature of human language, knowledge, and experience. Hobbes believed he had originated a complete and demonstrable system by which politics could be analyzed scientifically and political life changed both practically and analytically.

Hobbes did recognize the difference between his basic geometrical or mechanistic philosophy and the less-than-completely-demonstrable propositions of his moral and civil philosophy. He believed that he could account for this difference in a way that would prove important politically. In chapter 6, article 7, of *De Corpore*, Hobbes connects the sciences of geometry and physics with moral philosophy because they all involve the study of motions, the latter being the internal motions that are the passions, while the former are the motions caused by external objects acting on the senses. However, he says, "For the causes of the motions of the mind are known, not only by ratiocination, but also by the experience of everyman that takes the pains to observe these motions within himself."[24] That is to say, we know the motions of the mind not only by reason, as we do all the other sciences, but also by experience, our own inner human experience. Hobbes preserves this notion of experience, even as he pares it down to its most basic elements. The best evidence of Hobbes's establishment of the independence of the science of moral and civil life is *De Cive*, published in 1642 as a separate book (the third of his three-part general philosophy), because it was able to be understood on its own, that is, without the support of his previous work on the natural sciences; it was "grounded on its own principles sufficiently known by experience, it would not stand in need of the former sections."[25]

Why does it matter how Hobbes justified the scientific rationality of his politics? Because Hobbes based the construction of both knowledge and politics on the independence of the human will. The "will" is the basis of agency in modern thought, even though its status remains fundamentally problematic in all modern philosophical theories. Hobbes asserted the free and primary basis of human action in the will: "the last appetite or aversion immediately adhering to the action, or the omission thereof, is that we call the will."[26] He does not see a contradiction between the assertion of the freedom of the will and the reality of causation. We choose the actions we will enact within the discursive and material conditions that partially determine our existence.

Tom Sorrell, in two especially useful articles on Hobbes's science, says that "the 'standard interpretation' is that Hobbes's social studies owe their scientific status to their links with the natural sciences. They have no independent claim to be sciences, no method of their own that qualifies them for scientific status." He also says, "the standard interpretation is reasonable, but it seems to me to be mistaken."[27] I concur; the standard interpretation is mistaken, not only because Hobbes does distinguish between the kinds of science involved in the mathematical as opposed to the natural sciences, and between these kinds of sciences and the moral and civil sciences, but also because

Hobbes asserts a crucial similarity between geometry and civil philosophy, namely, that they both are known because they are "made" by man. Sorrell says:

> In Hobbes's view, the science *par excellence* was geometry, not physics. Geometry was fully demonstrable and perfectly certain, whereas physics depended on hypotheses that could be controverted. Underlying this difference, Hobbes believed, was a difference in the relation to our wills of the subject-matter of each science. The figures of geometry are things of our own construction, and the properties of the figures are due to motions made by ourselves. We are the makers of the figures and have a maker's knowledge of their properties, that is to say, an ideal knowledge (EW, vii. 183–4). In the case of the things studied by physics . . . the motions that create the properties are God's, and we can only say what these might have been (EW, vii. 3, 88). . . . Since physics can at best second-guess God's activity while geometry is perfectly informed about the human activities that produce *its* effects, geometry is the surer science. And, Hobbes adds, civil philosophy is like geometry. For the things that civil philosophy studies, namely bodies politic, are likewise our own artifacts, and so of their properties we can have a maker's knowledge as well.[28]

This view may appear strange to us because we are not accustomed to thinking of geometrical knowledge as man-made in Hobbes's sense; its ideality lies in its pure analyticity. Hobbes distinguishes between analytical and synthetical knowledge in *De Corpore*, but not clearly. The important point for our purposes, however, is Hobbes's designation of the *will* as crucial to both the making of the knowledge of civil philosophy and to the construction of "that great Artificial Man," Leviathan itself, the state. The human will, which involves both knowledge and agency, is the most basic datum about human beings in the suffering and the politics I analyze in this book. Desire and the will to implement it are the roots of man's suffering and of his power, and hence at the root of any politics in the modern age that seeks to take responsibility for suffering. The full implications of this relationship will not become clear until we get to Nietzsche's analysis of the will to power. Here it is only important to note the importance of the will in this first version of a modern theory of politics. It is important because it puts the causes of our suffering in our own nature, and likewise it puts the remedy for it in our own power.

Hobbes's science of politics is a science not because it resembles or is derived from physics, but because "*Science* is the knowledge of consequences, and dependence of one fact upon another: by which, out of that we can presently do, we know how to do something else when we will, or the like another time; because we can see how any thing comes about, upon what causes, and by what manner; when the like causes come into our power, we see how to make it produce like effects."[29] Science is practical knowledge. It tells us how to do what we need to do. So is politics.

Hobbes understands science and knowledge as what we do: how we trace causes and effects and therefore how we can act to change those effects. He situates knowledge squarely in the context of human action, will, and power. In this sense, it was clear to Hobbes long before it was clear to anyone else that knowledge is power, one of the primary themes of this book and of much of contemporary philosophy. Hobbes sees knowledge as a kind of power and he also sees the passion that motivates it. He asserts that knowledge of causes also results in our power to destroy and re-create our world, and its most important effect in this regard is to enable us to create the political structures that can alleviate and mitigate our natural condition of violence, suffering and fear. He was also clear very early that both knowledge and power have to do with language. "Right reason" has to do with the way we assign meaning to words; there is no "right reason" in nature. Right reason, and all the things we can build upon it, including peace, begin in and belong to humans alone, that is, in culture and history. Although he does not put it in these terms, this remains Hobbes's most fundamental epistemological, moral, and political insight.

4

The State of Nature as an
Ever-Present Origin

The lack of a common language and the absence of any given standard of value or right reason in the state of nature leads to an endless series of conflicts, the "war of all against all"—the human condition as a condition of unmitigated suffering at its most fundamental level. Hobbes calls the state in which men live "without a common power to keep them all in awe" the "state of nature," and this construction is linked to its necessary opposite state, "the social contract. "The state of nature is a myth of origins, a fiction, a model, an ideal type, a hypothetical logical construction, an abstract regulating, universalizing principle, a giant metaphor, and one of the most potent and important rhetorical devices ever devised. It is also an origin that is not historical but rather an originary presence that perpetually accompanies all social development. It marks the beginning of a movement that is always already there.

The state of nature is a trope that has held vast sway over readers for centuries. It is interesting to me that in a book of 477 pages, devoted to the scrupulous analysis of the background of classical and humanist rhetorical theory as the context in which Hobbes wrote, as well as a close reading of every rhetorical turn, trope, irony, metaphor, joke, sarcasm, and punchline that Hobbes ever used for persuasive effect, Quentin Skinner didn't see fit to include, as at least an appealingly original and perfectly "far-fetched" rhetorical device, Hobbes's "state of nature."[1] This is not something Professor Skinner merely overlooked.

Skinner, like virtually all philosophers in the Western tradition, sometimes including Hobbes himself, takes the philosophical concept as primary and fundamental to meaning, and classifies metaphor as rhetorical and figurative, poetic language not proper to precise, definitional, conceptual philosophical meaning, as Aristotle taught. So he carefully differentiates and helpfully traces Hobbes's changing valuations of the relationship between science/philosophy and rhetoric. He deftly shows how Hobbes kept changing his mind about how he thought about and ranked these opposing forms, but he follows the mature Hobbes, as most modern philosophers do, in maintaining the philosophical priority of logical and conceptual language, and he views the power of rhetorical language as giving punch to the point, but not as inherent in it.[2]

More important, it might be said that most philosophers see logical argument as the ideal form of philosophical thought, and metaphorical or rhetorical language as a second-best sort of language for expressing philosophical ideas, one that is much less exact, much less susceptible to logical proof, in fact, not susceptible at all to logical proof, and therefore significantly inferior to logical argument for providing reasons for thinking certain things or for thinking them to be true.

One of the issues at stake in the quarrel between analytical philosophers and others of several postmodern or poststructuralist kinds has to do with this question of the kind of language to be used to make true, scientific, or logical philosophical arguments, which involves what kind of an enterprise philosophers think philosophy is. This is an argument that has been going on, in various forms, since philosophy's inception. While I am not seeking to make a direct contribution to that argument in this book, Hobbes does begin to delineate the rudiments of the modern conceptualization of the problem, and he makes a significant contribution to setting it up, with ambiguous consequences. Nietzsche, moreover, makes a particularly strong case for the use and the necessity of a wide variety and even wildly varying assortment of styles to convey philosophical thoughts properly, and he sees conceptual and logical language as *inferior* to metaphorical and symbolic language for expressing primary meanings. He argues that logic is useless for conveying the most important kinds of experiences and the thoughts that can communicate them.

In arguing that suffering, passion, will, and power are the most important elements in political philosophy, I am arguing, following Nietzsche, that metaphorical expressions in the largest sense are indispensible for actually conveying what is at stake in political experiences. Metaphors are necessary to the way we configure and construct political experience and contribute to the philosophical conclusions we can draw from them. Political order is practical, and political theory is political work. It exercizes an agency that can only operate by means of metaphor. I am also trying to show that in fact the figures of speech, language and thought that do the real work in modern political theory are the great founding metaphors of Hobbes, Locke, and Rousseau, "the state of nature" and "the social contract." I suggest that there is a reason for that and that this reason has to do with suffering. Suffering is not easily conceptualized. Logical arguments about it both miss and mistake the point. It has a bodily, existential, experiential and inexpressible quality of presence that cannot be pinned down in syllogisms. Hobbes is the first theorist to make that clear. Nietzsche is the one who most completely drives that reality home.

Suffering always exceeds expression in words and is not merely a metaphysical but rather a physical, bodily, and psychological, even spiritual matter. It is an experience of bodies and souls, beyond reason and not located in the mind alone. Thinking about suffering only does justice to suffering when it thinks through usages and expressions that go beyond thinking alone. Human suffering occurs in bodies in nature and in time, in the historical political bodies of the world, and it involves bodily feelings and needs, actions and reactions. Suffering has to do with desire and power, as both Hobbes and Nietzsche differently insist. Men suffer from their desire and their power, and from their lacks, from the objects they desire and the doubling back of desire's frustration against the self in self-hatred and *ressentiment*. That is to say, suffering and the vicissitudes of desire are not rational and not logical, and that itself is a problem—because human suffering exceeds rational expression, it constitutes a moral and political reality that reason alone cannot adequately address. Only action is adequate as a response to suffering, and it is not always that.

In Nietzsche's genealogy, it is the nature of suffering, will, and passion that ultimately calls into question the entire Western tradition of philosophical metaphysics. He attacks this tradition as misguided, as deceptive, and as a cruel attempt to give meaning to suffering in a world in which there is no such meaning, no meaning at all that we, as humans, have not invented and imposed for our own purposes. I address Nietzsche's arguments in the last four chapters of this book. Here, I am concerned to show that, even in relation to his scientific knowledge and intentions, Hobbes was also fully cognizant of the political foundations of public knowledge, action, and the will to power that informs all philosophizing. He proved prophetically able to envision hypothetically the conditions of chaos that ensue with the collapse of all transcendentally sanctioned beliefs and values. He depicted this chaos by means of the great metaphor of the state of nature, which he projected back as the original condition of men's life. It is original not in a factual sense, but in a political one. He thus shows us politics itself as originary, as a domain of human life irreducible to any other and as constitutive of the human.

Hobbes has shown the relativity of language and meaning to the position and power of its users and the lack of any inherent "right reason in nature," thereby making evident the political construction of meaning, including his own. He does see science as being able to provide demonstrated conclusions about moral and political life, but he bases that ability on the fact that it is our will that is responsible for truth-making. Hobbes makes a good deductive case for his system of politics, but it depends for its success on a powerful metaphor, the state of nature, a metaphorically constructed configuration symbolizing the human condition, an image that compels rational action and sets the terms for the achievement of a political solution, the social contract. Although Hobbes sees logic as superior to metaphor in both truth and exactness, he in fact unites both conceptual and rhetorical power in his most important theoretical creations, and it is this that makes them work.

Hobbes's deductive system carries the force that it does not because the logic is flawless, but because he reasons by means of these great metaphors, which depict and express in vivid and unforgettable terms the most crucial aspects of the conditions he is using in his argument. These images provide both the clarity and the power that the argument needs to persuade.

It might well be argued that Hobbes's metaphorical power, especially his uses of "the state of nature" and "the social contract," is far greater than his scientific or conceptual power, even though he may not have desired that to be so. While his logical arguments in defense of monarchy, for instance, are easily and perhaps best forgotten, being limited by the historical context into which he intended to inject them, his metaphors, beginning with the Leviathan itself, and especially those of the state of nature and the social contract, have proved to be timeless and unforgettable; they still live in the active imaginations of contemporary theorists. They also pervade the ordinary language of most members of contemporary liberal societies. The language of the social contract prevails up to the present day. Human experience for thousands of years has made it indelible to us that in nature we suffer. I argue in this book that suffering is and has been most powerfully conveyed in metaphors that carry philosophical weight, rhetorical figures like the state of nature that do the philosophical heavy lifting, and this is surely the case with Hobbes. (Nietzsche later lays open the relation between metaphor and concept with a scalpel.)

Hobbes himself, of course, is trying to articulate a new relationship between newly reconceptualized philosophic forms. He asserts the primacy of mathematics, of geometry, as true and certain knowledge, and views all other forms of knowledge as less exact, less certain, and less true than mathematics. Hobbes designates hypothetical/experimental reasoning and rhetorical/metaphorical language as more derivative, less sufficient, and more fallible representations of truth than pure deduction, without the precision or self-evidence of mathematical proof. Mathematics, since Plato, has formed the standard against which all other kinds of truth have been measured as inadequate, and in the early modern age, the new sciences of geometry, astronomy, and optics revitalized this hierarchy of knowledge once again enthroning (modern) science as the *ne plus ultra* of truth. The grounds of scientific truth have been debated incessantly in the modern age, but its supremacy as the truest and most universally valid form of knowledge has remained largely unchallenged until perhaps very recently, although Rousseau mounted a heavy attack on the value of the arts and sciences, not as knowledge but in relation to virtue. Nietzsche calls into question not only the grounds (or lack of them) for science, but also its value in terms of the ascetic ideal and the unconditional will to truth that drives it.

The opposition between philosophy and poetry (or rhetoric) is as old as Plato's banishing of the poets from the Republic. It is only with Nietzsche that thought is again able to conjoin religious, philosophical, scientific, and moral reasoning all together as thoroughly metaphysical, as different aspects, versions, or incarnations of one ascetic ideal. On the basis of his genealogical analysis of the origins of the ascetic ideal and the purposes of metaphysics in relation to suffering, time, and the will to power, Nietzsche then finally exorcizes metaphysics. Nietzsche, as we will see, opts for music and rhythm, poetry, art, and metaphor as the best expressions of the ultimate stratum of human consciousness and the real. He understands art as the necessary means toward the creation of value, and as the only possible effective response to suffering. This inarticulate stratum of life is the basis for any further conceptualizations.

Nevertheless, a case can be made that Hobbes, read as a precursor to Nietzsche, himself repudiates what he knew as metaphysics, at least as he knew it in both Aristotle and Descartes. Hobbes was a scientist and a materialist and explicitly denied the existence of incorporeal metaphysical entities. For him, modern metaphysics encompassed logic and mathematics, but not immaterial existence and not normative qualities. He did not mistake categories for entities. While Professor Skinner is no doubt correct that Hobbes moved consciously away from classical and Renaissance forms of rhetoric, which prevailed in some political theories of the sixteenth and seventeenth centuries, it is also clear that he loved and used many and various rhetorical and metaphorical tropes, realizing their potency in his most compelling creations.

Philosophers invent analogies not merely for "rhetorical" purposes, which traditionally meant in order to make an emotional appeal rather than a rational case. Philosophical metaphors approximate an image or representation of that which is beyond words or concepts. Hobbes wanted an image to set out graphically the salient conditions of human existence he was trying to elucidate. Such an image cannot be refuted; it can only be traced to its ground, or replaced by another image. That is to say, the image is a representation or interpretation of the way things are seen from some particular perspective. An image expresses elements of experience, not an argument, logical or otherwise. If it works, it conveys the sense it creates immediately and renders the conditions it seeks to depict instantly intelligible. It works intuitively, in the imagination, and not only, or not merely, as a logical concept. As for the image of the state of nature, the consequences we draw from our reception of the image come from our having suffered in numerous ways the experience of nature it describes, our knowing or experiencing intuitively, bodily, what it would feel like, perhaps did once feel like, and what necessities it would provoke in us. This is what it means that the experience of order and that of chaos necessarily accompany each other; we know them both simultaneously, always. Fear and its remedy, peace, are inherent in our subjectivities.

The state of nature is an originary metaphor, a condensed myth of origins, one that grounds human existence in imagination and feeling. In Nietzsche's sense, it is a this-worldly, anti-ascetic, anti-ideal ideal. That is to say, it posits an "ideal" origin for human society in the sense that it is the opposite of a "real" or factually historical origin. And it is idealized in that only essential theoretical elements are considered; "extraneous" particulars are left out. It is an abstraction. But the state of nature as origin is not idealized in the ordinary meaning of that term—it is a dystopia, an unhappy chaos of fear and misery, a terrifying reality out of which order has somehow to be wrested.

Nevertheless, Hobbes's conception of science was science, however incomplete, and it can be read as a new and more rigorous modern incarnation of the ascetic ideal, a prime instance of what Nietzsche calls "the will to truth." We will consider this when we explore the implications of Nietzsche's critical analysis of modern science. This paradox about what the idea of science means, its origins, purposes, and value, situates Hobbes right in the center of the struggle to define the new discourses and perspectives of his age.

In all of the readings I have studied concerning Hobbes's state of nature, I have found virtually no references, analyses, or interpretations that make clear the metaphorical, rhetorical, and imaginary aspects of his primary construction. Hobbes declared it a hypothetical, rational model, a scientific "thought experiment," and that is what it has remained for contemporary writers. But it is a great deal more than that, as I have been trying to suggest. The established, ancient opposition between science and rhetoric, between concept and metaphor, begins to be reconfigured here.

By showing the origin of meaning and morality in language, and language as symbolizing the drives, desire, will, and power, Hobbes sets the stage for the kind of radical deconstruction of the truth of abstract conceptual systems that is decisively launched by Nietzsche in the nineteenth century and is carried over into late modern phenomenological, poststructuralist, and psychoanalytical philosophies in the twentieth century. Hobbes moves beyond classical metaphysics with his conception of science, even though science in the modern age characteristically became the basis for modern metaphysics, as that culminated in Kant and Hegel.

The metaphysical problem was always to join mind and the world, subject and object, to establish truth as a "correspondence" between some abstract, unified conceptual system and empirical experience. Hobbes shows how difficult this is to do. Nietzsche later demonstrates more completely the dependence of all truth conditions and conceptual systems on will to power and desire, on the writer's perspective, on history. This is best seen in his doctrine known as perspectivism. All concepts have histories; they cannot simply be defined. Nietzsche argues that nothing that has a history can be defined, and concepts, words, all have histories, as all good philologists know. Nor do concepts translate some object or experience transparently and immediately into words. They too are derived from metaphors. In so far as concepts have histories, it makes sense to ask what in the nature of their histories, in our histories as the makers of conceptual systems, determines the way we construct them and determine their value. One answer to this question, as I attempt to demonstrate in this book, is that we do so as a response to suffering.

THE SUFFERING SELF AND OTHER IN NATURE: SOCIALITY AND HISTORICITY

In their natural condition, Hobbes argues, men are radically equal, "in their felicity, and misery." "Nature has made men so equal, in the faculties of the body, and mind" that "when all is reckoned together, the difference between man, and man, is not so considerable, as that one man can thereupon claim to himself any benefit, to which another may not pretend, as well as he." And Hobbes does mean men here.[3] He "presupposes" that these men are heads of families. Women are so far from his mind, so absent from his estimation of the fundamental nature of things, that he can write, completely unselfconsciously, that he imagines "a company of men at the very first to have been all created together without any dependency one of another, or as mushrooms (*fungorum more*) they all on a sudden were sprung out of the earth without any obligation one to another."[4] Men are like mushrooms, sprung out of the earth, without any obligations, and, it must be noted, without any mothers.

Men are not happy in this natural state. They are more aggressive than mushrooms. "Hereby it is manifest, that during the time men live without a common power to keep them all in awe, they are in that condition which is called war; and such a war, as is of every man, against every man." It is not just the actual condition of fighting that counts as war, but the "tract of time, wherein the will to contend by fighting is sufficiently known." Men who live "without other security, than what their own strength, and their own invention, shall furnish them withal" live in perpetual uncertainty, in "continual fear, and danger of violent death; and the life of man, solitary, poor, nasty, brutish, and short."[5]

The chaos and insecurity, the violence and fear, the brutishness and aggrandizing motivations of the state of nature need not be perpetuated by all men, but only by a vicious few, in order to establish a condition of terror and suffering for all. Man's agency leads to natural war. Hobbes begins with natural freedom, where "in such a condition, every man has a right to everything, even to one another's body." This means that "there can be no security to any man, how strong or wise soever he be, of living out the time, which nature ordinarily alloweth men to live." For the sake of self-preservation, then, it is the first and primary law of nature that "every man, ought to endeavor peace, as far as he has hope of obtaining it."[6] From freedom, the subjectivity of words, and the passions of men, Hobbes deduces the war of all against all—a state of nature that expresses the human condition as a condition of suffering at its most fundamental level, not in spite of but because of men's natural state as free agents.

The traditional response to suffering was natural law as a reflection of divine law, and moral knowledge was understood to be available to men as part of their reason, so that even if they could not find a remedy for their pain, fear or affliction, they could at least understand its meaning in terms of God's law and human sin. They could take take priestly instruction as to how to live a moral life, which might reward their suffering in a better world beyond this life.[7]

For Hobbes, by contrast, in nature there is no moral knowledge. Knowledge is right reasoning, and it could only come from proper human ratiocination about the causes of things, including human suffering. Hobbes's construction of the state of nature was meant precisely as a diagnosis of the causes of human suffering, especially violence, as innate to the human condition. It is necessary to unpack what that means, however. First, Hobbes was very explicit that moral knowledge was not possible under these conditions— that the inherent subjectivity of language and the conflicting interests of men made any agreement on the meaning of words or the demands of justice impossible. In the state of nature, there is no justice and injustice—these concepts can have no meaning. "To the war of every man, against every man, this also is consequent; that nothing can be unjust. The notions of right and wrong, justice and injustice have there no place. Where there is no common power, there is no law: where no law, no injustice. Force, and fraud, are in war the two cardinal virtues. Justice and injustice are none of the faculties of the body, nor mind."[8] Then what are they faculties of? "They are qualities, that relate to men in society, not in solitude." It is necessary, then, to look at men in their primary relationships with each other as represented in the construct of the state of nature and the movement into the social contract.

By using the concepts of mechanical causation to construct his originary notion of human beings as bodies in motion, caught in physical causality, Hobbes radically emptied individuals of both their sociality and their historicity. That is to say, bodies in motion don't have histories or social relationships, even if they do collide. But human bodies, that is, human selves, do have histories and social relationships. Hobbes used the metaphorical devices of the state of nature and the social contract in order to represent human selves in their necessary sociality and historicity, specifically, as conjoined configurations that represent the problem of getting individuals to function as a community, as a commonwealth. Concepts of justice and morality are "qualities that relate to men in society, not in solitude." In the state of nature, Hobbes starts with a "multitude" of men as beings, as bodies in motion, and figures the process by means of which they can become a society, that is, an organized unity comprising a single collectivity, rather than a mere conflicting chaos of multiplicity, suffering bodies and souls. Hobbes believed in souls, but not in their incorporeality. Corporeal souls need to find common ground.

Hobbes's state of nature is a hypothetical construction, a fiction, a model of origins for the representation of the necessary and sufficient conditions, the causes and effects that bring about a society. It is a metaphorical representation of nature, and that is to say that part of the idea of "nature" to Hobbes is what is primordial, basic, animal, instinctual, atemporal, immemorial, given by God, the minimum zero-sum state of things as they are. It is not a representation of trajectories through time, not a history exactly, but it is an image or representation of a diachronic process. However oversimplified, the movement, or jump, from the state of nature to the social contract, as an event, represents our historicity; it is perhaps the first modern representation of our historicity. It is the primordial event.

While Hobbes could not fully elaborate a modern conception of time, he did conceptualize an originary state that perpetually accompanies a political founding. He recognized the need to give a temporal dimension to human sociality without being able to fully theorize it. Both Hegel and Nietzsche, in opposite ways, try to begin a modern theory of time in relation to history. It has been argued that no modern theory of time has yet been achieved in political theory.[9]

Machiavelli talked about history, and personified "her" as Fortuna, stressing her unpredictability. But he had no concept of human historicity—that is, of the idea that we carry our pasts, our temporality, within us as part of our being.[10] The state of nature and the social contract do encompass this sense of an originary process, a beginning and a completion that is always already there. They carry the past within them, which is why Rousseau can get busy disentangling various stages of the long past that he envisions as part of this structural set-up. Rousseau greatly differentiates temporality in his narration of this process, placing the state of nature in a far-away, prehuman past, and the ideal social contract in a new dimension of political theory, the future. He links these states through revolution—and revolution precisely on behalf of the suffering masses, the unfortunate. In this way he locates suffering for the first time decisively in a history, albeit a rather fanciful one. He understands history as what we carry within us, and as what makes us, problematically, human social beings.

Causation did not, by itself, for the men of the seventeenth century, connote history, but it did entail movement in time, and the state of nature is a state in time. It is a rather hypothetical kind of time, abstract, originary, imaginary, metaphorical. Hobbes is clear that it is not history, but it is not, for him, fictional either. It is a necessary part of the structural/functional moment he is designating; it does imply a movement through or in time, and in this sense, he shows temporality as integral to human sociality. It is a diachronic, mechanical picture of historicity, and since historicity, as we presently somewhat theorize it, is not very mechanical, it seems an oversimplified or unfinished model.

Nevertheless, Hobbes constructed an enduring representation of the movement of human nature within itself from one state to another, from one primordial location or subject position to another. It shows such movement as integral to our nature. It is mythopoetic. It can even be said to be psychoanalytic, insofar as it represents the original, repressed, suffering subject of time, the fearful, violent self, and the fractured or traumatized unity of the collective subject of time (society), fragmented (dismembered?) and in pain, seeking to resolve itself into unity "once more." The collective is always already there and its lost unity is always felt and thereby suggested. As a conceptualization, it verges on the developmental, but is not quite there. Rousseau will take us much further toward a working narrative history in the next century.

The "state of nature" and "the social contract" are both abstract ideal types, genetic, originatory, proto-historical images and metaphors for politics. They function politically as well as philosophically. They represent certain elements of human nature as naturalized, rationalized, and justified. They normalize certain political conditions and not others. It should be noted that, putting Hobbes's own authoritarian political conclusions to the side, these representations themselves are radically democratic. In the state of nature, bodies are free-moving, self-willed, and of equal mass and velocity. They participate equally, ferociously, in their own interactions, and they eventually all acquire the consciousness to get from a state of chaos to a state of unity, however rough and coerced.

So it could be said, Hobbesian men learn. There is a qualitative difference between the original selves in the state of nature and the "educated" selves of the social contract. We can't help being reminded of Nietzsche's dictum about the cruelty necessary "to breed an animal *with the right to make promises*. . . . If something is to stay in the memory, it must be burned in."[11] It takes cruelty, both thinkers agree, to make a memory and hence a promise. The whole register of man's historical and ethical being lies here, in suffering, memory, and time. We will return to the cruelty and coercion both Hobbes and Nietzsche see in the "right to make promises" shortly. It is an important convergence between these two theorists, widely separated in time, and it reveals the violence inherent in making contracts "voluntarily," which subsequent liberal theorists successfully concealed.

Hobbesian men contract voluntarily, but Hobbes insists that this is perfectly consistent with force, fraud, and fear. "Covenants entered into by fear, in the condition of mere nature, are obligatory."[12] Fear is our natural condition—there is no other. We will look at this obligation more closely in the next chapter. For Hobbes, the gain that is made by the self in the process of transition, by learning to make and keep promises, includes self-consciousness and rational self-discipline, as well as submission to the power of the sovereign for the creation of a secure commonwealth in which to pursue one's purposes. Significantly, he affirms that this promising is brought about through the effects of terror on the will.

In contrast, however, to Nietzsche's and Hegel's master/slave relationship as the primary political trope (also a myth of origins and a model of human historicity, but one integrating hierarchy and domination into the beginning), the state of nature and the social contract, which must be taken together, constitute a collectivity, a sociality and historicity based, at least abstractly, on equality and freedom. The coercion and terror and the promise are shared by all equally, except for the sovereign himself, who remains outside the compact.

Freedom in Hobbes is "the absence of external impediments" to the movement of bodies and wills. It is an uneasy amalgam of the free movement of the body and the self-determination of the will, all within the conditions of material causation. The will is free insofar as it chooses, within the constraints of its condition, which include necessity and coercion. What it would mean to have a will that is free in the sense of being unconditioned is inconceivable to Hobbes. (And to me, I must confess.) But the will is unconditional in Hobbes, that is, it has the right to all things. The obstacles to freedom are external. The will learns fear, and suffering, through collisions with other bodies and wills. The free movement of equal bodies (and wills) leads to conflict and war, and then, through the painful acquisition of self-conscious rationality, to equal participation in the authorization of legitimate sovereignty and to the establishment of a stable political order, peace.

This outcome is in many ways a very idealized version of the primary political condition in the modern age. It is the generic version of politics, or has become so. However, this is not the only way to look at this progression, and I will burden this picture with many of its unconscious and excluded shadows and unacknowledged underpinnings shortly. Still, it is influential, and has proved to be the definitive, historically consequential interpretation of this originary founding. It is not an accident that democracy was derived from this particular model. Equality is inherent in the initial conception of natural bodies freely in motion. These bodies do not bear different statuses, personalities, or histories. They are natural bodies in motion, self-driven and

equally effective. Power is included in their nature in roughly equal increments, as the very energy of their embodied wills. As Rousseau will show,
inequality is an acquired social characteristic. But, Hobbes argues, it is a
necessity of the establishment of any order at all.

Hobbes's state of nature and social contract are the beginnings of the
theorization of the conditions of modern subjecthood. Hobbes begins to give
us language to be able to describe the self in its inner and outer conditions.
Even as Hobbes focuses on the individual *in situ*, indeed as he fantasizes the
dreadful feelings of aloneness and fear of the radically subjective individual,
he shows that this subjectively alone individual is in fact socially situated and
concretely surrounded, in necessary and constant relations with his equally
mistrusting fellows. By separating out these elements analytically, Hobbes
problematizes the relations between the individual and others (not yet "a
society" but already "social"), and he dramatizes the necessary and simultaneous "differences and sameness" of these conjointly operating selves.

While Hobbes shows the sameness of "free and equal bodies in motion,"
in the multitude, he shows social collectivity, and its differences, as the only possible context of the individual. He shows the effects of this necessary sociality
on the fear and imagination of these violence-prone and narcissistically bur-
dened, self-interested, and self-conscious selves. The image of conflict inherent
in Hobbes's basic intuition of the state of nature has been so indelible, and it
has so well exemplified the lived experience of modern "autonomous" bodies
and coercively socialized selves, that it has dominated the imagery of modern
political theory ever since.

Hobbes's idealized autonomous, free individual beings, interacting time-
lessly, universally, and fearfully, with others of their kind, could not be in
greater tension with later theoretical depictions of human historicity, beginning
with the somewhat fantastic efforts of Rousseau to narrate a more strictly
developmental version of this conception. As human historical selves came
to be more fully theorized as such, the process of subject-formation came to
be understood to involve the inextricable mixing of self and others, in the self
and in collectivities, over time. Human historicity was said to include subjects/
objects who developed and changed over time through desire, fantasy, projection, and introjection—selves who weaved in, around and through each other,
permeable, if not transparent; subjects who imposed on themselves and
others narratives of identity and difference, victory and defeat, domination
and subjection, and power in all its forms, as part of their inner lives, constituting internal obstacles to freedom as well as external ones. The self as historical,
as layered, accumulated and culturally produced, as coerced, tormented, subjected, and projected into imaginary realms of release and submission, exul-
tation and suffering—it will take Rousseau at least another century to begin
to get there.

Hobbes had no real conception of human historicity when he tried to invent a science of politics, partly because his own science was geometrical and mechanical. But he did have confidence in his own intuitions, and, unlike Descartes, he did have a notion that he had somehow to include a historical dimension in his model, which, given the biblical traditions out of which the whole modern age climbed, readily took the form of a myth of origins. It worked. The state of nature as a model of the myth of origins has functioned up to the present day, in one form or another. It is a working representation of the logical and psychological requirements, or the necessary and sufficient conditions, for the establishment of social unity, cooperation, and political right. It still lacks a fully historical dimension, as contemporary critics of contract theory tirelessly point out, but it represents historicity as the operational function of the prior position: the structure that is an event, and vice versa.

Rousseau and later theorists of the Enlightened eighteenth century move this originary model much closer to one of genuine historical development. Rousseau develops a narrative of moral progression that reverses the normative values of the two states—the noble savage with his innocent pity exists in the state of nature in stark contrast to the corrupted, tormented, and degenerate subjects of modern civil society. Hobbes's social contract is originary in the past. It is a past that "progressed" out of the state of nature; but the social contract institutes the original covenant, the originary promising by which any society, a united commonwealth, is necessarily first brought into being.

Nietzsche as well locates the origin of promising in the past, an archaic and brutal past, which utilizes bloodshed, violence, and religious rituals of cruelty to teach men to be regular and calculable, to "breed a man with the right to make promises." Rousseau, in contrast, sees a gradual development of natural men into an unjust inequality, into hierarchy, servitude, and subjection. He adds a third dimension, an ideal future, to this historical development—the new social contract of the general will, which can remedy the deformations of existing civil society.

The social contract, for Rousseau, does not represent the way a society was first formed, but on the contrary, the way a future, just society will be formed. Rousseau seems fully to recognize that human nature is an historical achievement, a project as yet unfinished. He does not see it, however, as having been an historical achievement of virtue, but rather one of vice and decadence. He brings the perspective of the public spectator to bear on the sight of the still suffering masses of men, and he denounces their oppressors from his position as witness and mediator. This new perspective brings into play many of the dimensions of the public spectacle of suffering which have become so charged in our time. For Rousseau, only the social contract of the future, the contract of perfect freedom and perfect submission, will bring justice to history. As it turns out, the social contract he envisions is not, for all that, less violent or paradoxical than the ones projected into the archaic and brutal past.

Hobbes began with a concern, historically, for the dissolution of commonwealths. He lived through a particular history that made that problem clear to him. He was looking for the causes of the destruction of the political order, and in order to understand that, he had to reconstruct the original conditions out of which political order would seem to have arisen in the first place. Misery and suffering were self-evident to him as the result of the dissolution of commonwealths, and it was logical that such conditions obtained originally, that is, primordially and universally, as well, since such misery and suffering logically accompanies and arises from nature, which is disorder. He reasoned that men had been forced to come to terms with their sameness and their differences and had agreed to submit to authority only because they had been so naturally wretched and violent, in such inherent difficulties in the first place. Their fear, passion and suffering was always the beginning.

Living through the tragic effects of more than a century of European religious and civil war and the societal chaos and ideological changes of the English Revolution, Hobbes knew intimately the violence and confusion, the superstitious irrationality and the bloodshed that attended the destruction of secure political order. If his days were not literally a war of every man against every man, they felt like it. In his historical books, Hobbes denounced the factional partisan machinations of ambitious and unscrupulous party men, the "democratical gentlemen," and the fanaticism and folly, superstition, cupidity, credulity, and plain bad faith of the Presbyterians and sectarians that he thought drove the people into civil war. He saw that men grouped themselves into opposing factions and parties according to passion and interest and ideology. He saw that subjects were moved by emotion and rhetorical excess to destroy what they most needed. They were led away from clear thought and reasoning about their condition to outrageous hatred and folly. He feared "the Outworks of the Enemy," who "impugn the civil power," and cause a "fundamental derangement of the psyche, of the way in which men and women think of themselves and of their relationships and connections with the world."[13]

Hobbes's science is an abstraction that allows him to isolate the elements of politics that he sees as natural, as ever-recurring, and as always in danger of recurring. The dissolution of the commonwealth is an ever-present possibility, and Hobbes wants to understand the interactions of human bodies, consciousnesses, and wills that condition this reality. Hobbes used both science and what he knew of history to come to the political conclusions he reached. It is not only the war of all against all in nature and the suffering that entails, but the powers of the imagination and the derangement of reason that can be generated by unscrupulous men using unfounded and irrational religious beliefs for their own advancement and power, which led him to propose an absolute, undivided sovereignty as the only rational solution to the situation. What he seeks to show is the genesis of the state, whether it be a monarchy or a legislative assembly. But he shows this not as virtue or vice, just or unjust, but as the natural and logical necessity of the way men are, that is, violent and delusionary. The state is an artifice, a creation of human ingenuity to ensure order, a painstaking construction out of original natural elements that allows for some surcease from pain, but at a considerable cost.

There is a large critical literature focused on how the abstractions of social contract theory, and especially Hobbes's version, eliminate from human nature the history, particularity, and identity of actual people, the singularities of birth, training, education, family, culture, and previous condition of servitude, as well as mothers and other necessary items. It is argued that contract theory denies actual human beings in actual circumstances in favor of a falsely "essentialist" model of man, unconsciously expressive of masculinity, aggression, and an idealized and universalized rationality.[14] The critique is true enough, but it misses the point.

As Hobbes was one of the first to have pointed out, knowledge of whatever kind is always interested, always situated, always subjective and invested with the unconscious power and attributes of its devisers. Most forms of knowledge are not self-conscious about this fact, however, and in the modern age, the question of the objectivity of knowledge has constantly been reworked and reinterpreted. Philosophy has always billed itself as timeless, universal truth. Science does too, in a no less egomaniacal way. Science too depends on language and on clear "reckoning." The social contract model is hardly the only one that suffers from this "human, all-too-human" drawback. As Nietzsche makes clear, this is the way thought works: it is necessarily perspectival. Language itself delivers us, as we are, into a world of passions, deceptions, and organized mass productions. All philosophy, all science, all critique selects its elements and its perspectives, and it is never disinterested. Hobbes is one of the first theorists of the modern age to give us some of the elements of the analysis of self and passion, will, power, and language, which enable us to begin see how that production works. It's hard to imagine that he would have denied the interestedness, the politics, of his own production. How much stake he had in the posited objectivity of science, at the very dawn of the scientific age, is not clear.

In his construction of the state of nature, Hobbes demonstrates that morality comes into existence through language. He shows the motivations within the constructions of morality. Furthermore, Hobbes shows also that the most basic ground of human suffering necessarily occurs because we are part of a larger social multitude. We inhabit a world characterized above all by a violent, deadly clash of wills, one that with luck and skill and a bit of coercion can be turned into a political and symbolic order. Hobbes calls attention to the paradoxical nature of our sociality—that we are created, or create ourselves, however much we exist in theory as free bodies in motion, also as legal and moral persons, as social beings and as political subjects.

He intended that the rationality of the analysis he proposed would make us more rational about our politics. We behave rationally only because of the suffering we endure at one another's hands, and because the submission to community that we contrive can be used in order to relieve that suffering. Hobbes had political purposes in mind for his science of politics, not just at the endpoint, but all the way down. I am arguing that he began with the suffering he saw, caused or constituted by the disorder, the violence, and the irrationality he experienced around him. He thought that because of the magnitude and ubiquity of the suffering people endure from the lack of order, they would be willing to see reason and to submit to the necessity of promising itself, in order to relieve that suffering. We look next then to the powers of submission that constitute the social contract. We look to it as power, as coercion, and as right, as Hobbes did.

5

Coercion in the Social Contract

In the second essay of *On the Genealogy of Morals*, Nietzsche harkens back to an archaic time, the time of ancient, brutal, rude beginnings, for an explanation of the origins of contracts, what he calls "the right to make promises."[1] It is significant that a great majority of modern political theorists recognize the foundations of social existence and civil society in a human act, the act of promising. This foundation is thus taken out of nature and given over to human power and will. Promising is an act of will; one that does not come easily to men, as all philosophers have attested. Promising has a long history as a fundamental tenet of moral and political life. But promising in many theories tends to be read as a highest value that grows out of consciousness, reason, intention, and deliberation by free and equal individuals. Both Hobbes and Nietzsche show us the dark underside, the violence inherent in memory and in promising. Both, in different ways, see the ability of the individual to take responsibility for one's words and actions as the noble fruit of a very carefully cultivated and ruthlessly pruned tree.

For Nietzsche, the context of making promises is the active faculty of forgetting, something that men must have in order to be able to tolerate living. But the opposite, the creation of memory, of remembering, and hence of human reliability and calculability, was also necessary if men were not to remain "slaves of momentary affect and desire."[2] In order to come to agreement, men had to learn a great many things, which involved a great long "prehistoric labor":

> Man must first have learned to distinguish necessary events from chance ones, to think causally, to see and anticipate distant eventualities as if they belonged to the present, to decide with certainty what is the goal and what is the means to it, and in general be able to calculate and compute. Man himself must first of all have become *calculable, regular, necessary*, even in his own image of himself, if he

is to be able to stand security for *his own future*, which is what one who promises does! . . . His entire *prehistoric* labor finds in this its meaning, its great justification, notwithstanding the severity, tyranny, stupidity, and idiocy involved in it: with the aid of the morality of mores and the social straight-jacket, man was actually made calculable.[3]

As both Hobbes and Nietzsche argue, in different ways, the ability to make and keep promises is only created by force and pain. As Nietzsche so famously remarked, "If something is to stay in the memory it must be burned in: only that which never ceases to hurt stays in the memory." As Hobbes says:

> Hereby it is manifest, that during the time men live without a common power to keep them all in awe, they are in that condition which is called war, as if of every man against every man. For war, consisteth not in battle only, or the act of fighting; but in a tract of time, wherein the will to contend by battle is sufficiently known . . . so the nature of war consisteth not in actual fighting; but in the known disposition thereto. . . . In such condition, there is no place for industry . . . no arts; no letters; no society; and which is worst of all, continual fear, and danger of violent death; and the life of man, solitary, poor, nasty, brutish, and short.[4]

And so men come through violence, fear and war to promising, to contract. Nietzsche says: "the terror that formerly attended all promises, pledges, and vows on earth is *still effective*: the past, the longest, deepest, and sternest past, breathes upon us and rises up in us whenever we become 'serious,'"[5] And Hobbes says: "Therefore before the names of just, and unjust can have place, there must be some coercive power, to compel men equally to the performance of their covenants, by the terror of some punishment, greater than the benefit they expect by the breach of their covenant."[6]

Nietzsche also lodges the meaning of covenant or contract in the context of punishment, debt, and injury, and he shows how they look to us, looking back: "When we consider these contractual relationships, to be sure, we feel considerable suspicion and repugnance toward those men of the past who created or permitted them. . . . It was here that *promises* were made; it was here that a memory had to be *made* for those who promised; it is here, one suspects, that we shall find a great deal of severity, cruelty, and pain."[7]

All this sheds considerable strange light on Hobbes's original notion of the social contract; it is clear that the promises made to bring about a social contract are coerced, driven by pain and terror, and afterwards backed up by the continuing force of sovereign power. "Covenants entered into by fear, in the condition of mere nature, are obligatory."[8] What other sort of contracts could there be? How else could promises be wrested from warring, vainglorious, and deluded men?

THE COERCIVE CONTRACT

Hobbes shows that the individual comes into organized community only through fear, violence, betrayal, and the instinct for self-preservation; only in this way does conscious rationality lead to submission, to mutual consent, to agreement, and to the authorization of legal power for protection. Men come to covenant, to promising, by submitting their wills to one another through mutual fear, violence, and sustained necessity. Therefore, "covenants being but words and breath, have no force to oblige, contain, constrain or protect any man, but what it has from the public sword."[9]

The state of nature is an "idealization" of primordial politics in the basic sense that it "highlights some of its principal features and makes others disappear."[10] There is no image or concept that is not an idealization in this sense. If we add a specifically Nietzschean or Freudian inflection to the notion of idealization, then idealization is a defense mechanism, a defense against negative (or sometimes positive) qualities, a defense against feelings of aggression and the repression that entails. Hobbes's state of nature is a de-idealization, or negative idealization, in that it constitutes a return of the repressed (also a version of the eternal return of the same). Hobbes exposes the hypocrisy and the deception of philosophers who (will) argue that in this "best of all possible worlds," men act out of virtue and unselfishness, are peaceful and altruistic, law-abiding, and morally obedient, and that natural law and natural reason provide perceptible rules for life and assure the tranquilities of natural justice. Hobbes insists on the naked instinctual activities of appetite and aversion, the will to power, which he calls "a restless search for power never ceasing until death." He insists on the use of language to further desire, to escape from fear, and to gain power. Hobbes's image of the state of nature exposes the raw conflict and egoism that the philosophers' putative virtues have concealed and denied. Without the umbrella of illusions furnished by religion and morality, nature for men is constituted by impulse and drive, instinct and raw cunning, fear, violence, and the calculations of instrumental rationality.

Students always protest that Hobbes leaves out of his picture of human beings those qualities of love and altruism, family affection and trust, generosity, friendship, and sympathy (not to mention women and children and all the varieties of race and class) that make all the difference. What Hobbes selects has to be seen in context, against the background of what had previously been rhetorically, philosophically, and institutionally affirmed since Aristotle and Augustine. He felt no need to reaffirm what was on all sides

defended: natural law. He needed to respond to the illusion of natural morality by revealing what was on all sides defended against: the acknowledgment
of basic fear, violence, and pain as primary experience.

Hobbes's image is an effort of transposition that brings certain experiences
of life into vivid, lived intensity. Unlike the physician who adds sugar to a
bitter medicine to make it more palatable, Hobbes takes away the sugar so
that the bitterness of the medicine—the coercive contract as a remedy for the
violence of human nature—can finally be perceived.

We could argue that Hobbes's idealization of men's "original" freedom
and equality, read abstractly as universal and true, is, from our perspective,
just as false and deceptive as the truths of the previous tradition. But no one
had ever affirmed freedom and equality in quite the modern way before, nor
made it politically efficacious. If modernity's values of autonomy, equality,
and independence, of self-directed agents and selves has actually never been
historically true, nor indeed universal, it aspired to be so. Locke later ameliorated the logic of the state of nature to make it more comfortable, disguising
and concealing the bitterness, the violence and the suffering Hobbes had
revealed. In substituting the protection of property for sheer self-preservation
as the structural justification for civil society, he made the medicine much
more palatable for some, and even more bitter for others, more natural for
those who owned property, and more intractible for those who were themselves property (women and slaves).

The state of nature is metaphorical; it is imaginary history, a narrative
slice of putative archaic life, of what came "before." Because it is originary, it
reproduces memory. It is the "original position," necessary to the process of
founding. But it is not as if there could have been one original position, factually or historically; it is nature "before" society; it is what is logically and
morally prior, what comes "first" in an ontological and axiological and not
an actual way. It metamorphises history and morality in the image of natural
desire. The social contract is the pact, the pact of the brothers against the
fathers for the possession of the women.[11]

The social contract is what comes "after" the state of nature; it is the
founding moment, the moment of sacrifice and the moment of promising,
which grows out of the lived experience of terror, violence, and suffering. It
regularizes suffering and institutionalizes sacrifice, specifically, as Locke enjoins,
the sacrifice of the right to be one's own enforcer, one's own revenger for harm
and injury, by placing that remedy in the power of the community as a whole
in the form of public power. The moment of contracting leaves the private
forms of suffering unremarked. It sets up a public space for the remedy of
public harm, and it is very careful to delineate what counts as public harm.
This division of public from private remains continually contested. Nature,
faith, and property are the domains of the private self. But only political power

can establish the public peace of free agents and citizens as they deliberate the public good. Hobbes's remedy does show the power of power, that is, the force that must be mustered from individuals and combined to form a society that can use organized violence to mitigate and redistribute the raw violence of nature.

The state of nature and the social contract go together and are inseparable. All versions of contract theory require some version of the state of nature as original position and as premise—and all versions naturalize some values as positive and some as negative. The positive values in Hobbes's version are, in the state of nature, freedom, equality, autonomy, and individual rights, and the negative values are fear, violence, and conflict. Power is at stake and actively wielded in both states, as a function of free agency.

The social contract instantiates order, authority and law, protection and security. It can be used to justify democracy and popular representation as well as monarchy, although that was not Hobbes's version. Order, authority, and law can be good or bad, depending on the perspective of the subject, of course. Hobbes shows clearly how these values depend on prior subjection and submission. The fundamental structural conflict between freedom and authority, between the individual and the community, remain indemic problems in the politics and philosophy of the modern age. Hobbes gives some clues as to how this problem will evolve.

Hobbes shows that it is language that intervenes or mediates, or even produces the relations between the individual and society. Hobbes's theory of language, by showing language to be essentially and necessarily subjective as well as social, previews a much later understanding of language as the ultimate agency of socialization and individuation. He is prescient about the inability of the individual to sustain private meanings; he shows the individual forced by language to submit to collective norms, agreed-on usages, meanings, values, and rules as sanctified by consent and authority. He doesn't yet see the individual as formed by language, or as contained in it. He sees each man giving his own meanings, subjectively and even arbitrarily, to words, but also understands that there is no private language, only public language whose meanings are in contention. He sees that the fight in the public realm is over meanings. He shows the public realm itself as established for the sake of resolving by power the struggle over meanings.

Hobbes does not, however, really see the development of the individual through language, through discursively mediated interactions with others. He does see the development of society, however, as the development of public language and law. He does see that what the public realm does is develop public language and law. He does see that the individual can only join society by submitting to society's language, norms, and rules. He does see that the submission of the self to society is submission to a symbolic order which stands as the Other against the subject, to which he must submit in order to survive. More so than most other modern political theorists, who tend to overestimate quite optimistically the happy qualities that come with human sociality, the gains of joining the community and maintaining order and property by the demand of "free consent," Hobbes makes clear the coercive aspects of this submission, the hidden costs of self-discipline and self-control involved. One does submit to the definitions, even of oneself, of others. He does make it plain that the individual's survival is at stake, and that entering into society is a submission, a "forced choice." Of course, Hobbes argues that covenants undertaken out of fear, at the point of a sword, are valid. No other sort of "free choice" exists. And this is so because of human drives for power and gain, for reputation and vanity, on behalf of imaginary triumphs and defeats. He insists on the violence and pain they cause. And because we are always already in it, in our very language, and we wish to survive, we do submit. This is what we call free will.

AGENCY, FREE WILL, AND SUBMISSION

In the modern age, science gives man knowledge, and his own free will gives him right, the right and the power to make his own world. Hobbes asserts, and Rousseau and the Enlightenment philosophers reiterate, that the most fundamental and necessary protection there is against the abuse of power and the tyranny of rulers rests in human agency and human right. In Hobbes's philosophy, the right is prior to the good, and right inheres in the individual— "the right to everything, even one another's bodies." What greater guarantee could a man have that he will not be injured by another than his absolute right to defend himself, by all necessary means, his freedom to do "whatsoever he will" to pursue his own goals and his life?

Of course, things being what they are, man's agency is limited by what he in his own individual power can accomplish, and in conflict with many like wills, he "soon" realizes the wisdom of relinquishing, laying down, alienating that absolute right to do anything, giving it up to join the others in the group through the social contract, so that they collectively become a body politic, authorizing the sovereign. The individual subject can still then be harmed by the sovereign, but only technically, because he has authorized the actions of the sovereign. The sovereign, however, prevents him from being harmed by the others. Furthermore, Hobbes insists that a man never reliquishes his right to defend himself and his life, even against the sovereign (however fruitlessly), and the social contract allows for the establishment of public space, protection, security, peace, and law that will allow the pursuit of individual and commercial interests.

What is important here is that agency, both public and private, is Hobbes's (and with him, the modern age's) generic, chief, and overriding remedy for suffering or injury. The individual has primary, even primordial agency over his life, and this agency comes to be understood for the next several centuries as the fundamental and best guarantor of human welfare and as the foundation for a humane politics. The sovereign is given agency for the protection of the community and embodies that collective agency. This ideal of agency requires the value of freedom, which becomes the most central and important value of the modern age.

This modern ideal of free agency is grandiose, exaggerated, even hallucinatory, of course, and it is certainly ideological in that it denies its opposite, that is, what it costs, what it suppresses, and what it harms. The first thing one does with one's free agency is submit. Even the notion of a free agency suggests an unconditioned will, which Nietzsche will argue is unintelligible. Freedom of choice only occurs in such narrow and constrained circumstances, under such coercive and limiting conditions, that this freedom seems sometimes more of a technicality than anything else. Nevertheless, it is a technicality that has had great weight and effected prodigious political effects. It has established the modern liberal state. Free agency is a performative stipulation that will create, historically, a legal space for the individual and/or the public. It was a performance that proved to be not at all historically negligible, however much it remains linguistic, fictional, constructed, metaphorical, perhaps even self-contradictory.

Even when sovereignty is democratized and vested fully in the community, as it is with Rousseau, this collective will to which a free agent submits freely is still highly coercive, and the conjunction of perfect freedom with perfect submission is such a contradiction as to be almost unintelligible, as we will see in the following chapters. Nevertheless, philosophically, autonomous agency is the principal normative characteristic for the modern self and the modern polity, and this has important consequences for understanding both private pain and public authority. This self or subject is a free-moving, free-willing, free-choosing, autonomous, rational, self-reflecting self, at least in theory, and this is the most optimistic of self-portraits. It is a declaration by the subject that "by nature," "by right," I will relieve my own suffering, or have revenge on what caused it.

Hobbes believed he had distilled into a complex abstract formula the most basic elements of the human situation as that had been experienced by the inhabitants of the warring countries of Europe over many decades. With no commonly accepted rules or God-given rulers, no agreed-on standards, and no way to enforce unity, the principles of morality proved useless or worse, disguises for vice; they became mere private opinions and no match for force and fraud and the "restless search for power after power never ceasing until death" that seemed to afflict all parties in these religious and civil wars. There was, then, in this natural state "no propriety, no dominion, no *mine* and *thine* distinct; but only that to be every man's that he can get: and for so long, as he can keep it."[12]

It should be noted that the right of conscience, which was the first right to be articulated in the private realm, the first right that began to construct the private realm as private in the modern sense, that is, as a defense against the public state, is an equalizing right. All men, and women for that matter, have consciences and all consciences count equally, as Luther made clear. In this sense, all humans suffer equally as well.

The right of private property, on the other hand, the "second" right to be articulated in theoretical terms in the seventeenth century, and the economic realm as a private realm which it helped to construct, was an unequalizing right and the realm it protected a realm of inequalities. As Sheldon Wolin reminds us, "property signified inequality—inequality of capacities and, consequently, of power. The determination to protect property by constitutional guarantees was understood to mean the protection, perpetuation, and encouragement of inequality."[13] As Rousseau demonstrates, people suffer greatly from inequality, a source of suffering that the state preserves and defends.

SUFFERING, MORALITY, AND POLITICS

Perhaps the most significant influence Hobbes has had in the long run comes from his interpretation of morality. In contrast to Luther's Christian morality of suffering, Hobbes detaches morality from any natural or divine foundation and attributes it to profoundly situated and corporeal language-users. Rousseau remoralizes suffering and renaturalizes morality; Nietzsche constructs the genealogy of morals, tracing the needs, stemming from the will to power, that shaped the social construction of moral values.

Ian Shapiro argues that "Hobbes isolated the individual morally by making him the only meaningful subject of moral predicates, and by considering his wants, needs, and aspirations in isolation from those of all others, except insofar as these latter can assist or retard the pursuit of his own goals."[14] This is getting it wrong, however, and backwards. It holds the meaning of morality as constant, as self-evident, as the values generally incorporated in traditional religious and philosophical interpretations, when in fact what Hobbes and modern theory in general do is rewrite the meaning of morality, again and again.

Hobbes rewrites morality by making it a predicate of self-defining individuals as opposed to a God-given code of law that applies to a whole community. This changes the meaning of morality in a fundamental and not an incidental way. What morality means when it is generated out of the subjectivity of the individual rather than the unselfconscious culture of the group is exactly the point that Nietzsche makes in *The Birth of Tragedy* and *On the*

Genealogy of Morals. The modern meaning of morality wants very much to be related to traditional morality, but it keeps floating away, because it keeps losing its moorings. The individual subject proves quite elusive and unreliable as a source of morality, a reality that Descartes and Hobbes both immediately confront.

Furthermore, the way morality is structured at any given historical moment in any historical context very much determines the way suffering is construed. The meaning of morality and suffering varies widely across the spectrum of modern political thought. The reconstruction of morality is very much the unfinished task of the modern age, one that a reconsideration of the problematics of suffering is designed to shed light on.

Morality doesn't mean the same thing when it is predicated of individual wills as it does when it is predicated of God, or the *Eidos*, or Transcendent Reason. Morality had a unified and coherent content when it derived from a pure, "true world," located beyond this world, as a code of law expressly given by God, who commanded good and evil. Hobbes and modern philosophical and political theory, taking their cues from science, eviscerated this morality. As Hobbes demonstrates, science can give us a new kind of truth, or knowledge, but it cannot give us morality, for morality is not empirical, mathematical, or scientific. Or, to put it another way, when morality becomes empirical, it becomes historically and culturally relative; it becomes positivist. Insofar as science is empirical, it can tell us what is the case, but it can never demonstrate or prescribe what should be the case for the sake of the good. Science cannot prescribe what values ought to be lived for or defended, certainly not what values should be prescribed once and for all, for all peoples, in all times and places. Morality as empirical is mere cultural relativism, the problem modernity has been confronting since its inception.

According to Hobbes, for men in this world, morality has no meaning at all except utility in the largest sense; we call good and evil what we like and dislike, what advantages or disadvantages us, and there is no sameness as a basis for morality except the sameness of our passions, or perhaps, our suffering. We judge our pain and our pleasure from our own perspectives, and what conditions those perspectives is power. If utility seems too naked or too shallow a reading, and it has often been declared to be so, we can say that morality is a reflection of our passion, or a mirror of the depth, pain, or the meaninglessness of life without transcendent ideals, purposes, and guardians. This is where Nietzsche in late modernity will take us, but Hobbes made it perfectly clear in 1651.

Who is the subject of morality? What is the purpose of morality, or even the purchase of morality, in the modern economy of human life? These are questions that modern philosophy and political theory has posed to itself again and again and has yet to answer. Nor is it any longer to be expected that there could be one answer, one adequate, straightforward and stable answer, one unified or lasting or universal answer, one construction of meaning or value that could hold good for any length of time. As Hobbes shows metaphorically, metaphysically, and politically, the moral subject is constructed anew with each promising. And at no time is promising "free" or without the costs of subjection.

Luther asserted the independent reign of transcendent, divine morality in the individual conscience, with politics left behind. Hobbes constructs the human world of power and knowledge out of nature, human suffering, and will, but insists that there is "no right reason in nature." There is no morality, except what we create from our own desires and subjectivities and from our own power. By submitting our wills to the discipline of promising, we can create value and order. We can thereby relieve some kinds of suffering, while magnifying other kinds, or increasing the suffering of others.

In the next chapter, we will see how Rousseau translates nature into culture through a retelling of the story of history. Simultaneously, he reinstitutes morality both as instinct and as social norm, valorizing natural innocence and condemning social vice. Suffering is caused by reason in history, according to Rousseau. Rousseau indicts knowledge itself as deforming our natural needs and instincts, and he devises a construction of justice in the general will, which he constitutes as an ideal and perfect equality. As I will argue, he has to leave history behind to do it, however, and the perfect will and unity of the general will constitute a new form of tyranny.

Hobbes forms the crucial transition from the religious interpretation of life that preceded and instituted the modern age to the secular and scientific interpretation of life that truly demarcates the modern age as modern and as different from anything that preceded it. Hobbes sets the agenda for modern politics. He diagnoses the suffering of autonomous individuals in constant violent conjunction with each other and in constant terror and aggression over the objects of their conflicting wills and desires. He validates scientific knowledge and dismantles moral knowledge, constructing a philosophy of language that places the creation of value and of values in human hands. He brings agency out of the darkness of sin. He also constitutes politics as the proper arena for the resolution of human conflict, the determination of human meaning, and the institution of power—all proper remedies for human suffering. But he leaves the question of morality, and the subject of morality, in a perilous condition.

Hobbes locates suffering and the problem of the political response to suffering in two places: (1) the body, its passions and its will, and (2) language, its artificiality, subjectivity, and arbitrary connection to both mental and physical events. More important, he locates the nexus of the problem of suffering and politics in the conjunction of these two problematics—that of bodies, with passions and wills that conflict, and that of meanings, particularly the language of morals and politics, which cannot be decided, known, or agreed on by men. Language cannot be relied on for naming either the passions themselves or their connections with specific events, because these are precisely what is always at stake in the highly contested arenas of politics. Nor can moral meanings be determined as justice or injustice, good or evil, as the outcomes of these conflicts of wills and meanings. Moral meanings cannot even name the conditions of rage or fear, hurt or suffering, which engender them, without the political establishment of public power for producing agreement on meaning, and hence for resolving in some sense the problem of suffering, both by conferring individual agency (protected by rights) and by founding political order.

Both causation and responsibility are new problems in the modern age when the mantle of divine sanction is lifted. While natural causation can be understood scientifically, moral causation is much more problematical. Nevertheless, Hobbes gives us the rudiments of the modern configuration of suffering and politics, and hence the foundations of moral causation or meaning, by giving us bodies and wills in conflict, with language as the medium of the contest, of moral and political struggle. Although he disparages metaphor when compared to geometry, he instantiates the great metaphors of the modern age—the state of nature and the social contract—as ways to imagine the historical event of the constitution of human selves in society. The great metaphors give vivid expression to the problem of power and promising as the ground for modern political solutions to suffering, establishing both its meaning and its remedy. If Hobbes did not get all the way to property and history proper, he nevertheless deftly configured the journey and provided the basic necessary elements of what was to prove the most fundamental as well as intractible problem of the modern era.

6

The Death of God—
Theodicy and the Enlightenment

In Part IV of *Thus Spoke Zarathustra*, Zarathustra meets an old wanderer, and they speak of "what all the world knows today." "What does all the world know today?" asked Zarathustra. "Perhaps this, that the old god in whom all the world once believed no longer lives?"[1] The old man agrees, and Zarathustra thus recognizes the old pope, a "venerable one," whose hand always dispensed blessings.

Zarathustra asks, "You served him to the last? You know how he died? Is it true what they say, that pity strangled him, that he saw how *man* hung on the cross and that he could not bear it, that love of man became his hell, and in the end his death?" They speak of this god who is gone, whose "ways were queer," "a concealed god, addicted to secrecy," of his vengefulness and anger, his equivocation, and his bungling. "Let him go!" urges Zarathustra. The old pope wants to accompany Zarathustra back to his cave, but "a cry of distress" calls Zarathustra away, and he goes in search of "the distressed one who cried out."

He enters a valley, one "that all animals avoided," except ugly green snakes who come here to die. The valley was called Snakes' Death. And there Zarathustra sees something "scarcely like a human being—something inexpressible," who fills Zarathustra with shame. And the being calls out, "What is the revenge against the witness?" Zarathustra is seized with pity. "I recognize you well," he says in a voice of bronze. "*You are the murderer of God!* Let me go. You could not bear him who saw you—who always saw you through and through, you ugliest man! You took revenge on this witness!"[2]

The ugliest man asks him to stay. "But it is their pity—it is their pity I flee, fleeing to you." He adds, "I am too rich, rich in what is great, in what is terrible, in what is ugliest, in what is most inexpressible. Your shame, Zarathustra, honored me! With difficulty I escaped the throng of the pitying, to find the only one today who teaches, 'Pity is obtrusive'—you, O Zarathustra. Whether it be a god's pity or man's pity offends the sense of shame. And to be unwilling to help can be nobler than that virtue which jumps to help. But today that is called virtue itself among all the little people—pity. They have no respect for great misfortune, for great ugliness, for great failure." In contrast, Zarathustra is "ashamed of the shame of the great sufferer" and teaches that "all great love is over and above its pity."

The ugliest man explains why he killed God: "But he *had* to die: he saw with eyes that saw everything; he saw man's depths and ultimate grounds, all his concealed disgrace and ugliness. His pity knew no shame: he crawled into my dirtiest nooks. This most curious, overobtrusive, overpitying one had to die. He always saw me: on such a witness I wanted to have revenge or not live myself. The god who saw everything, *even man*—this god had to die! Man cannot bear it that such a witness should live."[3] So God is dead, and we have killed him.

In the next two chapters of this book, I want to look at the morality of pity and the politics that arises from the morality of pity, especially as that emerged in the eighteenth century in the philosophy and political theory of Jean-Jacques Rousseau. There is deep irony in introducing Rousseau by means of the ugliest man, who couldn't bear to be seen as he was, because Rousseau was a man obsessed with being seen and not being seen, with the inability of those around him to see him as he "truly" was. He was also a theorist who placed pity at the center of his moral and political theory. He saw pity as a quality that allowed humans to be "human," to share a common world and to create a just, perfect social contract, which would undo the effects of human history, a history of domination, inequality, and suffering. Rousseau is also a philosopher of paradoxes, in some respects even more so than Nietzsche. For the purposes of this book and from the perspective of suffering, he is one of the most important modern theorists, because suffering and the injustice that causes it are the explicit objects of his thought and political practice, and because he brought entirely new perspectives to bear on this question. Of Rousseau it must be asked, as it was asked by the one who killed God, "What is the revenge against the witness?"

This is because it is from Rousseau that we first begin to learn some additional perspectives on suffering that come into being and become politically important at this time in history. Rousseau gives us the perspective of the public man, the spectator and the witness; not one who suffers or one who acts, but one who witnesses the suffering of others and apportions blame. It is the spectator who demands justice, for others, and brings into play the related perspectives of the accuser, the denouncer, the persecutors who are denounced, and the benefactors who are moved to help. It is in the new public spaces of the city, and of the masses, that the voice of the modern spectator is first heard, and the roles of the victims, the predators, and the rescuers are given a new and modern life. These roles all come into being with the existence of the spectator, who suffers vicariously, watches, pities, mediates, and accuses; one who becomes after all a veritable connoisseur of suffering and vengeance.

The problem that the death of God caused for the thinkers of the Enlightenment, and especially for their ability to articulate a moral theory and a foundation for moral judgment, was not unremarked by those thinkers themselves. One way it was understood was as their inheritance of the problem of theodicy: the question of the goodness of God, of the suffering of the innocent, and of the obvious pervasiveness of evil in the world. With God's renewed hiddenness, transcendence, and absence from the temporal world in the modern age, the question of the possibility of criteria for moral judgment and the problem of evil loomed ever larger on the horizon of philosophical thinkers. The context of the problem of theodicy in the Enlightenment is one way to situate Rousseau in the larger tradition of which he forms an integral part.

As guide to this exploration, I will take one of the masters of the thought of the Enlightenment, Ernst Cassirer.[4] Putting Rousseau's philosophy into the context of the Enlightenment and its inheritance of the problem of theodicy allows us to focus on the relation between Rousseau's moral politics and the question of suffering, which he, for the first time, identifies specifically as an historical and political problem. Historical suffering becomes the defining moral problem of the modern age with Rousseau. It destabilizes the connection between what is and what ought to be, the representation of the factuality of the world and the moral evaluation of those facts. Rousseau is one of the first theorists to struggle with some of the differentiations of that relationship. Looking at the context of theodicy in the Enlightenment allows us to anticipate how that relation (between fact and value) intersects with his characterization of the state of nature as a kind of proto-history, and with his development of a new ideal of the social contract, not in the past but for the future. The dimension of time here makes its first self-conscious and problematical entrée.

In contrast to Hobbes, who denies the existence of "right reason" in nature, Rousseau greatly stretches the concept of nature to include both biology and anthropology, so much so that it might be said that he stretches it to the breaking point. Human nature is so paradoxical for Rousseau that he is not able to decide when nature becomes "human," thus exemplifying the difficulties of transporting morality into nature, and of judging what is "natural" and what "unnatural" to men. Seeking to preserve "natural goodness," he ends up having to deny humanness to what is "not good," or even "not yet good." He tries to identify the precise point at which immorality enters the narrative, and then he seeks to trace the consequences of that development in its disastrous effects for the self and civil society. He also seeks a political and

moral remedy for the "unnatural immorality" that it seems human development must entail. Rousseau is a moralist, and it is as such that he most significantly enters this account of the politics of suffering in modern political thought.

REASON AND THE ABYSS

In the eighteenth century, called the century of Enlightenment, or of "The Enlightenment" as a specific movement and time period in European cultural history, the problem of theodicy was confronted, reconfigured, and rethought;
it was secularized, revolutionized, deepened, and given new meaning. Modern
thought rejected the mystery of original sin and gratuitous grace as answers
to the question of the meaning or purpose of human suffering. The religious
response to suffering in the Western traditions has always been to categorize
it as punishment for sin and as to see it as inextricably tied to divinely judged
human failure and guilt. Modern thought, in its many trajectories, sought to
relocate the causes and sources of evil or guilt in some other quarter, within
the bounds of nature and reason. Modern philosophy was required to interrogate the necessity of evil and of suffering through the eyes of reason rather
than those of faith. Both nature and history remained stubbornly, irrecover-
ably, unreasonable, and that was the sticking point.

As Cassirer reminds us, it was Pascal who set forth the problem most
starkly in the seventeenth century. Without revelation, reason falls back into
the *abyss*. "The node of our condition has its folds and coils in that abyss, in
such a way that man is more inconceivable without this mystery than this mystery is inconceivable to man."[5] Pascal insists on the complete powerlessness
of reason to defend any kind of certainty or to arrive at any definitive version
of the truth. With his powerful logical and mathematical mind, Pascal dissected
the profound contradictions inherent in man's nature. Cassirer explains:

> These contradictions are the stigma of human nature. As soon as
> he attempts to understand his position in the cosmos, man finds
> himself caught between the infinite and nothingness; in the presence
> of both he is incapable of belonging to either one of them alone.
> Elevated above all other beings, he is also degraded below all; man
> is sublime and abject, great and wretched, strong and powerless, all
> in one. His consciousness always places before him a goal he can
> never reach, and his existence is torn between his incessant striving
> beyond himself and his constant relapses beneath himself.[6]

The only way man becomes comprehensible is through the unutterable mystery
of the Fall. All existing phenomena are based on the absolutely unknown.
Reason, without revelation, argues Pascal, is powerless to understand man
or his suffering.

What will become of you then, O man, who try by your natural reason to discover what is your true condition? . . . Know then, proud creature, what a paradox you are to yourself. Be humble, impotent reason; be quiet, imbecile nature: know that man surpasses man infinitely and learn from your Master of our true condition, of which you are ignorant. Hearken unto God![7]

The Age of Enlightenment, the Age of Reason, was hardly likely to take that as the final word on the subject. But Pascal here poses the most profound problem of the modern age. No Leibnitzian "best of all possible worlds" could deceive us, as moderns, into ignoring the depth and pervasiveness of evil in human life. Nor, without God, was there a persuasive response to it. In *Candide*, Voltaire concludes that "we cannot avoid evil and we cannot eradicate it . . . we can keep up a constant struggle against it."[8]

It was clear to the philosophers of the eighteenth century that their philosophy and their metaphysics hinged on this problem. No simple calculus of pain and pleasure, no merely utilitarian theory, would really meet the demand or solve the problem of evil and of moral value philosophically. It is Kant who presents the new perspective:

It is easy to decide what value life would have for us if its value were estimated in terms of what we enjoy, that is, according to the natural end of the sum of all inclinations to happiness. This value would sink below zero; for who would start life anew under the same conditions, or even according to a plan of his own (though according to the natural course of things), if life's purpose were merely pleasure? . . . Hence there is evidently nothing left but the value which we ourselves place upon our lives, not only through what we ourselves do, but through what we perform independently of nature in a purposive manner, if the existence of nature is to be meaningful only under this condition.[9]

Some purpose or goal, some value of value, must lie beyond pain and pleasure, but how shall it be known and how is it to be grounded? There is nothing left "but the value we give ourselves," moreover, "through what we perform independently of nature in a purposive manner"—but how shall we do that? What can we be said to perform, independently of nature? Where does nature leave off and we begin? Both Rousseau and Nietzsche are forced to struggle with the nature of value, with the relation of value to nature, or to "what we do independently of nature," which Rousseau attempts to describe, and Nietzsche declares inconceivable, a lie. Both, in opposite ways, occupy themselves with what values we give ourselves or create in the world. These are the questions that will be occupying us centrally for the remainder of this book, because the question of value is posed and can ultimately be posed only from the place of suffering.

What once had its foundation in theology was now floating untethered in the soup of human nature and the passions. Knowledge, which had once looked to the Absolute for value, now turned its analytical eye toward the complex examination of the formative forces within the self, as these represented the limits of the intellect, of the valuer. Two possible avenues or resources were devised for construing a solution to the problem of value, and thus to the problem of suffering and its sources, in the modern age—aesthetics and politics. Cassirer argues that neither of these realms of human practice looked immediately relevant to the problem, and yet the problem "takes root" in them.[10]

It is Rousseau, following Hobbes, who leads the way into an opposing exploration of politics as the solution to the problem of value and of suffering, beginning with the politics of the self, the history of the passions, and the suffering caused to human beings by social relationships. In Rousseau the politics of pity begins to take root.

In our time, Hannah Arendt, following Nietzsche, has rendered the most telling and notable critique of the politics of pity, especially as regards Rousseau and the French Revolution. Her analysis of the politics of pity emphasizes that it is based on a crucial distinction between those who suffer and those who do not, and that it focuses on the spectacle of suffering, which is seen, looked at, witnessed, as opposed to what is experienced in action. For Arendt, what is important is that this politics of pity does not center on action, on deeds and foundings, but on mere observation, on spectacle, and, more tellingly, on a necessary distance and difference between the spectator and the sufferer. It is this distance that Rousseau both depends upon and seeks again and again to remove. As Arendt argues, this distance of the spectator puts politics at a remove from any notion of justice as what would be enacted by free agents. It is a politics of spectators rather than of agents, and this changes fundamentally what is at stake in politics. There is the possibility of a totalizing vision here that does not occur with agents who are engaged in enacting justice.

Arendt traces the terror of the French Revolution of Robespierre and Saint-Just back to the work of Rousseau. She argues that the politics of pity depends on this distancing for producing the spectacle of suffering. This allows the witness to judge and direct politics according to the exigencies of the imagination, which can take it beyond limits that any active participant in the actual agon of politics would recognize and respect. Action imposes limits that the imagination, the spectator, does not and cannot know. A politics of pity, of suffering as spectacle, turns out to allow, in the distance between spectator and sufferer (who can be alternately victim and persecutor and is frequently both) a cruelty and an infinite emptiness, a nihilism in fact, which it was Nietzsche's business to unravel. We will get to that. Here we might only recall the haunting question of Zarathustra's ugliest man, in the opening passage from this chapter: "What is the revenge against the witness?"

While Rousseau, as witness, believes himself to be acting on behalf of the suffering masses from the perspective of the good-hearted neighbor, the spectator who, in all good conscience, calls down revenge on those who persecute, there will follow, necessarily, the revenge against the witness too. What are the values of those who witness the spectacle? How are those values fed by revenge?

Nietzsche will most profoundly question this good conscience of the spectator and its assumptions of disinterested pity. He will restructure in genealogical critique both the aesthetic and the political dimensions of the question of value, in a critical rage against the metaphysics of morality, developing in response the question of value in relation to the will to power.

No less an authority than Kant credits Rousseau for having justified the moral law: "Rousseau first discovered beneath the diversity of human shapes the deeply hidden nature of man and the latent law according to which Providence is justified by Rousseau's observations.... Since Newton and Rousseau, God has been justified."[12] No small accomplishment. How did Rousseau "justify" God and Providence?

Like Hobbes, Rousseau turned his critical gaze upon society as the "decisive feature of the meaning of human existence, of human happiness or misery."[13] He understood politics as the key, however, not only to human misery, but also to human virtue:

> I saw that everything depended basically upon political science, and that, no matter how one views the problem, every people is just what its government makes it. The great question of the best possible form of government seemed to lead me back to the other question: "What form of government is most suited to produce a nation which is virtuous, enlightened, wise—in short, in the highest sense of the word, as perfect as possible?"[14]

As Cassirer affirms, "a new norm for human existence appears here; instead of the mere desire for happiness, the idea of law and social justice is made the standard by which human existence is to be measured and tested."[15] That is, the standard for judging, testing, valuing *life* is to be the idea of human law and reason. This is the true heritage of the Enlightenment in both politics and morality—a new norm of human social justice is proposed, a new realm of human social justice is to be founded, and a new society and a new history begun. The answer to human suffering is to be constructed as a new society. It is to be man-made and perfect, a perfect will in a perfect commonality, the perfect society in a perpetual present, a balance of perfect personal and political proportions, in which suffering and inequality, dishonesty and domination, anguished personal ambivalence and public political injustice can truly be, once and for all, eliminated.

7

Suffering:
From Nature to History

Jean-Jacques Rousseau is a moralist, and that's what makes him part of our story. He is explicitly and passionately concerned with the evils of suffering and the misery of the people, especially with the suffering caused by political domination, social inequality, and moral deformation as these are embodied in modern political society. Rousseau, according to the standard interpretation, idealizes natural man, and nature itself, as innocent.[1] In fact, his concept of nature and of man in nature is more complex and paradoxical than the usual reading suggests, as we will see. Still, it is clear that for Rousseau, nature is a realm of original authenticity, of prehuman simplicity, which he holds to be morally preferable, however unrecoverable, to the artifices and deceptions, the injustices and dishonesty of the self that is created in, by and through society.

In his *Discourse on the Arts and Sciences*, Rousseau explicitly condemns the arts and sciences, knowledge, and cultural development in general as causes contributing to the degeneration and decadence of human beings in society. Also, it must be emphasized, Rousseau suffers, and he communicates his suffering as deeply integral to his project of social diagnosis and reform. He recommends his book, *The Confessions of Jean-Jacques Rousseau*, to his readers on the basis of "my sufferings and your entrails, and in the name of the entire human race."[2] He does not hesitate to identify himself as the first, the only, real *homme*. He has confidence in his diagnoses of the sources of suffering in modern selves on the basis of his own personal experiences of suffering. Even though he "in no way resembles other men," he is paradigmatically human, as other men are not, and thus he can recognize what is amiss, as other men cannot. It will take us some work to unravel what these paradoxical pronouncements amount to.[3]

In all of his works, Roussseau explicitly points to the pain he himself suffers. He offers us a powerful vocabulary of suffering, what Luc Boltanski calls a vocular of sentiment—"authentic tears are by definition *involuntary* and *irrepressible*."[4] He is torn and tormented by artificial needs, that is, needs created by social appetites, and by vainglorious desires, by the deleterious effects of social inequality, and by the spectacle of the domination of the poor by the wealthy and powerful. He himself experiences the dissipation of his natural virtue in social dishonesty and moral falsity, and thus he himself can discern the prevalence and depth of decadence and moral decay in those around him.[5] He anguishes over these properties in himself and uses them to point the way toward another kind of life. He presents himself as "an honest man who knows nothing and esteems himself none the less for it."[6] He wants to prove that he is the "common man," who turns out to be very uncommon. This is an idealized version of himself and of the common man, to be sure, but it is the nature of the idealization that proves to be so intriguing and politically signficant.

As a political thinker, Rousseau adds to the literature of political theory a powerful critique of the suffering caused to human beings by others, especially by coercive modern social institutions and by destructive economic and political inequalities, fixed in enduring hierarchies. He adds to the politics of modernity the politics of pity for suffering, which, in its later Marxist versions, has formed a fertile and dominating idiom and framework of analysis since the nineteenth century. In eloquent and sweeping language, Rousseau condemns modern social values, institutions, and norms for creating false and degenerate human selves, and for the loss of soul this entails. Souls, for Rousseau, are not immortal, but they are moral and they can be lost. He details the agonies suffered by the highly subjective, highly passionate, and emotionally overwrought souls he sees around him, of which he himself is surely the most supreme example. Rousseau takes his own subjectivity entirely seriously and he universalizes it into a theory of what it means to be human and to be political. He brings a searing critical moral feeling and judgment to bear on modern political life. By bringing exquisitely crafted moral and political formulas (even equations) to bear on history, he positions himself as the first self-conscious modern revolutionary.[7]

In terms of the relations between suffering and political theory and the argument of this book, Rousseau's work is critical for several reasons. First, he imagines the state of nature as a process of temporal development from a relatively painless and innocent natural condition to a permanently painful, debilitating state of society. He demonstrates that both subjects and societies have histories, and he analyzes the history of his society in terms of a contrast between the virtues of nature and the vices and corruptions of culture. In his concept of the state of nature, he does not give us a real history (which he points out explicitly), but he does give us a kind of "essential" history, a developmental anthropology that functions like a history. It gives us the origins, the drives, and the processes that bring about society as we know it, at least as he imagines that process from his own very strange and unique perspective. He shows that social qualities and social actors are themselves historically achieved. That is, in his terms, they are not natural.

All the terms of his analysis are explicitly (as well as implicitly) normative; they are meant to describe and evaluate simultaneously. Rousseau dichotomizes opposing pairs of qualities, dualistic polarities, contrasting nature with culture, equality with inequality, the authentic self with the deceptive or false self, always valorizing one side of the pair and condemning the other. He is a moralist; his analysis of suffering is a moral one.[8] And he locates the deepest meaning of suffering in history. Evil in the world comes about in and through history, and he concludes that the struggle against evil must be waged against history itself.

Second, Rousseau shows the self as we know it as being intimately created and constituted by the social processes of history, especially by the development of language, the relations betwen persons, the division of labor, the relations between the sexes, and relations between classes of wealth and power. He contrasts the natural self to the cultured or social self, to the extreme detriment of the latter. The natural self, as he imagines it, is innocent, solitary, male (preferably), free, and not very intelligent; the moral or cultured self is formed through the erosions, truncations, and twistings of human nature as it is forced through the deforming processes of unequal socialization and education to become utterly other than it is in itself. Tracy Strong argues that, according to Rousseau's criteria, the natural self is not "human," and neither really is the cultured self. The truly human self has somehow been lost or is still to be achieved.[9] There are clearly paradoxical consequences of this interpretation that need to be examined.

Third, Rousseau advocates a new political ethos, a moral (even ascetic) ideal of civic freedom and responsibility, of equal human willing, of commonality and participation among citizens. Rousseau's question is the question of human justice, where the meaning of "human" is as problematical as is the meaning of "justice." He asks whether there can be any "legitimate and sure principle of government."[10] Political *legitimacy* can only be brought about by the willing agreement of men to join together into a community made just by its radical equality and the common will of men and citizens exercised in moral freedom. Rousseau defends radical political reform and even revolution in order to bring such a new polity into being. That is to say, the correct modern response to suffering is to create a new and perfectly just political order. If history itself is the source of suffering, a new political founding, one that can somehow escape history by being perfectly balanced in the present by the continual exercise of the general will, will enable its healing. This too requires some crafty explication.

Finally, as we have seen, like Hobbes, Rousseau faces the problem of theodicy, the suffering of the innocent and the nature of evil, as this question was handed down to modern secular thinkers by the distancing transcendence of the Hidden God of the Reformation. Like Hobbes, Rousseau thinks that only new social and political arrangements can address the problem of suffering in the modern age. The politics of pity that Rousseau develops provides for the justification for radical political change. Because of the suffering of the masses in social and economic oppression, history must be overturned and created anew, with the intention to save the suffering and to redeem them. Rousseau's ideal arrangement is considerably more utopian than Hobbes's. The response to suffering does not lie in science's power to devise a minimal political order and to promote a rational political culture, but rather in earthly redemption through the establishment of the kingdom of the just, transforming human selves and society here on earth, in this world, in a transformed history. Rousseau is a true believer and a revolutionary. He wants to do away with the social classes and conditions of division that cause human misery and he wants to erect a just, free, and equal society, to free men from domination and dependence once and for all, so as to allow them to arrive at their ultimate and authentic selves.

Rousseau presents, if not an actual or factually accurate history of Western society, at least a proto-history, a moral developmental narrative, showing the past as a process of change, the present as a process of power, and the future as a process of virtue. In contrast to many philosophers of the Enlightenment in the eighteenth century, Rousseau does not take for granted that we are, as a civilization, improving and progressing into ever greater rationality and enlightenment. On the contrary, he argues that what has been called "progress" has been a falling away from an originary ideal. History has delivered man into slavery and misery, and only the enlightened wills of virtuous and far-seeing lawgivers and the good habits of common citizens can remake the world into a place fit for human beings to live.

From the perspective of this book, Rousseau is a moralist, in explicit contrast to both Hobbes and Nietzsche. That is to say, he carries into theory a moral standard, an ethical and political ideal, which he asserts as right, true, and universal. He attacks the causes of suffering in modern society as arising from false values, destructive property relations, and deformed cultural structures, the inegalities, servitudes, and deformations of the selves and institutions that modern society has produced. He does so on behalf of the suffering of the subjective self and of the people, especially those who are marginalized, excluded from power, and dominated by others in society (except women, who need to be dominated). He defines domination as being under the control, or even the influence, of others, a loss of self that he himself experienced as an unparalleled agony. Domination is not only external but also internal. It is a disease of the will. He proposes a radical political and moral solution for such suffering. Suffering, for him, is a moral and political problem and must be remedied by a moral and political human transformation, a transformation of the will and of the polity. This makes him important for the argument of this book, for seeing how suffering is constructed and how it is changed by its manner of construction in the modern age.

Suffering and morality are intricately and inextricably related. It is in terms of suffering that morality and political revolution are justified. While both Hobbes and Nietzsche see suffering as natural and human power and agency as the proper response to it (however differently they interpret both nature and agency), Rousseau sees suffering as historical and man-made, and he develops a politics of pity to condemn the oppressors and rescue the victims. He creates a moral ideology to explain the connections among victims, exploiters, oppressors, and rescuing benefactors. He develops a political narrative drama with three of four opposing roles and a plot that explains to the public spectator who is good and who is evil. He devises a politics that will be a remedy for evil because it involves the transformation of a society based on evil into a society based on good. It is a moral tale he is telling, motivated by pity for the suffering of others. He thus begins taking us down a long road toward ideologizing theories that will first condemn and then redeem the world through political revolution. This perspective takes for granted the ability of the spectator to identify who are the deserving poor and suffering ones, as well as who are their persecutors, and which also takes for granted the righteousness of the witness and his right to call down violence and wrath upon the latter. Luc Boltanski quotes Adam Smith, another participant in the construction of this moral theory of the spectator and the politics of pity, who describes and creates in language morally opposing forces, and takes sides:

> When we bring home to ourselves the situation of the persons whom these scourges of mankind insulted, murdered, or betrayed, what indignation do we not feel against such insolent and inhuman oppressors of the earth? Our sympathy with the unavoidable distress of the innocent sufferers is no more real nor more lively than our fellow-feeling with their just and natural resentment. . . . Our sense of the horror and dreadful atrocity of such conduct, the delight that we take in hearing that it was properly punished, the indignation which we feel when it escapes this due retaliation, our whole sense of feeling, in short, of its ill desert, of the propriety and fitness of inflicting evil upon the person who is guilty of it, and of making him grieve in his turn, arises from the sympathetic indignation which naturally boils up in the breast of the spectator, whenever he brings home to himself the case of the sufferer.[11]

It is important to note that this politics of pity and revenge pertains across the board of liberal and radical thought in the eighteenth century. It is very much the status quo perspective that we in the West have naturalized as our own inheritance. The roles it identifies and their moral and causal connections, the sentiments and values it counts on, and the violence it displays in the name of righteousness, are nevertheless completely unstable and contested. Only the narrowest areas of moral clarity presenting such a connection between particular oppressors and particular victims can subsist in our world. The ambiguity and difficulties of identification that surround such ideological narratives set the stage for the problematics of suffering we encounter at the present time.

Rousseau is the perfect foil, the *bête noir*, for Nietzsche. He is the ultimate modern example of what Nietzsche despised and wanted to expose and condemn. Nietzsche mounts his most important and decisive attack on the modern age against the moral, metaphysical, and political traditions represented by Rousseau. Nietzsche will propose an entirely different reading of history and its participants, a different understanding of suffering and its vicissitudes, and a radically paradoxical response to it, a response even more deeply paradoxical than the one we find in Rousseau.

We are the heirs of the Enlightenment and of Rousseau far more so than we have ever yet been of Nietzsche, although perhaps this is beginning to change. Rousseau, at any rate, speaks for modern consciousness, and he presents what has come to be its normative categories and familiar typical analysis of the causes and remedies for social suffering. He speaks in the terms of a justice with which we are all familiar, and he employs judgments that we find unexceptional, to reach conclusions we see as obvious. Inquiring into the way Rousseau conceptualizes suffering and the politics of suffering shows us ourselves and our habitual and reflexive responses to suffering. The difficulties and contradictions inherent in this position are just beginning to be articulated. With Nietzsche we will try to demonstrate the nature of these difficulties, to show both the flaws in the argument as well as the powerful motivations embedded in the reasoning that forms this foundation for modern metaphysics and politics. Whether such a foundation can endure, or whether it proves to be a chimera, constitues a crucial nexus in postmodernist argument. We will also imagine a new perspective, a new interpretation, even a new politics, one that Nietzsche called "beyond good and evil."

THE STATE OF NATURE AND THE DEVELOPMENT OF HISTORY

Rousseau's *Second Discourse, The Discourse on The Origin and the Foundations of Inequality Among Men*,[12] is an extended meditation on the difference between nature and culture, between what is given to men as their "original" endowment and what is "artificial" in their social and moral development. While it is certain that it was Rousseau's intention to make that difference clear, it is not certain that he was successful in doing so. What is "natural" and what is not remains very problematical in Rousseau's argument and in all subsequent arguments about the politics of suffering. It is not simple to decide what is "generic" about human suffering and what is the result of "causes" (including structures and classes) that can be changed.

One of the reasons for Rousseau's difficulty is that he confounds the difference between nature and society with the difference between the individual and society. He is forced to imagine a natural creature, an individual, so removed from others of his kind that he ceases to be "human." Rousseau posits an opposition between "social" and "natural" that is impossible to sustain.

In order to save the goodness and innocence of nature, in contrast to Luther's original sin, Rousseau resorts to a highly imaginative, if impossible, conceptual separation of the individual from society, in order to reconstitute "natural man." This assumption of a primordial individuality in nature, and of social relations as a kind of problematical add-on to individuality, is one of the most questionable assumptions of the whole metaphysical framework of modern political theory. It was Marx who most brilliantly called the question by insisting that human species-being is always intrinsically social, and that it is through human *praxis*, which is always both natural and social, that history is made. Marx did continue in Rousseau's radical line of political theory, however, also dividing humanity into the suffering oppressed and the ruthless persecutors and calling for violent revolution to bring about a classless society. When the victims turn into the persecutors, as they did in the Stalinist gulag, for example, then sorting people into the proper categories becomes particularly excruciating.

Rousseau understands moral (as opposed to physical) inequality to be the source of misery among men, and in the *Second Discourse* he lodges the sources of such inequality in history in explicit contradistinction to nature. His problem is in getting from nature to history. He attempts to isolate a conception of the state of nature that is logically and ecologically distinct from social development, and yet also to chart the course by which the natural species develops itself into a social species. The question of the relation between nature and society, and how history unites them, is one of the most difficult knots in Rousseauian scholarship and in modern political thought. What is at stake is the relation of human nature and power to time. The concepts of nature, power, and time change with each theory, each attempt to reconfigure their relations. These configurations will occupy us for the remainder of this book. Suffering as a *pathos* of power in time, and as the site of ethical-political decision, which founds the possibility of language and justice, is what we require to understand.

Rousseau insists that it is possible, hypothetically, to disentangle what is natural from what is not, from what "circumstances and [man's] progress have added or changed in his primitive state. . . . For it is no light undertaking to disentangle what is original from what is artificial in man's present Nature, and to know accurately a state which no longer exists, which perhaps never did exist, which probably will never exist, and about which it is nevertheless necessary to have exact Notions in order accurately to judge of our present state."[13]

Rousseau is going to delineate a conception of the state of nature that is in the nature of an "*experiment*." He is going to give us the history of the foundations of human society as these evolved in contradistinction to the original condition of men, and he is going to do so by "hazarding some conjectures" about a state of nature which "no longer exists," "never did exist," and "will never exist," but about which it is nevertheless necessary for us to have "exact notions." This is no sort of history. It is a kind of philosophical anthropology, an imaginary one. It is also, of course, an idealization, created "exactly" in order to furnish us with criteria by which to judge our present condition. It is a conjecture that will allow us to evaluate. It is a moral fable.

In his narration of the conditions of the state of nature, Rousseau offers a mythological reconstruction of an imagined original world. He is clear that it is not a history, that is, a narrative of the facts, that is needed here. "Let us begin by setting aside all the facts, for they do not affect the question." What is there left when one sets aside the facts? What is at stake here are "hypothetical and conditional reasonings . . . comparable to those our Physicans daily make regarding the formation of the world."[14] Once again, the medical model is needed for distinguishing modern methods of analysis from previous ones. Rousseau is going to construct a narrative that will serve as a normative model as well as a diagnostic tool for discovering the origins of moral inequality.

In describing the emergence of society and culture from nature, and of social man from original man, Rousseau created not a history, but theory of human nature that makes possible, "not necessary but inevitable," in Strong's paradoxical formulation, man's moral and political development.[15] Rousseau transformed the concept of human nature, diachronically represented in Hobbes by the transition from the state of nature to the social contract, into the story of a process, and he gives us some, but not all, of the elements and kinds of events that form the engine for the movement of that process.

Rousseau initiates an exploration of the development of human society by means of the analysis of the (proto-historical) production of basic social and political activities, such as the division of labor, the invention of language, the separation and distinction of the sexes by their sexuality, the elaboration of the social ego, and the establishment of the family. In the process he describes humanity as a biological species, but not one that is yet really "human." It is a humanity innocent of all guile and blame but also caught in the necessities of instinct. This species turns itself, by chance concatenations of circumstances and the function of the human capacity for perfectibility, into a self-conscious, laboring, hierarchical, social, and cultural being, and a suffering one. The innocent prehuman creatures of nature form themselves into an inhuman, suffering society. He describes this society thus:[16]

> The extreme inequality of ways of life, the excess of idleness among some, the excess of work among others, the ease with which our appetites and our sensuality are aroused and satisfied, the excessively exotic dishes of the rich, which fill them with inflammatory humors and wrack them with indigestions, the bad food of the Poor, which most of the time they do not even have, and the want of which leads them greedily to overtax their stomachs when they get the chance, the late nights, the excesses of every kind, the immoderate transports of all the Passions, the fatigues and exhaustion of the Mind, the innumerable pains that are experienced in every station of life and that constantly gnaw away at men's souls; Such are the fatal proofs that most of our ills are of our own making, and that we would have avoided almost all of them if we had retained the simple, uniform and solitary way of life prescribed to us by Nature. . . . The state of reflection is a state against Nature, and the man who meditates is a depraved animal.[17]

The state of reflection is a state against nature. Thought itself is depravity. We are not thinking beings by nature, but thinking beings against nature. We are natural "before" thinking. It is a heady conceit. The contrast between nature and society could not be greater. But how did this species get from such a happy, thoughtless nature to such an ill-governed, knowledgeable, and miserable society? That is the question Rousseau must address. It should be noted, however, in reference to suffering, that Rousseau insists that "our ills are of our own making," that there is no cause of our suffering outside ourselves, and that our knowledge, reason, and reflection are "against Nature," leading us into depravity. It is not in knowledge, therefore, but in will, without reflection, that we will find our freedom.

Rousseau starts from what he sees as a correction of Hobbes. In the state of nature, as "first principles prior to reason," what he will later call "instinct," Rousseau posits not only Hobbesian self-preservation, but also "a natural repugnance to seeing any sentient Being and especially any being like ourselves, perish or suffer," a principle of pity.[18] As should be clear by now, Rousseau sees pity as the natural source of moral goodness, and he moralizes politics into a series of encounters between morally differentiated armed camps. Pity leads to political vengeance, righteous vengeance. (We will return to pity many times in the following chapters.) He also recognizes, as the engine of historical change and as what differentiates human beings from animals, "the faculty of perfecting oneself":

> a faculty which, with the aid of circumstances, successively develops all the others, and resides in us, in the species as well as in the individual, whereas an animal is at the end of several months what it will be for the rest of its life, and its species is after a thousand years what it was in the first year of those thousand. Why is man alone liable to become imbecile? . . . It would be sad for us to be forced to agree that this distinctive and almost unlimited faculty, is the source of all man's miseries; that it is the faculty which, by dint of time, draws him out of that original condition in which he would spend tranquil and innocent days; that it is the faculty which, over the centuries, causing his enlightenment and his errors, his vices and his virtues to bloom, eventually makes him his own and Nature's tyrant.[19]

Because they can change, because they can learn, because they can grow, men can "perfect themselves," they can become "other than themselves." Instead of "becoming themselves," they become "other than themselves," that is, they can become false and corrupted selves. What does it mean to "become other than oneself"? Rousseau's entire oeuvre can be seen as an attempt to understand this question. Becoming oneself has to do with will, with pity, and with human commonality. But it is not yet clear that his formulations actually can or do apply to human beings.

At the beginning of the *Second Discourse*, Rousseau provides the ingredients needed to generate his complicated story of man in the state of nature and to show how that condition gradually and over time "develops" into primitive and then advanced bourgeois society. I put "develop" in scare quotes because there is some question as to whether "development" is actually what Rousseau has in mind in relating this process. Strong says, "for Rousseau, nature and society are different categories with no rational or necessary link between them."

> It should be noted that Rousseau is not interested here in "natural society." In the first place, Rousseau is clear that society as we experience it is not "natural" to human beings. It depends on human actions, on the recognition of others, and most important, on the specific character of those interactions. Society is constructed for Rousseau: but it is constructed in a way that it is only available to human beings in a manner that dehumanizes human beings. Thus, second, society is a convention that keeps its members from being human beings, and it keeps them from being human beings because

it lacks what for Rousseau is the single human element that would make it real: It lacks commonality.[20]

We will return to the question of commonality and of society as a convention. We need to be clear that what is at stake first is the question of whether Rousseau is talking about development, that is to say, about history. While he makes clear that it is not "real" history he is describing (and that will become evident), Rousseau is talking about development, as in continuous interrelated change in an "entity" or historical subject over time. He is trying to constitute an historical subject, but he wants to differentiate it in some way from its natural origins. The gap between nature and history, or how and whether human development is necessitated, is what is at stake. Whether the development of society is "necessary" or not is what is at issue. The question is twofold: is any development at all necessary, and is the particular development that resulted in this society, modern European bourgeois society, necessary? In what way can society be necessary? What sort of necessity rules historical development?

Rousseau cannot fully connect the circumstances of human interaction as he presents them in the state of nature to the causes of the changes that result in the creation of society. He does not want to so connect them. He wants to preserve the freedom of the will, that is, the freedom to create a different sort of society. But what does this have to do with history? What he can do, will do, is to cast the question of the difference in perfectly ideal terms. In the *Emile*, Rousseau says:

> Natural man is complete unto himself: he is the numerical unit, the absolute whole that has relation only to himself or to one like him. Civil man is only the fractional unity dependent on the denominator, and whose value is in his relation with the whole, which is the social body. The best social institutions are those that know best how to denature man, to take away his absolute existence to give him a relative one, and to transport the I into the common unit, such that each particular no longer believes itself to be one, but part of the unit and is only sensible in the whole.[21]

This is a formulation that comes from the time when Rousseau was preparing *The Social Contract*, and it is in some sense prematurely introduced here. We will return to it again in the later context. I use this formulation here to alert us to what Rousseau sees as the "absolute" ontological status of the individual natural man, his complete wholeness and self-sufficiency, his existence in and for himself. Rousseau's moral and critical condemnation of historical society, and his impetus for constructing the ideal social contract, derives from this conception of the almost mathematical perfection of the absolute individual in nature. This "absolute whole" contrasts starkly with the individual's partiality, in even the best social institutions. In the far-from-best social institutions that history has in fact so far produced, man is not only partial but deformed. Rousseau suggests that any social interdependence whatsoever is contaminating. Further, he wants to argue that such institutions are not necessary, that is, that they are contingent and can be changed.

Rousseau seeks to construct a new kind of absolute whole, the general will, into which the individual will fit, "denatured," no longer absolute, but relative, "only sensible in the whole." I want to suggest that this attempt to bypass history, to deny the necessity of social development, and to seek an atemporal perfection in a general will that will not be contaminated by history, betrays its own kind of inhumanity. If becoming human requires this kind of perfection, it is neither human, nor common, nor ordinary, nor desirable. We have to take the argument in steps.

We might begin, in relation to suffering in history, with Rousseau's insistence that in the state of nature, it is only the will, without reflection, that is relevant to change. "To will and not to will, to desire and to fear, will be the first and almost the only operations of his soul."[22] Rousseau, like both Hobbes and Nietzsche, asserts the primacy and freedom of the will, but it is a very different concept of both the will and of freedom from Hobbes's, and the opposite of the will to power of Nietzsche.

Rousseau's primitive men are not bodies in motion who can think their way to a promise of order. The autonomy of the *moral* life that Rousseau wants to defend has to be created, not out of knowledge and rational decision, but out of passion, need, and pity. Hobbes, of course, hardly denies the impetus of passion and fear. But while Hobbes saw moral knowledge as following only from language and from the submission of men to a common power, who was authorized to define meanings and values, because "there is no right reason in nature," Rousseau still seeks an indigenous moral order in nature, now ambiguously understood as man's "instinct" for pity, also eventually his "conscience."

The relation of instinct to a free and moral will, and of will to conscience as well as to consciousness of the whole, is another way of putting Rousseau's problem. Knowledge, for Rousseau, is an historically intermediate relation between instinct and conscience, between desire and morality, but for Rousseau, knowledge in history deforms "natural" human needs and desires and undermines the foundations of morality, which originate in nature as instinct. Rousseauian man needs to get out of history, out of time altogether, to achieve moral unity.

For Rousseau, as for Hobbes, knowledge is biologically rooted in desire. As Cassirer explains, "The will is not founded on the idea, but the idea on the will."[23] Rousseau says:

Regardless of what the Moralists may say about it, the human understanding owes much to the Passions, which, as is commonly admitted, also owe much to it: It is by their activity that our reason perfects itself; We seek to know only because we desire to enjoy, and it is not possible to conceive why someone who had neither desires nor fears would take the trouble to reason. The Passions, in turn, own their origin to our needs, and their progress to our knowledge; for one can only desire or fear things in terms of the ideas one can have of them, or by the simple impulsion of Nature; and Savage man, deprived of every sort of enlightenment, experiences only the Passions of this latter kind; his Desires do not exceed his Physical needs.[24]

Rousseau here gives us the basic elements of his historical anthropology. Reason is rooted in the passions: it is only because we have desires and fears that we seek knowledge. The passions, in turn, are rooted in needs, and in the *Second Discourse*, Rousseau will develop a theory of true and false needs that in many ways anticipates Marx's theory.

Knowledge in turn educates the passions, "for one can only desire or fear things in terms of the ideas one can have of them; or by the simple impulsion of Nature." So men are moved either by simple natural impulses, which constitute innocent and hence true needs, or in contrast by impulses that are developed by means of knowledge into more convoluted, and, Rousseau will argue, finally false, perverse needs. This is where the historical development of human nature and society begins. Where it finds its natural standard of value is in nature, where man's desires do not exceed his physical needs. In society he develops desires that are not true needs, but which are rather the result of social comparisons, of vanity, or what Rousseau calls *amour-propre*. Rousseau does not see historical or social development as natural. The ground of his moral critique of existing civil society lies not in history but in nature's inherent morality. What can this mean?

THE STATE OF NATURE AND NATURAL MORALITY

Rousseau's state of nature is a narrative about the ever-increasing suffering of "natural animals" as they gradually come to be socialized, to have relations with others like themselves, and begin to get organized in terms of language and families, the division of the sexes and of labor, which lead eventually to various social stratifications and property differentiations. Leaving aside for the moment the question as to whether this process is natural or necessary, or what its connection to nature or history might be, it is critical to the argument I am making to recognize that Rousseau's conception of the initial state of nature involves an extreme "dehumanization" of humans, at least as we usually understand them. Rousseau's creatures exist in a situation of impossible lack. They have will, the instincts of both fear and pity, but they live utterly alone, an impossibly isolated, unconscious, solitary, memoryless, timeless, and perhaps pointless existence in nature. Rousseau seems to find this existence idyllic in many ways, which is all the more striking because it seems so completely unreal. He certainly affords this state an absolute ontological and moral status.

It is not just that Rousseau's idealization of original man is more than a little like an adolescent male fantasy—the perfectly noble, strong, agile, and fearless male beast, loping through the forest, getting the best of all the animals by stealth or flight, unencumbered and totally independent, indeed virtually unable to imagine a tomorrow, mating fleetingly whenever and wherever and with whomever he likes, and then forgetting all about it, barely able to remember the tree under which he slept last night. "His imagination depicts nothing to him; his heart asks nothing of him. . . . he can have neither foresight nor curiosity . . . wandering in the forests without industry, without speech, without settled abode, without war, and without tie, without any need of others of his kind and without any desire to harm them, perhaps even without ever recognizing any one of them individually. "[25] Even your dog can do that. Even geese mate for life. Even mice have family relations. Even ants recognize their nest. It is important to make note of just how strange a projection this is. These are not humans; they are not even animals. Creatures so denatured, so "unnatural" are hardly conceivable. It is not only, as Strong argues, that "there is literally nothing to humans in the state of nature. Thus the defining quality of the human is not to be defined or fixed."[26] It is not just that they are not defined, however. It is that these are not creatures as we actually experience them on this earth. These creatures are defined by the fact that they lack all that we know of animal life, of social life, of sentient and instinctual life. They are an abstraction that can only function as a philosophical device to support Rousseau's moral ideal of perfect freedom and absolute self-sufficiency.

Rousseau, nevertheless, likens the passage from the state of nature to society to the growth of children out of childhood and into adulthood and of adults into old age, a growth that Tracy Strong characterizes as "not necessary but inevitable." I simply don't know what it means to say that this process, growing from a child to an adult, aging itself, is "not necessary but inevitable," except to say that the alternative to it is not to grow old, but rather to die. Unless we die, we age. Those are the only alternatives.

Strong quotes Rousseau's response to "Monsieur Philopolis"(Charles Bonnet, a Genevan naturalist who had attacked the *Discourse on the Origins of Inequality*), that is, to the argument that anything that comes from human faculties would have to be natural. Rousseau responded:

> Society is natural to the human species like old age is to the individual and peoples need Arts, Laws, Government as the old need crutches. The whole difference comes from the fact that the state of old age derives from the nature of the human being, whereas society derives from that of the human species, not directly as you assert, but only as I have shown with the assistance of certain external circumstances that could have been or not have been.[27]

Strong interprets this claim strongly to mean the "the existence of and need for civil and political society is the product of circumstances that did not have to be. . . . We have grown old, but we did not have to. . . . the aging process has been set in motion by various accidents. . . . It is a *dénaturation.*"[28] It was not necessary. I am at a loss to understand what this could actually mean. Is it a kind of astonishing wishful thinking, to imagine that human beings do not have to age, that we could stay forever young? On what terms could it be said that we age only by accident? What circumstances could have been otherwise such that we do not age? Death is the only alternative circumstance. What nature do we know that does not include old age, disease, and death? What nature do we know that does not include time and suffering? There are several aspects of Rousseau's theory, and of Strong's interpretation of it, that lend themselves to this kind of puzzlement. What fear of nature, of history, of time, of the processes of natural maturation and normal sociality, of mortality itself, motivates this uncanny conception? What does it mean to restrict the appellation "human" to something that is so completely opposite to what we as humans "ordinarily" experience?

The function of Rousseau's myth of the state of nature is moral. It is to exhibit clearly and in dramatic fashion the moral ideal—absolute independence, absolute freedom coupled with complete instinctual satisfaction, and complete moral innocence. It is important to this ideal in nature that according to Rousseau it can only occur in perfect solitude. If it is to be combined with any kind of commonsense sociality, then such sociality will have to be designed in such a way as to retain these perfect, and perfectly unreal, qualities. It is not an ideal that would appeal to everyone.

As a description of nature, it is perhaps worth making the point that it has virtually nothing to do with natural history as we usually describe it or with observed animal behavior. Rousseau criticizes Hobbes for reading social characteristics back into nature, but Rousseau, far more than Hobbes, projects a profoundly denatured version of happiness, as imagined by at least one very peculiarly civilized man, back into nature. It might be noted that in actual human and animal behavior, isolated individuals do not last long. Mammals, just to take the most obvious example, live in families, packs, herds, gaggles, prides, and groups. There may be intervals in the life cycle of some animals and some species when adult males travel solo. But on the whole, animals, and certainly humans, live together in groups, in extended families, and they use language even before the time when they are counted as humans. Neanderthal man buried his dead in Paleolithic times. Human evolution is social evolution and the origins of language are the origins of the species. Although individual humans exist before they use language, which is perhaps what gives us the illusion that there could be a species-whole state of such a kind, individuals are born into language and into language-using social groups, who initiate them into language and the cultures and practices it constructs.

The point of this is not to dispute Rousseau's biology, but rather to point to the moral life that lives in this conception, despite all "the facts." Rousseau insists that in his original state, man knows no language, no families, no society, no moral life at all. But it is because he separates the individual from all others of his kind, because he depicts his noble savage in such radical and total isolation, that *contra* Hobbes, Rousseau is forced to posit an instinct of natural goodness, that is, pity, as well as an instinct of natural selfishness, self-preservation, to get this solitary biped out of the state of nature.

Hobbesian men are always already in contentious relationship to others. Hobbes never shows us man in isolation; however much his individuals are individuals, they exist always already in relationship to others. They may be confused, fearful and prone to fantastical imaginings, but their "virtue consisteth in comparison." Hobbes does not even deny men altruistic motivations; he only argues that these are not the politically problematical ones. The problem comes with the interaction of independent wills in conflict, with each having a "right to all things," a necessary as well as inevitable accompaniment to men who live together in a "multitude" in nature.

Like Hobbes, Rousseau wants to argue that natural men are not moral. "It would at first seem that men in that state having neither moral relations of any sort between them, nor known duties, could be neither good nor wicked, and had neither vices nor virtues."[29] But he has a different reason than Hobbes for so arguing:

> Above all, let us not conclude with Hobbes that because he has no idea of goodness man is naturally wicked, that he is vicious because he does not know virtue, that he always refuses to those of his kind services which he does not believe he owes them, or that by virtue of the right which he reasonably claims to things he needs, he insanely imagines himself to be the sole owner of the entire Universe . . . . There is another principle which Hobbes did not notice. . . . I speak of pity (*pitié*) . . . a virtue all the more universal and useful to man as it precedes the exercise of all reflection in him, and so Natural that even the Beasts sometimes show evident signs of it. . . .

> From this single attribute flow all the social virtues . . . generosity, clemency, humanity.[30]

Perhaps it should be reiterated that Hobbes thought no such thing; on the contrary, Hobbes expressly argued that men give the names of "good" and "evil" to the things they like or dislike. He did not think men vicious or immoral any more than they were moral. These are names we give to qualities from our own perspectives. His point was rather that morality cannot come into existence until society and language is organized as such. His reputation for wickedness arose because he denied the existence of natural morality, precisely the problem Rousseau is trying to resolve. Where does morality reside in nature?

Rousseau pictures a natural state outside of or beyond all social relations. In a situation of complete isolation, with no language and no relationships to anyone else, natural man, according to Rousseau, still has both good and bad instincts. Rousseau develops a complicated psychology, contrasting *amour de soi* with *amour-propre*, to show how natural goodness and natural badness are changed into social goodness and social badness. But it should be clear that both definitions import into the instinctual sphere traditional moral conceptions.

To oversimplify, Rousseau solves the problem of the relation between instinct and virtue, the problem of morality, by simply dividing a "moral" instinct from an "immoral" one. This is not really a solution, but more a restatement of the problem. We still need to inquire into the relation between instinct and morality, and Nietzsche will sharpen the question of this relation to a razor's edge in his genealogy of morals. As Nietzsche reminds us also, the traditional moral conceptions that Rousseau imports into nature associate goodness with caring for others and badness with egoism and selfishness. Nietzsche also offers a powerful critique of this morality and the politics that goes with it.

Rousseau associates pity with recognizing another being as like oneself, and as prompted by identification with the suffering of that other being. Suffering is crucial for the active imagination that pity involves. In the *Essay on the Origin of Language*, Rousseau argues that pity sets us in motion by

> transporting ourselves outside ourselves; by identifying with the suffering being. . . . How could I suffer when I see another suffer, if I do not even know that he suffers, if I do not know what he and I have in common? Someone who has never reflected cannot be clement, or just, or pitying; any more than he can be wicked or vindictive. He who imagines nothing feels only himself; in the midst of mankind he is alone.[31]

There seems to be some contradiction here with Rousseau's earlier character-ization of reflection itself as depraved. Here he means imagination. He wishes to contrast the good spectator, who identifies with the sufferer, from the spec-tator who does not care, who "remains alone." How do we identify the moti-vations of the spectator? "How could I suffer when I see another suffer?"

The politics of pity must always concern itself with the authenticity, the caring, or the disinterestedness of the spectator as well as those qualities in the sufferer. None of these is self-evident. Does the spectator who suffers suffer "the same" as the victim? What is his interest—how are his needs served? What does it mean to the sufferer to be observed? Even the question of how one decides which is which, and what the motivations of the witness really are, come into question with the new territory opened up by the spectator in a public space. Boltanski stresses that the spectator only comes into existence as a perspective with the opening up of this kind of public space, and vice versa.

> By means of unhindered movements, observation from an invisible position and close relationships with an indefinite audience, the spectator fashions the public space. In fact, the ideal of the public sphere is inseparable from the possibility of moving around in an open and homogeneous special space and of conveying "without deformation," . . . observations made at any point in this space, within the exteriority of a relationship available to anyone. The public sphere thus presupposes the existence of a detached, casual observer who can survey the peculiarities of society in the way that the geo-grapher, cartographer or painter, inspired by the cartographic ideal surveys the peculiarities of the landscape."[32]

It almost presupposes an aesthetic of suffering. And this of course is the ques-tion Nietzsche raises.

Rousseau is unsure how detached this observer has to be. He needs him to be both disinterested and sympathetic, and those are always conflicting features of the spectator's perspective and also of the public space he produces and makes real. Rousseau wants to argue that because pity is a natural instinct in the state of nature, it forms a natural link to both reflection and moral consciousness, which come with relating to others. Morality cannot exist in isolation, it needs the presence of others and the reflection and feelings, includ-ing both pity and envy, which social relations always bring about. If pity is a natural instinct, it surely seems to lend itself to the supposition that the sociality that calls it forth is somehow also natural. Strong says:

> Pity is the archetypal activity that makes the commonly human and the humanly common available. Nor can one experience the common (or the human) alone. Pity involves seeing someone else and seeing

that one is like that other being. There is a theatrical presupposition to pity: It requires the witnessing of an action. It requires that I have differentiated myself from another whom I recognize as like myself. Nothing, however, follows from it, except that humans have the capacity to see that which is human as human.[33]

How do we see what is human as human? It is not at all clear that "nothing follows" from these theatrical presuppositions. They have special salience for us, who witness the spectacles of suffering from great distances and have to wonder about our own motives and interests as well as those who mediate the suffering of others for us. We are not so sure of these identifications, of what is human and what is not, or even what is real and what is not. Rousseau was highly critical of the feigned emotions of the theater, its falseness and vanities. We are even more conscious of the difficulties of morality that attend the spectacle of suffering. There is a difference between the spectacle of the mass media and the spectacle of the theater, one that Nietzsche will bring to our notice. Here, we still need to know what the "common" and the "human" are in this connection. The likeness that we see in the other, what we and the other have in common, is highly problematical. It might be argued that the disymmetry between the position of the sufferer and the observer makes them irreducibly different, as well as similar. It is also hierarchical. What we might note here is that Rousseau wants to believe that suffering is obvious and recognizable to us, and that this recognition expresses itself through pity and self-recognition. Rousseau builds his moral theory out of this recognition of suffering and the pity it calls forth in like individuals. The nature of this likeness still needs to be explored.

Rousseau argues that pity is at the core of the social virtues, and that self-regard, *amour-propre*, is at the core of the social vices. He does not yet entertain the idea that pity could itself be understood as vanity, as a form of egotism. Nietzsche definitely describes it as such. He calls pity an expression of superiority and the will to power. Morality itself, on this reading, is a larger form of the same force.

Neither sympathy nor vanity can arise, however, except when men are in relation to each other, in each other's company, when they identify with and compare themselves with one another. While Rousseau has some trouble getting men into this social state, he has no trouble identifying the problems that grow out of it.

It is worth trying to understand what was at stake in the notion that men are not moral until, actually unless, they are social, a point on which both Hobbes and Rousseau insist and which some modern commentators want to preserve.[34] Rousseau wanted to separate nature from society, but he needed to find the foundations of morality in nature, and he was in some perplexity as to whether nature could be moral. He was clear that society was immoral, but he insisted that only social beings could make moral distinctions. He didn't quite know how we got from nature to society, except by way of instinct. His solution was to moralize instinct, but that doesn't take him very far. We still don't know how to judge whether an instinct is moral or not. The question seems to be a category mistake.

At any rate, today, in like contexts, we (late modernists, at least) generally do not think of nature as moral. Our concept of nature is different from Rousseau's. Morality refers to man-made values. Moral language comes from human attribution and we don't usually attribute moral qualities to natural forces, although there are certainly exceptions—we tend to think of cancer or of hurricanes, for example, as bad—but we mean by this that they harm us, not that they are immoral. Still, we might be tempted to see them as evil. That's a holdover from our religious history, or a sign of our irreducible need to moralize what harms us. In this sense, we have become more like Nietzscheans. We recognize moral terms as referring to ourselves. Rousseau would not have agreed.

It should be said as well that we *do* tend to think of nature as social—that is, we recognize social attributes in sentient beings, although not in matter itself. That is, we divide nature into organic and inorganic nature, and reserve attributes of sociality to higher organic life forms. Or maybe all life forms—sponges are social, but are viruses? When we speak of clusters of galaxies, we don't usually mean that they hang out together.

When we confront the eighteenth century's differentiations of these conceptual usages, we are apt to get confused ourselves. We are still close enough to those thought systems to get caught up in them, and some would argue that we should be. We are still relentless moralizers, still perplexed, to say the least, about the foundations of morality. We are, however ("we"in the affluent and rapidly changing, relativistic, global cultural economies of the West), much closer to understanding that these foundations are in ourselves, as humans. That is what Hobbes and Rousseau are trying to get at when they insist that men are really moral only in society (that is, when they are human). To be human is to be social. To use language is to be human and social. It is also to be "moral," but not only *one* morality counts as such. There is no universal, rational, or self-evident morality that is non-negotiable. Sociality precedes language on the evolutionary ladder. Morality is a linguistic function, which is natural to all humans, cultures, and histories.

Keith Ansell-Pearson, a contemporary defender of Rousseau and the primacy of the question of political legitimacy, wants to preserve this "fundamental ambiguity" in Rousseau's work. He says that "It cannot be denied that there are passages . . . where it would seem that he is questioning the very authenticity of all and any social relationships." Nevertheless, he argues, it would *not* be "wise for any interpreter of Rousseau to resolve once and for all the ambiguity that lies at the heart of his thinking. . . . These paradoxes and tensions define our experience of what it means to exist as 'modern.'"[35]

Ansell-Pearson is right that the tensions and paradoxes he finds in Rousseau's work define us as moderns. And who but a modern would think to resolve them "once and for all"? It will take Nietzsche's genealogy to put this aspect of morality and modernity, and the impossibility of "once-and-for-all" solutions, into perspective. Perspective is the heart of the matter. From what perspective can one view morality as a whole? From whose perspective is such a view valid? The problem of morality "as a whole" is not helped by being divided into a "natural" as opposed to a "social" morality. What is lacking is perspective, or rather, the possibility of a universal perspective is taken for granted. It seeks a ground in nature, but nature, by definition universal, is not moral.

Rousseau does want to have it both ways. He wants to argue that nature involves a pre-moral natural innocence (goodness) in man, who, in complete isolation, nevertheless experiences instinctual goodness (pity) and instinctual selfishness (self-preservation). At the same time, he wants to demonstrate the historical development of both morality and immorality in society. He means this to apply to all social relationships, but he saw these relationships through the lens of his own European society.[36] Rousseau exhibits a certain confusion about nature and culture, good and evil, and their interrelations, a confusion which has been characteristic of the modern tradition as a whole and its profound struggle over where to site and how to ground morality. Rousseau believes that if morality can be grounded in nature, it is truly "grounded." But then what is "natural" simply overtakes the domains and claims of the "moral," and then what is "natural" has no more universal meaning or obvious reference than does morality. The others become "unnatural." But by introducing history into the story, Rousseau nevertheless complicates the problem in the right direction. At least the images start to move.

In order to preserve a natural ground for his moral condemnation of civil society, to show its historical development, and to open up the possibility of reversing the destructive and unjust effects of this political history by means of a new social contract, Rousseau has to preserve a natural morality for which he has no ground but only a history.

Only men, situated in particular histories and cultures, create values, and they do so "from the beginning" in language. Their history is the history of particular cultures and particular values and how they change, and of the languages devised to justify these values. Rousseau comes at a particular juncture of Western history. He inherits the problem of morality without a firm religious basis for anchoring or justifying it.

The belief in a natural moral order and also in an immoral history, a contradiction that Rousseau effectuates, paradoxically means that morality has to be read into both the nature part and the culture part of history—natural pity versus social pity, unconscious natural law versus rational natural law, innate goodness and badness versus socially acquired virtue and vice. Is history moral or immoral? When we put the question this way, we recognize the problem. Whose history? Which morality? As Nietzsche says, "The value of life cannot be estimated."[37] From whose perspective shall we decide whether history, as such, is moral or immoral? That turns out to be our question. Rousseau does, however, offer us a valuable answer to this question, to which we now turn.

The real paradox, however, occurs according to Nietzsche's dictum that "only that which has no history is defineable."[38] Rousseau attempts to define man's basic nature in terms of the instincts of pity and self-preservation, while at the same time demonstrating, via his narrative of the history of the state of nature, that man's instincts, having a history, cannot be defined.

THE SUFFERING SELF IN A DEGENERATE SOCIETY: A MORAL HISTORY

Rousseau gives us a resounding and impassioned answer to the question of whether history is moral or immoral. He argues that history is immoral, because it progressively increases human suffering and culminates in moral degradation and political servitude. Rousseau emphasizes two dimensions of this suffering: First, the suffering of the individual self, because it has been marked by changes in the basic composition and moral quality of its self-esteem as it becomes deformed from a natural *amour de soi* into an unnatural *amour-propre*. Second, the increasing misery of civil society, as it gradually comes to be established historically on the bases of property, inequality, domination, and despotism. A brief review of these arguments will take us to *The Social Contract*.

Rousseau interweaves these two narratives, of the individual and of the society, the anxiety of one and the fragmented hierarchization of the other, as he tells us about the development of civil society as we know it. The self and society are the two continously self-reflecting and self-constituting poles of a structural process of psychosocial and political development. Rousseau establishes goodness in the fundamental nature of man, even though he denies the name "morality" to such goodness. As we have seen, he roots this goodness in pity. "Pity is a natural sentiment which, by moderating in every individual the activity of self-love, contributes to the mutual preservation of the entire species. It is pity that carries us without reflection to the assistance of those we see suffer; pity that, in the state of Nature, takes the place of Laws, morals and virtue."[39] A quality of authentic sentiment forms the place for law, morals, and virtue. Pity is the natural form of virtue. Caring for others as opposed to caring only about oneself repeats the underlying moral dichotomy.

Rousseau locates a special sensitivity to suffering in the unconscious drives of individuals, and thus he is able to use this affect as a moral standard by which all further developments can be judged. He analyzes the self as it advances into ever more complex social relationships, focusing particularly on the individual's relation to himself.

> *Amour propre* [vanity] and *Amour de soi* [self-love], two very different passions in their nature and their effects, should not be confused. Self-love is a natural sentiment which inclines every animal to attend to its self-preservation and which, guided in man by reason and modified by pity, produces humanity and virtue. *Amour propre* is only a relative sentiment, factitious, and born in society, which inclines every individual to set greater store by himself than by anyone else, inspires men with all the evils they do one another, and is the genuine source of honor. This being clearly understood, I say that in our primitive state, in the genuine state of nature, *Amour propre* does not exist.[40]

Rousseau here contrasts the kind of self-regard that can be "guided by reason and modified by pity" so as to be harmless (*amour de soi*) with the kind of self-regard, lacking pity, which seeks only its own self-interest and power over others (*amour-propre*). But it's not so clear how the natural man he depicts could be capable of this kind of *amour de soi*.

What Rousseau wants to show is that human nature is constructed by social practices in history. Asher Horowitz explains: "Each form of social labour is expressed in and corresponds to a form of social individuality. Each form of social individuality in turn demands a particular modification of human instinctual life. The social modification of desires is predicated upon the existence of the quintessential social passion—the desire for recognition—which in turn presupposes the ability to substitute symbolic gratification for the direct expression and satisfaction of the 'savage.'"[41]

Amour de soi implies a satisfied unity of self, without the intrusion of others. But what sort of self can there really be without others? This is the question to which Rousseau returns again and again his whole life. The *Emile* is an entire text about a self that could grow without others. For a post-Freudian age, it seems at best a kind of lunacy. No child raised as Emile was would be sane. It is, in this sense, a devastating fantasy, always already lost, always longed for, always impossible, utterly self-contradictory. Selves becomes selves by interacting with others. *Amour-propre*, on the other hand, instantiates an anxious, restless division in the self, and between the self and others, which drives the subject to ever greater efforts toward connection, transparency, and wholeness, and of course necessarily also toward their perverse opposites.[42]

Rousseau locates the nexus of self and other in relations of dependence, and draws the origins of inequality, and thus of misery and domination, out of this nexus. "Since ties of servitude are formed solely by men's mutual dependence and the reciprocal needs that unite them, it is impossible to subjugate a man without first having placed him in the position of being unable to do without another; a situation which, since it does not obtain in the state of Nature, leaves everyone in it free of the yoke, and renders vain the Law of the stronger."[43] (He certainly seems to be forgetting the necessary, natural dependencies of infancy.) Rousseau situates this servile dependence between the unreal self-sufficiency of the nullity of the self in the state of nature, and the carefully wrought, precariously balanced perfection of the equal and mutual total dependence of all wills in the general will. What lies in between these two philosophical abstractions is actual history.

In the famous opening of Part II of the *Discourse on the Origins of Inequality*, Rousseau lays the origins of inequality at the doorstep of the first property-owner. "The first man who, having enclosed a piece of ground, to whom it occurred to say this is mine, and found people sufficiently simple to believe him, was the true founder of civil society."[44]

What is at stake here is the moment of violence: "to mark the moment when in the progression of things, right succeeded to violence, nature was subjected to law; and to explain by what linkage of wonders the strong could resolve himself to serve the weak, and the people to purchase the idea of repose at the price of true happiness."[45] Violence lies in the constraints exerted by one man over another. There are no equitable, and hence no nonviolent, relations between men. This is why law is instantiated.

Strong calls this the "moment of inequality," and ties it to history: "Rousseau is concerned to show how it is that inequality has become the dominant, even the only, form in which society makes itself available to its members. Inequality is the structure of what we experience of history, that is, of the way in which the human past is present to and in humans."[46] History, for us, as our past in us, as individuals and as a collectivity, is founded in violence and the establishment of domination. The grounds for our suffering lie in that past, both personally and politically.

As Nietzsche will argue, however, there is more than one past and more than one history, and which we identify as "ours" is highly problematical, both as to its reference and to its identity. Suffering lies in the past, our particular past, as excavated genealogically. It lies in time passed and passing, in our temporality, our historicity, our finitude. We, with our beginnings and endings, make the past; we may even make time itself.

Rousseau exhibits a double aspect of the growth of social relations, the institution of property, and the division of labor. He stresses the "reflection" that is produced in men's minds as the result of repeated interactions among them and repeated comparisons between them. And he emphasizes the labor that is the basis of all social interaction and dependence:

> In a word, so long as they applied themselves only to tasks a single individual could perform, and to arts that did not require the collaboration of several hands, they lived free, healthy, good, and happy as far as they could by their Nature be, and continued to enjoy the gentleness of independent dealings with one another; but the moment one man needed the help of another; as soon as it was found to be useful for one to have the provisions for two, equality disappeared, property appeared, work became necessary, and the vast forests changed into smiling Fields that had to be watered with the sweat of men, and where slavery and misery were soon seen to sprout and grow together with the harvests.[47]

By grounding inequality and injustice in the rights of property, the necessities of labor, and the relations of production they entail, Rousseau establishes himself as the first in a long line of social revolutionaries, of whom Marx is the most significant. Rousseau is the true progenitor of this radical, deep, and powerful tradition of social revolution, as the true and just political response to the suffering of the oppressed. He explained the nature of that oppression, both politically and psychologically, as a denaturing, an alienation, of man.

The first division of labor that Rousseau distinguishes is the division of labor between the sexes. In what he calls the period of the "first revolution," husbands and wives, "Fathers and Children," are brought together in one dwelling, giving rise to "the sweetest sentiments known to man, conjugal love, and Paternal love." (No mothers here.) "The first difference was established in the ways of living of the two Sexes. . . . Women became more sedentary and grew accustomed to looking after the Hut and Children, while the man went in quest of the common subsistence."[48] This institutes something of a golden age of primitive society, the "happiest and most lasting epoch." Here cooperation grows, but so does contention; fatal *amour-propre* arises as people compare themselves with one another and compete for public esteem, producing all the ills of competitive public egos, vanity, contempt, shame, and envy. As Rousseau famously describes it:

> It became customary to gather in front of the Huts or around a large Tree: song and dance, true children of love and leisure, became the amusement or rather the occupation of idle men and women gathered together. Everyone began to look at everyone else and to wish to be looked at himself, and public esteem acquired a price. The one who sang or danced the best; the handsomest, the strongest, the most skillful, or the most eloquent came to be the most highly

regarded, and this was the first step at once toward inequality and vice: from these first preferences arose vanity and contempt on the one hand, shame and envy on the other; and the fermentation caused by these new leavens eventually produced compounds fatal to happiness and innocence.[49]

Structural inequality and personal vice, pity and envy, public and private evil, seem to be generated together out of sheer social proximity. Rousseau is presenting a more nuanced and subtle psychological rendition of the condition which Hobbes began to describe; what follows fellowship is a "restless search for power never ceasing until death." (Hobbes, we remind ourselves, did not characterize this as evil.) In Rousseau's words, "black inclination to harm one another, a secret jealousy that is all the more dangerous as it often assumes the mask of benevolence in order to strike its blow in greater safety: in a word, competition and rivalry on the one hand, conflict of interests on the other, and always the hidden desire to profit at another's expense." And the cause of these evils: "all these evils are the first effect of property, and the inseparable train of nascent inequality."[50]

As Horowitz insists, Rousseau is answering "in advance the arguments of Adam Smith and Kant concerning the salutary effects of the division and competition of interests as the motor of progress in human affairs." Nor is he merely presenting some "backward-looking, moralistic critique of economic development."[51] Rousseau sees that this "nascent inequality" necessarily hardens into permanent hierarchies of wealth and power and ends up as systematic exploitation.

the stronger did more work; the more skillful used his work to better advantage; the more ingenious found ways to reduce his labor; the Plowman had greater need of iron, or the smith greater need of wheat, and by working equally, the one earned much while the other had trouble staying alive. This is how natural inequality unfolds with unequal associations . . . their different circumstances become more perceptible, more permanent in their effects, and begin to exercise a corresponding influence on the fate of individuals.[52]

The society divides into the rich and everyone else, into capital and labor, because of all the forms of inequality, wealth "can most readily be used to buy all the rest." The rich, under pressure from the chaos and violence unleashed by growing inequalities and scarcities, conceive of the most ingenious scheme of deception: "Let us institute rules of Justice and peace to which we are all obliged to conform, which favor no one, and which in a way make up for the vagaries of fortune by subjecting the powerful and the weak alike to mutual duties."[53]

So in the name of justice and formal legal equality, the most horrendous injustices are preserved and protected, and the powerful subjugate the weak by the permanent institutions of the state. "Such was . . . the origin of Society and of Laws, which gave the weak new fetters and the rich new forces, irreversibly destroyed natural freedom, forever fixed the Law of property and inequality, transformed a skillful usurpation into an irrevocable right, and for the profit of a few ambitious men, henceforth subjugated the whole of Mankind to labor, servitude and misery."[54]

Why is this history important? Rousseau identifies the causes of human misery and suffering as derived from injustice in history. He may even be said to have laid them at the door of history itself. I will explore that interpretation in the next chapter. Even though his mythological version of history is far from what we today think of as any factual or actual history, and it is even more bizarre in its purported contrast with an impossibly pure nature, the addition of the dimension of time past, of history, to the analysis and construction of the meaning of suffering is indispensable. Suffering has its deepest roots and meaning in history, as Nietzsche will demonstrate in his own idiom.

In the terms so far developed in this book, the deepest dimension of suffering lies in history, both in the individual's personal history, as that is generated psychologically by the power of subjection in the formation of the subject, and in the history of a culture and community, in the relations of domination and subjugation that create culture and community. We know of no community not constructed through the effects of power. Even Rousseau's perfect contract, is, in its very perfection, a perfect subjugation. Suffering takes its ever-renewed force from the power of the past, from memory, from what has been engraved on the body, burned into the unconscious psyche and soul of each and of all together: "If something is to stay in the memory it must be burned in," as Nietzsche puts it. Every self and every society are formed by violence. These theorists tell us, each in his own language, that it is through subjection to others and to the norms of society, by language, thought, and identity enforced by communal authority that we are forged as subjects. It is because we are historical beings, because we live one-way lives in time, that we are selves. Formed by forces and by names over which we have no control, our suffering necessarily comes about through desire, will, and power, and through the power of time to change us.

Rousseau made the strongest possible case regarding the historical origins of suffering in injustice, and for the creation of a modern response to that suffering: social justice. If history has created despotic, coercive, hierarchical, and destructive societies, full of personal misery and institutionalized social agony, the mind of man can nevertheless devise a formula for a new society, a true ideal and just society, by which suffering, at least of the historical kind, can be ended forever. Who could argue against that?

8

Social Justice and the General Will: In and Out of Time

Rousseau's first and most fundamental question in *The Social Contract* is "if, in political society, there can be any legitimate and sure principle of government, taking men as they are and laws as they might be." If the philosophical question is about the grounds for legitimacy, as Rousseau presents it, the reality he sees around him is decidedly illegitimate: "Man is born free, and he is everywhere in chains." Society, as it exists at present, is illegitimate. "How can it be made legitimate? That question I believe I can answer."[1] Rousseau claims to know how to determine what is and is not legitimate, and how to change what is not into what is.

A clue to his derivation lies in his next distinction: "The social order is a sacred right which serves as a basis for all other rights. And as it is not a natural right, it must be one founded on covenants." Here the sacred order is contrasted with the natural one, and legitimacy, belonging to the sacred realm, comes not from nature but from covenant. Hobbes also bases legitimacy on covenant, meaning promises, but he does not attach it to any kind of sacred right. That is to say, he uses "legitimacy" as a term of art, not as a term of moral right. In light of our discussion in the previous chapter, it is clear that Rousseau has moved here beyond trying to ground morality in natural instinct, although no doubt he still believes it to be so grounded. Nevertheless, constructing the social contract is a philosophical enterprise, and as such it takes its grounds from rational consent, from human will.

Rousseau needs to clarify the nature of right. He criticizes Hugo Grotius for his "characteristic method of reasoning . . . to offer fact as a proof of right." Critique depends on the distinction of fact from value. Rousseau means to distinguish fact strongly from right. Slavery, the paradigmatic example, is a fact, but that does not make it right:

But if there are slaves by nature, it is only because there has been slavery against nature. Force made the first slaves; and their cowardice perpetuates their slavery. . . . The strongest man . . . transforms force into right. . . . Hence "the right of the strongest." . . . But shall we never have this phrase explained? Force is a physical power; I do not see how its effects could produce morality. To yield to force is an act of necessity, not of will; it is at best an act of prudence. In what sense can it be a moral duty. . . . If force compels obedience, there is no need to invoke a duty to obey, and if force ceases to compel obedience, there is no longer any obligation. Thus the word "right" adds nothing to what is said by "force"; it is meaningless.[2]

It is important to be clear. There are no slaves by nature, but only by force. Is force not natural then? In any case, it is not right, that is, it is not moral. Rousseau is defending one of the most basic philosophical distinctions in the Western tradition, the distinction between what is and what ought to be, between fact and value. The motivation is to preserve value; to reserve the right to moral judgment even, or especially, in the face of what is. The argument is that what has value, what ought to be, what is right and moral, can never be derived from what is merely the case, from what Rousseau calls fact and "force."

In contrast to the moment of violence, the moment of inequality as it occured in history, as society was in fact established in domination, which Rousseau demonstrated in the *Second Discourse*, here he produces the question of the grounds for such an establishment. How could sheer force produce moral obligation?[3] This resolution begs the question of what can produce obligation, of how obligation can be produced at all. If fact or force cannot produce obligation or right, that is, value, how can it be produced?

Sacred covenants are what create value, right and wrong. Value comes from covenants, from promises made by men. Men oblige one another by their agreements. "All legitimate authority among men must be based on covenants."[4] So here clearly, the meaning and criteria for legitimacy, for right and for obligation, is covenant. That is to say, Rousseau will not use "right" (as Hobbes does) to refer merely to physical fact, to will, to force, to the mere ability to act; he will define right as legitimate power only, power based on covenant, agreement, consent, free will.

The contrast to Hobbes is instructive. Hobbes says that liberty is a natural right; that liberty is what "right" means. A right is a liberty. Rousseau seems to agree when he says that men are born free, that their liberty belongs to them, and that no one but they themselves have the right to dispose of it: "To renounce freedom is to renounce one's humanity, one's rights as a man and equally one's duties."[5] Freedom of this sort is the very mark of humanity. Without it, we are not human.

But for Hobbes, natural right is the freedom and power, the will, to move, to take what one needs, which in the state of nature entails a "right to everything." It does not possess or exert an extra-empirical moral meaning; on the contrary, right is power. Morality, "right" in the sense of "just" or "legitimate" power only comes later, with the political imposition of names for good and evil in the instantiation of the commonwealth, and the imposition of these names is always greatly contested. But Rousseau argues that "without freedom of the will, you strip a man's actions of all moral significance."[6] So, for Rousseau, moral significance inheres in the very exercise of the individual's free will. Morality inheres in free human action, in the freedom to choose, to make promises. Free choice, in and of itself, is moral, is legitimate. Even before there is a contract, there is free will and the choices of man. But what distinguishes free action as force and free action as moral choice? Must there not be a covenant before there is moral freedom to act?

First, what is at stake here is a disagreement about the meaning of "right" or "moral." For Hobbes, right means free action, motion, power, ability. It is force and will. Morality enters the picture with the social naming of things. Rousseau, on the other hand, sites morality in the freedom of the will—will not just as power, but as moral choice. But how are we to determine whether a man's choice is free or not, is right or not? Rousseau wants morality to inhere in the freedom of the will itself and not the content of the choice, but he also wants to deny that certain choices are legitimate. A free choice for slavery, for instance, is not legitimate. How do we know which choices, however free, are wrong? The background of this conception of right is religious morality, because the realm of the will was originally the realm of God's will.[7]

Rousseau aims at restoring natural moral order. Slavery, conquest, mere force are wrong, even if they are based on choices. No amount of force or time can make them right, that is, good, just, or legitimate. Force is not justice. So then, he must tell us, where does legitimacy, justice, moral significance come from? From the freedom of the will. From free choice. And from covenants freely entered into. Therefore, "The words 'slavery' and 'right' are contradictory, they cancel each other out." A covenant of slavery, either between one man and another or one man and a people, "would always be absurd."[8]

Therefore, Rousseau argues, "We Must Always Go Back to an Original Covenant," the title of chapter 5 of *The Social Contract*. "A people is *a people* even before the gift to the king. . . . we ought to scrutinize the act by which people become a people, for that act, being necessarily antecedent to the other, is the real foundation of society."[9] In the state of nature, men reach a point where the obstacles to their preservation prove greater than their means to preserve themselves. "The only way they can preserve themselves is by uniting their separate powers in a combination strong enough to overcome any resistance, uniting them so that their powers are directed by a single motive and act in concert."[10] Stong says: "The ability to contract is what makes an individual human. As Rousseau elaborates, what makes one human is the ability to consent to a social pact, that is, to become a citizen. . . . The insistence on the contractual basis of society is an insistence that there be individuals who are capable of contracting, as slaves are not, and that there be important social relations that are the proper subject of contract."[11] Where do such individuals come from? Is this "original covenant" quite different from the society founded in history? And is it, as we have been led to believe by previous writers and texts, inherently coercive?

The problem posed by history and by the domination and inequality Rousseau perceives in history set the crucial question: How are men to join together and yet still preserve their own strength and liberty? The difficulty, in historical society, was that even the simple proximity of men, the most basic human interactions, changed the nature of men from free but vacuous solitaries to snarling, envious, vain, and vengeful dogs. Only complete and total independence, total self-sufficiency, could ensure the free and proper operations of instinct and action. How can men join together and retain their independence? If moral significance inheres in the freedom of the will, how can that freedom and the morality of the will exercising that freedom be preserved in submitting to union in a community? That is the question as Rousseau formulates it:

> How to find a form of association which will defend the person and goods of each member with the collective force of all, and under which each individual, while uniting himself with the others, obeys no one but himself, and remains as free as before. This is the fundamental problem to which the social contract holds the solution.[12]

Rousseau is articulating the ideal form of the covenant, the social contract whereby men create a society that is capable of perfecting their freedom, and he will argue, ending their suffering. He asserts that the terms of this contract are so precise that the slightest modification makes it null and void, and that these terms "are everywhere the same. . . . if ever the social pact is violated, every man regains his original rights." The articles of the association are a single whole: "the total alienation by each associate of himself and all his rights to the whole community."[13]

The alienation of all the rights of the individual to the community is "unconditional," no man has any longer any rights left. Because "each man gives himself to all, he gives himself to no one; and since there is no associate over whom he does not gain the same rights as others gain over him, each man recovers the equivalent of everything he loses, and in the bargain he acquires more power to preserve what he has."[14] The essential formula for the social pact is this: "Each one of us puts into the community his person and all his powers under the supreme direction of the general will; and as a body, we incorporate every member as an indivisible part of the whole." Thus this body acquires "its unity, its common ego, its life and its will."[15]

Now there are numerous problems with this formulation, on any interpretation. We shall start with some of the contradictions inherent in Rousseau's terms and usages and branch out to the wider issues that are consequential to these definitions. It is possible to interpret Rousseau's social contract, the general will, and the sovereignty of the general will in such a way that they make logical sense. The question is whether they make human sense.

Rousseau's first problem is with the relation between natural liberty and civil liberty, and it goes back to the difficulties he first had with defining "right." Rousseau affirms that "passing from the state of nature to the civil society produces a remarkable change in man; it puts justice as a rule of conduct in the place of instinct, and gives his actions the moral quality they previously lacked."[16] As we saw in the last chapter, in nature instinct rules, and even though man's instincts are both benevolent (pity) and malevolent (self-regarding) (*amour de soi*), they are not yet, Rousseau insists, "moral." There is some quality of morality that can only be had in society, in either the corrupt society of history or the just society of the new social contract.

In chapter 8 of *The Social Contract*, Rousseau wants to draw up a balance sheet of the losses and gains man exchange by joining the social contract: "What man loses by the social contract is his natural liberty and the absolute right to anything that tempts him and that he can take; what he gains by the social contract is civil liberty and the legal right of property in what he possesses." We must clearly distinguish, he says, between "natural liberty, which has no limit but the physical power of the individual concerned, and civil liberty, which is limited by the general will."[17] Shades of Thomas Hobbes. Precisely the notion of right advocated and described by Hobbes (and Grotius), which Rousseau indignantly repudiated in chapters 2 and 3 of his own book, now becomes "absolute." What happened to his insistence that "The word 'right' adds nothing to what is said by force; it is meaningless"? That is to say, Rousseau himself cannot use the term "right" consistently to mean only what is sanctioned by covenant. Natural liberty, contrary to his first definition of it as comprising a moral freedom of the will and not mere force, is now said to be the "absolute right to anything one can take" (by force) as opposed to civil liberty, which presumably can only be had after the compacting of the covenant.

Contrast as well the statement that "man acquires with civil society, moral freedom, which alone makes him master of himself" with his earlier statement, "without freedom of the will, you strip a man's actions of all moral significance," asserted in the context of slavery.[18] Rousseau wants to argue both that simple freedom of the will has moral force and significance and also that only in civil society can moral freedom be obtained. This is again the problem we addressed in the *Second Discourse*, the complicated differentiation between nature and society, both moral and both immoral in different ways. Moral judgments hold only under the legitimate authority brought about by contract; but nature is moral too, in another way, in that man's free will, whatever his condition, is always "right," in the moral sense of the word. How?

Greater difficulties arise in trying to understand what is entailed in men making the social contract, and in the curious fact that Rousseau sees only liberation in contracts, in marked contrast to both Hobbes and Nietzsche. Compared with the societies of history, Rousseau wants to establish a social bond on the basis of a profound, atemporal, conception of human equality and human commonality. "It is what is common to those different interests which yields the social bond; if there were no point on which separate interests coincided, then society could not conceivably exist."[19] And if there is no such point? It is precisely in interpreting what it is that is common to humans, as Strong insists, that the beauty and the *pathos* of Rousseau's conception is found.

Tracy Strong spends a good deal of time on "the thought of the common" in his book. His own translation of Rousseau's formulation of the social pact makes clear how important it is to be able to understand the politics of the social contract as what is common to us as equals and as humans:

> *Each of us puts in common his or her person and all his or her power under the supreme ordering* (direction) *of the general will; and we receive corporeally* (en corps) *each member as a part indivisible from the whole.* At this moment, instead of the particular self (*personne*) of each contractant, this act of association produces a moral and collective body composed of as many members as the assembly has voices, a body that receives from this same act its unity, its common ego (*moi*), its life and its will.[20]

One implication of this reading is that "at the moment of the social pact we take into ourself, as our self, a self that is common or general, and that each individual engaged in the pact does exactly the same; each self has, one might say, the same melody."[21] The problem with this interpretation is how to make sense of "a self that is common or general," especially as something that we can each, separately, take into our own self, as "our self." Is it obvious, or to be taken on faith, that there is such a thing, even such a possibility, as a "self that is common or general"? Is it possible to explain what it is that each does "exactly the same"?

The problem is not that we must have unified selves. It is clear that Rousseau sees himself and everyone else as having multiple, divided, and even conflicting selves. And it is not quite the problem of getting from the "I" to the "we," although Strong attempts to explicate the common self in terms of difficulties Rousseau has with pronouns.[22] In the act of associating, "each" puts in, and "we" receive out again.

Still, Rousseau resolves the problem of the *moi commun*, the common self, through the notion of a common will. The general will is a common will—that is to say, "it has the common as its object and springs from a will that is common." As we saw, the will for Rousseau always has the character of freedom and morality. "The general will, to be really such, must be general in its object as well as in its essence," is the way Rousseau puts it.[23] So the proper subject and object of the general will is "the particular form of our commonality," which is apparently unproblematically arrived at, for instance, by several people considering themselves as a unity, as a whole, for certain common purposes.[24] We have particular forms of commonality and presumably also a generic form of commonality, the general will. So the subject and the object of the common will coincide. Our commonality is what we hold in common, in particular, as a unity, both of wills and of what we will, as subjects and an object. Is this coincidence so easy as that to bring about? Are subject and object brought together in a simple movement, or is it a complicated maneuver? Is there always a commonality we somehow, or sometimes, share? Do we necessarily hold something in common? What happens if there is no such thing?

Of course, it is clear that several people can have a common purpose "in mind" (separate minds, presumably, but with one thought?) and that they can unite their actions, and even their wills (metaphorically speaking?), to accomplish such a purpose. But does this amount to a common self? Not exactly, not in the way we usually use the word "self." We attach selves to bodies, and Rousseau as well wants to use the metaphor of a common body for the general will. Does it make sense to think of a common will as a common body or a common life? We do speak of the "body politic" in precisely this way. We can think of a common way of life, but life itself we tend to take literally. We die individually. Do bodies politic die? Are not all these bodies and wills metaphors, language for counting or gathering something together as a unity, which is only constituted as such by language? These questions lead us naturally in the next chapters to Nietzsche's reconsideration of the meaning of the "will," and the "body," both for individuals and peoples, as metaphors, names that have an uncertain reference, which speak for and to energies and powers that are only loosely, perspectivally, and provisionally, grouped together under such a name.

The question of the physical or moral nature of the unity of the general will arises naturally, inevitably, when one person differs from another as to what the common purpose should be or what the common will should do exactly. Strong says, "The general will is the thought of the humanness of the human being, ontological rather than (merely) moral."[25] Is it the thought that is ontological, or the will? The general will, being both moral and ontological, would strongly justify exercising the force of the common will against the dissenting individual will. Rousseau indeed asserts such a justification:

> whoever refuses to obey the general will shall be constrained to do so by the whole body, which means nothing other than that he shall be forced to be free; for this is the necessary condition which, by giving each citizen to the nation, secures him against all personal dependence, it is the condition which shapes both the design and the working of the political machine, and which alone bestows justice on civil contracts—without it, such contracts would be absurd, tyrannical and liable to the grossest abuse.[26]

It is the generality and the commonality of the general will, essential and genuine, which justify for Rousseau the use of force to "make free" the dissenter. It is hard to escape the conclusion, however, that, from the perspective of the one forced, at least, there is a certain amount of tyranny in this use of force, some level of violence inherent in the union of each with all that conjoins "force" and "freedom" in this way. And this in marked contrast to Rousseau's beginning in this book, where force and freedom are unalterably opposed.

Rousseau says that the general will is always opposed to particular wills, as a general interest is always opposed to particular interests. But, for the individual, "my will (any will) is general if and only if it has as its object that which is common to all concerned, that is, that which all concerned have in exactly the same way."[27] What do all concerned have in exactly the same way? What is at stake in the assumption that there is something that all concerned have "in exactly the same way"?

Of course, there is that corporate metaphor: "one body that receives from this act its unity, its ego, its life and its will." It is hard to imagine that we remain separate bodies and wills while incorporated into this general body, ego, life, and will. And Rousseau implied as much in the quotation previously cited from the last chapter from the *Emile*, which finds its true force in this context of the general will:

> Natural man is complete unto himself: he is the numerical unit, the absolute whole that has relation only to himself or to one like him. Civil man is only the fractional unit dependent on the denominator, and whose value is in his relation with the whole, which is the social body. The best social institutions are those that know best how to denature man, to take away his absolute existence to give him a relative one, and to transport the I into the common unit, such that each particular no longer believes itself to be one, but one part of the unit and is only sensible in the whole.[28]

The sovereignty of the general will is the way Rousseau expresses the legitimacy of the moral and political force of the general will, exercised "legitimately" against any opposing individual or group will. The sovereignty of the general will is a technical concept that carries a huge punch: "the sovereign, by the mere fact of being, is always what it ought to be."[29] Sovereignty is the action of the general will; it is the ongoing presence of itself, in itself, for itself. It cannot be alienated or represented or delegated or transmitted through another. Strong likens it to "grammar," as that which makes speech possible. It can only exist in the present insofar as each wills it. The will cannot be divided, or held over in time. This is perhaps the most perplexing and paradoxical of all the qualities of the general will: "sovereignty collapses the time dimension of political society into the present. Sovereignty, I might say, takes over the ambitions of the *Second Discourse*: It makes all our history present to us, and thus frees us from history."[30]

The sovereignty of the general will does not exist in time and does not last over time. Rousseau goes so far as to claim that "yesterday's law carries no obligations today."[31] The citizens of this social contract enact their sovereignty in their general will only insofar as they act as citizens, as members of the community, as a common body and a common will, and only in the actual moment of their willing and acting. There is no holdover, no binding, no obligation that persists through time. This unseating of the duration of the body and of the political, this defiance of the persistence of law and the relevance of history, derives from the "nontemporal quality of sovereignty."[32] It exists only in the actual activities of those who embody it. It exists only in the present. Bodies, of course, notoriously age. They wear their past on their sleeves. It is here that the metaphor breaks down. Timeless bodies are something from the age of film—simulacra. Nietzsche will take us there.

Perhaps the most appalling consequence of this understanding of the general will is expressed by Strong in this way: "The argument against representative sovereignty is consequent to Rousseau's understanding that the political life must be *one's own* life and that no life that is shaped by structures that have duration in time and extension in space can possibly be one's own."[33] What can it mean to say that no life that is shaped by structures that have duration in time and extension in space can be my own? Am I not, as a body, a structure that has duration in time and extension in space? Am I then only a mind, only and forever a mind? A thought, an image, a virtual reality? All *cogitans* and no *extensa*? Is there no world that I inhabit, no space and time that I can call my own? No earth that I love and cling to? No life that is lived in time and space that I can, and wish to, call my own? Am I a disembodied will, with no history, no past, no future, no weight and height and breadth? Are we, together, a disembodied will, with no history, no past, no future, no specific or lasting institutions, no cultural and historical particularities, no polis? Do we not endure? Is our suffering not suffered, that is, endured, that is, temporal?

What is it that is so feared in this philosophy? Body, time, corruption, duration, and the cessation of duration, mortality, *enfin*, suffering. Rousseau can only give legitimacy to the body politic if it is not in fact a body at all. The only legitimate rule he can recognize is a rule that exists only in the moment and in the mind and then is gone, never to materialize again. Materiality, we might say, is a problem for Roussseau. The only freedom worth having is the moral freedom of the will to choose itself again and again in each moment; "all attachment is insufficiency," literally. Only in the perfect moment of perfect willing, when each is separately but simultaneously embodying whatever, wordlessly, they share as one will, one body, one life, is there that "agreement of obedience and liberty" that consitutes the perfect citizen.

Anticipating Nietzsche's critical assault, it might be argued here that Rousseau hereby opts out of history, out of time and human temporality itself. His is precisely an ideal beyond life, beyond the world, this world, with its full, rich, and enduring imperfections. His perfectly just contract is way beyond the common and ordinary temporal and historical conditions of actual human beings living on an actual earth. While philosophy may have a hard time pinning down the reference, ordinary language does not.

Far from bringing to realization the common or the human, Rousseau has shown how far one has to go to escape the human. He has envisioned an unimaginably perfect balance of I and we, which couldn't exist even in one soul and never in any number of them, however momentarily united in good intentions. And the perfect moral right and sovereignty of this perfect "we" allows a perfectly justified coercion against gainsayers. This more-than-human perfection exercises a tyranny that has no limit.

Nevertheless, Rousseau has given us the lineaments of the problem, including his solution. The intention of social justice, as a perfect balance of wills to be exercised against injustice, locates for us the problem of the will and the body, and as the suffering of bodies in history, as a kind of space where discourse itself, perhaps even will itself, fails. Rousseau can only locate justice in the moment, a unity of intentions that cannot endure and must be perpetually, virtually, eternally renewed. The problem of time for us rises here to its full dimensions. As we know well, intentions only last a moment, and it takes more than will to construct something in time, and more than will to construct something out of time as well. As Nietzsche will affirm, it takes will to power and the mastery of time, and even then, time is our master. Rousseau's is indeed an ascetic ideal, immaculate, incalculable, inconceivable if one would respect the common, ordinary, messy, and (never transparently) overlapping lives we in fact live.

9

Nietzsche:
Suffering and Tragedy

Friedrich Nietzsche was one of the strangest thinkers ever known. He wrote incomparable, enigmatic, tragic, dangerous, and elegant prose, and carved up with a razor-sharp knife the metaphysical, moral, and political assumptions that had structured Western civilization for two millennia. At the end of his life, Nietzsche went mad; even his cool sanity was often outrageous, paradoxical, lyrical, ecstatic, dark, and sometimes beyond comprehension. His legacy to us is only now being unravelled, his sly, ironic, triply encoded codes, partially decoded, his songs sung by a crazy crew of commentators, some of whom are quite brilliant, some driven by curious winds to hound him or rage against him. This would not have surprised him. Having famously identified himself as having been "born posthumously," Nietzsche always found it difficult to find readers, and wanted only choice ones, with "good ears." In the century since his death, he has found some of the best there are, and some of the worst. All Nietzsche interpretation, even more than for other philosophers, is a reading of one's own life and work in his. He insisted that one could only see what it is given one to see.

It is impossible to prove a case in regard to Nietzsche, or rather, it is possible to prove many contradictory cases concerning the same question. In the end, one puts together a reading of Nietzsche that fits many incongruous pieces together in something like a collage, or a melody, which maybe accounts for disparate elements better than some other arrangements, but is all ultimately perspectival and never achieves logical consistency. That's what he wanted it to be like. For Nietzsche, nothing was ever finished once and for all, and logic was a hindrance rather than a help for many tasks of interpretation. There is never, nor can there be, a final word, an ultimate interpretation that saves the day. That is the blessing, he might say.

Nietzsche's intricate and paradoxical probings, his profound psychological, physiological, and philological analyses, what he called genealogy, gave us a new way to do history and philosophy and a new way to put them together as they had never been put together before. But Nietzsche's genealogy virtually gutted the primary buildings of metaphysics and morality within which traditional religion, philosophy, science, and politics had been housed. In doing that demolition, he opened up a gateway, dark and strange, to an entirely new reading of the past, to a reconfiguration of the task of art, philosophy, and politics, and to a struggle toward a difficult new beginning for both thought and action in a postmodern world. It is my contention in this book that the power behind his probing, the rage behind his evisceration of antecedent structures and practices, the point of all his poetry, was suffering.

Very few philosophers in the history of the Western tradition have been so little fathomed or so profoundly misunderstood as Nietzsche. No thinker ever did so much himself, deliberately and with malice aforethought, by means of style and paradox, irony, allegory, parable, satire, ridicule, and hyperbole, to keep from being understood. Despite his incessant efforts to mislead and the wildly contradictory stories he told, it is really only now, a hundred years after his eclipse by madness, that he is beginning to be interpreted in a truly serious way. There are many competing interpretations of Nietzsche. I will not be centrally concerned with making sense of these or taking sides, although I have my preferences; I will be developing a new perspective whose time, I think, is right.[1]

The central experience of Nietzsche's life was suffering and he made it the core of all his work, both explicitly and implicitly. Part of my task in this book is to show how suffering suffused all Nietzsche's thinking and lay behind his most classical philological investigations and his searches into modern knowledge. The question of suffering informed all his strategies to uncover the hidden and perverse motivations and meanings behind religion and philosophy, science and morality. It led him to try to find a place anterior to or beyond language, perhaps even beyond time, for a new kind of ethics. Even when Nietzsche is not speaking explicitly of suffering, the need to render account of it, to take it into account, to say how it can be accounted for, even beyond discourse and reference, pervades his constructions of meaning and sense in very widely disparate areas of inquiry. The question of suffering and the proper response to it, including his consideration of pity as the moral but deeply harmful and misguided response to it, underlies not only his life and how he lived it, but his every expression of that life in words, music, and poetry. It is through suffering that we read Nietzsche best, and through Nietzsche that we read suffering in our history and traditions best.

At the end of *Thus Spoke Zarathustra*, Nietzsche's haunting, uncategorizable masterpiece, Zarathustra says that his "final sin" was "Pity! Pity for the higher man! . . . Well, then, that has had its time! My suffering and my pity for suffering—what does it matter? Am I concerned with happiness? I am concerned with my work!"² I will come back to the question of pity several times in these next chapters. For Nietzsche it was a very intense personal concern. In Nietzsche's life, he experienced extreme illness and pain, rejection, despair, and utter loneliness, and when he finally went mad, he was found in the street, embracing a horse being beaten by its owner.³

Pity and tragic suffering were the most impenetrable mysteries of his life, his most enduring experiences, and the source of his deepest meditations. He used the question of suffering, its meaning, and even more significantly, its ultimate meaninglessness, as the finely calibrated razor by means of which he cut through the elaborate and deceptive wrappings of religion and philosophy to get at the core irreducibility of human need, mortality, and pain. He showed art and religion, philosophy and science all as having been developed out of the indomitable human desire to understand and explain, master and justify, mask, deny, and eliminate human suffering. He insisted on evaluating all thought and all practice in terms of its value for human life, and especially in terms of its value in relation to human terror and pain, for confronting the abyss, the nihil, the most unfathomable and unbearable aspect of human life. He pried open our "highest values" to show the pain and the power over pain that these values embody, bear, translate, encompass, sustain, and deny. In so doing, he gave us a key to the past: an unprecedented, difficult excursion into the unconscious roots and archaic rites of European culture, a journey that once taken, cannot be taken back. Once one looks back through that gateway, nothing ever looks the same again.

Nietzsche gave us the past itself as our most real context and our deepest problem. Through the lens of suffering, he understood the past itself as what forever passes and yet is never gone, whether we will it so or not. He viewed human temporality as that which preserves our deepest traumas and regrets, which we cannot reach; as that which epitomizes our hopelessness and powerlessness, which we cannot define; as that which we cannot change, however much we reiterate or rememorialize it. The past is the "It was" against which our will and our desire strive in vain. It is the very shape of our will and our desire.

Nietzsche interpreted our history, the history at least of the Western world centered on Europe, as the elaboration of monumental defenses against terror and pain, against human finitude, mortality, and temporality, and against the cruelty that creates both memory and personality. Religion, philosophy, politics, and morality are revealed as constructions erected against the dark, as perverse yet indispensable guardians against the emptiness and purposelessness, the chaos of life itself.

Nietzsche did not deny joy. On the contrary, he was the philosopher of the utmost joy, although not of the erotic-aesthetic ecstasies of darkness and cruelty some have made of him. He was the philosopher of a complete affirmation of life, despite its cruelties, especially in his doctrine of eternal recurrence, about which there remains endless mystery and debate. But he would never accept happiness, optimism, honor, or ideals of redemption or truth on their own terms, except as they are forever accompanied by their opposites, except as they are historically and psychologically conditioned, and except as they owned up to their debt to life and their purposes as responses to suffering. He took suffering and the very notion of time itself as suffering, to heart, and he forged of it a new vision, brilliant and paradoxical, of the eternal recurrence of the same as a new kind of response to suffering in time, one that opens up its corporealization into the self in a Dionysian moment of choice for life itself.

In these next chapters, I am going to consider central topics in Nietzsche's work that pertain to his understanding of suffering and to his genealogy of the history of values as engendered to respond to suffering. I will develop new close readings of *The Birth of Tragedy* and *On the Genealogy of Morals*.[4] I will reconsider the relations among culture, tragedy, and philosophy; I will critically examine the nature of Nietzsche's genealogical critique of morality and the metaphysics of morality. I will attempt an interpretation of the will to power and the will to truth and their relation, and of the politics of pity and nihilism. Finally, I will attempt a reinterpretation of Nietzsche's doctrine of the eternal recurrence of the same, which I argue for Nietzsche is always the return of difference. I am seeking the elusive elements of a new kind of politics and a new space for an ethics of suffering and responsibility. I want to delineate something of what a Nietzschean, postmetaphysical political response to suffering might be like.

THE BIRTH OF TRAGEDY: DIONYSUS AND SOCRATES

In his "Attempt at Self-Criticism," written in 1886 as a preface to a new edition of *The Birth of Tragedy* (originally published in 1872, when Nietzsche was twenty-seven), Nietzsche, in one of his finest pieces of writing, apologizes for the weaknesses of what was self-evidently a "first book," but affirms again the importance of the question the book raises, "to look at science in the perspective of the artist, but at art in that of life."[5] He says he finds it in hindsight "an impossible book." It was, when he published it, anything but what his colleagues in classical philology expected from the brilliant young philologist, called to the chair at the University of Basel in Switzerland in 1869 when he was twenty-four. It was scathingly attacked. Nevertheless, the book has had a lasting impact, not least on Greek studies and philology, because, however idiosyncratic is was by ordinary scholarly standards, its profound imaginative insight into the origins of tragedy and philosophy make it indispensable to anyone working in the field and to all who seek to understand the contradictory relationship between art and philosophy. This has been a controversial question of ultimate importance since Plato banned the poets from *The Republic*.

In *The Birth of Tragedy*, Nietzsche draws for the first time his famous distinction between Apollonian and Dionysian art and culture. It is not so much the contrast but rather the nature of each that is of interest to me and their relationship together as a response to the experience of suffering in Greek culture. The focus of the book, and it might be said of Nietzsche's work in general, is Dionysus. "Indeed, what is Dionysian—This book contains an answer: one 'who knows' is talking, the initiate and disciple of his god." The question of the origin of tragedy in the Greeks must be approached through Dionysus, because "the question of the Greek's relation to pain, his degree of sensitivity, is basic."[6]

Nietzsche sees tragic drama growing out of the Greeks' special relation to the "earliest" craving: "The *craving for the ugly*; the good severe will of the older Greeks to pessimism, to the tragic myth, to the riddle of everything underlying existence that is frightful, evil, a riddle, destructive, fatal."[7] Nietzsche locates the most basic and fundamental problem for human beings here, in this riddle of the pain and evil of life, of life's fatality; and he diagnoses everything that comes afterward, religion (especially Christianity), philosophy, morality, science, all of Western and particularly modern culture, as both failed and deformed attempts to come to terms with this quality of destructive fatality in human life. He sees Greek tragedy as having embodied a balanced, healthy response to the tragic suffering of life, and he begins to demonstrate a correlative belief in the hypothesis that the later "triumph of *optimism*, the gradual prevalence of *rationalism*, practical and theoretical *utilitarianism*, no less than democracy itself which developed at the same time, might all have been symptoms of a decline of strength, of impending old age, and of physiological weariness." This leads to his most important question: "What, seen in the perspective of *life*, is the significance of morality?"[8]

It is important to bear in mind the difference between the pity of Rousseau's humane spectator in the public sphere, who nevertheless takes sides and issues accusations on behalf of the victims against the victimizers in the name of authentic humanity, and this very different and much older model of artistic or tragic (rather than merely aesthetic) suffering. We will have to return to the question of aesthetic suffering. Here it is wise to note Nietzsche's valorization of tragic suffering, the Greeks' "craving for the ugly, their 'severe good will' to everything frightful, evil, riddle, destructive, fatal." This is not the response of either an idle spectator or a moralizing accuser, nor of one who easily identifies what is authentic in humanity. Nietzsche wants in fact to draw attention to the origins of a healthy culture because of its willingness to face up to the authenticity for humanity of evil and suffering and even to embrace it. Art is able to grasp suffering, to apprehend and magnify it, and to give it its deepest and most creative significance. Tragic drama shows suffering as an ineradicable and necessary dimension of life and as an intrinsic experience of human community. The ancient theater was the public space for the sacred enacting of suffering and fate in relation to the gods, especially Dionysus. Tragic drama integrated suffering into life.

Rousseau hated the theater. He condemned it for falsifying and even mocking the emotions associated with suffering and pity. Nietzsche, by contrast, insists that tragic suffering has nothing to do with either pity or catharsis—it has to do with the grandeur and self-overcoming of suffering and fate and teaches the noble soul how to live. It is not about witnessing or judging the suffering of others, morally or otherwise, but rather of experiencing our own limits through the transforming power of art. It involves no oversimplified idea of justice as fairness or equivalence, but rather one of spirit, which is a different king of justice.

In *The Birth of Tragedy*, Nietzsche first expresses one of his most basic philosophical contentions, that "art and not morality, is . . . the truly *metaphysical* activity of man," and that "the existence of the world is *justified* only as an aesthetic phenomenon."[9] Nietzsche has been interpreted as having *aestheticized* and thus justified evil, but I think it can be shown that that is not exactly what he means. Because he can critique genealogically the notion of the "metaphysical," he will profoundly transform the meaning of any possible "justification" for existence. Luther said we are justified by faith alone. Nietzsche asserts that we, and he, can never be justified at all. He shows that the attempt itself is deluded. We can see the matrix of his lifetime of work in this first book.

In the new preface, Nietzsche stressed the artistic meaning of the book, and what he took to be the meaning behind all events in life, the activities of "an entirely reckless and amoral artist-god . . . one who, creating worlds, frees himself from the *distress* of fullness and *overfullness* and from the affliction of the contradictions compressed in his soul." Creation, typically for Nietzsche, comes out of affliction. It may even be said that Nietzsche speaks from the perspective of the creator, one who combines the perspectives of the sufferer, the knower, the agent, and the spectator to create new values for life. Nietzsche sees the world, "the world—at every moment the *attained* salvation of God, as the eternally changing, eternally new vision of the most deeply afflicted, discordant, and contradictory being who can find salvation only in *appearance*." The spirit of this artist's metaphysics is "a spirit who will one day fight at any risk whatever the moral interpretation and significance of existence."[10]

This contrast between artistic creation and the moral interpretation of existence, especially as existence is experienced by the afflicted soul, is perhaps the most basic and important contrast developed in Nietzsche's philosophy. This difference is one that he draws out of what he experienced as the deepest and most vibrantly alive strata of life, which he characterizes in terms of an ecstatic Dionysian dance of affliction and contradiction, the discordance and the inseparability of joy and suffering, the dancing of the dismembered god, in contradistinction to a derivative or secondary, epiphenomenal, intentional, conscious, cognitive, conceptual level of life, linguistic, even metaphysical, but necessarily derivative, which includes the dichotomizing logical structures of philosophy and transcendental religion and morality. These discourses are later or belated events, which grow out of and are used to configure and find terms, in order to displace, disguise, deflect, and deny the deepest strata of life and its irreducible, ineliminable fatality and pain.

In this earliest book, Nietzsche establishes the meaning of the most important destructive and reconstructive point of his work on the basis of an experience of suffering that goes deeper than words and which ultimately cannot be met by thought. He identifies suffering, this kind of suffering, the suffering that is best characterized as the dismemberment of a god, as what is at stake in the most fundamental, urgent experiences of human life. It is a suffering that can only be approached with music and dance, ecstasy, tragic drama, with rhythm, with movement, with metaphors and symbols and images and allegories; it is a suffering that is rendered strangely, falsely, self-deceptively, and self-negatingly when it is rendered morally and metaphysically. Nietzsche establishes here and in other early writings that this most basic and chaotic level of life is what all other levels of life are about; all other levels of life are built on this most fundamental contradictory one. Even the simple level of appearances, of phenomena as such, grows out of this most primordial world of chaos, suffering, and creation.

The world of appearances is "at every moment the *attained* salvation" of the god, Nietzsche says—at every moment. That is, redemption is always here and now, in the world that we can see and touch around us. It is in our time, in every moment. There is no other salvation. Salvation is already *attained* in the world. This is Nietzsche's ultimate answer to all ascetic ideals, one he will develop through the next sixteen years that encompass his working life. The complicated higher layers of consciousness, language, and institutionalized symbolization come later and are reactive developments. Representation itself is a secondary elaboration of deeper and more contradictory energies. These are positions it will take Nietzsche his whole life, and ultimately his sanity, to work out, but they are present here, embryonically but clearly, from the first.

Nietzsche's explanation of the birth of tragedy has to do with tragic drama's ability, rare and fragile, to bring to a satisfactory staging and resolution the confrontation of consciousness and culture with this most basic level of experience of suffering. Tragedy, Nietzsche says, pertains to the extreme experiences of suffering in life, which defy all rationalization. It presents the provinces of life that are cruelty, terror, chaos, and fate, what Nietzsche calls "the heartbreaking and cruel character of human life."[11] In *The Birth of*

Tragedy, Nietzsche shows Greek tragedy as a complicated, difficult, dramatic response to the unrepresentable dark side of human existence. Early in the text he presents this dark side by telling the legend of Silenus, the companion of Dionysus:

> There is an ancient story that King Midas hunted in the forest a long time for the wise Silenus, the companion of Dionysus, without capturing him. When Silenus at last fell into his hands, the king asked what was the best and most desirable of all things for man. Fixed and immovable, the demigod said not a word, till at last, urged by the king, he gave a shrill laugh and broke out into these words: "Oh, wretched, ephemeral race, children of chance and misery, why do you compel me to tell you what it would be most expedient for you not to hear? What is best of all is utterly beyond your reach: not to be born, not to be, to be *nothing*. But the second best for you is—to die soon."[12]

It is for this knowledge, knowledge of the nihil, the nothing, that Greek tragedy was created. The ability of a culture to respond to life at this level is what makes it a "healthy" culture, or not.

We will pursue Nietzsche's conceptions of "health" and "illness" throughout his work, over hill and dale, through forest and stream. Health and sickness are primordial tropes in Nietzsche's life and his thought. Still it might not be too early to note that Nietzsche, although he employs the notions of "health" and "illness" as ultimate values in his work, warns against their reification both explicitly and repeatedly:

> There is no health as such, and all attempts to define a thing that way have been wretched failures. Even the determination of what is healthy for your body depends on your goal, your horizon, your energies, your impulses, your errors and above all on the ideals and phantasms of your soul. Thus there are innumerable healths of the body; and the more we allow the unique and incomparable to raise its head again, and the more we abjure the "equality of men," the more must the concept of a *normal* health . . . be abandoned by medical men. Only then would the time have come to reflect on the health and illness of the *soul*, and to find the peculiar virtue of each man in the health of his soul. In one person, of course, this health could look like its opposite in another person. Finally, the great question would still remain, whether we can really dispense with illness— even for the sake of our virtue—and whether our thirst for knowledge and self-knowledge in particular does not require the sick soul as much as the healthy, and whether, in brief, the will to health alone, is not a prejudice, cowardice, and perhaps a bit of very subtle barbarism and backwardness.[13]

We will return to many of the questions raised here several times over, in different contexts. We should note several things, however: (1) there is no health as such; (2) it is different and even opposite for every person (which democratic norms obscure and deny); (3) it is the health of souls (which are connected to bodies for Nietzsche) that he is interested in; (4) knowledge, and life itself, require the sick soul as much as the healthy one; and (5) the will to health alone is a kind of barbarism. While it is often the case that Nietzsche lionizes the healthy, who have very particular characteristics, and excoriates the sick and weak, also very particularly defined, he fully recognizes not only the different actions that vitiate all such general prescriptions, but also insists on the necessary connection and co-determination of sickness and health, even their interpenetration. His genealogy depends on it. Ultimately, his whole contextualization of the modern soul and of nihilism depends on it. For Nietzsche, in his life and in his thought, health and illness are always integrally and powerfully related; they form a great interwoven text and context, and always a test, for his evaluations, and especially for his genealogy of morals, which we will consider next.

In *The Birth of Tragedy*, Nietzsche identifies health with the necessary combination in art of the Apollonian impulse with the Dionysian one, which together create tragic drama. He identifies the Apollonian artist with dreams and images and the "plastic energies" that create form and with the creation of the entire Olympic world—"For there is nothing here that suggests asceticism, spirituality, or duty. We hear nothing but the accents of exuberant, triumphant life in which all things, whether good or evil, are deified."[14] The Dionysian impulse, especially evident in music, "which excited awe and terror," comes from the wild frenzies of the Dionysian festivals as they descended on the ancient world. These festivals "centered in extravagant sexual licentiousness, whose waves overwhelmed all family life and its venerable traditions; the most savage natural instincts were unleashed, including even that horrible mixture of sensuality and cruelty which has always seemed to me to be the real 'witches brew.'" In tragedy, however, the "witches brew" is rendered by art to be efficacious, "only the curious blending and duality of the Dionysian revelers remind us—as medicines remind us of deadly poisons—of the phenomenon that pain brings joy, that ecstasy may wring sounds of agony from us. At the very climax of joy there sounds a cry of horror or a yearning lamentation for an irretrievable loss."[15]

Nietzsche's point is that the Greeks, "so singularly capable of *suffering*," could only have endured existence because their suffering was revealed to them in their gods: "Thus do the gods justify the life of man: they themselves live it—the only satisfactory theodicy!"[16] It is the unsatisfactory theodicies of Western religion and philosophy that will henceforth be the targets of Nietzsche's greatest attacks. Apollonian culture, "which always must first overthrow an empire of Titans and slay monsters, and which must have triumphed over an abysmal and terrifying view of the world and the keenest susceptibility to suffering through recourse to the most forceful and pleasurable illusions," enabled the Greeks, by mirroring beauty, to combat their "artistically correlative talent for suffering and for the wisdom of suffering."[17] Unlike all of the thinkers we have so far studied, Nietzsche alone speaks of a talent for and a wisdom of suffering. We have to figure out what he means by that.

I have dwelt at length on Nietzsche's understanding of life as "suffering, primal and eternal, the sole ground of the world,"[18] not only because it is central to the argument of this book, but because it is indispensable for understanding the ground, or perhaps the underground, of Nietzsche's genealogy and recovery. The only adequate response to primordial suffering, "the sole ground of the world" is "the most sublime artistic symbolism, that Apollonian world of beauty" which is "necessarily interdependent" with "its substratum, the terrible wisdom of Silenus."[19] In this his earliest conception, the terror of the world is only answered and redeemed by beauty, by artistic creation.[20] The comingling, necessary interrelatedness of joy and pain, agony and ecstasy, is one of the primary sources of Nieztsche's more fully developed conception of a life lived "beyond good and evil," out of the shadow of morality and justification, into the midday of creative possibility.

The artist, "with his sublime gestures, shows us how necessary is the entire world of suffering, that by means of it the individual may be impelled to realize the redeeming vision, and then, sunk in contemplation of it, sit quietly in his tossing bark, amid the waves. . . . The Apollonian Greek . . . had to recognize that despite all its beauty and moderation, his entire existence rested on a hidden substratum of suffering and of knowledge, revealed to him by the Dionysian. And behold: Apollo could not live without Dionysus!"[21] Suffering is necessary because it engenders the redeeming vision—all existence rests on Dionysian knowledge. It is Nietzsche's task to explicate such knowledge.

There are then related issues of knowlege, which I attend to at length in later chapters, having to do with Nietzsche's "epistemology," a philosophic misnomer because Nietzsche expressly denies the possibility of epistemology (what one commentator called his "epistectomy"), and develops a method of genealogy that corresponds to his understanding of life as primordial, physiological impulses, rhythms best expressed in sound and music, a will to power and energy only secondarily translated into perceptions and appearances, into metaphors and parables, and then only very belatedly into language and concepts, or knowledge.

Philosophers are noticeably discontent, sometimes irritably impatient, with Nietzsche's philosophy, which produces itself in passionate images, stories, parables, ironies, analogies, exaggerations, and contradictions, and they try to hammer out a straight line of argument, insisting all the way on Nietzsche's being a kind of idiot who cannot shoot a straight arrow at a definite target.

We might then note here, at the beginning, that Nietzsche sees life as lived expressions of movement, energy, music, power, pain, and passion, that his genealogy is a *pathos*, and that he does not seek a theory of knowledge, to put it blandly, that will straighten out this contradictory lived reality. We will come back to this question of methodology and interpretation, knowledge, perspective, and style. It is a fallacy to fault a philosopher for not doing what you want him to do, which he expressly denies as his intention or goal.

Here I want to show how Nietzsche came to understand philosophy and abstract conceptual arguments as dead things, as icons of misunderstanding, as defenses against human helplessness and incomprehension of the contradictoriness and impenetrable movements of life, and also as revenge, as twisted instinct, a denial of the quality in life that brings us irrational suffering. Nietzsche sees the entire philosophical edifice of Western thought, and of Western religion as its source, as an extraordinary effort to escape the consequences of our profound and irrevocable duality. Language itself is inadequate to translate the basic rhythms and music of experience, feeling and impulse into sense.

> The poems of the lyricist can express nothing that did not already lie hidden in that vast universality and absoluteness that compelled him to figurative speech. Language can never adequately render the cosmic symbolism of music, because music stands in symbolic relation to the primordial contradiction and primordial pain in the heart of the primal unity . . . beyond and prior to all phenomena. Rather, all phenomena, compared to it, are merely symbols: hence language, as the organ and symbol of phenomena, can never by any means disclose the innermost heart of music; language, in its attempt to imitate it, can only be in superficial contact with it and cannot bring the deeper significance of it one step nearer.[22]

Nietzsche locates the origin of Greek tragedy in the satyric chorus. Contrary to contemporary interpretations, the chorus does not derive from the idea of an "ideal spectator." Rather, the chorus of satyrs, embodiments of Dionysus, come from a realm of "religiously sanctioned reality under the sanction of myth and cult":

> The metaphysical comfort—with which, I am suggesting even now, every true tragedy leaves us—that life is at the bottom of things, despite all the changes of appearances, indestructibly powerful and pleasurable—this comfort appears in incarnate clarity in the chorus of satyrs, a chorus of natural beings who live ineradicably, as it were, behind all civilization and remain eternally the same, despite the changes of generations and of the history of nations. With this

chorus the profound Hellene, uniquely susceptible to the tenderest
and deepest suffering, comforts himself, having looked boldly right
into the terrible destructiveness of so-called world history as well as
the cruelty of nature, and being in danger of longing for a Buddhistic
negation of the will. Art saves him, and through art—life.[23]

The chorus "beholds its lord and master Dionysus . . . sharing his *suffering*,
it also shares something of his *wisdom* and proclaims the truth from the
heart of the world."[24] Nietzsche explicitly emphasizes the "terrible destructiveness of so-called world history," as well as the "cruelty of nature" and
the "contradiction and pain" at the heart of existence, to which the eternal
satyric chorus bears witness. He asserts that, nevertheless, life is at bottom
"indestructibly powerful and pleasurable." How is it possible to affirm life in
the face of the magnitude of human suffering and the nihil? That is the ultimate question we must address with Nietzsche.

In the tragedies of Aeschylus and Sophocles, the tragic heroes experience
the depths of terror, sacrifice, and suffering, and the ultimate ethical reality
they show is this: "All that exists is just and unjust and equally justified."[25] It
is according to the measure of this truth that Nietzsche will judge the metaphysical morality of the philosophers and history itself.

Nietzsche locates the death of tragedy, a "death by suicide," in the emergence of two new "spectators" of the art, the poet Euripides, "as *thinker*, not
as poet," and the "newborn demon," Socrates. It is "the new opposition"
between the Dionysian and the Socratic that accomplished the destruction of
Greek tragedy and defined the world-historical struggle of art against reason
that would come to define the next two millennia of Western culture, and as
well, Nietzsche's lifework. Nietzsche's relationship to Socrates is notoriously
ambivalent; he sees him as the pivotal point of Western culture, carrying philosophy off in the fatefully wrong direction, but also as the first great questioning
one, despite all, a prototype and progenitor for Nietzsche himself.[26]

Nietzsche decisively situates the origins of philosophy in a weakening,
declining, and deformed will, one that can no longer attain the strength and
clarity of a true, healthy, and largely unconscious cultural response to the
chaos, terror, and suffering of life. Philosophy, in a kind of insane detach-
ment from the unity of the soul with its culture, projects a spectator's logical
analysis by which to dissect and measure the authority or justification of the
community's ways of life. Nietzsche is concerned to show just how strange
this new philosophical approach is.

Socrates brings into being for the first time a mode of life and a kind of
knowledge or inquiry that will vanquish tragedy, and banish art altogether
from the ideal city, and which will become the dominant mode of intellectual
thought in the West for the rest of Western history. Tragedy, as Nietzsche

makes clear, did not depend on "epic suspense" or on "uncertainty as to what was to happen next," but rather, "everything laid the ground for *pathos*, not for action: and whatever was not directed toward *pathos* was considered objectionable."[27] It is in this sense that Nietzsche says that from the point of view of the artist, the philosopher's dialectic is vulgar, in poor taste. It misses the point. But what is the point? *Pathos*, suffering, which is set not in the context of time's uncertainty, the unknown future, but rather in time already encompassed, the future already laid down by the past, the *pathos* of this future already tragically fated, as it is, for instance, for Oedipus or Antigone. Nietzsche's relating of suffering to time, his doctrine of eternal recurrence, is already prefigured here.

The question Socrates asks and answers in an unprecedented way is whether the beautiful is intelligible. His point is not *pathos*, but logos. How do we know what is right? The Socratic dictum, "Knowledge is virtue," followed from Socrates' interrogation of his fellow citizens, statesmen, orators, poets, artists, where everywhere he found "the conceit of knowledge."

> To his astonishment he perceived that all these celebrities were with-out a proper and sure insight, even with regard to their own pro-fessions, and that they practiced them only by instinct. "Only by instinct": with this phrase we touch upon the heart and core of the Socratic tendency. With it Socratism condemns existing art as well as existing ethics. Wherever Socratism turns its searching eyes it sees lack of insight and the power of illusion; and from this lack it infers the essential perversity and reprehensibility of what exists.[28]

"Only by instinct"—with this phrase Socrates condemns existing art and existing ethics, existing life. Nietzsche's emphasis here is on already existing culture—art and ethics already exist, they already work, live, function, have authority, command obedience, provide meaning and membership in a com-munity, instinctively. That is to say, the practices and assumptions of culture are not altogether conscious, cognitive, or rationally chosen; they are, and Nietzsche insists, ought to be, instinctive, that is, unconscious, natural, pre-supposed, understood, engrained, integrated, bodily, whole, passionate, alive, known, lived, and suffered.

It is the collapse of culture that produces the need for a rational justifi-cation for life, for culture, for what was once instinctive. It is this need, this gap, this absence of what was once taken for granted that Nietzsche wants to explore. What is the origin or source of this need for rationalization—where did the authority and innate power of culture and communal life within us and upon us go? How did its ungrounding come about? How did instinct get so twisted around that it tried to look for itself over its own shoulder?[29]

Socrates applies a "penetrating critical process, this audacious reasonableness" as the measure of all things, to correct them according to rational principle. "Basing himself on this point, Socrates conceives it to be his duty to correct existence: all alone, with an expression of irreverence and superiority, as the precursor of an altogether different culture, art, and morality, he enters a world, to touch whose very hem would give us the greatest happiness."[30]

Nietzsche looks with longing back to the world we have lost as a result of the irremediable finality of the Socratic intervention. A world of instinctual balance and belonging, not in spite of its terrors but in accordance with the nature of the world, including its terrors; this world, which tragedy had preserved, finally deteriorated and degenerated to the point where the functions of instinct and reason became reversed, and where reason could bring instinct up before the bar of judgment.

> The "*daimonion of Socrates.*" This voice, whenever it comes, always dissuades. In this utterly abnormal nature, instinctive wisdom appears only in order to hinder conscious knowledge occasionally. While in all productive men it is instinct that is the creative-affirmative force, and consciousness acts critically and dissuasively, in Socrates it is instinct that becomes the critic, and consciousness that becomes the creator—truly a monstrosity per defectum.[31]

We should imagine "the one great Cyclops eye of Socrates fixed on tragedy. . . . To this eye was denied the pleasure of gazing into the Dionysian abysses." Nietzsche does not deny that there is pleasure to be found in the abyss. But it is the meaning of that pleasure that has been lost. What did Socrates see in tragedy? "Something rather unreasonable, full of causes apparently without effects, and effects apparently without causes; the whole, moreover, so motley and manifold that it could not but be repugnant to a sober mind, and a dangerous tinder for sensitive and susceptible souls."[32] To the logical mind, the fate of Oedipus is not only incomprehensible, it is repugnant. Life should, it seems, make sense.

To Socrates and his eye of reason, art is unreasonable, nonsensical, inefficient, inexplicable, and not very intelligent. It is not logical. It is not clear. It is not arranged in an orderly fashion. And most important, it does not "tell the truth." Literalness, logical equivalence, clear-cut causation, and moral resolution, these are to be the hallmarks of the new ideal of philosophic truth. This notion of truth, however, misses the point of tragedy. *Pathos*, passion, the mystic duality of primordially contradictory human experience is precisely the point of tragedy, Nietzsche wants to argue. Truth values cannot be applied.

Philosophy is an evasion, an untruthful and cowardly evasion, Nietzsche says, of the real, of the cruelty and suffering and drunkenness of the world.

It insists on seeing or setting straight what is not straight; it insists on analyzing straightforwardly what is never straightforward. The consequences of Socrates' inversion are enormous: "'Virtue is knowledge; man sins only from ignorance; he who is virtuous is happy.' For now the virtuous hero must be a dialectician; now there must be a necessary, visible connection between virtue and knowledge, faith and morality; now the transcendental justice of Aeschylus is degraded to the superficial and insolent principle of 'poetic justice' with its customary *deus ex machina.*"[33]

Nietzsche wants above all to deny Socrates' equation of virtue and knowledge, and of both with happiness. It may be that happiness sometimes promotes virtue, depending on what one means by "virtue." It can be argued that Nietzsche is saying that. He sometimes seems to see virtue, which he interprets as courage and healthy vitality, as resulting from an overflowing of well-being and happiness. But the reverse is certainly not the case. On the contrary, Nietzsche's genealogy of morality finds that virtue, morality feeds on and instills unhappiness in suffering souls; it depends on and deepens debt, guilt, sin, punishment, and misery. Virtue, as we know it from Christian morality, is built on self-denial and suffering, and the exploitation of suffering for the sake of power, according to Nietzsche. Happiness is altogether different. It is instinctual, not rational. Furthermore, knowledge, especially in the Socratic sense, will not yield happiness, but rather the opposite. Clear knowledge and the will to truth, especially in the modern age, lead to the knowledge of the death of God, the failure of belief in morality or any moral purpose underlying history, and to nihilism, the collapse of all values. That is the problem we face in our time as a result of the influence of Socrates, "spread over posterity like a shadow."[34]

Nietzsche is clear that it was "a profound *illusion* that first saw the light of the world in the person of Socrates: the unshakable faith that thought, using the thread of causality, can penetrate the deepest abysses of being, and that thought is capable not only of knowing being but even of *correcting* it." This metaphysical illusion "accompanies science as an instinct and leads science again and again to its limits, at which it must turn into art—*which is really the aim of this mechanism.*"[35]

In future books, especially *The Gay Science, Thus Spoke Zarathustra, On the Genealogy of Morals,* and *Beyond Good and Evil,* [36] Nietzsche will develop this understanding of the suspicious origins of philosophy's will to truth, and he will track its development into science as an "instinct" for truth in the modern age. He will diagnose the nihilistic undoing of meaning and the power of the philosophic illusion that thought or reason can penetrate being and even measure life and find it lacking. (Nietzsche exploits all the resources of the medical model for thinking, for both cognition and ethics.) He will demonstrate even more powerfully the nihilistic effects of the shattering of this illusion by the very operation of the will to truth itself, truth turned ultimately against itself, until it reveals, unceasingly, the error, falseness, and untruth of all absolute values.

I have stayed so intensively with *The Birth of Tragedy* because the crucial lineaments of Nietzsche's genealogy of morals and metaphysics and the importance of his conclusions and the space they open up for understanding suffering are presented so clearly and well in this early work. While Nietzsche does not propose that we could or even should return to tragedy as a way of confronting life and its abyss, he does see in art, "*which is really the aim of this mechanism,*" the point not only of his enterprise, but of the history of the civilization he both uncovers and overturns. Nietzsche does sometimes seem to say that life itself, or human life, had to work its way through these torturous turns and illusory monuments of human defense against pain in order to produce at least the possibility of a higher kind of human being. We turn then to this analysis.

10

On the Genealogy of Morals

Nietzsche gave us the past itself as our real context and our deepest problem. He worked through the notoriously difficult conundrums of the concept of time, from several different perspectives all enigmatic. His most important insight into the relation of human life to the past came through his profound apprehension of human suffering. Through the lens of suffering, he saw the past as what forever passes, which has been interpreted as what, therefore, deserves to pass. He understood the power of this idea through a fragment of Anaximander:

> The Unlimited is the first-principle of things that are. It is that from which the coming-to-be of things and qualities takes place and it is that into which they return when they perish by moral necessity, giving satisfaction to one another and making reparation for their injustice according to the order of time.[1]

Nietzsche understood as perhaps no one before him had that even from the very beginning, the concept of time had coincided with and been inextricably mixed with that of justice. He himself reached back before Plato for his own reconfiguring of the relations between time and justice. He wanted to express this relation not in terms of blame or first principles, but in terms of will and power and the eternal recurrence of all things. He wanted to open up a new space, not of moral presence, but of absence and choice, in which the human values of justice and injustice could be created in the moment at which the past and future meet. These are highly paradoxical notions that we will explore in the following chapters, especially in relation to Nietzsche's notions of will to power and eternal recurrence.[2]

Nietzsche saw human temporality, and human memory which preserves our temporality, as history; not simply as events past and passing, irretrievable, but as what preserves, within us and in our language and systems of analysis, our deepest traumas, hurts, and regrets. Time registers our hopelessness and powerlessness to change what cannot be changed, the great "It was" against which our will and our desire strike in vain. It is what has already made us what we are, whether we like it or no. He didn't at all think of history as merely the contingent succession of moments, although from certain perspectives, it retains this character. He saw time rather as what which was always fated to happen (and will, strangely enough, happen again and again). Time is what made us and formed us, the conditions that bring about the present and will condition the future. Furthermore, he interpreted our particular history, the history at least of the Western world centered on Europe, as an elaborate working out of philosphical, moral, and scientific defenses against the inexhaustible pain and inevitable suffering of human life, against our mortality, our transience, our finitude, and as disguises for the cruelty and domination that are needed to create memory, personality, and culture. Nothing, for Nietzsche, was easier than forgetting.

Religion, philosophy, politics, and most of all morality, all stand revealed, beneath his genealogical onslaught, as displacements of desire, of forgetting, and therefore as mendacious and deforming constructions erected against the dark, quick passage of time and the night. He saw them as perverse but also indispensable strategies, guardians against the emptiness and purposeless of life itself, the chaos of becoming. His notion of will to power is the site where all purpose lies, but it is our will to power and our purposes that live there. Life, time, the world as a whole have no meaning in themselves, no underlying purpose, no destiny by which we will be carried toward truth.

Nietzsche became in the end the philosopher of joy as well as suffering. He advocated an all-encompassing and urgent affirmation of life, accepting all its terms. He did not underestimate what was entailed in such an acceptance. In his doctrine of the eternal recurrence of the same, about which there remains endless debate and mystery, he tried to articulate a thought that, while it was the "weightiest burden," was also a chance, by means of the paradoxical gateway of the moment, to affirm and transform both past and present, to give rise to an unanticipatable future. But the moment has value only as we give it such, and we can only do that by not only accepting but also revaluing suffering. A new way of thinking about valuing and suffering is the key to that new beginning. Nietzsche took suffering, and the *pathos* of power in time itself, as our deepest dilemma. He sought to imagine a new art of the self out of the incorporation of all of life, its heights and depths, into the self, a Dionysian affirmation of the already "attained salvation" of the world.

THE DEATH OF GOD, NIHILISM, AND GENEALOGICAL CRITIQUE

When he turns to the modern age, Nietzsche finds not culture, which he understands as an organic unity such as was embodied in Greek tragedy, but rather the absence or active disintegration of culture. This disintegration, decay, degeneration of culture both portends and symbolizes the great danger from which the modern age suffers, the danger of nihilism. While he located the advent of nihilism in the ancient world, which eventually produced both Socrates and Christianty as its products, the great danger of present nihilism in the modern European West arises as the power of the will to truth, of science, which undermines and exposes all previous truths as false. God is dead and all that he stood for for us, "that is *all over* now, . . . the decline of the faith in the Christian god, the triumph of scientific atheism, is a general European event. . . . unconditional and honest atheism is simply the *presupposition* of the way he [Schopenhauer] poses his problem, being a triumph achieved finally and with great difficulty by the European conscience, being the most fateful act of two thousand years of discipline for truth that in the end forbids itself the *lie* in faith in God." It is through science that we "forbid ourselves the *lie* of faith in God." Moreover, "what it was that really triumphed over the Christian god: Christian morality itself, the concept of truthfulness that was understood ever more rigorously . . . scientific conscience, an intellectual cleanliness at any price."[3] The discipline of truth is what brought about the death of God, at last, and left us alone with ourselves in the emptiness. This is just one of the stories Nietzsche tells about the death of God.

Because of the collapse of culture under the onslaught of the discipline of truth, Nietzsche understands the goal of human thought to be the necessity for "an unprecedented *knowledge of the preconditions of culture*,"[4] in order that culture may somehow be rebuilt and the disastrous conditions of modern nihilism, not averted, but at least in some instances overcome. Nihilism for Nietzsche is not only the twisted underlying logic of European philosophy and history, but a critical, pathological condition, one come to fruition through the indispensable domination of the will to truth in our day. To know what was needed to oppose this ever-more invasive nihilism was a very large task, and it is no wonder that Nietzsche experienced himself as heroically overburdended. He thought he bore the responsibility for changing human history. He made a good beginning at it.

The grounding, or what serves as one in the absence of any such possibility, for Nietzsche's investigations into the forces that formed and then destroyed civilization in the West is the ultimate context of present-day nihilism, what he characterized as the death of God. Nietzsche first told the story of the death of God in that famous passage in *The Gay Science*, called *The Madman*:

Have you not heard of that madman who lit a lantern in the bright morning hours, ran to the market place, and cried incessantly: "I seek God! I seek God!"—As many of those who did not believe in God were standing around just then, he provoked much laughter. Has he got lost? asked one. Did he lose his way like a child? asked another. Or is he hiding? Is he afraid of us? Has he gone on a voyage? emigrated?—Thus they yelled and laughed. The madman jumped into their midst and pierced them with his eyes. "Whither is God?" he cried. "I will tell you. *We have killed him*—you and I. All of us are his murderers. But how did we do this? How could we drink up the sea? Who gave us the sponge to wipe away the entire horizon? What were we doing when we unchained this earth from its sun? Whither is it moving now? Whither are we moving? Are we not plunging continually? Backward, sideward, forward, in all directions? Is there any up or down? Are we not straying as through an infinite nothing? Do we not feel the breath of empty space? Has it not become colder? Is not night continually closing in on us? Do we not need to light lanterns in the morning? Do we hear nothing as yet of the noise of the gravediggers who are burying God? Do we smell nothing as yet of the divine decomposition? Gods, too, decompose. God is dead. God remains dead. And we have killed him.[5]

Finally, the madman, looking at the astonishment of his listeners, says, "I have come too early, . . . my time is not yet. This tremendous event is still on its way, still wandering: it has not yet reached the ears of men. . . . This deed is still more distant from them than the most distant stars—*and yet they have done it themselves*." At the opening paragraph of Book Three of *The Gay Science*, Nietzsche cautions us that even though God is dead, "there may still be caves for thousands of years in which his shadow will be shown.—And we—we still have to vanquish his shadow, too."[6]

The death of God is not merely a matter of seeing through and putting aside previous religious beliefs. It is not just a matter of now knowing that something is false which once we took to be true, namely, God's existence. God's existence has served as the foundational framework for Western civilization for millennia, and the death of God that Nietzsche announces is an apocalyptic historical event. An event is neither false nor true, it simply is. But it takes a discerning historian to see events over such a long duration. This event, a long time coming and a long time passing through us and around us, changes everything. As Nietzsche explains, it is a fate, what was and cannot be undone in the modern age. What Nietzsche means by fate will be made clearer as we proceed. But what Nietzsche means by history is quite particular. History is precisely not what is contingent or accidental, it is not about numerous chance possibilities, rather the opposite; it is about what out of all those numerous possibilities actually happened, fatally happened, happened once and cannot be changed. It is the throw of the dice, what actually came up on the dice as they were cast, in fact, and not any other. In this sense, our history is our fate and it lives in us.

The death of God is our history; it encompasses a history of our values and these values are fateful for us, a fateful inheritance. What is the meaning of the death of God? How do events have meaning, and for whom do they have meaning? What meaning does a death have for us? It depends, as in all things, on our relationship to the deceased. This is part of what Nietzsche will recover in *On the Genealogy of Morals*. He wants to expose to us the underside of our long relationship with God, especially now that he is dead, and we have killed him.[7]

Nietzsche shows us that our relationship with God was largely unconscious, although its conscious elements were vast and conspicuous. It has been the most significant relationship in the history of Western peoples. Even after the death, the relationship goes on, as it does with the deaths of fathers and mothers. The shadow of God stays on the wall of the cave for centuries; the shadow of God haunts us, and his memory, engraved in rituals and suffering on our bodies and rites, still determines many actions and events. The customs and habits we have accrued from our long relationship to God have a very long half-life. And they are, in a sense, radioactive too. That is to say, as Nietzsche argues, they can burn with a malignant force, a vengeance and cruelty and suffering that lingers in the bone. The death of God is surely as significant as the birth of God, which is an event still quite alive in our memories and practices. The living God is different from the dead God, but we have to be able to trace the effects of his life to begin to fathom his death. Do we merely believe that God is dead, or do we know it and practice it? How do we practice the death of God—that is Nietzsche's deadly question. In the parable, men cannot yet hear the news that God is dead. The event is still coming from afar. Its repercussions are still reaching us, like the premonitions of an earthquake.

In order to understand how Nietzsche understands this fateful and vastly overdetermined event in human history, the death of God, and to trace its implications for our lives, we must first look at Nietzsche's analysis of the historical and psychological processes that brought us to this event. His most accessible and famous book on the subject, *On the Genealogy of Morals,* is also one of the most easily misinterpreted of his works. The particular perspective that the question of suffering affords us, for the book is filled to the brim with suffering and the genealogy of suffering, may allow for a more nuanced and more penetrating interpretation of this work than has so far been offered.

In *On the Genealogy of Morals*, Nietzsche begins by asking what seems to be a simple question. He wants to know how values which are, on the face of it, neither attractive nor natural to human beings in terms of their instinctual animal nature—values that he calls "unegoistic," like pity, self-abnegation, and self-sacrifice, values that do not directly preserve or benefit the one who performs actions of this kind—how such values could ever have become so important, in fact, dominant, in the history of human civilization as we know it.

Nietzsche says that he has grown ever more mistrustful and skeptical of such values, which constitute what we have come to call morality, and of the way such values are justified, connected, and used. He wants to ask the largest question about morality, namely, "what is the value of morality?" He wants to offer not only a "transvaluation of all values," but a new kind of evalutive thinking, evaluative thinking that is not moral. He sees the "ever-spreading morality of pity that had seized on philosophers and made them ill" as a "sinister symptom" of "sinister European culture," that is, of nihilism.[8] Nihilism is a reality that constitutes an ever-growing problem for man.

Nihilism is not only for Nietzsche the exhaustion, defeat, and emptiness that lives in the vacuum left by the evacuation of all values, the draining away of all belief and credibility from our most potent, long-lasting truths and faiths. It is also the point zero of the human will to truth. Nihilism lives in the unconditioned and unconditional will to truth that drives us into the future. We will return to the question of nihilism as we find it in Nietzsche's genealogical critique of the history of ascetic values and value-creation in our civilization. We will analyze with Nietzsche the ways in which this genealogy of values, of morality, culminates in the death of God, the crisis of "highest values" in the modern era.

In the *Genealogy*, Nietzsche excavates the history of European morality in order to satisfy a *"new demand,"* which is raised by the suspicion of pity and of the highest values of morality. It is a demand for "a *critique* of moral values, *the value of these values themselves, must first be called into question."* In asking this question, he brings into being a new way of doing philosophy, namely, *genealogy*—"for that there is needed a knowledge of the conditions and circumstances in which they [values] grew, under which they evolved and changed (morality as consequence, as symptom, as mask, as tartufferie, as illness, as misunderstanding; but also morality as cause, as remedy, as stimulant, as restraint, as poison), a knowledge of a kind that has never yet existed or even been desired."[9] This is genealogy. We will look in the end at the ground, and at the impossibility of grounding, and even at the underground, of genealogical critique.[10]

In order to explain the value of values or of morality, Nietzsche will have to dig out the means by which human beings find, invent, create, assign, discover, constitute, construct, deconstruct, and deploy value, that is to say, how they evaluate, and from what sources and needs, what hidden crevasses and contortions of motivation their evaluating activities stem. The great originality of Nietzsche's work here is to see values not as given, not as things or as goods, but rather but as the effects of evaluating activities. Humans evaluate objects and events and thus create values by so doing. He looks for the "physiological" and psychological roots of such human evaluating. In uncovering these roots, Nietzsche shows why we have normally come to see values as given, as external to us and our actions, and in fact as standards, given from "above" by God or fate or reason or history, such that we have been "obliged" to judge our actions according to them. He reveals the sources of that "obligation." Nietzsche's task is digging out the genealogical underground, the origins, motives, and needs, the instincts of life and death, of fear and power, which accomplish themselves in the creation of metaphysics and morality as deeds. Simultaneously, these moral values self-deceptively and necessarily disguise themselves as outside of and beyond human dispensation, decision, and will. Only that distancing makes them work for the purpose for which they were designed—to give meaning to suffering.

In the first essay of *On the Genealogy of Morals*, Nietzsche sets the stage for his entire three-part investigation of the question of value by bringing into explicit contrast what he says are two different kinds of morality, what he sometimes calls master versus slave morality, what he sometimes calls Rome versus Judea, or perhaps more benignly, classical as contrasted to biblical morality. Nietzsche crucially frames this contrast on the basis of a mythological story about how these conflicting moralities (only one of which turns out to be a morality in the conventional sense of the word) handle aggression and suffering.

From the perspective we have established in this book, it is significant that the way they handle suffering lies at the heart of both of these moralities, and directly contributes to the way they are formed—one as the lordly active propagation of cruelty and the easy "forgetting" of suffering, and the other as the interiorization and self-reflexivity of cruelty and suffering on the part of the victims, the slaves. Slave suffering, Nietzsche says, is suffering turned back against the sufferer in a situation of powerlessness, both political and psychological. Slaves are powerless to *act* to relieve their suffering or to express their anger over it. This powerless, inexpressible suffering is therefore ontologized, and compensated for, first, by being blamed on "the others," and second, by inventing rewards and punishments projected onto another, ideal moral world beyond this one, a world in which complicated and eternal revenges are exacted, in retribution for the sufferings endured, helplessly, in this world.

Nietzsche sets up a dichotomy between an "active" as opposed to a "reactive" way to express human aggression in its relation to suffering. He uses language that strongly praises one sort of morality, the master-Roman-classical sort, and even more strongly condemns the other, the slave-Judean-biblical sort. But, as we will see, this is not only an oversimplification of what Nietzsche is doing, it is a deliberately misleading one. And it is Nietzsche himself who is responsible for its being misleading, of course.

Nietzsche exhibits a typical neurasthenic intellectual's admiration for unthinking, rashly acting natural predators, who have no second thoughts about their actions, but he also makes it quite clear that nothing still living has come from anything so uncomplicated, and also that any person, including he himself, only temporarily achieves anything like mastery of this sort. It is important, at least for some readings, not to take Nietzsche too literally when he talks about masters and slaves, however much commentators relish doing so. Not only does he make it clear that he is not talking about social classes as we think of them, but also the deeper psychological and metaphorical meanings of the opposition are lost when they are oversimplified or reified into rigid psychological or sociological types. This is not to deny that Nietzsche certainly does mean that some, the rare few, are more capable of his kind of nobility than others; and that the many, the herd, are always naturally caught in slavishness. But there is nothing simple or commonplace about what he means by "noble" and "slave," and nothing intuitively familiar about those to whom in particular he assigns such qualities.

Nietzsche sets up the contrast between master and slave morality in such a way as to tread on our most sensitive sensibilities. Our own history of slavery and the guilt we carry for it makes it virtually impossible for us to get the context of Nietzsche's remarks right, or to miss his point. He understands the provocative nature of his defense of nobility and his contempt for slaves, and he uses the dis-ease of our (previous slave-owning now resolutely democratical) defenses to pry open closed moral boxes and preconceptions. My suggestion will be that Nietzsche lives, and knows that he lives, as we all do, on both sides of this divide.

Like all of Nietzsche's oppositions, these types too turn out to be not only inextricably linked, but also virtually unintelligible unless they are considered together, as divided parts of one whole.[11] It is master-slave morality that Nietzsche is considering here, and both master and slave live in the individual self as well as in the body politic (although "outside every existing social order"). Nietzsche shows the interconnections between masters and slaves and the forces they symbolize in his analysis of pain, memory, and bad conscience in the second essay, and in his powerful overview and diagnosis of the ascetic impulse, the ascetic ideal as a version of the will to power in religion, philosophy, and science, in the third essay.

Nietzsche frames his analysis of master-slave morality with two important observations: first, that philosophical thinking is by its nature "unhistorical," to which we must contrast his own genealogical method, which is both historical and psychological, and second, with a brief aside on the origins of language:

> It was out of this *pathos of distance* that they first seized the right to create values and to coin names for values. . . . (The lordly right of giving names extends so far that one should allow oneself to conceive the origin of language itself as an expression of power on the part of the rulers: they say "this *is* this and this," they seal every thing and event with a sound and, as it were, take possession of it.)[12]

This conception agrees entirely with Hobbes's analysis of the origins of language and the authoritative determination of meanings by rulers, especially moral meanings, and seems equally to set up a kind of value relativism. But as we saw with Hobbes and will see with Nietzsche, it is not relativism that is the end point of this analysis, but rather the politics of language and of culture that is at stake. Relativism is a kind of philosophical translation of a political reality; it cannot be made into mere metaphysics. Politics creates the grounds for meaning. Practice sets up the possibility of truth. Nietzsche calls it perspectivism, which is not mere relativism; Nietzsche's perspectives are context-producing. They may be multiple, and true, and contradictory to one another all at the same time. (We will return to perspectivism in the next chapter.) That is, perspectives, expecially philosophical ones, are a function of power and the will to power. Perspectives necessarily have to do with winners and losers, the politics of establishing "legitimacy." Nietzsche's politics, which we will also consider in the next chapter, requires "a *pathos* of distance," conquest, and of time.

ON DUALISM AND SIMULTANEITY

Nietzsche's own investigations are genealogical, both historical and linguistic, involving both bodies and philology—and suffering, because the link between the body and the ideal is pain. Genealogy seeks the origins of our moral usages in language, and then ties those usages to practices, even and especially instinctual practices. Nietzsche deploys those instinctual practices and the way they are organized or disorganized to try to differentiate "healthy" and "sick" ways of practicing human emotion, drive, need, desire, aggression, and suffering. But I put those qualities in scare quotes because Nietzsche warns interminably against the reification of any configurations of instinct and energy into fixed, antithetical types—his purpose is "to remove antitheses from things after comprehending that we have projected them there."[13] Genealogy means to diagnose "our highest" values as symptoms of underlying disease and health, but there is no fixed or systematic meaning that Nietzsche or anyone else can give to either sickness or health. Despite numerous commentators to the contrary, Nietzsche recognizes, in many texts, not only the necessary interdependence of health and illness, but even the difficulties and complications of telling one from the other. It is worth quoting again this passage from *The Gay Science* in full:

> For there is no health as such, and all attempts to define a thing that way have been wretched failures. Even the determination of what is healthy for your *body* depends on your goal, your horizon, your energies, your impulses your errors, and above all on the ideals

and phantasms of your soul. Thus there are innumerable healths of the body; and the more we allow the unique and incomparable to raise its head again, and the more we abjure the dogma of the "equality of men," the more must the concept of normal health . . . be abandoned. Only then would the time have come to reflect on the health and illness of the soul, and to find the peculiar virtue of each man in the health of his soul. In one person, of course, this health could look like its opposite in another person. Finally, the great question would still remain whether we can really dispense with illness—even for the sake of our virtue—and whether our thirst for knowledge and self-knowledge in particular does not require the sick soul as much as the healthy, and whether, in brief, the will to health alone, is not a prejudice, cowardice, and perhaps a bit of very subtle barbarism and backwardness.[14]

Nietzsche certainly seems to be reaching for a kind of perspectival relativism here: there is no health as such and it is certainly not the same for all people: what is healthy for one may be the opposite in another. Even what is healthy for one person changes from moment to moment and depends on the context, the diagnosis, on the history and the "ideals and phastasms" of his body and soul. That is why it is at bottom political, not metaphysical, reality that determines meaning. Context is produced, and only in context can one evaluate health. For the purposes of self-knowledge, all contexts help. So there are "innumerable" healths of the body, not to mention of the soul, and the concept of "normal" health must be abandoned as a prejudice of democratic thought. Nietzsche certainly argues that the concept of "normal" should be abandoned anyway, as a deceptive cover-up for what is in fact only a prevailing norm. He does not think we can do away with illness or weakness, which are necessary to the process of growth.

Nietzsche argues that health and sickness are part of the same story, even part of the same person and historical epoch. How one comes to evaluate a condition of health or sickness, strength or weakness, depends on many different factors, not least of which is the position of the questioner and the goals being pursued. There is no doubt that Nietzsche sometimes uses the language of sickness and health or strength and weakness roughly, loosely, outrageously, or "experimentally," but when he speaks directly to the issue, he cautions: "health and sickness are not essentially different, as the ancient physicians and some practitioners even today suppose. One must not make of them separate principles or entities that fight over the living organism and turn it into their arena. That is silly nonsense and chatter that is no good any longer. In fact, there are only differences in degree between these two kinds of existence: the exaggeration, the disproportion, the nonharmony of the normal phenomena constitute the pathological state."[15]

For all of Nietzsche's rantings about the healthy, cheerful cruelty of the strong and morbidly sick *ressentiment* of the weak, here as always, Nietzsche does not decisively separate the two or give them opposing ontological statuses. He is always seeking to incorporate both, and especially health and sickness, into some more intelligible, integrated life, for both good and evil, and beyond both.

> *Overall insight.*—Actually, every major growth is accompanied by a tremendous crumbling and passing away: suffering, the symptoms of decline *belong* in the times of tremendous advances; every fruitful and powerful movement of humanity has also created at the same time a nihilistic movement. It could be the sign of a crucial and most essential growth, of the transition to new conditions of existence, that the most extreme form of pessimism, genuine *nihilism*, would come into the world. *This I have comprehended.*[16]

The extremes imply, create, and condition each other. We reopen the question of nihilism when we consider the will to power and the will to nothingness. But consider that this "overall insight" can be applied to individuals, peoples, and psychological seasons as well as to historical periods.

I want to offer a different interpretation than usual in relation to Nietzsche's sometimes extreme or provocative splitting of the world into the dominant and dominated, the active or reactive, healthy or sick, strong or weak, and his obvious preferences for the former. It is easy to posit Nietzsche as a defender of beasts of prey; it is slightly more difficult, but not really hard, to argue, as some have done, that one can ignore his more overt and alarming reactionary political statements and derive a more progressive politics out of his powerful genealogical analysis.[17] But in good Nietzschean fashion, it might be worthwhile to ask what interests are served, whose power is generated by these human-all-too-human interpretations.

Making Nietzsche a good guy is making him tame and like us, the good guys. It produces a comfortable fellow-feeling with him that helps relieve our anxiety and dis-ease with some of his more hateful and cruel pronouncements. Identifying Nietzsche with the builders of the master race, or the insane, serves our pleasure and power even more, either (or both) because it allows us to identify with these powerful predators and/or because it allows us to differentiate ourselves from them and identify with our own superior gentleness and goodness. Nietzsche pinpoints precisely that *ressentiment*, that kind of revenge, in the *Genealogy*. This is not to say that it isn't possible to garner prooftexts all day to prove either one of these readings, and many others. If one wants to win, it is not hard to win with Nietzsche. He lends a hand to every cause sooner or later, especially taken out of context. And it is very difficult to say what constitutes Nietzsche in context. But that very ease of gathering should warn those with "good ears" of the hollowness of such victories when struck with the hammer, or the tuning fork. It is better to dig deeper into the nature and power of this conflict. It is this conflict, inner and outer, that Nietzsche finds interesting.

I want to propose that, while it is undoubtedly true that some people are more "naturally" victimized than others (children?), and others more "naturally" predators (drugdealers?), the conventional meanings of these qualities are not what Nietzsche has in mind, and what is "natural" is for him completely reconfigured. Furthermore, all people, like we, his scholarly-type readers, are like Nietzsche in being by turns varying combinations of both types. This could be seen as a psychoanalytic approach, and Nietzsche was certainly a psychoanalyst *avant la lettre*. We can justly interpret Nietzsche's texts as overdetermined and open to multiple interpretations, which do not cancel each other out but rather deepen each other. It is important to remember that Nietzsche and we ourselves, with our histories, have many times been both lambs and birds of prey, displayed both healthy and sick impulses, lived as both masters and as slaves, at different times and in different contexts. This is helpful because it precludes our immediately identifying finally with either the good guys or the bad guys, and more important, with the moralizing drive that underlies such identifications. It forces us to question what purposes, what needs, these different motivations, dispensations, dispositions, or proclivities serve. In this sense, taking these forces as internal to every agency, subject, or timeframe induces us to differentiate ourselves further, to enlarge our capacities for experience and endurance. It urges us toward the next question, which is how these attributes got separated , externalized and eternalized in things in the world, reified in one way or one place or one people or another. It allows us to see how the constant interaction of these forces fills not only our lives but the world. It complicates things enough to push us beyond dichotomies.

We explore Nietzsche's oppositions and the conjunctions between health and sickness and will to power and will to truth in later chapters, especially in relation to the indispensability of morality and of nihilism, despite or because of their perversion of instinct and culture. We might want to keep in mind, however, that Nietzsche's conception of the strong is the one able to circulate "a tremendous number of different interests in a single soul"—"Who will prove to be the strongest in the course of this? The most moderate; those who do not require any extreme articles of faith; those who not only concede but love a fair amount of accidents and nonsense; those who can think of man with a considerable reduction of his value without becoming small and weak on that account: those richest in health who are equal to most misfortunes and therefore not so afraid of misfortunes—human beings who are sure of their power and represent the attained strength of humanity with conscious pride."[18]

MORALITY AS REVENGE

In the first essay of the *Genealogy*, Nietzsche contrasts the moral valuations of a kind of prototypical noble ruling class, loosely identified with classical Greece and Rome, with the valuations of the lowborn, the oppressed, the slaves, but above all, the priests, closely bound up with Judaism and Christianity.

> The knightly-aristocratic value judgments presupposed a powerful physicality, a flourishing, abundant, even overflowing health, together with that which serves to preserve it: war, adventure, hunting, dancing, war games, and in general all that involves vigorous, free, joyful activity. . . . the priests are the *most evil enemies*—but why? Because they are the most impotent. It is because of their impotence that in them hatred grows to monstrous and uncanny proportions, to the most spiritual and poisonous kind of hatred. . . . the spirit of priestly vengefulness.[19]

Vengeance is the deepest sickness of man Nietzsche knows. Although he vehemently condemns "the slave revolt in morality," he is also explicit about the great value, coming from the power of life itself, of the "highest values," those which emerge out of slave morality: "It is only fair to add that it was on the soil of this *essentially dangerous* form of human existence, the priestly form, that man first became *an interesting* animal, that only here did the human soul in a higher sense acquire depth and become evil."[20]

Nietzsche's great allegory of the difference in moral viewpoints involves, as might be clear by now, little lambs and birds of prey: "That lambs dislike great birds of prey does not seem strange: only it gives no grounds for reproaching these birds of prey for bearing off little lambs. And if the lambs say among themselves: 'These birds of prey are evil; and whoever is least like a bird of prey, but rather its opposite, a lamb—would he not be good?' there is no reason to find fault with this institution of an ideal."[21] Nietzsche's point is that there is no *blame* for the birds of prey, or for the opinion of the lambs either. Things are what they are. It is natural that in their helplessness, lambs should condemn birds of prey. It gives them a feeling of power and revenge. It is when they go on to create a religion of lambs, which compensates for their suffering by consigning the evil "other" to eternal damnation, that things get a little twisted.

Nietzsche's explanation for the origins of slave morality have to do with suffering and power. The suffering of the lambs and their inability to enact their rage directly at their devourers fills them with *ressentiment* and revenge. It is the "impotence grown to monstrous proportions" of the priests that fills the world with vengefulness. Impotence breeds vengeance, and priestly vengeance is the most subtle and potent kind. This is an allegorical oversimplification, of course. Men are not lambs or birds of prey, or rather, they are both lambs and birds of prey, both masters and slaves. Nietzsche is elaborating a complicated hierarchy of forces of action and reaction in this text. Nevertheless, Nietzsche also reveals his affinity not only with the aggressors, but also with the "cleverness" of the slaves and their spite, and his awareness of its value for human history: "Human history would be altogether too stupid a thing without the spirit that the impotent have introduced into it."[22]

Nietzsche cites the "most notable example" of slave morality as the Jews:

> the Jews, that priestly people, who in opposing their enemies and conquerors were ultimately satisfied with nothing less than a radical revaluation of their enemies' values, that is to say, an act of the *most spiritual revenge*. For this alone was appropriate to a priestly people, the people embodying the most deeply repressed (*Zurückgetretensten*) priestly vengefulness. It was the Jews, with awe-inspiring consistency, dared to invert the aristocratic value-equation (good=noble=powerful=beautiful=beloved of God) and to hang on to this inversion with their teeth, the teeth of the most abysmal hatred (the hatred of impotence), saying "the wretched alone are the good; the poor, impotent, lowly alone are the good; the suffering, deprived, sick, ugly alone are pious, alone are blessed by God, blessedness is for them alone— and you, the powerful and noble, are on the contrary the evil, the cruel, the lustful, the insatiable, the godless to all eternity; and you shall be in all eternity the unblessed, accursed, and damned!" One knows *who* inherited this Jewish revaluation.[23]

Out of this protracted process of development, there grew from Jewish hatred "a new love, the profoundest and sublimest kind of love" as the "crown" of this hatred. Can anything equal, he asks, "the enticing, intoxicating, overwhelming, and undermining power of that symbol of the 'holy cross,' that ghastly paradox of a 'God on the cross,' that mystery of an unimaginable ultimate cruelty and self-crucifixion of God *for the salvation of man*?"[24] Christianity is the ultimate flowering of this great tree, watered by revenge, cruelty, and hatred for life itself. Nietzsche's assault on Christianity is tireless and grows only more bitter throughout his life.

Over time morality won a complete victory, Judea triumphed over Rome, the "grand politics" of revenge culminated in the domination of the Christian ideal over all other ideals. Morality begins "when *ressentiment* itself becomes creative and gives birth to values: the *ressentiment* of natures that are denied the true reaction, that of deeds, and compensate themselves with an imaginary revenge."[25] Imaginary revenges create religion, philosophy, and all ideals. It is the creation of values with which Nietzsche is ultimately concerned. He is looking here at the original, archaic creation of values out of the impotence of slaves and priests, but he will be concerned, at the end of this genealogical narrative, with how new values can be created in relation to new responses to suffering.

Morality is originally created out suffering, suffering which is stifled and repressed, and in which the hatred aroused by cruelty suffered is turned backwards, inwards against the self. The process, the turning, itself creates the self. Morality comes from "the very opposite of *happiness* at the level of the impotent, the oppressed. . . . the man of ressentiment is neither upright nor naive nor honest and straightforward *with himself*." He develops a secret, hidden, inner life, where he learns "how to keep silent, how not to forget, how to wait."[26] Values are created out of the need to do something with stifled aggression, suffering and cruelty, where these energies or powers cannot be directly unleashed. Not being released, they circle round and round and create an inside, a space of inwardness and secrecy, the self. Nietzsche implies that personal identity, whatever that might be, is formed by the play of forces, the action and reaction of physiological impulse, instinct, and will aroused and directed inward by suffering and cruelty. In this way he places suffering at the root of the self. The interpretations and evaluations, the ideals and "highest values" that issue from this self, with its derivative productions of metaphysical consciousness, are expressions of suffering in elaborate, disguised forms.

The "blond beasts," outside the circle of their own noble equals, express directly and actively the ferocity of "uncaged beasts of prey . . . of innocent conscience, as triumphant monsters who perhaps emerge from a disgusting procession of murder, arson, rape, and torture, exhilarated and undisturbed of soul."[27] Is Nietzsche saying that these monsters are as free of blame as birds of prey are for killing little lambs? Not exactly. He is arguing, however, that our ready moralizations of these actions are as murderous as the actions they condemn, and that their elaborate disguises as sacred duties and higher truths make them even more dangerous in their killing cruelty and the violence and suffering they embody and generate. As victims, we allow ourselves no limits on what we justify doing to others.

Is it difficult to see that morality, born of *ressentiment* and forged in vengefulness, was nevertheless necessary to life and to the birth of culture? Nietzsche says that these instincts of reaction and revenge are "the actual instruments of culture." Nietzsche nevertheless sees them as a disgrace, an accusation against "the ill-constituted, dwarfed, atrophied and poisoned" people of Europe today. His indictment of morality culminates in a genealogy of modern nihilism: "The sight of man now makes us weary—what is nihilism today if it is not *that*?—We are weary *of man*."[28] Culture that is forged out of inverted instinctual life ends up very depleted, weary and sick.

Nietzsche wants to stress the innocence of natural forces, of action and reaction in the universe, a simple play of strengths and weaknesses—these things just are as they are. This is not the moral innocence of Rousseau's nature. It is the amoral innocence of the sheer itness of the world as it is. "To demand of strength that it should not express itself as strength, that it should not be a desire to overcome . . . is just as absurd as to demand of weakness that it should express itself as strength." Strength and weakness are natural states and they manifest themselves in many ways; they can only be evaluated according to explicitly given contexts and goals. All is naturally *will to power*, as we will examine in detail. There are only forces —"quantums of force equivalent to a quantum of drive, will, effect." What values these forces have, they have been given by us. One of our tasks now is to uncover the motives of the value-givers and to track the origins of values. It is not to read into the multiplicity of forces in action and reaction some inherent value, meaning, or purpose. There is nothing more in the world than "this very driving, willing, effecting," and it is only "the seduction of language (and of the fundamental errors of reason that are petrified in it)" that misconceive actions as the effects of a "subject" who acts or wills or causes things to happen. In one of his most important philosophical innovations, Nietzsche declares that there is no such subject: "So popular morality also separates strength from expressions of strength, as if there were a neutral substratum behind the strong man, which was free to express strength or not to do so. But there is no such substratum; there is no 'being' behind doing, effecting, becoming; 'the doer' is merely a fiction added to the deed—the deed is everything."[29] The doer is merely a fiction; there is only the deed. The subject of action is a popular fantasy and an effect of language; there are only acts.

Still, it is suffering that results from the havoc wreaked by the strong beasts of prey, and suffering that cannot be returned, or expressed, or even understood by those they subjugate, which leads to the deep and dark interiority of the "clever" ones, those who construct languages with subjects and doers, who contrive judgments of the guilty and the innocent, who invent justice and injustice, heaven and hell—who devise eternal bliss and eternal punishment "to console them for the suffering of life."

But if "subjects" are illusions, invented to give "the right to make the bird of prey *accountable* for being a bird of prey," then what meaning are we to give to suffering? Who is it who suffers? Who is it who can be held responsible, not only for suffering, but for actions of any kind? The question of responsibility won't go away, regardless of the innocence of birds of prey. Nietzsche does give us an answer to this question, but we have to go the long way around to get to it.

With the abolition of the "subject," the ego, or the doer behind the deed, Nietzsche moves decisively beyond traditional metaphysics and morality.

Without getting too caught up in the complicated philosophical issues this entails, which I consider briefly in the section on the will to power, it is necessary to emphasize that without a "subject" in the ordinary sense, the question of responsibility, of critical accountability, becomes entirely problematical. For the present, let's approach the question of "who suffers?" from a perspective Nietzsche offers in *The Gay Science*:

> Every art, every philosophy may be viewed as a remedy and an aid in the service of growing life; they always presuppose suffering and sufferers. But there are two kinds of sufferers: first, those who suffer from the *over-fullness of life*—they want a Dionysian art and likewise a tragic view of life, a tragic insight—and then those who suffer from the *impoverishment of life* and seek rest, stillness, calm seas, redemption from themselves through art and knowledge, or intoxication, convulsions, anesthesia, and madness.[30]

Nietzsche himself falls into both of those categories, as perhaps we all do. There are no fixed identities, and no fixed and eternal values in Nietzsche's life or ours, as he teaches. Our strategies to answer the questions "Who suffers?" and "Who is responsible?" require us to take apart the self, the subject, the doer, and all simple or traditional explanations or attributions of responsibility. We can reconstitute something like the strategic equivalents of the self or the subject, and its obligations, from multiple perspectives and contexts, in relation to the problematics of time, through the consideration of the will to power and eternal recurrence. But this is a very long philosophical journey. Nietzsche does not expect that we will be able to do without language and its metaphysical accoutrements, but he does not expect us to continue to be taken in by objectivist claims either. We need still to attend to the way Nietzsche reconstructs the story of the self, how memory and the cruelty that creates it, seasoned over time, succeeded in slowly forming a "sovereign individual," one who can take responsibility, if not for the suffering of others, at least for himself. Nietzsche shows us what unrequited suffering has wrought.

THE *GENEALOGY*:
CRUELTY, PROMISING, AND BAD CONSCIENCE

In the second essay of *On the Genealogy of Morals*, Nietzsche explores the actual processes by means of which moral man was bred. Once again, the forces of cruelty and suffering lie at the crux of the business. Nietzsche defines the original task of man in the opening sentence of the essay: "To breed an animal *with the right to make promises*."[31] The genealogy of the right to make promises devolves upon a struggle between forgetfulness and memory, that is, upon the relationship between consciousness and time. "Forgetfulness is no mere *vis inertiae* . . . it is rather an active and in the strictest sense positive faculty of repression." Health requires a strong capacity to "close the doors and windows of consciousness for a time." An active forgetfulness allows for breathing, for room, for planning, foresight, and premeditation; it preserves order and repose; there could be "no happiness, no cheerfulness, no hope, no pride, no *present*, without forgetfulness."[32]

Nietzsche implies that unless consciousness actively represses memory, the past would be utterly overwhelming. Consciousness creates the present; it opens a space for thought and response. The present is the space created by forgetting so that an ethical response is possible. Still, however much the healthy animal needs forgetfulness, it is also the case that "an opposing faculty, memory" is required, "namely in those cases where promises are made." Nietzsche stresses that promising requires an active desire, "a real *memory of the will*: so that between the original 'I will,' 'I shall do this,' and the actual discharge of the will, its act, a world of strange new things, circumstances, even acts of will may be interposed without breaking this long chain of will."[33] A whole interior world, a world of memory and intention and identity and purpose is necessary to this kind of willing. The capacity for this kind of willing, "to ordain the future in advance," requires that a world of personal and historical development comes into being: "man must first have learned to distinguish necessary events from chance ones, to think causally, to see and anticipate distant eventualities as if they belonged to the present, and to decide with certainty what is the goal and what the means to it, and in general be able to calculate and compute. Man himself must first of all have become calculable, regular, necessary, even in his own image of himself, if he is to be able to stand security for his own future, which is what one who promises does."[34]

How is this dependability to be achieved? Nietzsche says that it takes pain to create a memory for the human animal. "If something is to stay in the memory it must be burned in: only that which never ceases to *hurt* stays in the memory." It is the pain and terror that accompanied promises, pledges, and vows that created the human past, "the longest, deepest and sternest past." In the history of the individual soul and in the history of the species, of a people or a community and culture, pain and the deliberate infliction of pain establish and constitute the past, the past that cannot be forgotten, the past that lives in the moral inscriptions and codes, the rules, precepts, and laws, the identities and contracts which are necessary for the institutions of personhood, politics, and culture. Pain is required "to impose a few primitive demands of social existence as present realities upon these slaves of momentary affect and desire."[35] Men as natural animals are the slaves of instinct. "Man could never do without blood, torture, and sacrifices when he felt the need to create a memory for himself; the most dreadful sacrifices . . . the most repulsive mutilations . . . the cruelest rites of all the religious cults—all this has its origin in the instinct that realized that pain is the most powerful aid to mnemonics."[36]

When Nietzsche speaks in Zarathustra about human hatred of the past, of the great "It was" that cannot be changed and cannot be willed, it is necessary to remember that the past as he conceives it is a past of pain, terror, and suffering. It is not only that what has already happened cannot be changed; the will is impotent to alter in any way what has already taken place. It is also that the past, what has already taken place, and the memories it generates or of which it is composed, is constituted by suffering. We remember trauma. We are made as selves out of trauma. Nietzsche is saying that memory itself, in the individual consciousnessness and in the dogmas and practices of the cult, is created by trauma. The self is made from its memories, and its memories bring the pain and its myriad consequences that it cannot escape or deny. The institutions of justice, of religion, of sacred gods and rituals all stem from the installation of memory, of habit, routine, regularity, calculability, of promising, by means of pain, inflicted, repeated, and embedded in the collective bones of human memory. "The whole of asceticism belongs here," he says.[37]

Nietzsche locates pain, cruelty, and suffering at the core of the creation of promising, conscience, the free individual, and the creation of values. The ethical space of responsibility is created by pain. It may be signified by language, but it is created by flesh too, burned into the memory of the body. He likens the relationship between guilt and punishment to the compensations of debtor to creditor, to the idea of an equivalence between injury and debt. Even the categorical imperative "smells of cruelty. . . . It was here that that uncanny intertwining of the ideas 'guilt and suffering' was first effected—and by now they may be inseparable. To ask it again: to what extent can suffering balance debts or guilt?"[38] Or we can ask it another way—To what extent can guilt, debt, and punishment balance suffering? The equation between them, suffering and guilt, is what Nietzsche uncovers as the always original site of memory, religion, and philosophy.

This is also the nexus of guilt and suffering that I have been examining through the words of Luther, Hobbes, and Rousseau, as reconstructed in the images of the state of nature and the social contract in the politics and political theory of the modern age. The unbreakable interconnection between guilt and suffering infuses the religious interpretation of suffering as it was felt in Luther's afflicted soul, judged by a remote and unfathomable God, abandoned to temporal authorities to whom the soul is enjoined simply to submit. Hobbes recasts suffering and the conditions of its propagation in nature; he analyzes the power needed to erect an authority by forced submission to a social contract that can contain the fear and chaos of men in nature. The causes of suffering and the power to remedy it can be found by means of a new science of knowledge. Creating the great metaphors of the state of nature and the social contract, Hobbes embodies the nature of pain in time in an originary condition and in a diachronic movement toward the willed submission to necessity in an original social contract upon which political society and the meaning of justice can be founded.

For Rousseau, guilt and suffering arise with social humanity. Out of an almost inconceivable condition of natural isolation and innocence, individuals gradually gather; thus human sociality gives rise to human development, and human historicity, if not history proper, emerges. Out of history, inequality, egotism, vanity, and anguished self-consciousness rise the permanent institutions of injustice, domination, and servitude. Here history itself is the cause of suffering, and Rousseau's social contract, an ideal atemporal perpetual moment of perfect unity and tyranny, seeks an end to injustice and suffering once and for all and for all time by seeking to put an end to time, to temporality itself. History can be overcome by the creation of a perfect kingdom of the just.

Nietzsche explicitly identifies both the Reformation and the French Revolution as particular moments of the triumph of the modern ascetic ideal over the newly revivified classicism of the Renaissance in the modern age.[39] Nietzsche also analyzes modern science and the will to knowledge, as represented in the early modern age by Hobbes, as an even more complicated, "reified" manifestation of the ascetic ideal than religious or social morality. The genealogy Nietzsche is tracing between suffering, guilt, and normative morality, and between suffering, knowledge, and metaphysics, are connected because they involve "the spiritualization and deification of cruelty which permeates the entire history of higher culture (and in a significant sense actually consitutes it.)"[40] Suffering is the source of both signification and valuation.

Nietzsche cautions us against believing that our intuitive modern understanding of suffering is the only possible one. "Today, when suffering is always brought forward as the principal argument *against* existence . . . one does well to recall the ages in which the opposite opinion prevailed because men were unwilling to refrain from making suffer and saw in it an enchantment of the first order, a genuine seduction to life." He even asserts, perhaps ironically, that "pain did not hurt as much as it does now," and uses the example of Negroes' insensitivity to pain for proof.

His most important point is that "What really arouses indignation against suffering is not suffering as such but the senselessness of suffering." So the Christian "who has interpreted a whole mysterious machinery of salvation into suffering," and the ancient who interpreted suffering according to ancient gods did not suffer as we do, who have no longer any God or cosmos by which to absorb and define our suffering.[41] Like Marx, Nietzsche insists that we are now brought face to face with human suffering, purely, without social defense mechanisms to deny it.[42] Part of Nietzsche's case for the nihilism of the present age is its inability any longer to believe in *any* explanations for the justification of suffering. We can no longer be sure that any suffering, guilty or innocent, can be justified. We cannot think how to justify suffering, except for the most restricted areas of moral utilitarianism. Nietzsche implies that we suffer more because of the loss of our consoling frauds. Is nihilism worse for present sufferers than the fear of eternal damnation for one's irremediable sin was for traditional Christian believers?

Two points must be made here. First, suffering became and remains "the principal argument *against* existence" in our history. Perhaps Nietzsche's most central tragic insight is the way suffering stands for and has been used as the reason for negating, denying, and hating the human world and life as we experience it. Suffering is the argument we have made against life, and the reason we have invented other, "true worlds" beyond this one to make it up to us. Second, what most torments us about suffering is not so much pain itself as its meaninglessness. If we cannot make sense of our suffering, then we have to invent reasons for it, even if those reasons are false and even if they manifestly increase our suffering. We would rather have greater but purposeful suffering than less suffering that makes no sense. One way that Nietzsche puts this: "Man would rather "will nothingness than not *will*."[43]

In the *Genealogy*, Nietzsche implies that the point of the whole long story about how responsibility originated is "the breeding of an animal with the right to make promises"; that is, the point of the whole torturous exercise is the creation of the "sovereign individual," one who can "stand security for the future" (*für sich als Zukunft gut sagen zu kömmem*): "the ripest fruit is the sovereign individual, like only to himself, liberated again from morality of custom, autonomous and supramoral (for 'autonomous' and 'moral' are mutually exclusive), in short, the man who has his own independent will and *the right to make promises*— . . . a consciousness of his own power and freedom, a sensation of mankind come to completion."[44] Randall Havas, in his excellent book, *Nietzsche's Genealogy*, suggests that this means that "only someone who has the right sort of memory has a future." He translates "*für sich als Zukunft gut sagen zu können*" more literally than Kaufmann, as "to be accountable 'as future,'" which is as much to say that the one who has the right to make promises "is a future."[45] The right to make promises constitutes the future in advance, as it were, and this is the essence of taking responsibility for it, according to Nietzsche. If one can make and keep a promise, one is the future, is taking responsibility for it, not as morally accountable, but as creating the values and choices that will have life in the future.

For Nietzsche, the capacity to take responsibility for oneself, to give one's word and to keep it, even "in the face of fate," is ultimately *the opposite* of the moral and moralizing individual. The highest quality of man involves the "proud awareness of the extraordinary privilege of *responsibility*, the consciousness of this rare freedom, this power over oneself and over fate, has in

his case penetrated to the profoundest depths and become instinct, the dominating instinct."[46] When responsibility becomes instinct, it ceases to be morality
altogether, and as a second nature can create new values. But the ability to
become this highest type of human only results from the long and cruel
apprenticeship in the crucible of customary morality, in the "blood, torture,
and sacrifices" needed to breed a man with memory and calculability, one
with the right to make promises. This is not, *per contra*, a "natural" right. It is
an historical achievement. The "right to make promises" implies the capacity
to keep them, to be them. It implies a self of the highest, noblest kind.

Man first "measured himself" against another in "determining values,
contriving equivalences, exchanging . . . comparing, measuring and calculating
power against power."[47] It was in this weighing and measuring, valuing and
compelling that Nietzsche says the origins not only of justice but even of
thinking itself are to be found: "in a certain sense they constitute thinking *as
such.*" Thinking, according to Nietzsche, derives from assignments of terms
of identity, equivalence, or equilibrium, and the conceptual systems of metaphysics and science that thought produces likewise proceed from attributions
of sameness. In fact, Nietzsche argues, there exists no sameness and no identity, no equivalence or equilibrium in a world of constant flux and becoming,
the measuring of power against power. But human logic and justice assign
equivalences anyway, and thus establish order, even if it is, in essence, an
illusion.[48]

Nietzsche sees justice as an attribute of strength. This means not only that
lawgivers operate from a position of power, but also, he implies, that societies
become more just insofar as they are able more easily to overlook or dismiss
transgressions. Justice is a function of generosity, not retribution. "The 'creditor' always becomes more humane to the extent that he has grown richer;
finally, how much injury he can endure without suffering from it becomes the
actual *measure* of his wealth. It is not unthinkable that a society might attain
such a *consciousness of power* that it could allow itself the noblest luxury
possible to it—letting those who harm it go *unpunished.*"[49]

Nietzsche wants particularly to repudiate the notion that justice derives
from revenge. He sees justice on the contrary in strength, clarity, and objectivity. He also doesn't expect to see it on earth any time soon. "Being just is
always a *positive* attitude, when the exalted, clear objectivity, as penetrating
as it is mild, of the eye of justice and *judging* is not dimmed even under the
assault of personal injury, derision, and calumny, this is a piece of perfection
and supreme mastery on earth—something it would be prudent not to expect
or to *believe* in too readily."[50]

Justice always works to put an end to the "senseless raging of *ressentiment*" and to move the law beyond revenge. The powerful institute of the
law declares what is to count as just and unjust. "'Just' and 'unjust' exist,

accordingly, only after the institution of the law. . . . To speak of just or unjust *in itself* is quite senseless; *in itself*, of course, no injury, assault, exploitation, destruction can be 'unjust,' since life operates *essentially*, that is in its basic functions, through injury, assault, exploitation, destruction and simply cannot be thought of at all without this character."[51] Nietzsche is not saying that this is all that life is; it is also joy and the dance. But life cannot function without destruction, without death. This seems obvious to him.

Nietzsche agrees with Hobbes that the meaning of these terms only exists through the institution of law by the powerful. He argues further, *contra* Rousseau, "that every will must consider every other will its equal—would be a principle *hostile to life*, an agent of the dissolution and destruction of man, an attempt to assassinate the future of man, a sign of weariness, a secret path to nothingness."[52] All wills are not equal—to assert that they must be made to be so is death to difference and to quality. This is not only a decisive argument for the conventionality of justice, and for the willful delusion involved in counting things, or people, as "equal" or "the same." More important, it provides a decisive uncovering of the vengeful and tyrannizing effects of a conception of equalizing justice such as Rousseau's general will, from the point of view of the value of life itself, according to Nietzsche.

Nietzsche's politics is indeed the politics of the will to power. He is arguing that any conception of politics or of justice that does not include power, which necessarily includes domination and destruction as well as the imposition of order and the establishment of agency, is nonsense. It is attempting to consider the day without the night; the heights without the depths. There is no justice outside of time, none based on a perfect sameness. Only a politics that takes full account of the nature of life, *essentially*, is worth articulating. A fuller understanding of Nietzsche's politics is the goal of the next chapter, and we have farther to go to reach such an understanding. But it is well to note here the powerful nature of Nietzsche's critique of the deceptive, distorted origins and destructive aspects of the value of revolutionary social equality. This is not a conclusion that comes easily to social democrats of the twentieth century, but it is one which the circumstances of twentieth-century fascism and colonialism have made newly compelling. Nietzsche is arguing that this forced equalization of wills and effects is nihilism itself.

Nietzsche condemns not only the nihilism of popular equality and the democratizing impulse (of which statistical thinking itself may be the most drastic form), which destroy the value of difference, but even more important, the senselessness of any evolutionary or revolutionary idea of history, such that history is a "*progressus* toward a goal, even less a logical *progressus* by the shortest route and with the smallest expenditure of force."[53] There are several important points of this analysis. First, there is only the will to power operating in history. Second, the will to power operates in history by *becoming master*, imposing a new interpretation on an old one, such that "meaning" and "purpose" are fluid, "taken over, transformed, redirected . . . obscured or even obliterated" over and over again. And finally, history is not definable, and therefore, concepts that have a history are not definable. Nietzsche says: "all concepts in which an entire process is semiotically concentrated elude definition; only that which has no history is definable."[54] Are there concepts that have no history?

This is the essential philosophical insight of Nietzsche's genealogy, what makes it radically different from all previous philosophies, which posit their terms by definition, ahistorically, once and for all. As Deleuze would put it: "concepts are dated, signed and baptized, they have their own way of not dying, while remaining subject to constraints of renewal, replacement and mutation."[55] Nietzsche "deconstructs" philosophy by insisting on the historical constructedness of philosophical concepts, and by presenting us a history of crucial terms. He insists on the vicissitudes of the will to power in conceptual history, power that constructs, interprets, evaluates, and names states and events, structures and functions in a perpetual political struggle to determine what is to count as an equivalence, or even as a just equivalence.

Nietzsche calls morality the unwillingness to acknowledge history, because the essence of morality is its willingness to legislate totally, forever, for everyone, once and for all. The only way to preserve the absoluteness of moral (and philosophical) judgments is to deny their historicity, their conditionality, their conditioning and subjectivity, that is, their history.

Finally, in the second essay, Nietzsche gives us a more intimate phenomenology and genealogy of suffering as it effects the formation of the individual, and this enables us to ask again about the two different ways to experience suffering as the foundation for Nietzsche's critique of morality. Nietzsche calls the originary experience of suffering "bad conscience," and thinks of it as "the serious illness that man was bound to contract under the stress of the most fundamental change he ever experienced—that change which occurred when he found himself finally enclosed within the walls of society and peace."[56]

Like sea animals forced to become land animals, "suddenly all their instincts were devalued and 'suspended.' . . . A great misery descended on them, a dreadful heaviness." From depending on their "unconscious and infallible drives," they were reduced to "thinking, inferring, reckoning, co-ordinating cause and effect . . . they were reduced to their 'consciousness,' their weakest and most fallible organ!"[57]

But "all instincts that do not discharge themselves outwardly *turn inward* . . . what I call *internalization* of man: thus it was that man first developed what was later called his 'soul.' The entire inner world . . . acquired depth, breadth and height, in the same measure as outward discharge was *inhibited*."

Thus began "the gravest and uncanniest illness, from which humanity has not yet recovered, man's suffering of man, of himself."[58] Is it subjectivity itself that man suffers as his "gravest and uncanniest illness"?

This analysis certainly implies that all selves, sooner or later, undergo this kind of internalization, this change into an inner space of consciousness and reason. Freud, of course, will articulate some of the paths and detours of the process. Nietzsche calls this inferiority an illness that "man was bound to contract." This "animal soul turned against itself" was a new and profound innovation on earth, one that was *"pregnant with the future,"* which gives rise to "a tension, a hope . . . a bridge, a great promise." Clearly this creature, whose natural instincts of hostility and cruelty were turned back against himself to form conscience, is both the origin of the most deadly and poisonous ones, the ascetic priests, and of those in whom Nietzsche's hope for the future lies, those whose *"instinct* for *freedom"* will eventually emerge out of the bonds and despair of nihilism, who will "stand security" for the future.

This is important because it suggests what we will explore in more detail in future chapters, that the one who can make promises, who can take responsibility and therefore is a future, is one who takes responsibility for the past, and especially for the suffering of the past: "anyone who manages to experience the history of humanity as a whole as his own history will feel in an enormously generalized way all the grief of an invalid who thinks of health, of an old man who thinks of the dreams of his youth, of a lover deprived of his beloved, of the martyr whose ideal is perishing, of the hero on the evening after a battle that has decided nothing but brought him wounds and the loss of his friend."[59] It is suffering that afflicts the wounded soul; what one does with that suffering determines whether one is caught in the webs of the ascetic ideal, deformed and hollowed out, the "last man," or whether one can go on to take some kind of responsibility, a kind not yet determined, for mankind's history and especially its suffering.

THE *GENEALOGY:*
THE MORALITY OF PITY AND THE ASCETIC IDEAL

The entire third essay of the *Genealogy* is a profound meditation and deeply felt analysis of the question of suffering in history and the various remedies that have been invented in our civilization to cope with it. Such remedies fall under the general rubric of "the ascetic ideal," including the most important dimensions and manifestations of this ideal, especially religion (Christianity), philosophy, morality, modern politics, and modern science, and those who perform in their services.

Nietzsche's understanding of the world as *will to power* enables him to unify all of these wide-ranging disciplines under one heading, *the ascetic ideal,* and to show that morality is the essential motivation for all of them. Modern science requires special discussion, because science inherits the ideal of truth, the will to knowledge, which it seems to set against faith and superstition. In fact Nietzsche argues that the will to truth in science is the most refined version of the ascetic ideal, and that in the modern age, it carries us to the brink of nihilism and over into the abyss.

It is not necessary to give as close a reading of the third essay of the *Genealogy* as I have done with the previous two essays. The above has given us more than enough to work with for understanding the ways in which Nietzsche sees suffering and pain interact with power and cruelty in order to produce thought itself, and memory, bad conscience, the interior self, faith, heaven, and eventually religion, philosophy, metaphysics, and morality, including modern science and politics.

One issue does need to be more particularly resolved: the morality of pity. Nietzsche warns us against pity.[60] On the face of it, it seems a strange warning. Pity seems no bad thing. Surely the cruelty of which Nietzsche speaks so powerfully in the second essay would be better warned against. But Nietzsche uses pity to symbolize the very essence of morality, and as the quintessence of what the man of the future, like Zarathustra, must guard against. Pity is Zarathustra's "last sin." Why?

Nietzsche's point is a warning against the cruelty and self-reflection of pity. He condemns not only organized religion and the morality of pity, garnering suffering for some ultimate gain, as capital in heaven or as payback in "eternal damnation," spitefully and vengefully finding power and satisfaction in the suffering and guilt of others. Nietzsche also wants to genealogize the everyday variety of pity as a form of superiority and contempt. We might understand this more intuitively if we think of self-pity. Pity offends us when we see it turned inward, in ourselves or others; we comprehend it thus as self-hatred, as unhealthy and corrupting, as digging us deeper into our own pit, or preventing us from seeing past our own pain. Self-pity destroys something valuable in us, some form of self-respect.

Nietzsche wants to say that not only our own self-pity, our victimization, but that of anyone or any group should be seen for the ruse of power that it is. Victimization is a profession today in specular culture, and the cultivation of pity and self-pity feeds that profession. Suffering is not an identity, and treating it as one destroys the integrity of the experience of suffering and of the person who suffers. In this sense, Nietzsche contends, pity mocks and exploits suffering and sets the pitier on high in superior condescension. Is there no natural or genuine pity then? Is Rousseau entirely wrong; have we no natural and spontaneous pity for the hurt or pain of another being?

One reading of Nietzsche's intention is that he means for us to cultivate the strength to throw off our suffering, not to hold on to it as debt or as capital, nor to hold anyone else's suffering to them as a part of their debt or their capital. Suffering is natural to life, and comes to us all in ways that cannot always be seen or measured. There is presumption in claiming knowledge of another's suffering, or ranking it. But aren't these precious niceties, one might ask, when pity can move the strong to help the weak, or to give aid to those in pain? Nietzsche is notorious for arguing that, on the contrary, the weak are a danger to the strong, especially in the modern age, when no genuine culture obtains and what operates is the herd, massed under the auspices of nihilistic religions and political regimes, propagating weakness as goodness and claiming power under the guise of pity and love for the helpless. The leveling impulses of the masses endanger the creative powers of genius and singularity. He means to expose the fraud in that.

Nietzsche's deeper answer to suffering comes later. But I want to use his interrogation of pity to underline his notion of the profound inappropriateness, indeed even the obscenity, of pity for the victims of the vast cataclysms of history, especially the nightmares of the twentieth century. The mass annihilations of peoples, the advent of the abyss, the nihil, the nothing, into time, these are the ruptures in the fabric of life that Nietzsche's doctrines are above all designed to address. Whether he is successful in doing so, we will have to estimate as we penetrate to his "weightiest thought."

But as for misfortune and injury, Nietzsche declares that it is strength that can respond genuinely, actively, moderately to misfortune, in oneself and others—"those richest in health who are equal to most misfortunes and therefore not so afraid of misfortunes." Out of strength, overflowing healthfulness, and well-being that is able to ignore injuries and ignominies, the man of the future can respond to misfortune as fate and fatality, as a lucklessness that needs no pity, even if it requires help or aid. Pity is no necessary addition to the giving and forgiving that comes from strength of will, clarity, and justice. Whatever can be given should be given; whatever is given should be free. Pity costs, it exacts a charge against the sufferer, for the pleasure of the pitier. It is in this sense that it is always a cruelty and a revenge. We might give from sympathy, or generosity, or even some Buddhist-like form of compassion. This sort of compassion takes no such hold on anyone, does not grasp, does not define guilt or shame, and exacts no tribute.

Nietzsche argues that the core of morality is a "deadly hatred of suffering generally," and those who pity "want, if possible . . . to *abolish suffering.*"[61] This seems well enough. Who would not want to abolish suffering? But it is not so simple as that, as Nietzsche shows.

Randall Havas presents a careful analysis of the drawbacks of "an ethics whose only permitted motivation . . . was a desire to avoid suffering," and develops some obvious examples of the kinds of suffering that are valuable, which the one who pities all suffering, whom Nietzsche calls nihilist, would prevent. Havas speaks of an athlete who requires suffering as self-discipline for her training, or of someone who is seeking "self-enhancement," a development of her talent, or a new accomplishment, and even of someone undergoing psychoanalytic therapy, who must suffer to give up destructive images or behaviors. From the point of view of the morality of pity, anything that requires such suffering would be discouraged. Havas argues, moreover, that "the person inclined to pity is, according to Nietzsche, unable to let someone suffer. Letting someone suffer is Nietzsche's metaphor for a certain form of *reading*." It accords with a capacity for listening and with the ability to take responsibility for what we say.[62]

This analysis is correct as far as it goes, although I think the notion of "reading Nietzsche" as the key to our making ourselves intelligible and responsible is a bit overextended. The big problem with Havas's argument, and with all arguments that oversimplify the valuation or affirmation of suffering, is not taking seriously Nietzsche's claim that it is not suffering itself, but the *meaninglessness* of suffering that causes our greatest troubles with it. Any suffering like the suffering of surgery, or athletic training, or psychological therapy is entirely intelligible and purposeful, and therefore it is not harmful in the way Nietzsche wants to warn us against, as causing *ressentiment*, revenge, hatred of ourselves and of life itself.

When Nietzsche stresses the problem of the meaning of suffering, he points especially to its incomprehensibility. This passage from *The Gay Science* is worth quoting at length:

> Our personal and profoundest suffering is incomprehensible and inaccessible to almost everyone. . . . But whenever people notice that we suffer, they interpret our suffering superficially. . . . When people try to benefit someone in distress, the intellectual frivolity with which those moved by pity assume the role of fate is for the most part outrageous: one simply knows nothing of the whole inner sequence and intricacies that are distress for *me* or for *you*. The whole economy of my soul and the balance effected by "distress," the way new springs and needs break open, the way in which old wounds are healing, the way whole periods of the past are shed—all such things that may be involved in distress are of no concern to our dear pitying friends; they wish to *help* and have no thought of the personal necessity of distress, although terrors, deprivations, impoverishments, midnight's adventures, risks and blunders are as necessary for me and for you as are their opposites. It never occurs to them that, to put it mystically, the path to one's own heaven always leads through the voluptuousness of one's own hell.[63]

It is not only that one's suffering is always personal and part of an intricate and convoluted history in which it figures for growth and change; it is not only that what counts as suffering for my life may not be the same as for yours, and that it cannot be known, or assumed to be known, in others. It is that the function of suffering in life is deeply mysterious and necessary in ways that we cannot understand. Mystically, the spirit needs to find its own upward and downward path.

When Nietzsche speaks in the previous section of *The Gay Science*, already quoted, of "all the grief of an invalid who thinks of health, the old man who thinks of the dreams of his youth, a lover deprived of his beloved, the martyr whose ideal is perishing, of the hero on the evening after a battle that has decided nothing but brought him wounds and the loss of his friend," he is not thinking of functional suffering that serves a clear and present purpose. He is thinking of the suffering of failed dreams and lost love, of injury, anguish and death. When Nietzsche asks us to affirm suffering, he is asking us to affirm suffering that we cannot understand or account for, suffering that has no obvious use or purpose, suffering that is unfathomable, meaningless, and yet truer and deeper than any other experience.

Furthermore, the question of the morality of pity and the affirmation of suffering must not trivialize the great sufferings of history. We will only get to this level of depth in interpreting Nietzsche's affirmation of suffering from the perspective of his doctrine of eternal return, in the final chapters of this book. But let us be clear now about the problem of the morality of pity and the affirmation of suffering. It must answer the challenge of suffering as we actually know it today.

Bernd Magnus puts it this way: "Who could live, as some of us have had to do, in the midst of extermination camps and love that unconditionally? And who among us would not will the recurrence of our lives minus the deaths of tens of thousands of innocent children who died and are still dying brutal deaths in Iraq, Kuwait, El Salvador, and elsewhere throughout the Third World—and not only there? Who among us, in brief, would not prefer some other possible life and world, no matter how content one may be with one's present lot? How can eternal recurrence be willed after Dachau, Auschwitz, and Katyn Woods?"[64] Is there no pity due to all those senselessly and brutally silenced dead? Is it possible to affirm suffering of such magnitude and inconceivability?

In the third essay of the *Genealogy*, Nietzsche refines his simple question posed at the beginning of the book about the value of "unegoistic" values into a more pressing philosophical question: "What is the meaning of ascetic ideals?" He answers this question in several crucial ways. First, the meaning of the ascetic ideal is that it gives a meaning to suffering. Nietzsche articulates throughout this essay and emphatically reiterates at its end that man's problem was not merely his suffering, but his question *"why* do I suffer? . . . The meaninglessness of suffering, *not* suffering itself, was the curse that lay over mankind so far—*and the ascetic ideal offered man meaning.*"[65] Nietzsche shows how this meaning was accomplished by religion, philosophy, and science, and how the meanings offered deepened and worsened suffering, finally to the point of cataclysm.

Second, Nietzsche argues that the ascetic ideal protected the weak, the sick, the dispossessed, and he rails against them in the name of the strong and healthy, even as he himself must be considered among them. We need to come to terms with this paradox. Nietzsche himself must come to terms with this paradox, and he tries to do so by determining what purpose in life is served by the ascetic ideal. He digs even deeper for a third answer to the question of the meaning of the ascetic ideal, as an instinct, as will to power, as life itself wrestling with death and with the will to nothingness. I will look briefly at these answers.

Nietzsche considers the way the ascetic ideal manifests itself in artists, in philosophers, and especially in priests in this third essay. He also considers modern scientists, who seem to be the modern opponents of this asceticism, especially in its religious and moralistic versions, but turn out to embody its "last and noblest form." He dismisses artists as meaning "*nothing whatever*" to the ascetic ideal, with the ironic aside that artists are never independent and are always props, "valets" for other forces. In fact, Nietzsche thinks that artists are the only true opponents of the ascetic ideal, but he develops that opposition elsewhere.

A more serious question concerns the relation of philosophers to the ascetic ideal. Nietzsche understands philosophers to be intimately related to the ascetic ideal, but it is a kind of spiritual affinity, and just as he can imagine a "musical Socrates," Nietzsche can imagine a philosophy set free from the metaphysical impediments of traditional philosophy. He sees the ascetic motivation in philosophy residing in its fastidiousness, its "rancor against sensuality," its natural propensity for "poverty, humility, and chastity," as a kind of philosophical personality trait.

More important, Nietzsche sees in Kantian metaphysics, the prototypical, even archetypal philosophy, with its unworldly predicates of "impersonality" and "universality" and especially "disinterestedness" applied to beauty, truth, virtue, and knowledge, the motivated articulation of seeking surcease from pain: "he [Kant] wants to gain a release from torture."[66] Philosophy, as it began with Socrates' overestimation of reason and as it continued under the veil of Christianity, was a way to supply a meaning to the painful imperfections of this world by positing another world, a "true world," governed by ideal forms, absolute Truth, perfect Goodness, and eternal Beauty. Reason was to provide a governing universal moral purpose and agenda for history. Philosophers emerged in history under cover of darkness, wearing "the mask" of the "*previously established types*," namely, ascetic priests.

When the ascetic ideal seeks to philosophize, not only does it downgrade life's "physicality, pain, and multiplicity," in the light of "pure reason" and "knowledge in itself," it does so by "thinking of an eye that is completely unthinkable, an eye turned in no particular direction." In contrast, Nietzsche articulates one of his most important and contested doctrines, perspectivism: "There is only a perspective seeing, only a perspective 'knowing'; and the more affects we allow to speak about one thing, the more eyes, different eyes, we can use to observe one thing, the more complete will our 'concept' of this thing, our 'objectivity' be."[67]

Still, Nietzsche's essential question has to do with what purpose could be served by the ascetic ideal as an instinct and will for life: "life wrestles in it and through it with death and *against* death; the ascetic ideal is an artifice for the *preservation* of life." The ascetic ideal is a kind of death but it serves the purposes of preserving life against death. For whom? For the "herd," the "ill-constituted, disgruntled, underprivileged, unfortunate, and all who suffer of themselves," for whom the ascetic priest is their shepherd. The ascetic priest is the "predestined savior, shepherd, and advocate of the sick herd," their doctor. "Dominion over the suffering is his kingdom . . . his distinctive art, his mastery, his kind of happiness."[68]

It is the ascetic priest who is the "most repulsive and gloomy caterpiller form" out of which all other versions of the ascetic ideal grew, and it is here that Nietzsche seeks to come to grips with the real problem. The priest's "right to exist" stands or falls with the ascetic ideal. At issue is the "*valuation* the ascetic priest places on our life": he juxtaposes this world of becoming and transcience with another world, a mode of existence that will put this one right. What is wrong with this world? It is wretched.

In the third essay, Nietsche violently attacks the sick:

> The sick represent the greatest danger for the healthy; it is *not* the strongest but the weakest who spell disaster for the strong. . . . The *sick* are man's greatest danger; *not* the evil, *not* the "beasts of prey." Those who are failures from the start, downtrodden, crushed—it is they, the weakest, who must undermine life among men, who call into question and poison most dangerously our trust in life, in man, and in ourselves.[69]

Why? What is at stake in this anguished hatred of sickness and misery? What kind of sickness is this? The sickness of victims and their eternal self-pity? One answer, perhaps the most significant, is what Nietzsche calls the "most calamitous effect" of the taming and diminishing of man that he associates with modern culture, namely, that the nausea and the pity aroused by the sight of the suffering, by the bitter, poisonous "failures"among men, will unite and "inevitably beget one of the uncanniest monsters: the 'last will' of man, his will to nothingness, nihilism."[70]

What does "underprivileged" mean? Above all, physiologically—no longer politically. The unhealthiest kind of man in Europe (in all classes) furnishes the soil for this nihilism: they will experience the

belief in the eternal recurrence as a curse, struck by which one no
longer shrinks from any action; not to be extinguished passively but
to extinguish everything that is so aimless and meaningless, although
this is a mere convulsion, a blind rage at the insight that everything
has been for eternities—even this moment of nihilism and lust for
destruction.[71]

If life is a curse, one no longer shrinks from any action; one lusts for destruction. The underprivileged are not the politically downtrodden, but the most
spiritually debilitated. In all classes, those who care for nothing and nourish endless rage and futility—they are the breeders of nihilism, for whom no limits exist.

So Nietzsche's rage against the weak comes from his fear of the effects of
this weakness in the context of the age of the destruction of all values. There
is no doubt great rancor in some of Nietzsche's denunciations of the downtrodden, although he does not speak here of political but of spiritual decadence.
Still, this is Nietzsche and he always doubles back on himself. He insists that
there are no eternal or fixed identities in life, no health in itself, no strength in
itself, but only the mutual interchanges of identity and indebtedness of strong
and weak, master and slave, healthy and sick. We alternate captivities, and none
lasts forever. He is judging sickness and health from a particular perspective,
that of nihilism, and from a particular question, the question of the response to
suffering. Suffering deepens the self, he says, and it is that depth that he sought
at any cost.

Nietzsche suffered from illness and failure all his life. He was not a
stranger to what he attacked, and it is inconceivable that he could have
mounted such an attack had he not known intimately and dreadfully what
he warned against and feared. Nietzsche lived in pain; he endured intolerable
suffering in his life; and god knows his revenge against the religion of his
fathers was murderous. He aspired to strength, to health, even as he knew
his own sickness to be both productive and creative, and inextricably linked
to his "convalescences."

In the end, he did not succumb to his suicidal rage and despair, he endured
and posthumously prevailed; he became the most important philosopher of our
time. But he recognized in himself his own inmost demon, the cry of suffering
and the demand for its meaning and assuagement. He was intimately familiar
with all the ruses of power invented to console and to justify suffering. He despised the weakness that needed those consolations, and the strategies of ascetic
priests to console and preserve the weak and to justify their suffering, instead of
overcoming it. He recognized this need and this motivation as the danger, the
source of the catastrophe coming in Europe. He foresaw the horrors of the
coming century, and he named the force at work—the will to nothingness,
nihilism.

It is suffering that constitutes the crux of the problem, for the individual and for the culture, and has done so throughout our history. Civilization was built on cruelty and suffering and on the attempt to establish limits for it. It is suffering and the tortured justifications of the ascetic ideal, first devised to comfort the sufferers and finally in our time having exposed the fraudulence of that comfort and that justification, which led him to see and fear the abyss of nothingness opened up by the will to truth.

In the *Genealogy*, Nietzsche analyzes the many means used by the ascetic priest to *"alter the direction of ressentiment."*

> For every sufferer instinctively seeks a cause for his suffering; more exactly, an agent; still more specifically, a guilty agent who is suscep-tible to suffering—in short, some living thing upon which he can, on some pretext or other, vent his affects, actually or in effigy: for the venting of his affects respresents the greatest attempt on the part of the suffering to win relief, *anaesthesia*. . . . This alone . . . consti-tutes the actual physiological cause of ressentiment, vengefulness, and the like: a desire to *deaden pain by means of affects*.[72]

The priestly physician combats "only the suffering itself . . . not its cause."

Nietzsche discusses first the "innocent" means by which the ascetic priest alleviates suffering, and then the "guilty" ones as well: the "innocent" ways reduce feeling by abolishing will and desire, by extreme hypnosis, of which he says religious redemption itself is an example, and also by means of "mechan-ical activities" and the "petty pleasures" of social and political associations, communities, and congregations. They dull the mind and the senses and sub-stitute trivialities for experience. Nietzsche clearly puts democratic politics in this category of ways to alleviate envy and vengeance by mutual helpfulness. "The formation *of a herd* is a significant victory."[73] It consoles for emptiness.

The "guilty" means by which the ascetic priest alleviates suffering "all involve one thing: some kind of *orgy of feeling*." Priestly "inventiveness" in producing orgies of feeling "has been virtually inexhaustible." And "every such orgy of feeling has to be paid for afterward—it makes the sick sicker." That is what makes it guilty. But the ascetic priest has employed such means "with a good conscience," knowing its "indispensability."[74] Nietzsche seems to be suggesting that given the brutality at stake, this emotional bloodletting is pre-ferable to the more physical kind. One must invent seemingly harmless ways of enacting our will to power as a surcease for pain. Thus in this way excess is indispensable to life itself. But it is not harmless, as Nietzsche demonstrates.

The chief means by which the ascetic priest addressed suffering was by the "exploitation of the *sense of guilt*." "Sin" is the priest's name for "bad con-science (cruelty directed backward). . . . Man, suffering from himself, . . . thirst-ing for reasons—reasons relieve —thirsting too for remedies and narcotics."

The priest, knowing hidden things, directs him to the "cause" of his suffering: "he must seek it in *himself*, in some *guilt*, in a piece of the past, he must understand his suffering as a *punishment*." We saw this, of course, in Luther. Nietzsche condemns the religious conscience: "everywhere the sinner breaking himself on the cruel wheel of a restless, morbidly lascivious conscience; everywhere dumb torment, extreme fear, the agony of the tortured heart, convulsions of an unknown happiness, the cry for redemption. . . . one no longer protested *against* pain, one *thirsted* for pain; '*more* pain! *more* pain!' the desire of his disciples and initiates has cried for centuries."[75]

Nietzsche asks, "What is the meaning of the power of this ideal?" The ascetic ideal expresses a will—where is there an opposing will? Modern science is alleged to be the opponent of religion and morality—"we men of knowledge" distrust all believers and unmask the charlatans, proving the undemonstability and improbability of all religious faiths and dogmas. Science formalizes suspicion and skepticism toward all that cannot be proved. We saw the clean lines of this skepticism even in its early modern manifestation in Hobbes. Here Nietzsche praises the "intellectual cleanliness," the severe intellectual conscience of the men of knowledge, of science, and he never ceased to hold this kind of intellectual integrity as a source of the greatest value.

Nevertheless, Nietzsche uncovers at the deep core of modern science a faith that not only mirrors but also derives from the ideals it challenges—the "*faith in truth*." "That which constrains these men, however, this unconditional will to truth, is *faith in the ascetic ideal itself*, even if it is an unconscious imperative—don't be deceived about that—it is the faith in a *metaphysical* value, the absolute value of *truth*."[76] Metaphysical truth, he has demonstrated, "affirms another world than that of life, nature, and history, and devalues this world, this life."

The faith in truth depended on being, on God; "once the faith in the God of the ascetic ideal is denied, a new problem arises: that of the *value* of truth."[77] In the unconditional will to truth or will to knowledge, Nietzsche discerns, behind the defeat of faith as superstition and the contempt for the cruelty of the practices of religion, a will to unmask, a will to destroy, a will to tear down the "highest values" and to cut man down to size. "Since Copernicus," he argues, man has begun a long slide into a "penetrating sense of his nothingness."[78]

Nietzsche is making a fateful argument here. What is left as the core, as the heart, the driving will of the ascetic ideal, is the will to truth. It is the strictest, most spiritual, most demanding, most unforgiving, most esoteric and subtle, and most penetrating form of the ascetic ideal. It is the ideal as will to power, as will to mastery itself, as will to dominate by throwing open and tearing down, by digging into the deepest crevices of the human psyche and the natural world. It is a will to doubt, to tell the truth regardless of the cost.

"It is the awe-inspiring *catastrophe* of two thousand years of training in truthfulness that finally forbids itself the *lie involved in the belief in God.*"[79]

The will to truthfulness at all costs finally destroys the belief in the reality and the value of all the beliefs and values that have preceded it and prepared its way. Nietzsche expresses this as a law of nature and will: "All great things bring about their own destruction through an act of self-overcoming." Truthfulness was contained in the law of Christian morality and the law of philosophic reason. It draws one inference after another, slowly and inexorably, turning its critique against everything in its path, and then finally against itself. Nietzsche's own genealogy is also a descendant of this spirit of truthfulness and uncovering. Genealogical critique is ruthlessly critical and turns its suspicion again and again against itself. "In us the will to truth becomes conscious of itself as a *problem.*"[80]

Morality, Nietzsche says, "will gradually *perish* now: this is the great spectacle in a hundred acts reserved for the next two centuries in Europe— the most terrible, most questionable, and perhaps also the most hopeful of all spectacles."[81] Characteristically, Nietzsche sees the greatest danger and the greatest hope arising out of the most extreme conditions.

It now remains to face the consequences of this will to truth, to explore the politics of the will to power, as it manifests itself in both the will to truth and the will to nothingness. The politics of nihilism is the result, and it is pervasive in our day. Nietzsche also suggests in some people a rare opposite, the will to power, which takes shape as self-discipline and the right to make promises, and which can, perhaps for some, become a will to take responsibility for oneself, for history, and for suffering.

11

The Will to Power and the
Will to Nothingness

Nietzsche draws the connection, powerfully and eloquently, between the death of God and the liberation of the world through knowledge or the will to truth—the liberation of history from any underlying moral purpose, especially for those "free spirits" for whom this event is most important. For Nietzsche, science in its deepest aspirations means the ultimate destruction of the religious metaphysics of morality that has dominated Western history. It inaugurates the beginning of a new time. In the opening section of Book Five of *The Gay Science*, Nietzsche explains the effects of the death of God in uncanny and deeply contradictory terms:

> The greatest recent event—That "God is dead," that the belief in the Christian god has become unbelievable—is already beginning to cast its first shadows over Europe. For the few at least . . . some sun seems to have set and some ancient and profound trust has been turned into doubt; to them our old world must appear daily more like evening, more mistrustful, stranger, "older." But in the main one may say: The event is far too great, too distant, too remote from the multitude's capacity for comprehension even for the tidings of it to be thought of as having *arrived* as yet. Much less may one suppose that many people know as yet *what* this event really means—and how much must collapse now that this faith has been undermined because it was built upon this faith, propped up by it, grown into it; for example, the whole of European morality. This long plenitude and sequence of breakdown, destruction, ruin, and cataclysm that is now impending—who could guess enough of it today to be compelled to play the teacher and advance proclaimer of this monstrous logic of terror, the prophet of a gloom and an eclipse of the sun whose like has probably never yet occurred on earth?

And yet there are those who do see it coming, "we philosophers and free spirits," and the effect on them is not one of gloom and cataclysm, but inexplicably, one of lightness, of "dawn":

> Even we born guessers of riddles who are, as it were, waiting on the mountains, posted between today and tomorrow . . . we firstlings and premature births of the coming century, to whom the shadows that must soon envelop Europe really should have appeared by now—why is that even we look forward to the approaching gloom without any real sense of involvement and above all without any worry or fear *for ourselves*? Are we perhaps still under the impression of the *initial consequences* of this event— . . . They are not at all sad and gloomy but rather like a new and scarcely describable kind of light, happiness, relief, exhilaration, encouragement, dawn.
>
> Indeed, we philosophers and "free spirits" feel, when we hear the news that "the old god is dead," as if a new dawn shone on us; our heart overflows with gratitude, amazement, premonitions, expectation. At long last the horizon appears free to us again, even if it should not be bright; at long last our ships may venture out to face any danger; all the daring of the lover of knowledge is permitted again; the sea, our sea, lies open again; perhaps there has never yet been such an "open sea."[1]

How can something that is doom, destruction, ruin, and cataclysm also be, for the lover of knowledge, a lightness, a happiness, a freedom, an exhilarating adventure—a new dawn? Some mark in time has been reached, some benchmark arrived at, according to which men will reckon before and after differently. But only the most discerning historian can see the signs of the change.

Nietzsche says in a note that "Nihilism can be a symptom of increasing strength or of increasing weakness."[2] That is, the destruction of all values in which men hitherto believed, which grows out of the death of God, may bring either strength or weakness; in fact, it will inevitably bring both. Not only do the greatest spirits and the worst both grow out of the most extreme conditions, but such conditions will necessarily bring forth both, because they belong together and necessitate each other. But for whom are these conditions best, and for whom worst? And what are these conditions? What is nihilism, finally? How can we know whether or under what conditions it will emerge as strength or as weakness, a sign of hope or one of decay? Of what is it the end, of what the beginning? For Nietzsche, it is always both, and differentiating the ways and means, the reasons why and how it is both, in different contexts simultaneously, is part of the task of his life's work.

We need to understand the death of God in relation to nihilism, and the relation of nihilism to the will to truth, especially as that involves the genealogy of Western ideals. Nietzsche means to demonstrate that "the entire history of mankind hitherto is on the point of changing suddenly into nihilism—into the belief in absolute worthlessness, i.e., *meaninglessness.*" Nihilism is our history. It is our fate. It is the nature of the world into which we have been born, and of the modernity we have inherited. In the face of "the destruction of ideals, the new desert," in the space of nihilism, we need to create "new arts by means of which we can endure it, we amphibians."[3] We also need to understand the genesis of meaning, such that it can be so readily changed into meaninglessness, and it is here that the crucial connection between knowledge and suffering is made.

> Nihilism stands at the door: whence comes this uncanniest of all guests? Point of departure: it is an error to consider "social distress" or "physiological degeneration," or, worse, corruption, as the *cause* of nihilism. Ours is the most decent and compassionate age. Distress, whether of the soul, body, or intellect, cannot of itself give birth to nihilism (i.e., the radical repudiation of value, meaning, and desireability). Such distress always permits a variety of interpretations. Rather: it is in one particular interpretation, the Christian-moral one, that nihilism is rooted.[4]

"Distress," that is, suffering itself, does not generate nihilism. Suffering is life, just as joy is. It is a particular response to distress that effects nihilism. That is to say, it is in this particular history in the West, this particular elaborately constructed interpretation of distress, of suffering, in which our present hopelessness and meaninglessness is rooted. As we have seen, this was not an accidental or contingent choice on our part, this religious-moral, idealist interpretation of suffering. It is one deeply rooted in our desire, in our need to deny or get rid of suffering or to find someone to blame. Our hatred of suffering and our revenge against those who seem more advantaged than us, or who rule, our *ressentiment* against our powerlessness, causes us to accuse someone or some other power, the other who oppresses us, or God, and eventually also ourselves, of blame as guilty and deserving of punishment. We must blame and name the nameless causes of our suffering. Luther called it sin; Hobbes nature; Rousseau history. Nietzsche names all three parts of the ascetic ideal and pronounces all of them as plays of self-deception on our part. When the illusions are torn down, the nihil, nothingness, enters into time. It is into the space that pain and emptiness opens up that all explanations and the giving and taking of responsibility fall.

He also asserts, however, that ours is the most compassionate age. We experience and witness suffering and begin the immense task of trying to differentiate not only its causes and agents, its spectators, malefactors, and benefactors; but we also seek to discern its deepest meaning for our psyches and spirits and bodies. All of these perspectives are necessary to this task, and that of the creator especially. It is a journey we have begun as a species. Is this not the meaning of Nietzsche's teachings?

In our powerlessness in the face of human suffering and meaninglessness, we gather our will to eliminate suffering from life or to project its justification and redemption onto a better, truer life elsewhere, one that will not have suffering in it. This history is ours, and we are only now experiencing the modern fruits of that history—nihilism, the uncanniest guest. In *Ecce Homo*, Nietzsche puts it this way: "To consider distress of all kinds as an objection, as something that must be abolished, is the *naiserie par excellence* and, on a large scale, a veritable disaster in its consequences, a nemesis of stupidity— almost as stupid as would be the desire to abolish bad weather—say, from pity for poor people."[5]

This is Nietzsche's most powerful and irrefutable indictment of the preceding ages: that they based their raison d'être in a monumental stupidity and lie—that suffering could be eliminated from human life. Kaufmann remarks: "Those who want to abolish all hardships because they themselves are not up to them are like sick people who wish to abolish rain, no matter what the consequences might be to others and to the earth generally."[6] Nietzsche's point is not only the incredible stupidity of trying to eliminate what is both necessary and intrinsic to life. He also insists that our centuries-long efforts to do something so self-evidently impossible have deformed us: "It is the lack of nature, it is the utterly gruesome fact that *antinature* itself received the highest honors as morality and was fixed over humanity as law and categorical imperative—To blunder to such an extent, not as individuals, not as a people, but as humanity!"[7]

Nietzsche tracks nihilism to the original creation of Christianity according to the sadistic, self-denying ministrations of priests, and also to Platonism, which became an integral part of Christian metaphysics. In the modern age, he sees the reemergence of naked and boundless nihilism in the death of God, the end of Christianity "at the hands of its own morality," the "youngest virtue," honesty, the sense of truthfulness or will to truth, which finally rebounds from "God is truth," to "there is no God," to "All is false." He reminds us that "all science and philosophy so far has been influenced by moral judgments," and that there are "nihilistic consequences of contemporary science."[8]

It is as lovers of knowledge, as men of science and the will to truth, that we philosophers and free spirits, we "godless antimetaphysicians," greet the new day and sail our ships out on the new and never-so-open seas. But Nietzsche is clear: "it is still a *metaphysical faith* upon which our faith in science rests— that even we seekers after knowledge today, we godless antimetaphysicians still take our fire, too, from the flame lit by a faith that is thousands of years old, that Christian faith which was also the faith of Plato, that God is the truth, that truth is divine.—what if this should become more and more incredible, if nothing should prove to be divine any more unless it were error, blindness, the lie—if God himself should prove to be our most enduring lie?"[9]

The will to truth, the drive of seekers after knowledge, as Nietzsche analyzes it in relation to modern life and the ascetic ideal, is will to power, and it is as will to power that it comes, late in the modern age, to be revealed as such. The unconditional will to truth is the cause and the effect, the essential motive, of the pursuit of knowledge and science, and it is this will to truth that will finally bring about the destruction of all values, all previous ideals and beliefs, culminating in the monstrous emptiness and cataclysm of the modern age, which is pure nihilism. In this chapter I want to look especially at the politics of the will to power and the will to truth, the will to nothingness, at the nihilism that forms the underlying political condition of the present day. The politics of the will to power, the will to truth, and the will to nothingness are Nietzsche's politics and his anti-politics, paradoxical aspects of his most fundamental thought.

THE WILL TO POWER AND THE WILL TO TRUTH

Usually we understand power as an object of representation and desire, as what the will wants, the way Hobbes understood power. It is a capacity that desire strives to appropriate and it is the force that desire strives to acquire in order to command and dominate others or to gain the representations of power, which are always the already established values of the status quo. We do not usually think of power or the will to power as creating new values, or as the force inherent in all values. But for Nietzsche, the will to power is the basic originary force in the universe, the very stuff of life, time, chaos, and becoming, the essence of motion, the striving, the drive, the sheer energy of the world and of life itself. Whatever there is in the world is will to power, and he affirms this even as he denies the existence of separate or "free" wills (an illusion of "subjects," created by grammar) and of power as something that can be possessed. All "will" is always a multiplicity of wills, of feelings, of affects, of appropriations in time.

The will to power, in Nietzsche's terms, preserves and appropriates anything that resists it and compels to obedience and submission any competing force that proves inferior to its will. It also submits to superior force. Gilles Deleuze separates the will to power as it enters history or sensibility into active and reactive forces, superior and inferior wills, affirmative or negative evaluations. I think his bipolarization of the will to power is too dualized—and too fixed, totalizing, and eternal. But Deleuze does work out an interesting, complicated schema by which to analyze how active forces become reactive, and even how reactive forces may, in certain circumstances, become active.[10]

The will to power always seeks its furthest extension, it always strives to go as far as it can go. Willing, for Nietzsche, is a supremely creative act and an act of joy: "any *willing* always comes to me as my liberator and bringer of joy. Willing liberates: that is the true doctrine of will or freedom—thus Zarathustra teaches you."[11] Power is the genetic and differential element in the will. That is why the will is essentially creative. "This is also why power is never measured in representation; it is never represented, it is not even interpreted or evaluated, it is 'the one that' interprets, 'the one that' evaluates, 'the one that' wills."[12] Power is in the will as its bestowing, acting, giving nature; it bestows, creates, posits, measures, interprets, conquers, and deciphers meaning and value. It is the verb, not the noun. Power is the very activity of life itself as it moves and changes and strives to establish itself. In this way, as we will see, Nietzsche employs as his most fundamental metaphor a political metaphor, the will to power. Life itself is a never-ending politics, a contest, a struggle for achievement, a battle between mastery and loss. The only way the very stuff of the world, the chaos of becoming itself, can be felt, construed, organized, or represented—put into images, words, or concepts, that is, made evident or comprehensible at all (to us and by us, as historical, temporal configurations of such energies, below the surface of consciousness, as bodies and beings, as subjects and agents, all metaphorical unities) is as will to power, as a politics of strength and weakness, of meaning mastered or lost, made and lost again, until it exhausts itself into meaninglessness. I will attempt at least a partial unpacking of these notions.

The will to power is affectivity that manifests itself as a feeling of power; it is the "primitive affective force" from which all other feelings derive.[13] More important, Nietzsche writes, in a note that is not as lucid as it might have been, "The will to power not a being [*Sein*], not a becomimg, but rather a *pathos* is the most elemental fact from which a becoming, a working first emerge."[14] The will to power is not being or becoming but rather a *pathos*, the elemental experience from which all becoming and being arise. From the perspective of suffering, as I have developed it in this book, this is Nietzsche's most crucial formulation. According to Nietzsche, the will to power, as *pathos*, as suffering, is the most elemental reality of the world: it is truth, it is nature, and it is politics. What does it mean that the will to power is not being or becoming, but rather *pathos*?

Tracy Strong, in his book *Friedrich Nietzsche and the Politics of Transfiguration*, turns for an explication of this formulation to *The Gay Science*, where Nietzsche draws the classical distinction between *ethos* and *pathos*: "as long as men continue in a particular form of life they tend to think of it as *ethos*, that is, as the 'only possible and reasonable thing. . . . ' A truer understanding, though, would be that life is *pathos*, that it is 'not one's lot to have (certain particular) sensations for years.'"[15] The importance of this contrast has to do with the contrast between the illusion of permanence and stability that men have in their ways of life, as opposed to the transience and impermanence which is their real lot. Their *pathos* is their experience as their lot, what has been given for a tme, what affects and effects them, and then passes. *Pathos*, in this sense, is what men *suffer*, what they undergo, in relation to time. It is what they suffer on account of the shortness and inevitable passing away of their things and of their lives. Nietzsche's doctrine of eternal recurrence is meant precisely to address this *pathos* of time and transience, the way men suffer the impermanence, the passing away, of all things, which is our fate.

Strong quotes a Greek lexicon to the effect that *pathos* can mean "that which happens to a person or thing, what one has experienced, good or bad." Strong explains that it does not really mean mere change or growth, however, or an origin or natural form. It is what one has experienced, not as origin, genesis or development, but rather what is experienced as human, as it is felt, known, and suffered. "The will to power refers then not to an ontological principle, nor to something that has evolved; 'it cannot have become,' says Nietzsche. It is rather the movement itself, and thus has neither being nor becoming." All organisms and matter have the most basic character of seeking to incorporate and interpret everything that they encounter. "'All the forms a thing acquires constitute its pathos, its will to power.'"[16] The very particularities of our accumulated subjectivities are our *pathos*. Our will to power is always a *pathos*, because any victory or ground gained is transient, temporary.

That is to say, all the forms that a thing acquires in its will to power constitute as well its *pathos*, what it suffers, because it gives its form to things, but only in passing, only for a time, only obliquely and temporarily, however powerful its will to power. The will to power is *pathos* as passion; it acquires things, gives values, and bestows interpretations, each one conquering the previous one, but still, it is only a moment, a *pathos* of power, in the flux of time, eternal becoming.[17] The will to power is a giving of form that necessarily dissolves in time. It is a *pathos* of all things, a feeling and suffering, in all things. This is the tragic knowledge that is inherent in Nietzsche's will to power. Nietzsche insists in *Zarathustra* that he wants not transience, but eternity for all things, hence his doctrine of eternal recurrence. In the next chapter we try to decipher what he means.

First, however, it is necessary to delve a little more deeply into the relations among Nietzsche's will to power, the will to truth, and the will to nothingness. We need to clarify where we stand and what we face in the politics of our time. The most problematical of all the formations that will to power can will is truth. Remember that Nietzsche says "*Truth is the kind of error* without which a certain kind of living creature could not live. The value for *life* ultimately decides. "[18]

Furthermore, Nietzsche's critique of modern science as the most refined and rarified version of the ascetic ideal rests on his estimation that "both science and the ascetic ideal stand on one ground . . . namely, on the same overestimation of truth (more correctly, on the same belief in the inestimability, the uncriticizability of truth."[19] How valuable for life, how indispensable is the necessary illusion of "truth"? What will does it serve? Nietzsche says:

> Will to truth is a making firm, a making true and durable, an abolition of the false character of things, a reinterpretation of it into beings. "Truth" is therefore not something there, that might be found or discovered—but something that must be created and that gives a name to a process, or rather to a will to overcome that has in itself no end—introducing truth, as a *processus in infinitum*, an active determining—not a becoming-conscious of something that is in itself firm and determined. It is the word for will to power.[20]

Truth comes about because man's life, his work, and his will to power require the oversimplification and even falsification that is entailed in creating unities and equivalences, that is, names—subjects and objects, causes and effects, the "enduring and regularly recurring things" which we attribute to the world with our logic and science, "but which are not, in reality, 'out there.' Man projects his drive to truth, his 'goal' in a certain sense, outside himself as a world that has being, as a metaphysical world, as a thing-in-itself, as a world already in existence. His needs as creator invent the world upon which he works, anticipate it; this anticipation (this belief in truth) is his support."[21]

Nietzsche's genealogy shows us the needs of man the creator at work. He adds the perspective of the creator to those of the sufferer and the knower, the actor and the spectator. The creator is in many ways the culmination of all of these previous perspectives and she needs all of them. Nietzsche showed us the origins of the values and ideals of the metaphysical world created by the drive to truth, this will to power, as it has done its work in our own history. He also showed us the importance of suffering and the will to eliminate or justify suffering as the ongoing origin of the "needs of the creator" to work.

Perhaps an even more pertinent question has to do with the genealogy of Nietzsche's genealogy—is not its provenance as well this indispensable, and illusionary, will to truth? David Farrell Krell puts the point this way: "This uprooting of traditional values, or moral prejudice, rests upon the conviction that a fundamentally nihilistic *provenance* expresses the *true* value of past systems, considered from the point of view of power; the truth of this true value is not groundable, but haunts the underground."[22] We must note, however, that Nietzsche's analysis of the "provenance" of metaphysics is, after all is said and done, an interpretation and an evaluation. This is not to say that Nietzsche does not claim for it "truth," but rather that he recognizes that truth is a *pathos*; it is something to which we give form by our will to power, which we suffer and which passes away.

Nietzsche wrote an unpublished document in 1872 called "On the Pathos of Truth." A fable from the preface of that work, in Krell's translation, reads:

> In some remote corner of universal space, glimmering with the numberless solar systems that were spilled out into it, there was once a star on which clever animals invented *knowing*. It was the most arrogant and mendacious minute of universal history but still only a minute. After nature drew a few breaths, the star congealed, and the clever animals had to die. It was also high time: for although they boasted that they had already managed to learn much, in the end, and much to their displeasure, they uncovered the fact that they had learned everything falsely. They died, and in dying they cursed the truth. That was the way of these despairing animals who had invented knowing.[23]

In dying they cursed the truth. Nietzsche does not curse the truth, but he shows the curse that the will to truth brings with it. This story recalls Nietzsche's famous "Fable" in *Twilight of the Idols*, "How the 'True World' Finally Became a Fable."[24] In this fable, Nietzsche tells the story, in six parts, of the "history of an error," the belief in the existence of a "true world," and how that error, the "true world," comes to be abolished. First, the "true world" is available to the wise, the pious, and the virtuous; this is the ancient world. It can be signified by "I, Plato, *am* the truth." Second, the "true world" becomes Christian. It is unattainable in the present, but promised for the wise, the pious, and the virtuous in the eternal hereafter. Third, the "true world" is understood to be unattainable and undemonstrable; it cannot even be promised, but even the "mere thought" of it is a "consolation, a duty, an imperative . . . . the idea grown sublime, pale, northerly, Konisbergian" (Kantian). Fourth, the "true world" is not only unattained, but entirely unknown. It cannot be known. There's no point in asking the question. We seek truth here, in this world. Scientific reason dawns. Fifth, the "true world" is no longer real, "it is an idea grown useless, superfluous, consequently a refuted idea, let us abolish it!" Nietzsche says that here "Plato blushes for shame; all free spirits run riot." Finally, then, we have abolished the "true world: what world is left? the apparent world perhaps? . . . But no! with the real world we have also abolished the apparent world! Mid-day . . . the zenith of mankind; *Incipit Zarathustra*."[25]

Whole books have been written to interpret this fabled history. Nietzsche abolishes the distinction between the real and appearance and this has a great many consequences. At present we live in a world where the difference between appearance and reality is blurred, erased, and reconstituted constantly—a world where images become data, turned into codes of electrons or DNA, bytes of information, messages transmitted in nanoseconds, simulacra that cannot be distinguished from their originals, where historical evidence is always more than meets the eye and is manipulated for innumerable purposes, where virtual reality constantly intrudes, where appearance is reality and vice versa, and there is no "other," there is the only "truth" and it is always a "lie."[26] The paradoxes of postmodern truth are legendary.

We will have to see what gift it is that Zarathustra brings. What was the purpose of the true world? Why was it necessary to invent it? What happened that it became possible to abolish it? What is the *pathos* of this truth, this knowledge, that turned out not to be true? In a long note he wrote circa 1887, Nietzsche explains what he calls the "Psychology of Metaphysics," the *pathos* of the true world.

> This world is apparent: consequently there is a true world;—this world is conditional: consequently there is an unconditioned world;—this world is full of contradiction: consequently there is a world free of contradiction; —this world is a world of becoming: consequently there is a world of being:— all false conclusions . . . It is suffering that inspires these conclusions: fundamentally they are *desires* that such a world should exist; in the same way, to imagine another, more valuable world is an expression of hatred for a world that makes one suffer: the *ressentiment* of metaphysicians against actuality is here creative.[27]

Why is there suffering? What reasons could there possibly be for the magnitude of human suffering? "Suffering as a consequence of error: how is error possible? Suffering as a consequence of guilt: how is guilt possible?" If this world is conditioned by another true and unconditioned world, who conditioned it? "The world of appearance, becoming, contradiction, suffering, is therefore *willed: what for?*"

Nietzsche cautions that the "real genesis of the concepts . . . derives from the practical sphere, the sphere of utility"—that is to say, the sphere of power. "It is suffering that inspires these conclusions." The essential drive of philosophy is politics, politics as the most basic kind of practice. Metaphysicians are preoccupied with suffering. "Even morality is so important to them only because they see in it an essential condition for the abolition of suffering."[28] The will to power, in the face of contradiction, conditionality, and suffering over which we have no control, leads to the creation of the institutions of religion and morality, metaphysics and the state. Our will to power serves us to relieve us and to effect our escape, to deny by giving meaning to our suffering.

If the will to power can create a false "true world," it can destroy it as well. How is the unprecedented magnitude of suffering and self-annihilation in our world related to the will to truth and the lie, the nihil, the nothing that it opens up?

Nietzsche reminds us, "Brave and creative men never consider pleasure and pain as ultimate values—they are epiphenomena: one must *desire* both if one is to achieve anything."[29] It is the capacity to take everything upon oneself and endure it, "the most comprehensive soul," which constitutes human greatness in Nietzsche's teachings.

Nietzsche suggests that in the will to power, both the will to truth and the will to lie come together; they are inextricable. What does this mean? How are we to evaluate it? In *Zarathustra*, Nietzsche asserts that "the inexhaustible productive life-will" is the "way of all living things." Krell observes:

> Living is a hearkening, listening, and responding; life is an obeying, *ein Gehorchendes*. Further, any living creature that cannot hearken and respond to itself falls under the command of another; commanding is more difficult than obeying, for one must bear the burdens of those who obey, and such burdens are crushing. Commanding is experiment, hazard, and risk of self. Zarathustra invites his listeners to test his claim: Is this not hearkening, this obedience, this commanding at the very root of life? Where one finds life, one finds will to power. Life herself whispers her secret to Zarathustra: "I am that which must always overcome itself."[30]

Insofar as will to power must always overcome itself, genealogy too must always overcome itself, and truth must always overcome itself as well. Zarathustra says to "the wisest ones"—"And you too, my knowing ones, are but a path and the footfall of my will: for truly my will to power walks on the feet of your will to truth!"[31] The will to power is always stronger than and drives the will to truth. The more unconditional the will to truth becomes, the more nihilistic it becomes. It is driven to unconditionality by will to power. It tears down all the idols, it reveals the shabby rags of all belief, in tatters. This is Nietzsche's point about truth: it pushes through all the remnants of the past, into the moment, into the future.

The will to power is not the will to life. It is the stuff of life; it does not will life. The living cannot will themselves into existence. They can, however, will themselves out of it. As Nietzsche has tirelessly demonstrated, they do will themselves out of it, and have done so for centuries, with every invention and construction of metaphysics, morality, and history that denies life and creates a "true world" somewhere else by which to judge this one. They can also will themselves out of it in an even more basic way. They can will nothingness—suicide, the abyss, the cataclysm that cuts time open. "For suicide is simply the will to nothingness deprived of the contrivances of asceticism; it is the praxis that corresponds to a metaphysics deprived of its piety and pusillanimity. Suicide is the final celebration of rancune and ressentiment. Suicide is rigorous science."[32] The will would rather will nothingness than not will. The will to nothingness, to meaninglessness is manifestly ubiquitous now in our world. Time is speeded up; annihilations accumulate faster and faster.

The will to power expresses itself in several different ways as will to truth: in the delusionary and power-laden "pseudo-truth" of metaphysics; in the will to art, which is a will to conscious, creative deception, knowing illusion, shaping appearance and becoming, which Nietzsche argues is "worth more" than truth; and in genealogy, which seeks origins and thereby shows up the fraud of the first and the necessity of the second.

Here our question has to do with the connection between the will to truth or knowledge as the most subtle incarnation of the ascetic ideal and the nothingness it repeatedly begets and uncovers. "Also we knowers of today, we godless ones and antimetaphysicians, our fire too is taken from the torch that enkindled a millenial belief, that Christian belief that was also Plato's belief, that God is truth, that truth is divine. . . . Yet what if precisely this becomes ever-more-unbelievable, if nothing suggests itself anymore as divine?"[33] All interpreting, all valuing is caught up, "embroiled in the stream of power."

I would perhaps not go so far as to say, with Krell, that "intellectual rectitude and philological probity reveal their nature as protracted suicide."[34] But he has a point: knowledge for Nietzsche is always tragic knowledge, and the will to truthfulness, insofar as it becomes unconditional and knows no limits, is a will to death and the abyss. What limits does Nietzsche devise for the will to truth: two important ones, art, and the fatedness, the historicity of all will to truth, the knowledge of its conditionality, its conscious limits by history and time.

History is very important for Nietzsche; he understands our world as constructed, as historical, as laden with memory and the past. History for Nietzsche is neither mere contingency nor purpose, both of which are nihilistic. Why? Because both contingency and purpose, conceived as intrinsic to history, are concerned with the possibility that what was could have been different. These conceptions of history privilege the concept of the possible over the concept of the actual. But the concept of the possible is a logical concept, even a statistical one, one that always dissimulates desire. And the concept of purpose in history, as Nietzsche has made clear, is derived from the fantasy of a world-historical subject, one unity that wills us into being and intends that we will triumph in the end, the One who will repay our suffering, or redeem it. In the name of this Absolute Eternal Presence, this world and its rich imperfections have been despised.

That which has been feared the most, the cause of the most powerful suffering (lust to rule, sex, etc.,), has been treated by men with
the greatest amount of hostility and eliminated from the "true"
world. They have eliminated the affects one by one. . . . they have
hated the irrational, the arbitrary, the accidental (as the causes of
immeasurable physical suffering). . . . In the same way, they have
feared change, transitoriness. . . . Against the value of that which
remains eternally the same . . . the values of the briefest and the
most transient, the seductive flash of gold on the belly of the ser-
pent *vita.*[35]

History, for Nietzsche, is by contrast always the realm of the irrational, the
arbitrary, the accidental, that which constantly changes. In what way does it
become unrecoverable, irrevocable? We have constructed a history against
history.

For Nietzsche, the concept of the possible is misapplied to history. History is not just a particular realized trajectory of events out of many (infinite?)
possible trajectories. History is the "It was," what actually happened, what
was actually in fact brought to pass in this world by the sum of the forces of
all previous conditions—the previous conditions that actually obtained and no
others. It is, as Deleuze insists, the throw of the dice that was actually cast.
We have no knowledge or access to other historical "possibilities," however
much we desire them. History is not, was never, as we experience it, optional.
It is what was fated and determined, not in the sense of meant to be, as in
some summing of reason or divine will, but in the sense of meant to be our
lot, our fate, always already created by our wills and all the past wills unconsciously operating in terms of the largest social and political forces that our
wills have created in history. History is what has already been willed into
actuality, the inextricably mixed and inexplicably peculiar concatenations of
circumstances that actually obtain; what is fated for us today and tomorrow.

Causality, which for Hobbes was an abstract conception of bodies in
motion, is always for Nietzsche a construction by and of actual particular
bodies in specific motions, and in largely unconscious, contexts—these ones
and then these ones and then these ones, and no others. Causality is another
delusionary human construction, like subjects and objects. There are no causes
and effects, but only what we read into events as causes and effects. And our
perspective changes what we count as causes and effects, as every physicist
and psychologist knows.

The unalterable sequence of certain phenomena demonstrates no
"law" but a power relationship between two or more forces. . . . It
is a question, not of succession, but of interpenetration, a process
in which the individual successive moments are not related to one

another as cause and effect—The separation of the "deed" from the "doer," of the event from someone who produces events, of the process from a something that is not process but enduring substance, thing, body, soul, etc.—the attempt to comprehend an event as a sort of shifting and place-changing on the part of a "being," of something constant: this ancient mythology established the belief in "cause and effect" after it had found a firm form in the functions of language and grammar.[36]

It is worth asking, then, how the moments of temporal succession are related to one another, if not as cause and effect. The question of the *pathos* of power in time, the question of the necessity of the will in temporal succession, is the subject of this book. It is best addressed by considering the thought of eternal recurrence, to which we turn in the next chapter. But first it would be well to look, briefly, at the functions of language and grammar in relation to will to power, before we apply these functions to the problem of Nietzsche's politics.

WILL TO POWER: LANGUAGE, BODIES, AND METAPHOR

Nietzsche sets in motion the play of truth and illusion, truth and lie, in his very construction of language as twice removed from original experience, which is rhythm, impulse, and drive, expressing itself in appearances and metaphors, and only belatedly in words and concepts. "We insert a word where our ignorance begins—where we can no longer see any further; for example, the word *I*, the word *do*, the word *suffer*—these words are perhaps horizontal lines of our knowledge, but they are not 'truths.'"[37] What language misses, among other things, is our *character* and our *fate*. [38] Our character, that is to say, our history, our fate, and our fatedness, and how we face them, cannot be put into language. But the structure of language assures that both idealism and metaphysics will remain with us. As Nietzsche so famously says: "I fear we are not getting rid of God because we still believe in grammar."[39]

It might be helpful to think back to *The Birth of Tragedy* to recognize the crucial importance of music and metaphor in Nietzsche's metapsychology. Metaphor for Nietzsche is not a rhetorical device, but rather a "live spectacle at which he [the god] is present."[40] Music is the most manifold and diverse symbolic range, which generates a thousand metaphors: "it discharges all its powers of representation (*Darstellung*), imitation, transfiguration, transmutation, every kind of mimicry and play-acting, conjointly. . . . Dionysian man . . . enters into every skin, into every emotion; he is continually transforming himself."[41]

We should also remember Nietzsche's celebration of rhythm in *The Gay Science* as what was meant by man "to impress the gods," its "elemental and overwhelming effect" bringing us "closer to the ears of the gods." Rhythm is power: "rhythm is a compulsion; it engenders an unconquerable urge to yield and join in; not only our feet follow the beat but the soul does, too—probably, one surmised, the soul of the gods as well!"[42] Here Nietzsche is very close to the elemental meaning of the will to power. It is the compulsion of the beat. In the end, there is only the eternally echoing heartbeat in the vastness of the universe. Life is the heartbeat that goes on and on, eternally recurring, however much one's own particular heartbeat suddenly begins and ends. That is the sense of our finitude and our *pathos* that Nietzsche addresses in his doctrine of eternal recurrence of the same. What is "the same" is the beat.

In contrast, "philosophical language is the most unsatisfactory there is, for it petrifies the 'music of the world' into concepts." As Sarah Kofman shows, Nietzsche from the beginning elaborates a "theory" of metaphor based on the unity and disunity of Dionysian experience, which is not an ontology, but a metamorphosis, and as will to power, a politics too. Nietzsche reverses the Aristotelian relation between metaphor and concept; for Nietzsche, "the essence of things is enigmatic, so genera and species are themselves but human, all-too-human metaphors."[43]

Nietzsche's metaphorical philosophy is connected from the start with the "shattering" of the belief in a linear or referential historical time. As Kofman and Blondel, Derrida and Foucault all point out, time for Nietzsche is not a determined march forward into an ideal future or goal; "it is a rhythmic play between opposing forces which prevail by turns, innocently constructing and deconstructing worlds. A rhythmic play which implies repression and the return of the repressed."[44] This "innocence" of the play between opposing forces involves the politics of domination and submission, but that is not, for Nietzsche, a guilty or immoral (or moral, for that matter) invocation. It is the fundamental politics of nature and culture, as translated through the body. The will to power can be used for a variety of purposes of our devising, and has been infinitely valued and devalued in our history. Nietzsche, in his "revaluation of all values," takes pride in provoking outrage not only by showing the will to power inherent in the "highest values" heretofore, but in insisting on the value of that which has been "judged most evil in the world."[45]

Nietzsche translates metaphors of consciousness into those for the body and vice versa, but the body is the guiding thread. We can trace the connections between consciousness and the unconscious, between consciousness and community, and between community and body through the workings of the will to power, Nietzsche's most basic metaphor for life and politics: "The multiplicity of drives—we must assume there is a master, but it is not in consciousness, for consciousness is an organ, like the stomach."[46]

the conscious world is a language which symbolizes a text written originally by unconscious activity, and which consciousness knows only in a masked and transposed form. The transposition is achieved by carrying over the "known" on to the unknown. It presupposes an activity of assimilation, of digestion, of reducing differences, which is a fundamentally "unjust" will to mastery (Nietzsche later calls it "will to power").[47]

Every event, every motion, every will and thought, is political, from its inception:

That commanding something which the people call "spirit" wants to be master in and around its own house and wants to feel that it is master; it has the will from multiplicity to simplicity, a will that ties up, tames, and is domineering and truly masterful. Its needs and capacities are so far the same as those which physiologists posit for everything that lives, grows and multiplies. The spirit's power to appropriate the foreign stands revealed in its inclination to assimilate the new to the old, to simplify the manifold, and to overlook or repulse whatever is totally contradictory—just as it involuntarily emphasizes certain features and lines in what is foreign, in every piece of the "external world," retouching and falsifying the whole to suit itself. Its intent in all this is to incorporate new "experiences," to file new things in old files—growth, in a word— or, more precisely, the feeling of growth, the *feeling* of increased power.[48]

Language develops under the impulsion of the need to communicate, but it is not a mere pragmatic need, but preeminently a political one, an exigency of human, living power over powerlessness.[49] Indeed, Nietzsche argues that the fixing and forcing of metaphor into concept, by philosophers, involves an effacing of the originary power of metaphor by violence: "The impression is petrified . . . it is captured and stamped by means of concepts. Then it is killed, skinned, mummified, and preserved as a concept."[50] As in all things, fixity is only gained by violence.

Nietzsche likens the ancient concept of equilibrium, based on equivalence, or a spurious sense of "sameness," to "the oldest theory of law and morality; equilibrium is the basis of justice. . . . the equilibrium of the disturbed power relationship is restored." The community punishes in order to restore its equilibrium after transgression.[51] In much the same way, thought establishes equivalences and meanings, conceptual schemas and metaphysical truths on the basis of the subduing of heteronomy and the fixing of canonical meaning:

What then is truth? A mobile army of metaphors, metonymies, and anthropomorphisms: in short, a sum of human relations which have been poetically and rhetorically intensified, transferred, and embellished and which, after long usage, seem to a people to be fixed, canonical, and binding. . . . To express it morally, this is the duty to lie according to a fixed convention, to lie with the herd and in a manner binding upon everyone. Now man of course forgets that this is the way things stand for him. Thus he lies in the manner indicated, unconsciously and in accordance with habits which are centuries old; and precisely *by means of this unconsciousness* and forgetfulness he arrives at his sense of truth.[52]

Community itself, of course, is a unity imposed by domination: "All unity is unity only as organization and co-operation—just as a human community is a unity—as opposed to an atomistic anarchy, as a pattern of domination that *signifies* a unity but *is* not a unity."[53] Here Nietzsche makes an explicit reply to Rousseau's concept of the general will—that such a concept is a pattern of domination that signifies unity, but is not a unity. We saw both the problem of establishing unity and the violence inherent in doing so in our previous interpretation of Rousseau.

Finally, it is the body, itself a hierarchy of forces, a perpetual unconscious struggle between drives and impulses, which propagates these representations and ideals: "Genealogically, these representations are the mask donned by the 'body,' which is the fundamental determining agency and uses ideal representations as disguised expressions of its desires. Culture is no longer 'merely' a collection of representations. It is all the *evaluation* of an age, a people or socio-historical grouping of some kind, the hidden face of the reality of a certain *bodily economy*, which Nietzsche sometimes calls 'idiosyncracy' or 'metabolism' (*Stoffwechsel*)."[54]

If we understand culture as a bodily economy, we can understand as well that genealogy leads us to uncover its vicissitudes, its place in and out of time, and its profound roots in suffering: "The discipline of suffering, of *great* suffering—do you not know that only *this* discipline has created all enhancements of man so far?"[55] Our suffering is in the body and the (mortal) soul, in history, memory, and culture, and in time itself, which no amount of willing can alter. The will to power is the expression of our need and our power; it is the force that makes meaning and community out of domination and struggle, and it is also the expression of our achievements and our fate. Out of the will to power comes the will to truth, and from the will to truth, courageously and ruthlessly pursued without conditions in the modern age, come the devastations of a nihilistic world. What Nietzsche sees around him and envisions for the future is the politics of nihilism.

NIETZSCHE'S POLITICS AND ANTI-POLITICS

What conclusions can we draw from the foregoing for the articulation of Nietzsche's politics? This is a most interesting task. Nietzsche does not value politics, what we normally mean by that term, although he uses a metaphor of politics, the will to power, to express his deepest insights and values. Many political theorists have attempted to reconnoiter the territories Nietzsche covers politically in order to fit him into a progressive, transformative or democratic political agenda; some have also taken pleasure in fitting him into the most ignoble, reactionary, and dangerous ones.[56] Scholars in general seem to be on the look-out for "misappropriations" of Nietzsche's texts for what they see as deviant political purposes, and one scholar calls such misappropriations "shameless."[57]

But this is exactly what Nietzsche's notion of will to power at work in life, and especially in intellectual life, is all about. All analyses are interpretations; all interpretations are will to power. They are all appropriations for political purposes. They are thus political in two ways, on two levels, at the least.

> The will to power *interprets* (—it is a question of interpretation when an organ is constructed): it defines limits, determines degrees, variations in power. Mere variations of power could not feel themselves to be such: there must be present something that wants to grow and interprets the value of whatever else wants to grow. Equal in that—In fact, interpretation is itself a means of becoming master of something. (The organic process constantly presupposes interpretations.)[58]

Interpreting is appropriation—it is a means of becoming master, of domination. All thought is will to power, any grasping of any text is an interpretation that seeks dominion. There is no interpretation that is not a political appropriation, that is, a domination, that is, a politics.

One interpretation prevails or succeeds against another by means of will to power—that is, politics. There is no separating the text from the appropriations that make it up, or from the politics of interpretation, a process of inherently political moves; each interpreter strategically seeks to appropriate for herself the profits accruing to "the correct interpretation." The contest is waged continuously from various competing vantage points in the larger social whole on behalf of widely divergent political ends. Discourse is will to power and discourses construct and produce the social and material world for themselves and their interpreters. Appropriation itself is political, and the conscious and unconscious purposes for which an interpreted text or event is used are political. How else? Where is "neutrality" to be found among human beings? Even the impartialities of science are protocols set up for protecting certain gains. (Even the human genome is patented.) Nietzsche insists that life itself is political through and through, and of course, shameless. "To impose on becoming the character of being—that is the supreme will to power."[59]

History, according to Nietzsche, is not a matter of either causality or necessity—"Necessity and universality can never be given by experience." And of course the same holds true for intellectual dogmas, for theories and facts, for texts and interpretations. The will to power is always at play in the will to truth. The value of the world lies in our interpretations:

> That the value of the world lies in our interpretation (—that other interpretations than merely human ones are perhaps somewhere possible—); that previous interpretations have been perspective valuations by virtue of which we can survive in life, i.e., in the will to power, for the growth of power; that every elevation of man brings with it the overcoming of narrower interpretations; that every strengthening and increase of power opens up new perspectives and means believing in new horizons—this idea permeates my writings. The world with which we are concerned is false, i.e., is not a fact but a fable and approximation on the basis of a meager sum of observations; it is "in flux," as something in a state of becoming, as a falsehood always changing but never getting near the truth: for— there is no "truth."[60]

All "truths" are in flux, and all are caught in the *pathos* of time. All purposes, aims, and meanings are effects of the will to power.[61] That is to say, they are political. That does not make them untrue, but only always conditioned, contextualized, established, and accepted as truths because we need and use them as such. It is we who need and make truth, as we need its opposites. We establish the horizons, the contexts and frameworks, for our facts, our histories, our methods, our truths, and our purposes. Sometimes Nietzsche is optimistic about the possibilities; sometimes not.

Nietzsche's politics, then, are not to be determined altogether by how one interprets what are taken to be his most overt political statements, because that takes for granted as given the already established meanings of the modern era in the realm of politics, namely, the structures and institutions of democratic rule, justice, right, and the state. Nietzsche deconstructs the references and reconstructs genealogically the disciplines of power and discourse at work in the construction of these institutions. Nietzsche is notoriously unfond of such structures, especially on the grounds of their hypocrisy. But politics, as being that is imposed by will on the world of becoming, that is also and more profoundly Nietzsche's politics, the politics of the will to power. Also profoundly political are the purposes of his attack on the nihilism that he sees underlying and protecting the normative realm of the political institutions and values of his day—and of our day even more. Nihilism is a political condition; one that breeds violence, emptiness, and danger, as well as opportunities.

Nietzsche is both the most political and the most anti-political of thinkers, because he shatters the blinders that the modern state and its apologists use— the virtues inherited from Christianity, from transcendental reason, from world-historical revolutionary justice, or even mere utility—to show that every move of every organism and every event, every thought and project, is an instance of the will to power. All the political ideals of modern life are empty of meaning in themselves except as exercises of the will to power, the will to survive, to grow, to master, which uses any device, rationale, or simulacrum for its exercise. Nietzsche warns that the will to power has found democratic ideals to be the most useful and blind.

Nietzsche is not, as political theorist Mark Warren, for instance, claims, simply mistranslating the will to power as a life principle into outdated and reactionary conventional political arrangements. Only if we hold "the political" to refer solely to those established characteristic relations between rulers and ruled, of the individual to society or to the state that the modern age has delimited as "political," can we separate the will to power from what is to count as "politics proper." Nietzsche does sometimes seem to speak that way, while cautioning us that language falsifies, and warning us still that we have to use it. When he addresses the political institutions of the age, he condemns modern liberal politics pretty unconditionally. This has to do with the question of value that is his deepest question—what is its value for life?

But Nietzsche's will to power is also his politics, the deepest politics and the most subversive. Nietzsche is saying that everything is politics and that nothing is politics, in fact, that nothingness is politics, which he finds truly alarming. (Like a book for all and for none, as he characterizes *Zarathustra*.) Nietzsche radically destabilizes what politics has been. He finds politics in every action and every decision whatsoever, thereby demanding that we choose our values consciously when we take action or make decisions.

In the conventional sense, politics relates to the state, which Nietzsche despises as the most shabby and base modern substitute for the dead God. "The state organized immorality—*internally*: as police, penal law, classes, commerce, family; *externally*: as will to power, to war, to conquest, to revenge."[62] This is modern politics, and it takes the place of the transcendental signifier with a vengeance. But in showing will to power operative in all of life, culture, and history, Nietzsche inaugurates the postmodern shattering of the traditional political boundaries and polarities—public/private, state/individual, self/other— and refashions all these relations as positions established for political purposes by the will to power, the politics of life itself. He repoliticizes all culture, philosophy, and art, and makes them transparent as objects of political will.

The temporary organization of contrasting, conflicting energies and wills that is the body, the ego, the self, and also the community, the culture and its ideals, all erected through the will to power in time, the will to mastery, the will to prevail, cannot be translated stupidly, oversimplistically, either into institutions of domination or institutions of submission, institutions of inequality or equality, institutions of democracy or autocracy or anarchy, however much Nietzsche may have had his own preferences. Neither does will to power translate readily into fixed types, castes, or classes of people or organizations, however much Nietzsche sometimes talks as if these types were established perpetually by time. He especially values the forces that have been historically discredited and "called evil," the ones that oppose the empty and vengeful platitudes and identities that dominate in the politics of the modern age. All institutions of whatever kind are brought into being by will to power and forced into and out of being again and again by the same forces, coming from different directions. All being is imposed on the chaos of becoming by domination, the domination of discordant wills, instincts, tendencies, and drives, forged into a signifying unity of one kind or another, for a time, as a *pathos* by human creativity and will to power.

In earlier ages political rule justified itself by divine right; in the modern age it has justified itself by popular authority and rights, lately sanctified by public opinion polls, mass marketing, media technology, biotechnology and the forces of global finance. Like Marx, Nietzsche sees all political positions and the intellectual, legal, and normative apparatuses used to perpetuate and align them as instruments of the will to rule, the will to power. Unlike Marx, he does not think that revolution will change any of this, or bring about justice. It will not bring about the kingdom of the just on earth or a classless society. History is not carrying us to the world-historical victory of the oppressed. It is not eschatological.

Not only does power and resistance circulate freely up and down, as Foucault insists, but will to power drives the motion of bodies of every sort in time, and every such motion is political in this much larger sense. Nietzsche shatters the boundaries that demarcate the political from everything else and places politics at the heart of everything; he uses the metaphor of politics, of will to power, as expressive of everything that happens in the world and of the world itself.

The modern epistemological dichotomies upon which political theory has based the differences between public and private, subject and object, or the individual will and general will, have ceased to be entirely functional, to contain what they were meant to contain. They are in fact being experienced in our time, like all other modern dualities, as more and more transparent and artifactual, self-reflexive, transient, manipulable, and politically constructed. They are demarcated relative to the perspective of the viewer, and, as in modern physics, the position of the object viewed varies in accordance with the movement of the viewer. In fact, the position of the object is only knowable as such from a certain perspective; from another perspective, there is only a wave. What it is depends on what we want to do with it. This is a bit reductive as a translation of Heisenberg, but it is not inaccurate. We live in a world of constantly moving images, translated into and out of code, into and out of light, into and out of history. The references multiply, get reconfigured, disappear and reappear in altered form. The distinctions between subjects and objects cannot be maintained, except for particular purposes by particular parties at particular moments. They require a great deal of both will and power to be maintained and defended.

It does no good to complain, as Mark Warren does, that Nietzsche doesn't understand the difference between the processes of individuals and "the essential features of modern society," the "autonomous, independent" collective functions of social and political life, like markets and bureaucracies.[63] Nietzsche doesn't misunderstand the difference, he denies the difference. He is not simply parroting the ancient analogy between the individual soul and the polis, an unconscious idiot Plato, as Warren seems to suggests. He is showing both individuals and collective functions to be organizations of the will to power, like all other unities, concepts, constructions, and organizations.

The will to power differentiates and establishes positions, interprets and evaluates texts and events in the temporal flux of history, within the essentially destabilized ongoing context of previous, remembered, contested moves of the same sort. Our interpretations of social processes or collective entities reconstruct them as we speak or write. We represent them, and enforce them, according to many different standards and discourses, some of which are and some of which are not compatible with or strictly analogous to the sort we might use to construct bodily or individual processes, and all of this is politics.

Nietzsche does not fail to recognize "permanent" or "necessary" structures of modern societies; he claims that the notions of the autonomy of market forces or the rationality of bureaucratic procedures we hold simply are, as are all other "things," manifestations of the will to power, organized and defended by some as "independent and necessary functions," which serves the purpose of their propagation and preserves their power of domination. They have no more independent, autonomous, or essential existence than anything else, which is none.

If, for purposes of our own, we choose to count, for instance, the market, either the global heterogenous systems of economic exchange or the financial markets that represent them, or the division of labor, or the structures of kinship, or any other structure as having "autonomous independence," or "permanent" effects, that's familiar and reassuring for some, depending on whose power is being served. Some effects last longer than others, of course, historically, especially if we keep calling them by the same names even while they change. But how long is long, Nietzsche wants to know? Philosophical, religious, and moral structures have certainly been constructed and construed as if they were absolute in the past. But nothing besides human decisions and language, interpretations and evaluations, the effects and products of will to power, bring such structures into existence and maintain them. That doesn't mean that they are not "real," but it forces us to question what "real" means. Their constructedness doesn't mean that we can just blow them away. Centuries of effort and fortified power have been and continue to be invested in them. Poststructuralism is the late recognition of the processes whereby structures get structured.[64] "Neither necessity nor universality can ever be given by experience."[65] The stakes we have invested in maintaining dominant concepts and structures can be and readily are contested and resisted by competing, opposing positions and perspectives. And we invent new ones all the time.

We operate, we live, among a welter of competing fictions as far as social formations go. For certain purposes, "private rights" might aid in the work of power to protect persons or spaces, turf and territory, gains and losses.[66] In other contexts, they can have the opposite effect. What we hold constant, historically, is what has served some powerful purposes longest—dominant purposes and hidden ones, forces of growth or of decay in Nietzsche's terms. Some structures and functions are the most familiar ones, the ones we call home, or like the best, or which serve life in various ways that we cannot fully understand. Often they are the ones that allow us most effectively to mask, deny, or alleviate suffering. Weber's theory, Marx's theory, Heidegger's theory—they are congenial to us (or not) as explicit organizations of thoughts for purposes of establishing ruling discourses and practices, the deep covert purposes of life, health and sickness, which Nietzsche intuits and tries to delineate. They have, as the saying goes, no essential existence, necessity, or universality, no sanctity or sanction inherent in the world. They have value because we gave them value and maintain it by power. They offer potent, useful interpretations that enable us to build up and tear down this, as opposed to that or the other. They are all, in other words, political.

Time is our canvas, our hunting ground, our playground. History is our home and we comfortably or uncomfortably inhabit it without taking notice of its historicity in every gesture. We fiddle with it constantly, making it more or less comfortable, safe, or more dangerous, for some. "In-itself" has no meaning, and the *pathos* of our power is time—nothing lasts, everything passes away. Our buildings and our theories outlive us, but they cannot establish a true or an everlasting bulkhead. Suffering is temporal. We are forever inventing and then investing in something "permanent" to assuage it.

I think it is interesting that Warren should choose, of all things, the market, as an essential and permanent structure of modern society that Nietzsche "misunderstands," since it seems to me the perfect image, the very metaphor itself, of the will to power, and especially of the nihilistic modern, democratic will to power, which creates and destroys values in every minute, incessantly. The financial market is made literally of millions of instant decisions to buy or sell, to win or lose, made by the anonymous impulses of anonymous egos in instantaneous electronic transactions all day and all night long all over the world—the indescribable and incalculable balance of forces, decisions, and acts of will, of power, transacted in milliseconds, up or down, victory or defeat, and then moving on to another and another, endlessly. Is there purpose or permanence there? Is there some overall intention in the market? Hardly. It is the register of pure will to power, inscribed through countless individual moments of choice, by countless impulses, desires, drives all continuously banked, counted, and then gone, change incessant, interminable, and impenetrable—reckoned up at the end of the day (whenever and wherever that happens to fall) as a number, electronically coded, standing in for innumerable entities, coming into and passing out of existence, and amounting to what? This is what Nietzsche fails to understand as a political game? This is what he can't account for critically by means of the will to power?

As to what this makes of politics, we have still to inquire. It is Nietzsche's charge regarding the nihilism endemic to modern politics that we have to take seriously.

NIHILISM: WHO ARE NOW THE MASTERS AND SLAVES?

In general, Nietzsche sees the democratizing impulse of our time as the leveling instincts of the herd in the modern age, as for instance effected in the mindless movements of markets and mass communications and media commodification, generated by nihilistic political and economic leaders for their own purposes of power. Democratic slogans appease and regulate the envy, *ressentiment*, and revenge of the "last men," who seek comfort and armed security, which they call freedom, from the relentless tearing down of ancient idols and the violent revenges of the hopeless, men who seek endless entertainments and intoxicants, including violence, the ephemera of the last days.

Nietzsche sees the state as having taken the place of God, a creation of the mighty, the barbaric and nihilistic mighty, who manipulate the slogans of nationalism and virtue for their own purposes, but barely even need anymore to disguise their will to power, to wealth and control of the world. Only the treacherous and ignoble values of nationalism and of militant group identities based on exhausted religious, class, race, and sex ideologies circulate in the political marketplace today, to lend a spurious "legitimacy" to the machinations of the strong and the weak. From whose point of view could we determine the moral "legitimacy" of rule?

This politics, according to Nietzsche's analysis, is itself the politics of nihilism. The virtues claimed in political struggle are sham, and are increasingly seen as sham, as bankrupt, dishonest, cynical, weary, without hope, meaning, truth, purpose, or integrity. They have a half-life of a week in the media circus of the world. These values and those who proclaim them live in the moment, offering momentary gratifications, and ever new gratifications for the voracious appetites of the nihilistic world, hungry for more affect, more entertainment, more pain and pleasure, which become indistinguishable. They do not, cannot, create—either culture, or art, or organic connections between people.

Arguments about whether Nietzsche is or isn't "political" tend to be relentlessly superficial.[67] I have argued that Nietzsche is deeply political, according to a changed meaning of that term, because he locates the will to power as the most fundamental force in all nature and life, and thus sees all willing, all deciding, all naming, as political, through and through and all the way down.

The problem with this, as Bonnie Honig suggests but does not quite argue, is that it constitutes a "displacement" of politics as we know it and as it has been conceived in the Western tradition since Plato. The "agonal" politics ascribed to Machiavelli, Nietzsche, and Hannah Arendt, primarily, as it has been conceptualized in recent years by Honig, Dana Villa, and others, is one way of "saving" politics from its modern sociological, administrative, and technical economic displacements in contemporary political theory.[68]

In relation to Nietzsche, this conception still doesn't help to solve two problems: (1) what to do with Nietzsche's contempt for democracy, liberalism, egalitarianism, and most important for leftist types like myself, for social revolution; and (2) the deeper and more urgent question of what happens to "the political," as it has involved the modern self and civil society, critical reason, freedom and authority, virtue and power, and the structures and institutions that translate these values into stable, enduring configurations, once all decisions whatsoever are understood as political. According to Nietzsche's deepest political instincts, all action, will, and thought are the exercise and effects of will to power in active and reactive, ever-changing and circulating patterns of "command" and "obedience." Doesn't making everything political make nothing political? How can one judge? Where is the critical lever to be applied?

As regards the first question, it is certainly possible to produce dozens of quotations from Nietzsche to show his contempt and hatred for democracy, for the leveling and herd-like characteristics of modern society and the "last men" who inhabit it, for the numbing sameness and destructive lack of creativity of modern politics, especially its mendacious and soul-destroying "idealism," derivative and recycled from ancient Christianity and modern Romantic anguish and envy. It is possible to find references, although they are usually more subtle than most commentators give him credit for, to aristocratic masters whom it is said Nietzsche thinks should be bred to rule the world. Recall his statement in the *Genealogy* that "to sacrifice humanity as mass to the welfare of a single stronger human species would indeed constitute progress."[69] The movement from "mass" to "species" is a significant one. I'm not going to wrestle with that here.[70]

It should be noted, however, that despite his most notorious pronouncements, Nietzsche is talking about the most spiritualized forms of will to power in his new type of man, not the most conventional or commercial. He was not a lover of the marketplace or the assembly. That is to say, it is precisely *not* the *political* type, as we understand it, whom Nietzsche sees as needed to rule. Nor is ruling others what interests him. It is the breeding of a kind of new spirit, a new kind of philosopher or truth-seeker, a musical Socrates, to which he is dedicated. It is hard to dissociate him from the obscene uses his work has been put to historically, but it should be done.

It should also be noted that even when Nietzsche speaks of future slaves and tyrants, he is trying to distinguish the making and preserving of distinctions, differences, between people. In one of his most infamous passages in *Beyond Good and Evil*, he speaks of "Europe's *democratic* movement" as a "tremendous *physiological* process," an historical differentiation such that "Europeans are becoming more similar to each other," which produces a counteraction—"a super-national and nomadic type of man is gradually coming up, a type that possesses, physiologically speaking, a maximum of the art and power of adaptation as its typical distinction." It can hardly be doubted that such a "type" is emerging on the global stage, but whether that adaptability constitutes mastery of the kind Nietzsche had in mind can be doubted. It is also in this passage that he goes on to say that

> the very same conditions that will on the average lead to the leveling and mediocritization of man—to a useful, industrious, handy, multi-purpose herd animal—are likely in the highest degree to give birth to exceptional human beings of the most dangerous and attractive quality. . . . But while the democratization of Europe leads to the production of a type that is prepared for slavery in the subtlest sense, in single, exceptional cases the strong human being will have to turn out stronger and richer than perhaps ever before. . . . the democratization of Europe is at the same time an involuntary arrangement for the cultivation of tyrants—taking that word in every sense, including the most spiritual."[71]

The kind of tyrants we have seen, unfortunately, have not been the most spiritual kind. Still, it is fascinating to think of who Nietzsche might see as the highest tyrants of spirit, the true masters of our century: Shostokovitch or Stravinsky? Mahler or Bela Bartok? Gauguin, Picasso, or Mark Rothko? Yeats or Joyce, Proust or Rilke? Never Virginia Woolf or Toni Morrison? What are the criteria for spiritual mastery that pertain to our world? Who are the "highest" human beings, who have mastered themselves and rule, not the herd, but rather the culture in which we all swim?

It must also be said again that when Nietzsche speaks of natural slaves he is not speaking of the poor. He does not mean by "underprivileged" what we mean by "underpriviliged":

> What does "underprivileged" mean? Above all, physiologically—no longer politically. The unhealthiest kind of man in Europe (in all classes) furnishes the soil for this nihilism: they will experience the belief in the eternal recurrence as a curse, struck by which one no longer shrinks from any action; not to be extinguished passively but to extinguish everything that is so aim- and meaning-less, although this is a mere convulsion, a blind rage at the insight that everything has been for eternities—even this moment of nihilism and lust for destruction.—It is the value of such a crisis that it purifies, that it pushes together related elements to perish of each other, that it assigns common tasks to men who have opposite ways of thinking . . . those who command are recognized as those who command, those who obey as those who obey. Of course, outside every existing social order.[72]

Nietzsche is talking about nihilists, not merely about the downtrodden; he is thinking of something other than what we intuitively or traditionally think of as the ruling and the ruled. It is not the politically, certainly not the economically dominant, of the present world in whom he discerns spiritual commanding, nor that sort of domination that is at stake here. He is not talking about economic classes or about the production of wealth. It is far too easy for commentators to slip carelessly from his usages to ours. Nietzsche is appalled by our ruling classes and their values. Like Plato, it is important always to ask what virtues he is seeking in his rulers, although "virtue" in the moralistic sense is precisely what he is not seeking. Yet what we see as non-moralistic virtues are not Nietzsche's either. Higher souls are higher in that they are self-overcoming.

Nietzsche is talking about "the great health" that is needed to overcome nihilism; he doesn't expect it to come from the ruling classes or ideas of today, nor would he find those who obey in the familiar places. The differentiation he is talking about comes about through living the terror and pain of the great crises of the end of modernity, crises brought about by the pressures of traditional values being annihilated in all social classes, and most especially in the ones in charge at present. It is "outside every existing social order" that his new ranks of spiritual command and obedience, masters and slaves, take shape. "It seems that the essential thing, both 'in heaven and on earth,' is that there be a protracted period of unidirectional obedience: in the long run, that is how something emerged and emerges and makes life on earth worth living: virtue, for example, or art, music, dance, reason, spirituality—something transfiguring, elegant, wild, and divine. The long constraint of the spirit; the reluctant coercion in the communicability of thoughts, the thinker's self-imposed discipline."[73]

Nietzsche's indictment of revolution is even more troubling. It seems only yesterday that revolution, in its traditional modern form, still seemed both possible and necessary to many, and yet his prescient understanding of revolution as a form of the state that devours its own children has proved all to the point in the century since his death.

In *Zarathustra*, Part II, "On Great Events," Zarathustra descends beneath the earth to speak to a fire-spewing hellhound, a revolutionary "overthrow devil," who is interested in the great task of overthrowing the modern state. Nietzsche counters that for him "the stillest hour" and "the greatest thoughts are the greatest events."[74] Furthermore, as Laurence Lampert makes clear:

> Nor does Zarathustra distinguish between the church and the modern state in this respect. All three—church, state, and revolutionary—believe that they hold conflicting views about the belly of things; but all three belong to the same camp as sects of the same religion, and each is possessed by the passion of sectarians against the heretics who stand nearest them. As a sectarian of the democratic religion, the only religion viable in the political ecclesiology of the modern world, the socialist or communist revolutionary sees himself as the fundamental opponent of the liberal state, with the church no longer relevant.[75]

But when Zarathustra repeats the rhetoric of the modern state, that it is the most important thing on earth, the revolutionary hellhound almost chokes on his envy, revealing what Nietzsche has maintained all along—that modern revolutionary ideology is based on envy and revenge and is looking to gain for itself the powers that the state wields. Revolution is not, in other words, according to Nietzsche, a genuine response to suffering, nor does it bring justice. It exchanges those who rule and are ruled, but the nature of rule remains. This is not all there is to say about revolution in Nietzsche. In this chapter of *Zarathustra* he hints at another kind of revolutionary, one who would create new values. But Zarathustra clearly sees existing modern revolutionaries as monsters of violence, malice and envy, who are merely the underground of the ground of the state, its necessary and connected opposites, inhabiting the same primary field, the field of nihilism. Power without real value is what Nietzsche sees as the field of modern politics, both official and anti-official—a barbarism of the crudest and worst, the "money-makers" and "military despots."

Nietzsche correctly predicted that our century would be the century of wars for control of the world, wars to give ideological meaning to the world, to dictate such meanings to the world. He predicted that it would be a world of polemical and technological manipulations in the face of ever-deepening alienation, isolation, terror, and suffering.

> competition for growth assumes a kind of tropical tempo and there is a tremendous perishing and causing-to-perish, owing to the wild egoisms that challenge one another with seeming explosiveness, struggling for 'sun and light,' and no longer knowing how to derive any set of limits, any restraint, any forbearance from their earlier moral code. . . . The dangerous and sinister point is reached where the greater, more differentiated, richer life *survives beyond* the old morality; the 'individual' is left standing, forced to be his own law-giver, to create his own arts and wiles of self-preservation, self-advancement, self-redemption . . . decline, decay and the greatest aspirations terribly entangled. . . . Danger is present once again, the mother of morality, the great danger, this time displaced into the individual, into the neighbor or friend, into the street, into our own children, our own hearts, into everything that is most secretly our own wishing and wanting: what will the moral philosophers who emerge during this period find to preach about?[76]

He did not look to "political" answers for these conditions—he gave politics over to the consoling illusions of old-fashioned liberalism and utilitarianism, to the fanaticism of the nihilists, and to the nihilism of the everyday commercial world, to the last men. He had no hope for political solutions, because the problems he diagnosed were not, in the traditional sense, political, except insofar as culture, values, the creation of values and the fate of souls is political. In our time, whether they are or they are not, and how that might be, presently constitutes the most ferocious battleground for political theory and practice.

The second question I raised, the question of whether seeing every decision and act, every event and creation, as political, is virtually or practically the same as seeing nothing as political, raises a further and related question—whether by dismantling the structures of principle, agency, rational critique, the metaphysics of morality, and the foundations of ethics and politics, whether Nietzsche, however thoroughly he reenvisions and reinvents a postmodern notion of the polical, of agency and responsiblility, doesn't destroy "modern" politics and its conditions of critique, agency, and responsibility. This is an exceedingly important question.

The answer, in a word, as Laurence Sterne would say, is yes and no.[77] Nietzsche wrestles time and again with the necessity of language and the fact that our language and history, our grammar and thought, are drenched in metaphysical categories and demarcations, and as much as he, and we, might like to do away with that, we cannot. The past, the "It was," accompanies and lives in us always. We construct unities and totalities by talking, whether we will or no. Nonetheless, the reifications of traditional metaphysical morality and politics are continually collapsing and the relativities of place and time continually evolving. New postmodern metaphors of meaning, agency, and responsibility are being invented. We learn to swim in the new open seas. Nietzsche suggests some new ways for such swimming, enigmatically, in his thought of eternal recurrence.

The power of his critique of ancient and modern idols and his revaluation of what has been most despised are powerful political tools, however. His dismantling genealogy of the politics of the individual and the state, as Hobbes, Rousseau, or Marx would recognize them, is what makes him the first "postmodern," and he certainly knew himself to constitute in his very life and work such a decisive break in history.

Nietzsche did not see such a break as inevitable, historically or philosophically. It forms part of an ongoing war, a struggle, which he expects to last hundreds of years. He does see that it follows from the will to truth, the noblest and most dangerous of all human versions of the will to power. It is the will to truth that grew out of Christian morality and yet accounts for the death of God, underway for centuries now. Moreover, Nietzsche diagnoses the problem of suffering that lies at the heart of religion, metaphysics, and morality and lays bare the meaninglessness, purposelessness, and powerlessness of our suffering and our finitude. He locates the creation of values in the space opened up by the disappearance of truth and purpose, in the moment, the gateway, at which past and future meet, and he places the moment in our hands.

Creative individuals are rare; that is one of Nietzsche's most persistent truths. They can't be produced, and certainly not by the political machines for the production of public values and commodities as we know them. Nietzsche saw no way to make creativity or responsibility "political" functions. Politics in our age comprises the worst conflagrations of suffering and will—suffering without end or meaning, and the will to exploit suffering while denying one is producing it. There is no will to truth in politics. Need we look farther than this week's headlines to confirm that? The imagination boggles when it tries to imagine applying real aesthetic criteria to these spectacles.

It is possible to imagine a politics of affirmation, of responsibility, of artistic creativity for individuals, as we will consider next in relation to Nietzsche's doctrine of eternal recurrence. It is a difficult unraveling, but worth the effort. But is it possible to imagine a politics of the creation of new values for peoples, or for the world as a species, which is what Nietzsche ultimately thought had to be brought about? The experiences of the twentieth century have not brought us closer to refuting Nietzsche's pessimism in this regard. We can see nihilism in a thousand masks and garbs, more than Nietzsche could ever have imagined, in our private and our public lives, the lines separating the two increasingly blurred, the suffering and loss in both increasingly impenetrable.

If we might be able, haltingly, to specify how an individual might make herself understood, might take responsibility for her history, and affirm even her own suffering, why can we not generalize such acts from an individual, who is, after all, already a multiplicity, to a concrete communal multiplicity that could be united, always only for a time, in a revaluing of values? Why and for whose sake would such a unifying take place? How could it be enacted, or even taught? By the will to power only. And whose will to power would that be? Where would new values come from? Whose history should we pick to choose them? Out of whose pain can they be created?

12

The Eternal Recurrence of the Same

If Nietzsche dramatizes genealogically that all moralities and metaphysics are the desperate, decadent, yet indispensable expressions of the will to power and the will to nothingness, dressed up as eternal truths, he indicates only two kinds of experience that can oppose or overcome this form of the will to power: artistic creativity, and an exceedingly enigmatic notion of time and self-overcoming that paradoxically involves coming to terms with who one is, with one's suffering, as an eternally recurring fate.

> that no one gives one's qualities, neither God nor society, nor one's parents and forefathers, nor oneself. . . . No one is answerable for the fact that one is there at all. . . . The fatality of one's essence is not to be disengaged from everything that was and will be. The human being is not the effect of a particular intention, will, or goal . . . .We have invented the concept "goal." In reality, the goal is missing. . . . One is a piece of fatality, one belongs to the totality, one is in the totality. . . . But there is nothing outside the totality. . . . The concept "God" was previously the greatest objection to existence. . . . We deny God, we deny the answerability in God: we thereby redeem the world for the first time.[1]

There is no reason that we are in existence and no one is responsible for it. "One is a piece of fatality," not only fated, but fatal, given in time as a gift with no giver, as in some sense the sum of all that has gone before, and finite, mortal. But why, or how is it that because we deny God and God's answerability for the future, we thereby "redeem" the world for the first time? Is it the lack of answerability that frees us for action or for the willing of some other future? And what kind of meaning can "redemption" have for Nietzsche or for us, if there is no god, no ideal world or coming of the kingdom on earth, no place for a final self-overcoming, and no possible end to suffering?

251

We might recall that Nietzsche in the *Genealogy* proclaimed suffering as man's greatest objection to existence. That thought is intimately related to this one: God's answerability, that is, man's positing the existence of the Absolute, as judgment and end, in a perfect world beyond this one as an answer to the meaninglessness of human suffering is what makes the combination of God and suffering the greatest objection to human existence in this world. It is the elaboration of that answer, the very conditions of that answerability, which has shaped our history. Suffering, and thus the need for God and for an ideal world (either divine or metaphysical) to justify and redeem this one, and the gradual exposure in the modern age, in both thought and history, of the unbelief, the lie, at the core of that answer, constitute the historical, nihilistic rejection of existence that Nietzsche's genealogy uncovers. Suffering fuels the rage of revenge in the nihilistic politics of the present.

Suffering is our passion. It is the *pathos* of our power and truth in time. It is this passion and *pathos* that has built a historical world of religious, philosophical, and political structures to endow our passion with sense and purpose. The will to truth that suffering and power generated, an unending skepticism and critique, finally tore that world apart and left us naked with suffering in the void, with no answer, no conditions of answerability even, from which to create a response to suffering. It is this fatality, which Nietzsche also called "indispensable," the inevitable inscription of our error and raging despair in our bodies and souls, which forms the context in which Nietzsche sets his doctrine of the eternal recurrence of the same. It is in the context of the genealogy that tears the heart out of every affirmation and every redemption that Nietzsche sets his paradox of eternal return. It is to the elucidation of this doctrine that we now turn.

SUFFERING AND THE ETERNAL RECURRENCE OF THE SAME

In the teaching of the eternal recurrence of the same, Nietzsche affirms the fatality of our existence as a kind of liberation. We are not responsible for our being here, nor was there ever any intention, god, or goal behind it or in front of it. There is only the totality of the world and we, swimming upstream, in it. Our profound realization of that reality constitutes, Nietzsche says, a "real redemption," although we need to decipher what that could mean in this context. Nietzsche despises the "cry for redemption" that arises from the inverted cruelty of the ascetic redeemer-type.[2] What other sort of redemption could he envision? It is certainly not obvious how willing the eternal recurrence of everything, especially of all the suffering known to the world in mankind's history as a whole, could be either liberating or redemptive, or how it could possibly constitute a meaningful response to suffering.

Nietzsche's insight into the paradox of our existence, our finitude, our suffering and our willing was most fully worked out, although it was by no means ever fully worked out, in terms of the experience that paradoxically combines fatality with eternity, the acceptance of life and especially of suffering with some new form of "already achieved" redemption, the thought Nietzsche called "the eternal recurrence of the same." Each term of this thought requires considerable working through to articulate what it might involve. As David Farrell Krell puts it, "The words *eternity* and *recurrence*, to say nothing of *the same*, militate against what Nietzsche is trying to think as *tragic* affirmation, as the adventure of immanence."[3] The thought of the eternal recurrence of the same, which he understood as his most "authentic teaching," his "destiny," he experienced both as the most intolerable burden and as the greatest liberation, simultaneously joy and terror, ascent and descent, and it remains his most difficult and controversial thought.[4]

Nietzsche first experienced the thought of eternal recurrence as an "explosive" epiphany in August 1881, "six thousand feet beyond human beings and time," walking along the lakeshore of Silvaplana, as he explains in *Ecce Homo*.[5] Nietzsche's first announcement of the doctrine, however, was made under the title *"The greatest weight"* [*Das grössye Schwergewicht*] in Book Four of *The Gay Science*:

> What, if some day or night a demon were to steal after you into your loneliest loneliness and say to you: "This life as you now live it and have lived it, you will have to live once more and innumerable times more; and there will be nothing new in it, but every pain and every joy and every thought and sign and everything unutterably small or great in your life will have to return to you, all in the same succession and sequence—even this spider and this moonlight between the trees, and even this moment and myself. The eternal hourglass of existence is turned upside down again and again, and you with it, speck of dust. Would you not throw yourself down and gnash your teeth and curse the demon who spoke thus? Or have you once experienced a tremendous moment when you would have answered him "You are a god and never have I heard anything more divine." . . . Or how well disposed would you have to become to yourself and to life *to crave nothing more fervently* than this ultimate eternal confirmation and seal?[6]

It is important that Nietzsche's first published mention of eternal return is cast in terms of the demonic, a demon who invades your "loneliest loneliness" and issues a challenge that is both a burden and a test, a test of health or of decadence, of self-love or self-hate, a test of one's ultimate attitude toward life, Dionysian affirmation or nihilistic nightmare. If one could "crave nothing more fervently" than that one's life, and all of the history that has gone before it that leads inexorably to this moment, would recur again and again unchanged throughout eternity, one would affirm, tragically and ecstatically, everything that the world is and ever has been; one would refuse any otherworldly redemption, and thus, unwittingly, bring "real" redemption into the world. The tragic insight of eternal recurrence is the insight of Silenus turned inside out; man's recognition and concurrence in Silenus's judgment, along with its simultaneous revaluation: "in spite of the flux of phenomena, life is at bottom indestructibly powerful and pleasurable."[7] The world is, in itself, the already "achieved redemption" of the god.

In *Thus Spoke Zarathustra* Nietzsche dramatizes the doctrine of eternal recurrence, and in the strange poetry of that book, he gives us the conditions and some intimations of the meaning of this almost unfathomable doctrine. In the chapter "On Redemption" in the second part of *Zarathustra*, Zarathustra speaks of what he sees among men: not only "to see that this one lacks an eye and that one an ear and a third a leg, . . . and human beings who lack everything, except one thing of which they have too much—human beings who are nothing but a big eye or a big mouth or a big belly or anything at all that is big. Inverse cripples I call them. . . . The now and the past on earth—alas, my friends, that is what I find most unendurable."[8]

It is the past, the deformations among men, the suffering they have caused, and the responses of self-deception and pity they have engendered, that Zarathustra finds intolerable. It is not merely that men are deformed; it is not merely that their responses to these deformations have led them to pity and revenge; it is not merely even that in that revenge the "last men" have come to dominate the earth; it is that all this has passed and is done and that no amount of willing can change it—that is what Zarathustra finds intolerable.

Zarathustra connects the inversions of the will, the fury and hatred of the will against the past, against the "It was," with both nihilism and a liberation of the will. "This, indeed this alone, is what *revenge* is: the will's ill will against time and its 'it was.'"

> The *spirit of revenge*, my friends, has so far been the subject of man's best reflection; and where there was suffering, one always wanted punishment too. For 'punishment' is what revenge calls itself; with a hypocritical lie it creates a good conscience for itself. Because there is suffering in those who will, inasmuch as they cannot will backwards, willing itself and all life were supposed to be—a punishment. And now cloud upon cloud rolled over the spirit, until eventually madness preached, 'Everything passes away; therefore everything deserves to pass away. And this too is justice, the law of time that it must devour its children.' Thus preached madness.[9]

If everything ends, then it must "deserve" to end. If man does not have ultimate value, inherent value, which his mortality denies, then nothing is worthwhile, nothing is of any value, nothing endures or protects or sustains us. Everything is worthless. This, Nietzsche says, is madness.

At the end of Christian piety, at the time of the now-occuring collapse of all previous values, a new problem emerges, the will to nothingness in the face of time itself, the will to truth, the will to the truth of nothingness, preferable to not willing at all. Time itself devours its children and renders meaningless all their truths and all their suffering. Krell says: "Titanic time eats its mortal and immortal children alike, devours its nymphs and daimons, all of whom *suffer* time. Yet the pleasure they take in the world and the earth, 'eating bread, tasting the earth,' wills the eternity of the time of the earth. Humankind honors the earth now, not the gods of Platonism and the Prophets, and so honors the immutable fate of this suffering of time—not contradicting it, as we shall see, but calling for it once again."[10]

Everything passes away and madness preaches that therefore everything deserves to pass away. What cannot endure has no worth, no value. And yet what, after all, endures? Without eternity, how shall anything be redeemed from time's utter destruction? And yet Nietzsche wants to affirm the transient world and our responses to it. Nietzsche's response, on our behalf, occurs through the will:

> To redeem those who lived in the past and to recreate all 'it was' into a 'thus I willed it'—that alone should I call redemption. Will— that is the name of the liberator and joy-bringer; thus I taught you, my friends. But learn this too: the will itself is still a prisoner. Willing liberates; but what is it that puts even the liberator himself in fetters? 'It was'—that is the name of the will's gnashing of teeth and most secret melancholy. Powerless against what has been done, he is an angry spectator of all that is past. The will cannot will backwards; and that he cannot break time and time's covetousness, that is the will's loneliest melancholy.[11]

The will itself is broken on time's wheel; the will cannot will backwards. Time is a one-way arrow. The will can change the present, and thus part of the future, but it cannot change what has already happened, what is finished once and for all and can never be undone. That is our fate and the burden of our finitude. Whatever the eternity of the world, we humans only go in one direction, from birth to death. What is past is beyond reach and beyond remedy. Or so it would seem.

We are caught in the stream of time, going eternally into the dark. Even Benjamin's Angel of History is blown backwards into the future, looking back at the ever-accumulating catastrophe that is blowing him forward. Nietzsche's Zarathustra is pinned likewise. It is only in the thought of the eternal recurrence that willing backwards becomes possible. How? It is only possible to speculate; I will try to put together a formulation, an articulation, that can translate into language what Nietzsche experienced, what he feared and found intolerable, exalted, inexpressible—what he hesitated again and again to put into language. This is the thought that Nietzsche saw as his particular and irreproachable destiny; a thought he never brought to an "ultimate conceptual formulation" (as if there were such a thing), because it is an experience that cannot finally be conceptualized.[12] So we must pick our way among metaphors and images to attempt to understand it.

Karl Löwith, in his pathbreaking book *Nietzsche's Philosophy of the Eternal Recurrence of the Same*, argues insightfully that "For answering the question of the philosophic meaning of this teaching, the context in which one places the teaching is decisive." He rightly places this teaching in the context of nihilism and the death of God: "for this work too [the plans for *The Will to Power*] the teaching of the eternal recurrence would have remained the definitive answer—that is, to the question of nihilism, which for its part arises out of the death of God. The overcoming of nihilism by means of the man who overcomes himself is the precondition for the prophecy of the eternal recurrence."[13]

The problem of nihilism, as I have conceptualized it in this book, has to do with meaninglessness, especially the meaninglessness of human suffering, the vacuum that exists after the death of God, and also that which arrives with the will to truth, which in conceiving itself in the modern age unconditionally, as unconditioned, wills nothingness. In Christianity, the *horror vacui*, the suffering of being-there and its emptiness, seemed to be filled. "*The will itself was saved*" precisely through the development of the ascetic ideal. The Christian conception of redemption was, Nietzsche argues, a twisted and willfully false salvation, a deception and a cruelty, but it was nonetheless a willing that preserved willing. It allowed us to go forward, to become interesting, to grow deeper; it was in the interest of life itself that this devotion to rarified cruelty and suffering was devised.

But for us as moderns, "To sacrifice God for the nothing—this paradoxical mystery of the final cruelty was reserved for the generation that is now coming up: all of us already know something of this."[14] Christianity was in itself a will toward nothingness, because it was a will toward a nonexistent reality, a nullification of this world for the ideality of a world beyond, which constituted as sacred a hatred for the actual world, a denial and a cruel contempt for human life and its wretched history.

But in the modern age, as we have seen through Hobbes, science has progressively revealed the untruthfulness and the untruth, the ungroundedness, of the ancient God and all the virtues of morality and metaphysics that flowed from and depended upon him. For what have we "sacrificed" God? To what have we sacrificed God? To truth, to truthfulness, to the kind of intellectual honesty and probity that Nietzsche honors as our finest capacity. And yet, this is a final, terrible cruelty. What is revealed in the death of God is nothingness, pure and simple.

Is it in nothingness that we are to find "redemption" from the endless history of our revenge—our revenge against ourselves which was God, our revenge against suffering, our revenge against time? "Liberation from revenge is the goal toward which Nietzsche directs his thinking of eternal recurrence,"[15] revenge not just from the cruelties and the sufferings of life, but from the hatred of time and transience, from the *pathos* of truth, and from the impotence of the will in the face of "it was."

> Metaphysical man seeks a *ground* for his suffering, for the *circle* of life, suffering and death. Not content with accepting suffering as his condition or situation, he devotes his life to a search for its cause, for a place to lay the blame. Suffering is experienced always as a *fait accompli*, with the cause in each case lying outside itself, back in time, in the 'it was.' . . . Time reveals itself as the absolute impossibility of the human will to overcome suffering. Time is that which the will cannot break, the will's insurmountable obstacle. . . . The thwarted will thus becomes enslaved to revenge: revenge foments a sort of counterwill to the forceful 'it was' of time, a counterwill or ill will that declares the sole justification of a world in which there is suffering to be its transiency, its passing away. . . . For Nietzsche, this counterwill is the origin of metaphysics, hence of nihilism.[16]

To understand how to free the will, how to overcome the revenge of the nihilistic will to posit permanent meaning and truth, and then to tear it down, it is necessary to imagine abandoning or relinquishing the goal of finding a cause, a transcendental source, or a meaning for human suffering. When suffering is not only accepted as a necessary condition of human existence, but affirmed as an ultimately desired and desireable part of human existence, it is possible to go beyond revenge. How?

In *Zarathustra*, in "The Wanderer," Nietzsche writes of Zarathustra's loneliest walk: "Only now are you going your way to greatness! Peak and abyss—they are now joined together. . . . now that which has hitherto been your ultimate danger has become your ultimate refuge."[17] The highest peak and the deepest abyss come together, and together they form the context for Zarathustra's vision, which comes in the next part, "On the Vision and the Riddle." But it is crucial to Nietzsche's most profound truth, the great *pathos* of truth, that the highest mountain and the deepest abyss are always one and the same:

> Before my highest mountain I stand and before my longest wandering; to that end I must first go down deeper than I ever descended—

deeper into pain than ever I descended, down into its blackest flood.
Thus my destiny wants it. Well, I am ready. Whence come the highest mountains? I once asked. Then I learned that they come out of
the sea. The evidence is written in their rocks and in the walls of
their peaks. It is out of the deepest depth that the highest must
come to its height.[18]

Even in the first part of *Zarathustra*, Nietzsche speaks to the young man,
who may become his disciple, of "the tree stretching upward into the light
by rooting itself deeper into the darkness of the earth, into evil."[19] In all of
Nietzsche's works, early and late, the necessary conjunction of good and
evil, of height and depth, is constant. It is not that good and evil are inextricably mixed, but that they are forever and necessarily co-determining. Each has
no meaning or reality without the other. Wishing away evil is like wishing
away rain or night, wanting only sunshine (if such an earth is even imaginable),
with no thought for the consequences for the things of the earth.

Nietzsche's uncanny insight is into the folly of imagining that man could
will a world or build one in which there could be only light, only height, only
goodness and justice, and no necessarily accompanying dark, depth, evil, and
injustice. What Nietzsche is seeking to bring us to accept, not as a bitter fact,
but as an obvious condition for all life, and as truth that is *pathos*, is that the
very meaning and reality of the good depends on the reality and meaning of
evil—not just as words but as experience. The suffering of evil is integral to
the enacting of good. We cannot know or enact one without the other. Getting "beyond good and evil" is, for Nietzsche, getting beyond the will to have
one half and not the other, which is a pointless thought, an idiocy. The goal,
as he sees it, is for human willing somehow to integrate both good and evil,
both day and night, into a life of striving for self-overcoming, for an ever-more-
encompassing creation. To choose, disregarding customary labels, according
to the context and the most far-reaching human purposes. To have control
of one's pros and cons, and to deploy them for the taking of responsibility or
the creation of new values. That requires a spirit that has suffered a long discipline in the widest possible ranges of human experiences.

Nietzsche does not argue that there is no good or evil, and certainly not
that they can be done away with, although he wants to mount a powerful
offensive against the traditional pieties and virtues, on behalf of the traditional
vices, at this point in history. What he wants is someone who can perceive
with subtlety and discrimination what might be needed in any given context,
and can choose, knowing the conditioned and conditional nature of all such
choices, disregarding what is traditionally thought of as good and evil. He
wants to transfigure the terms of choice—he retains the terrain, however, of
ethical choice in every context and from every perspective.

There is no joy without pain; there is no blissful dance of life without also and necessarily (how else?) its agony. If one wants one's destiny, and this is Nietzsche's most noble one's wish (it is of the essence of the strongest and most courageous will that it wants its own destiny), then one wants as well one's deepest pain; only out of the depths can the heights be attained. Nietzsche says that it is the capacity to "endure the most" that shows the greatest spirit. He asserts the value of suffering for mankind:

> The discipline of suffering, of *great* suffering—do you not know that only *this* discipline has created all enhancements of man so far? That tension of the soul in unhappiness which cultivates its strength, its shudders face to face with great ruin, its inventiveness and courage in enduring, persevering, interpreting, and exploiting suffering, and whatever has been granted to it of profundity, secret, mask, spirit, cunning, greatness—was it not granted to it through suffering, through the discipline of great suffering? In man, *creature* and *creator* are united: in man there is material, fragment, excess, clay, dirt, nonsense, chaos; but in man there is also creator, forgiver, hammer hardness, spectator divinity, and seventh day: do you understand this contrast?[20]

The deepest pain and the most terrifying descent as always also and simultaneously the steepest ascent and the most blissful joy, these together give a vision of life that is most fruitful, worthy, and glorious. Perhaps enough to count as something of a redemption, if a redemption of an altogether new kind? Perhaps, but who is it who is redeemed? What of the others?

Zarathustra, Nietzsche says, is "a friend of all who travel far and do not like to live without danger." On his own climb up the mountain path, Zarathustra has to bear the dwarf, the spirit of gravity, on his shoulder: "Upward—defying the spirit that drew it downward toward the abyss, the spirit of gravity, my devil and archenemy. Upward—although he sat on me, half dwarf, half mole, lame, making lame, dripping lead into my ear, leaden thoughts into my brain." The dwarf mocks Zarathustra: "O Zarathustra. . . . You threw yourself up so high; but every stone that is thrown must fall. Sentenced to yourself and your own stoning—O Zarathustra, far indeed have you thrown the stone, but it will fall back on yourself."[21]

Nietzsche echoes the necessary correspondence and complementarity of ascending and falling here, but the dwarf's taunt also carries the implication of Zarathustra's self-defeat—"Sentenced to yourself and your own stoning"—which attends the will to achieve the heights. Zarathustra is being set up, or is setting himself up, for a fall. Nietzsche is playing, gravely, with the proximity, indeed the coicidence, of the abyss, the nihil, the will to nothingness and suicide, nihilism itself, with the will to go onward, upward, to prevail. What is needed, he declares, is courage:

"Dwarf! It is you or I!" For courage is the best slayer, courage which *attacks*; for in every attack there is playing and brass. Man, however, is the most courageous animal. . . . With playing and brass he has so far overcome every pain; but human pain is the deepest pain. Courage also slays dizziness at the edge of abysses: and where does man not stand at the edge of abysses? Is not seeing always—seeing abysses? Courage is the best slayer: courage slays even pity. But pity is the deepest abyss: as deeply as man sees into life, he also sees into suffering. Courage, however, is the best slayer— courage which attacks: which slays even death itself, for it says, "Was *that* life? Well, then! Once more!"[22]

It is with courage, playing, and brass that man's courage overcomes even the deepest pain. Standing at the edge of the abyss, as we always are and especially as we are now in our time, even more nakedly than when we stood under the protective delusions of God and metaphysics, our knowledge has brought us to the edge and over into the abyss: "Is not seeing always—seeing abysses?"

We must slay even pity. As Nietzsche says in the conclusion of the passage from *Beyond Good and Evil* on the discipline of suffering: "And that *your* pity is for the 'creature in man,' for what must be formed, broken, forged, torn, burnt, made incandescent, and purified—that which *necessarily* must and *should* suffer? And our pity—do you not comprehend for whom our *converse* pity is when it resists your pity as the worst of all pampering and weaknesses? Thus it is pity *versus* pity."[23]

Pity for the necessary suffering of man is the deepest abyss, because seeing into the depths is always seeing suffering, and because wishing away that suffering is also and necessarily wishing away all that the discipline of suffering can attain, the heights and greatness and creativity of which man is capable. "*Your* pity," for the suffering creature, is to be opposed by "our *converse* pity," for the creator in man who needs his suffering in order to create, and who is gravely endangered, even destroyed, by the "preachers of pity." Suffering and pity, as we have seen, go together and they constitute together, for Nietzsche, our deepest danger. If we can replace our pity for our suffering with a pity for the difficulty of our task as creators and an appreciation of the necessity of our struggle, we can take courage and create new values. But how does this bring us some victory over time?

Our finitude itself, our mortality, Nietzsche affirms, is not to be wished away, but it is to be savored and celebrated as the tragic root of our life and our achievement. Even death does not in the end make us pitiful, or afraid— "Was that life? Well then! Once more!" Da Capo! From the beginning! The will to the eternal recurrence of the same is the willing of the most imaginative and almost unimaginable courage. Whatever life has brought, well, then, yes, let's have it once again.

Whatever life has brought? To everyone, everywhere?

Why? What could be the explanation of the meaning of this will to have it all happen all over again, eternally? One image that Nietzsche gives us comes in the next section of *Zarathustra*, "On the Vision and the Riddle." The dwarf jumps down from Zarathustra's shoulder, and there is a gateway where they have stopped. Here Zarathustra utters his "abysmal thought:" "Behold this gateway, dwarf!" I continued. "It has two faces. Two paths meet here; no one has yet followed either to its end. This long lane stretches back for an eternity. And the lane out there, that is another eternity. They contradict each other, these paths; they offend each other face to face; and it is here at this gateway that they come together. The name of the gateway is inscribed above: 'Moment.'"[24]

Zarathustra explains his thought to the dwarf, the spirit of gravity. From this gateway, the moment, the two eternal paths of the past and of the future meet and come together, in opposition, Nietzsche says, in contradiction. The past and the future confront each other in "the moment," the present. Something is in contention in the moment. The fate of the past and of the future are in contention in the present. In the moment, in the gateway that is the present moment, the past and the future are determined. There is a paradox and a choice in this moment. There is an opportunity to choose. It is a gateway, open on either end, infinitely. And can the choice alter both the past and the future? What could this mean? Behind lies an eternity, and ahead, contending with the past, the future also lies as an eternity.

> Must not whatever *can* walk have walked on this lane before? Must not whatever *can* happen have happened, have been done, have passed before? . . . And are not all things knotted together so firmly that this moment draws after it *all* that is to come? Therefore— itself too? For whatever *can* walk—in this long lane out *there* too, it *must* walk once more. And this slow spider, which crawls in the moonlight, and this moonlight itself, and I and you in the gateway— must we not eternally return?

For Nietzsche there can never be, there could never have been, a beginning or an end. Time is a curve, a spiral, a hyperspace. "Are not all things knotted together so firmly that this moment draws after it *all* that is to come?" From the moment of the present, the past is recontextualized and reconstituted, and the future as well, drawn by its being tightly intertwined with everything else, is also drawn through the moment of the present. In the present is the knot of the past and the future. And since time is infinite, everything has happened always already forever.

Whatever could have happened must, in the eternity of time, have already happened, and whatever could be yet to come, must in the eternity of time, have already come. If there were ever to be a beginning, it would have happened. If there were ever to be an end, it would already have taken place. That is what infinity means, he says. This is eternity. So there can be no beginning and no end. The eternal recurrence of the same. But it is not just a circle, a cycle, as Zarathustra's animals optimistically interpret. Zarathustra keeps silent. What is the meaning of the gateway and of eternity?

Zarathustra is afraid of his thoughts. Then he hears a dog howl. He remembers such a dog. "And when I heard such howling again I took pity again." So Nietzsche offers Zarathustra, and us, another image, even more terrifying and enigmatic:

A young shepherd I saw, writhing, gagging, in spasms, his face distorted, and a heavy black snake hung out of his mouth. Had I ever seen so much nausea and pale dread on one face? He seemed to have been asleep when the snake crawled into his throat, and there bit itself fast. My hand tore at the snake and tore in vain; it did not tear the snake out of his throat. Then it cried out of me: "Bite! Bite its head off! Bite!" Thus it cried out of me—my dread, my hatred, my nausea, my pity, all that is good and wicked in me cried out of me with a single cry.[25]

The shepherd "bit with a good bite." He spat out the snake and jumped up: "No longer shepherd, no longer human—one changed, radiant, *laughing*!"

These are not simple images to interpret, but they lead us in certain directions. Zarathustra's fear, his doubt, his hatred, and his pity, all his suffering and his revenge, they choke him. Biting through the head of the black snake, he is able to free himself, as the shepherd symbolizes him, from the heavy black snake of his dread. This leads to a Dionysian transformation, where one, "no longer human," emerges, radiant with laughter. How simple is that?

The context of eternal recurrence is the death of God, but also the genealogical critique of the ascetic ideal, and also the will to power, with its nihilistic eventualities. The possibility of the liberating dance and laughter do not undo their opposites or the context in which this decision, this biting through, takes place. In *Ecce Homo*, Nietzsche describes his discovery of Zarathustra (or vice versa), a book that he wrote in inspired creative bursts of ten days for each of the first three books, as burgeoning from a time of "great healthfulness" in his life.

Nevertheless, he complains that "everything great, a work, a deed, once completed, inevitably turns *against* the one who did it. . . . To have something *behind* oneself,—that is the cruelty of the 'it was' of time."[26] Krell says "one might have hoped and expected that the 'great health' could overcome any kind of suffering and resentment, and banish the chronic symptoms of human finitude. Perhaps it could, if like a crab it could go backward."[27] But no, the point is *not* to overcome suffering, as Nietzsche has been at such great pains to point out. It is the desire, the inexhaustible need to "banish" the "symptoms" of human finitude that is the essence of nihilism, which catches us out again and again.[28] And are the symptoms of our finitude the sources of our rancor and bitter revenge, or is their source our finitude itself? Are we expecting to banish that? Have we not tried and tried? However, Krell is perfectly correct to understand that no amount of healthful creation, willing, or affirming is going to reverse the reverses of time or our suffering them.

Nietzsche is very aware of the problem he gives Zarathustra. He speaks in *Ecce Homo* of the "psychological problem of the Zarathustra type," and it is necessary to keep in mind that Zarathustra is Nietzsche's literary character, and that he only symbolically and sometimes ironically stands in for Nietzsche himself.[29]

> The psychological problem of the Zarathustra type is how he who to an unprecedented extent says and *acts* "no" with regard to everything to which prior human beings have said "yes" can nevertheless remain the opposite of a no-saying spirit; how the one who bears destiny's heaviest burden, whose life-task is a fatality, can still be the lightest and most ethereal of spirits—Zarathustra is a dancer—: how he who has had the hardest and most terrible insight into reality, he who has thought "the most abysmal thought," can nevertheless find in these things no objections to existence or to its eternal recurrence; on the contrary, he finds still other grounds for *himself being* the eternal "yes" to all things, "the vast, limitless Yes-and-Amen saying. . . . " "Into all abysses I carry my yes-saying, which blesses. . . ." *However, to repeat: that is the very concept of Dionysus.*[30]

Is it that Dionysus dissolves all contradictions? And how is that to be interpreted, not to mention lived? How can eternal recurrence, experienced in Dionysian rapture, cure the symptoms of our finitude? In Nietzsche's account of his writing of Zarathustra in *Ecce Homo*, he describes this Dionysian rapture as the feeling that one is "beside oneself": "It is the sense that suddenly, with inexpressible certainty and subtlety, something becomes visible, something becomes audible, something that throttles one down to the depths and overturns one. One hears, one does not seek; one accepts, one does not ask who it is that gives; a thought flashes like lightning, with necessity, without hesitation in its form—I never had a choice."[31]

Nietzsche describes this experience not as intoxication or as impenetrable mystical dissolution, but as encompassing "an uncanny lucidity":

The Dionysian manifold does not peacefully submit to incarceration in pure concepts, nor even in impure "sensible concepts." Nietzsche conjoins two apparently contradictory words to describe it: *Glückstiefe*. *Glück* means happiness or good fortune, the ascendancy of one's star, precisely as the sounding of the word itself rises from the depths of one's gorge to the roof of the mouth; *Tiefe* names the depths, and descends to the depths, de profundis, in the throat. One scarcely knows how to pronounce the neologism *Glückstiefe*.[32]

As Krell's translation of Nietzsche's unpublished text makes clear, in this Dionysian rapture, "the most painful and foreboding things do not refute" its unconditioned, divine penetration; rather, "all terrors and tremblings seem to be conditions or requirements," "a necessary color within a such a spectrum of light."[33] It is important to pause here, to sound out the implications of this inexpressible but necessary requirement for the terrible and painful to be included in Dionysian rapture.

We might recall Nietzsche's more sober insistence in *The Gay Science* that "So far, all that has given color to existence still lacks a history. Where could you find a history of love, of avarice, of envy, of conscience, of pious respect for tradition, or of cruelty?"[34] History, as Nietzsche has demonstrated, is drenched in the "color" of suffering. Here, in considering *Zarathustra* and the experience of Dionysus that seems to ground the ungrounding and ungroundedness of the eternal recurrence, Nietzsche is trying to find a metaphor, where "the most powerful skill in metaphor that ever was is poor, is mere wordplay, in the face of this return of language to the nature of imagery . . . but where everything offers itself as the closest, most correct, and simplest expression. . . . Here all being wants to become word, all becoming wants to learn from you how to talk."[35] Here is the boundary between life and word, between language and being, a word Nietzsche rarely uses. Here is where language runs out.

He suggests, moreover, that suffering, like joy, or any most basic and fundamental affect, is a color, a tone, a rhythm, a beat; that it can never be expressed as a concept or even really as an image, and it certainly has never yet been given a history. What if its expression always has to be a construct, a narrative, a drama, an enactment, a performance, part of the story of a lived body, which after all begins and ends? What if it is not just a feeling but a pulse in the arteries, an outbreak of sweat, a rush of blood into or out of the extremities, a speeded up heartbeat, or one slowed down to a crawl? What logical concept will dress it up? It is, Nietzsche insists metaphorically, physiological, digestive, devouring. A flare of heat or a chilling into a deep cold; cramped bowels. How are we to give a meaning to life, to suffering, except by complicated, indispensable, and perverse falsehoods, fictions, stories?

And living in the middle, always, of the story, enmeshed and entangled in its plots and representations, its hidden agendas, where are we to stand to decide what is fact and what fiction, what happened and what didn't, and whether what happened, might have happened, is something of value? How are we to judge the story? "Becoming is of equivalent value every moment; the sum of its values always remains the same; in other words, it has no value at all, for anything against which to measure it, and in relation to which the word 'value' would have meaning, is lacking. *The total value of the world cannot be evaluated*; consequently philosophical pessimism belongs among comical things."[36]

One of the themes of this book has been that the experience of human existence, with suffering at its core, cannot be conveyed otherwise than through an "originary" metaphor (always of course accompanying the event)—the state of nature, the fall from grace, expulsion from the garden of Eden, the dismemberment of a dancing god. It is also, scandalously, as Nietzsche insists, always a politics. It is will to power, to rule, to conquer, to master, to prevail, as well, of course, as their opposites: to submit, to be ruled, conquered, mastered, dominated. Strategies of the will inherently involve both victories and defeats. But they are strategies. Is one truer than the other? As Krell says, "If the play has to do with knowledge at all, such knowledge is *tragic*."[37]

Nietzsche says:

> The point of view of "value" is inadmissable:—That in the "process of the totality" the labor of man is of no account, because a total process (considered as a system—) does not exist at all; that there is no "totality"; that no evaluation of human existence, of human aims, can be made in regard to something that does not exist; that "necessity," "causality," "purposiveness," are useful *unrealities*; that *not* "increase in consciousness" is the aim, but enhancement of power— and in this enhancement the utility of consciousness is included; the same applies to pleasure and displeasure; that the world is not an organism at all, but chaos; that the evolution of "spirituality" is only a means towards the relative duration of the organization; that all "desirability" has no meaning in relation to the total character of being.[38]

Krell submits Camus as one of the most thoughtful interpreters of the affirmative, liberatory power of Nietzsche's doctrine of eternal recurrence, but he faults him for not considering "whether the bipolarity of the will to power, the central conception of genealogical critique, constitutes or at least presupposes a 'standard of values' and therefore inevitably contains elements of the metaphysical slander."[39] Camus affirms: "From the moment it is recognized that the world pursues no end, Nietzsche proposes to concede its innocence . . . , to replace all judgments based on values with absolute assent, and with a complete and exalted allegiance to the world. . . . This magnificent consent, born of abundance and fullness of spirit, is the unreserved affirmation of human imperfection and suffering, of evil and murder, of all that is problematic and strange in our existence."[40]

I agree with Krell *contra* Camus, not only that there remain "a number of disturbing aspects—shades of decadence—to this supposedly full affirmation of human existence. . . . Eternal return . . . bears within itself virulent strains—infectious strains—of nihilism, at least as far as we, the last human beings, think it."[41] Not only is the "magnificent consent" to evil and murder clearly nihilistic, but it constitutes an alarming, totalizing interpretation of the thought of eternal recurrence, which Nietzsche never totalizes. There are always contending interpretations. Camus' version leaves us with no resources against the cataclysms of our time. In our time, the abyss is all too real; the cataclysm has already occurred beyond all redemption, the nihil remains unmistakeably with and within us and gathering speed. If all Nietzsche can offer us is the affirmation of the abyss, with a courageous smile, then our inquiry really has been "in vain."

We need to confront not only the contamination of this interpretation of eternal return with the nihilistic metaphysics Nietzsche indicts, but to venture another nontotalizing interpretation of what it means to overcome unity, totality, and finality in the real interplay of the dark and the light that is central to Nietzsche's thought of the eternal recurrence of the same.

Nietzsche connects meaninglessness with the thought of eternal recurrence: "Let us think this thought in its most terrible form: existence as it is, without meaning or aim, yet recurring inevitably without any finale of nothingness: *'the eternal recurrence.'*" He says that this is the most extreme form of nihilism. But he doesn't rest there. He goes on to suggest a way of conceiving of this process differently: "Can we remove the idea of a goal from the process and then affirm the process in spite of this?—This would be the case if something were attained at every moment within this process—and it is always the same."[42] What is it, then, that is the same and attained at every moment within this process?

Nietzsche promises that in the thought of the eternal recurrence there is an answer to the terrible destructiveness of the will to power as will to truth and to the nihilism of the politics of time in our time, a response, however enigmatic, to the abyss, the catastrophe, which has entered into our history as unprecedented disaster and torn it to shreds. In order to make good on that promise, to give an interpretation of eternal recurrence that can offer signification and responsibility in relation to suffering, Nietzsche has to respond to three powerful challenges to the thinking of eternal recurrence: the challenges of Deleuze, of Magnus, and of Wyschogrod, who all speak from the close of the twentieth century.

First, seemingly the most harmless, is the challenge of Deleuze, who simply asserts that we cannot imagine a world without *ressentiment*, without revenge. "And we do not really know what a man denuded of *ressentiment* would be like. A man who would not accuse or depreciate existence—would he still be a man, would he think like a man? . . . To have *ressentiment* or not to have *ressentiment*—there is no greater difference. . . ."[43] It is so far from anything we have known in life, that imagining human beings without the automatic, inborn responses of envy and resentment, remorse, and both subtle and violent revenge is virtually impossible. It evokes a world beyond anything we have ever known or even hoped for. So his question is, how can we imagine the world under the sign of eternal recurrence?

Second, Magnus gives us a more direct challenge, especially in relation to suffering. Magnus interprets eternal recurrence as imaginable only as the "defining disposition of an *übermensch*, the person who would crave nothing more fervently than the repetition of each and every moment of his or her life."[44] He quotes Nietzsche in *Ecce Homo*: "my formula for greatness in a human being is amor fati: that one wants nothing to be different, not forward, not backward, not in all eternity. Not merely to bear what is necessary, still less to conceal it . . . but to love it."[45] For Magnus, this unconditional love of each and every moment, which would entail the eternal recurrence of the most inconceivable horrors of human history, "that is what turns this requirement into a self-consuming human impossibility." Only a god—he says the God of the Judeo-Christian tradition, but surely that God has not been a god of unconditional love of every moment of existence, as Nietzsche has definitively demonstrated—could affirm such moments unconditionally. "Who could live, as some of us have had to do, in the midst of extermination camps and love *that* unconditionally? . . . To love each moment unconditionally . . . just is to will its eternal return. . . . for me at least, the thought *is* abysmal!"[46]

Finally, Wyschogrod, writing as the "heterological historian," trying to find a "non-space" of ethical response to the cataclysm of the Holocaust, and to the many genocides that have followed it, turns to a consideration of Nietzsche's eternal recurrence, his "Dionysian yes-saying to 'the world as it is, without subtraction, exception, or selection,'" and asks, "does it not also necessitate the affirmation of the century's slaughters, its development of weapons of unprecedented power?"[47] How can the affirmation of life, which Nietzsche sees as both abysmal and ecstatic at once, which means the affirmation of the eternal recurrence of a magnitude of suffering and annihilation that cracks open history and brings the abyss to every moment, how could that possibly be a response to suffering? That is our question.

Nietzsche's response, as I will interpret it, comes in several parts that have to be distinguished for it to be seen how they add up to and actually do constitute a response to the question of suffering. First, Nietzsche separates history into parts and layers; he separates the "event" from its signification or representation (while of course insisting that no such separation is ever really possible) and also from the impulses, the active and reactive forces, that give it life. For Nietzsche, life is a flux, a movement of differential forces, and the "ground" or place or point of these forces is suffering. It is suffering from which issue all the impulses that move or shape, interpret or signify, create or enforce, win or lose, dominate or submit as will to power and truth in this world.

Therefore, the ethical-political moment of choice and framing precedes and exceeds all images, names, metaphors, descriptions, inscriptions, all language and disposition in speech or writing or silence. The vortex forms around suffering; it is always already the "there" from which all form and content proceed. However much one deconstructs subject and object, meaning and reference, even images that have no memory or no body, the limit point of the "panic unleashed by images"[48] is suffering. Blanchot writes: "I call disaster that which does not have the ultimate for its limit; it bears the ultimate away in the disaster."[49] The ultimate is not, Nietzsche insists, an ultimate in time. It recurs, in the eternal curvature of time, as suffering.

We must go back to the Moment, the gateway in which the infinite past and the infinite future meet. Zarathustra is not to be understood as his animals understand him, that is, eternal recurrence is not a circle or a cycle. Zarathustra affirms instead "Being begins in every instant; the ball There rolls around every Here. The middle is everywhere. The path of eternity is crooked."[50] The Moment always bisects time, it is always the eternal now and here, the resonance where two infinities meet.

Furthermore, I agree with Deleuze, *contra* Heidegger, that there is no "self-same" in the eternal return of the same. Time's passing, both its stretching backwards and forwards and its punctiform uniformity as an endless succession of moments, implies difference, not sameness, in that there can be no identity, anywhere. It is only the simultaneity that is the same. Nietzsche has not stupidly overlooked the fact that consciousness changes each moment and that therefore each moment is unique, as some commentators have pleased themselves to imply. He first of all insists that there is no sameness in nature or in time, except what we devise as such, for our own pleasure and pain. It is the eternal recurrence of the moment, the beat itself, that "stamps itself" on the flux, "constituting being insofar as it affirms becoming. . . . Identity in the Eternal Return does not designate the nature of what recurs, but the fact of recurring difference."[51]

Further, *contra* Wyschogrod, I interpret Nietzsche's important insistence— "And are not all things bound fast together in such a way that this moment draws after it all future things? *Therefore* draws itself too"—not as indicating the "*primacy* of the past," but rather the primacy of what he calls "the Moment," the *present*, which draws forth both the past and the future, figures and reconfigures them, and binds them in discord in the choices of the Now.[52] The importance of the Moment is that it is here that suffering and choice constitute thought, agency, and responsibility, even especially in the absence of a subject.

There is no getting away from the necessity to choose. The thought of eternal recurrence revalues both the past and the future and makes them both permeable, elastic, redefinable, able to be remembered, interpreted, and anticipated anew. The past is curved into the future; what has passed is never past but is always also still to come. Its events and symbols recur and multiply in the speeded up production of images and interpretations. Every image and event recurs in a performance of itself and can be reiterated and recreated in an infinity of new ways. The images, signs, symbols, simulacra of the past can be read as symptoms or fetishes of any sort of desire or disease, of any forgotten trauma, of any object of remembered pain, wished for hope, or projected prophecy. The past does not stand still such that it can no longer speak. The future is not determined by anything, because anything can mean, or be made to mean, anything. Where are the limits to signification or the purposes of will to power? Nietzsche does not, cannot, provide any. He can hardly be blamed for the collapse of all values under the weight of history, which finally discredited all moral values whatsoever and turned them into currency in an endless cultural exchange.

Taking pleasure in pain, the aesthetic enjoyment of suffering, paradoxically increases both our courage and our power of creativity. It is not an accident, as Marx would say and Nietzsche shows, that this "aestheticizing" impulse, however badly or crudely misinterpreted, comes at the end of the day, at the time of the abyss, the cataclysm, "the writing of the disaster," at the time of the death of God and the void it unveils. It is a late invention, the mixing of pleasure and pain so as to increase the power of both and of their creators. Thinkers of the nineteenth century likened it to the degeneration at the end of the Roman Empire. But that was only the beginning of the end. We have gone through that mirror.

It is power that is wanted. It is a secret of our nihilistic time, one we dread to acknowledge, that cruelty, violence, and ruthless destruction, pointless pain suffered and inflicted, increase power. In a world where new powers are invented every day, the sacrifices that may be demanded to pay for them are as yet unknown to their inventors. We charge ahead, ignoring the pain, or stylizing it, using it, devouring it and it increases our energy and our time. If this is so, where shall we draw the line, set a limit, impose a boundary that can hold for what we can suffer or inflict as suffering, in the face of nothingness? According to what criteria shall we choose such a limit and who shall have the power to choose or to set limits? Only those conscious of the problem of suffering and its creation of the real have any option of grasping what is needed or possible.

For the heterological historian and the ethical-political theorist, this openness of the past and the future to infinite reinterpretation and reenaction is a deadly risk and danger. Can anything be proved actually to have happened? Can any catastrophe be erased from the record, or worse, recreated with new embellishments in some other place? Can any montage of images of destruction and annihilation be produced to tell any kind of narrative story whatsoever? No past is beyond reconstitution or recuperation, no future beyond imagination in virtual or hyperreality. Nietzsche puts the Moment squarely in our hands, that is, eternal recurrence is *willed*, and willing, he says, liberates. What then shall we will?

For Nietzsche in his life and his work, there was only one answer: self-overcoming, the overcoming of suffering. It is, as I have been trying to make plain, suffering that is to be overcome, and the old ways of overcoming it have proved bankrupt and worse. Nietzsche's response to suffering is to be taken from his own response to his own suffering—he overcame it, until it overcame him. The ethical-political response to "alterity" and to the "It was" that is unbearable is to overcome it in ourselves and incorporate it in our lives, un-"doctored," unredeemed by stories of eternal salvation out of time or absolute justice in time, but lived, performed, and reenacted, perhaps, with new inventiveness and purpose, for the sake of new values and perspectives.

We reconstruct the past and reconfigure the future for our own purposes, and there is no getting away from the necessity to choose, to create the values according to which we might overcome the intolerable. Our choice of how to do that depends on the nature of the suffering we face and the values we want to draw with us into the future. They cannot be specified in advance and they cannot be protected once and for all. They derive from our history, but we remember it differently in different contexts, and tell it differently for different audiences. We may use it differently when we learn how. That is just the condition of our lives now. And the ethical and political point that Nietzsche above all recommends: There is no blame. That is the hardest lesson of all to learn, and the one Nietzsche most wanted us to learn. There is no blame.

Notes

INTRODUCTION

1. See Philip Ariès, *Centuries of Childhood: A Social History of Family Life*, translated by Robert Baldick (New York: Random House, 1962).

2. In the contemporary world, the experience of suffering, however ineffable and inexpressible even to an isolated subject, becomes infinitely complicated by its innumerable, dubious representations and the mediated, artistic, and political productions, communications, and simulations to which it is submitted and by which it is presented. I will use only a few reasonably random examples from recent news sources to illuminate some of the difficulties of the problem. From *Newsweek*'s June 19, 2000 issue, in its weekly box entitled "Conventional Wisdom," the first item: "Africa — / — 1.7 million killed in eastern Congo in two years and we're finding out about it now?" In the context of *Newsweek*'s harrowing and extensive coverage of the millions dying in Africa from famine, civil wars, brutal insurgencies, and AIDS, a simple enough commentary, but one that highlights the everyday commonplace of 1.7 million people killed, anonymously. "We don't know about it." The global village misses a few facts of note, and that, not accidentally. The vast scope of tragedy and suffering in the world boggles the imagination. It is the concrete particulars that catch our imagination. Last week forty-eight Chinese were found dead in a container truck landing at Dover in England, having been shipped from China in an airless box overland through Russia and Europe to England; they finally arrived dead. How many more are there? What price are they willing to pay to get over here? Do we know about it now? What do we do about it? Whose fault is it?

3. Georgio Agemben, *Infancy and History*, translated by Liz Heron (London: Verso, 1993), 50–51.

4. Courtney Eldridge, "Better Art Through Circuitry," *New York Times Magazine*, June 11, 2000, sec. 6, 35.

5. Thomas Keenan and David Gelber, roundtable on Kosovo, Swarthmore, spring 1999. See Keenan's forthcoming *Live Feed*, for a more extended analysis of this question.

6. Emmanuel Levinas, "Time and the Other," in *The Levinas Reader*, edited and translated by Seán Hand (London: Basil Blackwell, 1989), 40.

7. Ibid., 39

8. Ibid., 40–41.

9. Ibid., 43.

10. See Michel Foucault, "Nietzsche, Genealogy, History," in *Language, Counter-Memory, Practice*, edited and translated by Donald F. Bouchard (Ithaca: Cornell University Press, 1977), 143.

11. Ibid., 145.

12. Ibid., 147–48.

13. Ibid., 154.

14. Luc Boltanski, *Distant Suffering: Morality, Media and Politics*, translated by Graham Burchell (Cambridge: Cambridge University Press, 1999).

CHAPTER 1. SUFFERING IN THE CONTEXT OF RELIGION

1. Friedrich Nietzsche, *Human, All Too Human*, translated by R. J. Hollingdale (Cambridge: Cambridge University Press, 1986), sec. 25, 25. Emphasis in the original.

2. Nietzsche, *The Gay Science*, sec. 125, 183.

3. Ibid., sec. 125, 183; sec. 108, 167. See also, Friedrich Nietzsche, *Thus Spake Zarathustra*, translated by Walter Kaufmann (New York: Viking Penguin, 1954), "The Ugliest Man," 370–79.

4. This reminds us, as a precursor, of Freud's famous tale of the primal horde and the killing of the Father, as in *Totem and Taboo*.

5. Nietzsche, *Thus Spoke Zarathustra*, 4, 378–79.

6. Ibid., 378–79.

7. Martin Luther, *Tischreden* (Weimarer Ausgaben), V, 5247. Quoted in Erik Erikson, *Young Man Luther* (New York: W. W. Norton, 1958), 202.

8. Martin Luther, "Preface to the Epistle of St. Paul to the Romans," in *Martin Luther: Selections from His Writings*, edited by John Dillenberger (New York: Doubleday Anchor, 1962), 24.

9. Charles Whitney, *Francis Bacon and Modernity* (New Haven: Yale University Press, 1986), 8.

10. Quentin Skinner, *The Foundations of Modern Political Thought*, 2 vols. (Cambridge: Cambridge University Press, 1978), 3–4.

11. For Erasmus's dispute with Luther, see particularly Marjorie O'Rourke Boyle, *Rhetoric and Reform: Erasmus' Civil Dispute with Luther* (Cambridge, Mass.: Harvard University Press, 1983), and John C. Olin, James D. Smart, and Robert E. McNally, eds., *Luther, Erasmus, and the Reformation: A Catholic-Protestant Reappraisal* (New York, 1969).

12. Martin Luther, *The Bondage of the Will*, 98, 176. Quoted in Skinner, *Foundations*, II, 5.

13. Luther, *Bondage*, 130, 175. Quoted in Skinner, *Foundations*, II, 5.

14. This begs the question for the moment of the famed optimism and enthusiasm of Renaissance humanists. While not disputing that an entirely different feeling pervaded the artists and scholars of the Italian Renaissance, we are coming into a more northern and far more pessimistic debate. In relation to politics, Machiavelli was hardly more jolly.

15. In what sense it is a ground or can serve as one is one of the great questions of the age. For both Luther and Hobbes, grounded as they are in opposing worldviews, suffering nevertheless forms the ground at least insofar as it stands as the starting point of all inquiry.

16. Skinner, *Foundations*, II, 5.

17. Erikson, *Young Man Luther*, 190.

18. Skinner, *Foundations*, II, 6.

19. Martin Luther, "Preface to the Complete Edition of Latin Writings," in *Selections from His Writings*, edited by John Dillenberger (New York: Doubleday Anchor, 1961), 11.

20. Luther, *Selected Writings*, 11

21. Skinner, *Foundations*, II, 8–9.

22. Jean Bethke Elshtain, *Public Man, Private Woman* (Princeton: Princeton University Press, 1981), 89

23. Ibid. Emphasis in the original.

24. Marcel Gauchet, *The Disenchantment of the World*, translated by Oscar Burge (Princeton: Princeton University Press, 1997), 76–77.

25. Erikson, *Young Man Luther*, 214.

26. Luther quoted in ibid., 238.

27. Martin Luther, *Heidelberg Disputation*, edited by E. Vogelsang, *Luther's Werke*, 5:388. Quoted in Peter Levine, *Living Without Philosophy: On Narrative, Rhetoric and Morality* (Albany: State University of New York Press, 1998), 194. See also Alister McGrath, *Luther's Theology of the Cross* (Oxford, 1985).

28. Luther, "the Freedom of a Christian," in Dillenberger, *Selections from His Writings*, New York: Doubleday Anchor, 1961, 31.

29. Luther quoted in Erikson, *Young Man Luther*, 210.

30. Elshtain, *Public Man, Private Woman*, 81.

31. Skinner, *Foundations*, II, 10.

32. Ibid., 11.

33. Ibid., 14–15.

34. Sheldon Wolin, *Politics and Vision* (Boston: Little, Brown, 1960), 149

35. Luther, *Werke*, 2: 262.

36. Barnes quoted in Skinner, *Foundations*, II, 71.

37. Skinner, *Foundations,* II, 17–19.
38. Ibid., 70.
39. Skinner quoting Tyndale, *Foundations,* II, 72.
40. Skinner quoting Tyndale and Barnes, *Foundations,* II, 67.
41. Wolin, *Politics and Vision,* 148.
42. Skinner, *Foundations,* II, 62.
43. Ibid., 247.
44. Ibid., 248.
45. John Locke, *A Letter on Toleration* (Indiana: Hacket, 1983), and see also Kirstie N. McClure, "Difference, Diversity and the Limits of Toleration" in *Political Theory,* Vol. 18, No. 3 (August 1990): 351–91.
46. Skinner, *Foundations,* II, 113.
47. Gauchet, *The Disenchantment of the World,* 143. Gauchet seems to place the beginnings of this movement in the fourteenth century. I have no argument with that. Beginnings are not given in nature but only in the questioning narrator.
48. Skinner, *Foundations,* II, 89.
49. Ibid., 89.
50. *Schleitheim Confession of Faith,* 133. Quoted in Skinner, *Foundations,* II, 78.
51. There was, in balancing contrast, the optimisim, confidence, and joy of the Italian Renaissance, which also influenced the jurists and scholars who designed the next stages of political invention. We will also touch on that in the following pages. But the subject is suffering, and Luther is the man, part-humanist, part-medieval, and part altogether idiosyncratic and new, who brought the question of suffering forward at the inception of this new world and who made it the religious question that could not be avoided or propitiated until it had torn down the world around him. He was not solely responsible for this result, needless to say.
52. Skinner, *Foundations,* II, 139.
53. Ibid., 139.
54. Ibid., 143.

CHAPTER 2. A SCIENCE OF SUFFERING BODIES

1. There are many excellent texts on the rise of science in the early modern age, and on its metaphysical presuppositions. See especially Alexander Koyré, *The Astronomical Revolution* (Ithaca: Cornell University Press, 1973); and idem, *From the Closed World to the Infinite Universe* (Baltimore: Johns Hopkins University Press, 1957). Arthur Koestler, *The Sleepwalkers* (London, 1959), gives an accessible version of these changes, as does Thomas S. Kuhn, *The Copernican Revolution* (Cambridge, Mass.: Harvard University

Press, 1957). See also Robert Mandrou, *From Humanism to Science 1480–1700* (Harmondsworth: Penguin, 1978); and Paul Hazard, *The European Mind 1680–1715* (Harmondsworth: Penguin, 1964) for basic accounts.

2. J. Peter Euben, "Preface," *Corrupting Youth* (Princeton: Princeton University Press, 1997), xiii.

3. It wasn't until the "Glorious Revolution" of 1688 that the English monarchy achieved its more permanent characteristics. There are some very good sources on the English civil war and the Restoration. John Locke is the major theorist of this transformation. See especially John Locke, *Two Treatises of Government* (Cambridge: Cambridge University Press, 1960); and more recently, Christopher Hill, *The World Turned Upside Down* (Harmondsworth: Penguin, 1975); Lawrence Stone, *The Crisis of the Aristocracy* (Oxford: Oxford University Press, 1965); J. G. A. Pocock, ed., *Three British Revolutions: 1641, 1688, 1776* (Princeton: Princeton University Press, 1980); Richard Tuck, *Philosophy and Government 1572–1651* (Cambridge: Cambridge University Press, 1993). There are many others, to be sure.

4. See Quentin Skinner, *Reason and Rhetoric in the Philosophy of Hobbes* (Cambridge: Cambridge University Press, 1996) for a more than thorough analysis of Hobbes's humanist learning and his struggle for and against it throughout his writing career.

5. Tom Sorrell, *Hobbes* (London: Routledge, 1986), 1.

6. Sources for Hobbes's life include the above-mentioned works by Skinner and Sorrell, and also Noel Malcolm's "A Summary Biography of Hobbes," in *The Cambridge Companion to Hobbes*, edited by Tom Sorrell (Cambridge: Cambridge University Press, 1996), 13–44; *Perspectives on Thomas Hobbes*, edited by G. A. J. Rogers and Alan Ryan (Oxford: Clarendon, 1990); and for the context of Hobbes's life and work, Johann P. Sommerville, *Thomas Hobbes: Political Ideas in Historical Context* (New York: St. Martin's, 1992). There are hundreds of volumes on Hobbes and various aspects of his work, and most of them include some biographical material.

7. John Aubrey, *Brief Lives, chiefly of Contemporaries, set down by John Aubrey, between the years 1669 & 1696*, edited by A. Clark, 2 vols. (Oxford: Clarendon, 1898). For Bacon, see Charles Whitney, *Francis Bacon and Modernity* (New Haven: Yale University Press, 1986); Paolo Rossi, *Francis Bacon: From Magic to Science*, translated by Sacha Rabinowitz (Chicago: University of Chicago Press, 1968). There are many others.

8. Malcolm, "A Summary Biography of Hobbes," 18.

9. It is not necessary to assert a direct influence of Bacon on Hobbes, but G. A. J. Rogers does. He juxtaposes quotations from Bacon and Hobbes in order to argue for "the force of the mathematical, and particularly the geometrical, model as it entered from the mathematicians and astronomers into the wider intellectual consciousness" (195). The quotations have to do

with the power of definition: "so it is almost necessary in all controversies and disputations to imitate the wisdom of the Mathematicians, in setting down in the very beginning the definitions of our words and terms." Rogers argues in "Hobbes's Hidden Influence," in Rogers and Ryan, *Perspectives on Thomas Hobbes,* 189–205. It does indeed sound like Hobbes, but it is from Bacon's *Of the Advancement of Learning.* Hobbes in *Leviathan* wrote: "The first cause of Absurd conclusions I ascribe to the want of Method; in that they begin not their Ratiocination from Definitions." It will become clear how important this argument about definitions was for Hobbes, and how important the problem of definitions and what can or cannot be defined was to become for modern thought. Of course, Bacon was not the only source for such methodological insight. As I will argue, both Galileo and Descartes, in quite different ways, were very influential in Hobbes's developing his scientific methodology and his understanding of right reasoning as demonstrable truth.

10. Christopher Hill, *Intellectual Origins of the English Revolution* (Oxford: Clarendon, 1965), 86. Emphasis in the original.

11. Francis Bacon, in *Works* (1826), vol. iv, 79. Quoted in Hill, *Intellectual Origins,* 87.

12. Francis Bacon, *Works,* iv, 32. Quoted in Hill, *Intellectual Origins,* 88.

13. Francis Bacon, *Works,* iv. 21, 247–48, and *Works,* iii, 592–94. Quoted in Hill, *Intellectual Origins,* 89–90. It is worth noting that centuries later Nietzsche would echo this judgment, indicting traditional religion and philosophy precisely as a "wicked effort to curtail human power" and as a production of "deliberate and artificial despair." We will inquire into this indictment in later chapters of this book.

14. G. A. J. Rogers, "Hobbes's Hidden Influence," 197. Skinner, in *Reason and Rhetoric in the Philosophy of Thomas Hobbes,* 254, confirms the report of this meeting, but finds it strange that Hobbes makes no mention of it in his autobiographies.

15. See Rogers, "Hobbes's Hidden Influence," 196, and Skinner, *Reason and Rhetoric,* 254.

16. Galileo Galilei, *Letter to the Grand Duchess Christina,* 1615. Quoted in E. A. Burtt, *The Metaphysical Foundations of Modern Science* (New York: Doubleday Anchor, 1955), 75.

17. Galileo, *Opera Complete di Galileo Galilei* (Firenza, 1842), vol. IV, 171. Quoted in Burtt, *Metaphysical Foundations,* 75.

18. Galileo, *Two Great Systems,* 96, 31. Quoted in Burtt, *Metaphysical Foundations,* 77.

19. Burtt, *Metaphysical Foundations,* 60–61.

20. It was Descartes who became obsessed with the difference between primary and secondary qualities and founded his philosophy on complete metaphysical dualism.

21. Burtt, *Metaphysical Foundations*, 83.

22. For his explanation of heat as caused by motion, see Galileo, *Opera*, IV, 333, and for the atomic theory of matter, see *Two New Sciences*, 40, both in Burtt, *Metaphysical Foundations*, 85–86. See Galileo's *Il Saggiatore*, 1623, for his discussion of heat and secondary qualities.

23. Burtt, *Metaphysical Foundation*, 93. Emphasis in the original.

24. It is Friedrich Nietzsche, in *Thus Spoke Zarathustra*, who in an indelible metaphor pictured the Moment as Gateway to the infinities of the past and the future, meeting and colliding in the Moment. Do the lines ever meet? he asks, thus establishing the setting for the doctrine of the eternal recurrence of the same.

25. Burtt, *Metaphysical Foundations*, 98.

26. Richard Tuck, "Hobbes and Descartes," in Rogers and Ryan, *Perspectives on Thomas Hobbes*, 10–41, 28.

27. Ibid., 20, 26, 28.

28. Ibid., 29.

29. Ibid., 29. Tuck quotes Miles Burnyeat to the effect that "the idea that sense-impressions could themselves be objects of knowledge—objects perceived by an observer in a necessarily veridical way—was one which never occurred to any ancient philosopher." See M. F. Burnyeat, "Idealism and Greek Philosophy: What Descartes Saw and Berkeley Missed," in *Idealism Past and Present*, edited by G. Vesey, (Cambridge, 1982), 19–50. Tuck also stresses that "The three principal figures in the 'Mersenne group,' Descartes, Gassendi and Hobbes, in fact all have some claim to be the first person to have the idea." All three, it should be said, also came by the idea via Galileo's discussion of heat and other noninherent properties, in *Il Saggiatore* of 1623 (p. 30).

30. Tuck, "Hobbes and Descartes," 32.

31. Ibid., 34. Emphasis in the original.

32. Ibid., 35.

33. See Aryeh Botwinick, *Skepticism in Maimonides, Hobbes and Nietzsche* (Ithaca: Cornell University Press, 1997); and also Richard Popkin, *The History of Scepticism from Erasmus to Spinoza* (Berkeley: University of California Press, 1979.)

34. Hobbes, Letter of 1636. Quoted in Tuck, "Hobbes and Descartes," 38.

35. Hobbes quoted in Tuck, "Hobbes and Descartes," 39.

36. Tuck, "Hobbes and Descartes," 39, 40, 41.

37. David Johnston, *The Rhetoric of Leviathan* (Princeton: Princeton University Press, 1986), 70.

38. Note the relevance of recent work, especially by Johnston and Skinner, on the conflict between philosophy and rhetoric in Hobbes's career on this question.

39. See Georgio Agemben, *Infancy and Destruction: Essays on the Destruction of Experience*, translated by Liz Heron (London: Verso, 1993).

CHAPTER 3. FOR THE LACK OF MORAL KNOWLEDGE

1. David Johnston, *The Rhetoric of Leviathan* (Princeton: Princeton University Press, 1986), 126–27. There are numerous classic works that deal with the far-ranging cultural and political changes of this time. Some of the most important are: Michael Walzer, *The Revolution of the Saints* (New York: Athenian, 1970); Lawrence Stone, *The Crisis of the English Aristocracy 1558–1641* (Oxford: Oxford University Press, 1965); idem, *The Family, Sex, and Marriage in England 1500–1800* (New York: Harper and Row, 1977); Christopher Hill, *The World Turned Upside Down* (Harmondsworth: Penguin, 1975); idem, *Milton and the English Revolution* (Harmondsworth: Penguin, 1978); J. G. A. Pocock, *The Machiavellian Moment* (Princeton: Princeton University Press, 1975); Quentin Skinner, *The Foundations of Modern Political Thought*, 2 vols. (Cambridge: Cambridge University Press, 1978); and Richard Tuck, *Philosophy and Government 1572–1651* (Cambridge: Cambridge University Press, 1973). There are many other valuable works on all aspects of this subject, some of which will be mentioned further on.

2. Thomas Hobbes, *Leviathan* (Oxford: Basil Blackwell, 1651), introduction by Michael Oakeshott, ch. 44, 397.

3. I have used David Johnston's *The Rhetoric of Leviathan* for this brief summary, but there are numerous other sources; see especially E. Eisenstein, *The Printing Press as an Agent of Change*, 2 vols. (Cambridge: Cambridge University Press, 1979) and L. Febvre and H.-J. Martin, *The Coming of the Book: The Impact of Printing, 1450–1800* (London: Basil Blackwell, 1976). For an especially interesting approach to such cultural change, see Peter Stallybrass and Allon White, *The Politics and Poetics of Transgression* (Ithaca: Cornell University Press, 1986).

4. Johnston, *Rhetoric*, 74.

5. Ibid., 75.

6. Ibid., 78, quoting Hobbes, *Leviathan*, ch. 29.

7. Hobbes, *Leviathan*, 211.

8. The recognition of this model owes everything to the work of Michel Foucault, especially his *Madness and Civilization* (New York: Vintage, 1965) and *The Birth of the Clinic* (New York: Vintage, 1975). But there are numerous works tracing these themes in various periods. See, for instance, Jonathan Sawday, *The Body Emblazoned: Dissection and the Human Body in Renaissance Culture* (London: Routledge, 1995); Walter Laqueur, *Making Sex* (Cambridge, Mass.: Harvard University Press, 1990)

and the wonderful, strange Barbara Stafford, *Body Criticism: Imaging the Unseen in Enlightenment Art and Medicine* (Cambridge, Mass.: MIT Press, 1994). There is a wealth of material on many dimensions of this subject in the modern age.

9. Hobbes, *Leviathan*, 7.

10. Ibid., 17, 20, 22.

11. Ibid., 24–25.

12. Ibid., 21.

13. Ibid., 67.

14. Ibid., 26.

15. Ibid., 29.

16. Ibid., ch. 44, and the Epistle Dedicatory.

17. Ibid., 81.

18. Ibid., 35.

19. Ibid., 32–33.

20. Ibid., 26.

21. Ibid., 63–64.

22. Ibid., 42, 57, 81.

23. Rousseau will make much of the idea that Hobbes has read back into nature what only comes from society, as if the demarcation were somehow fixed, not relative to culture, time, and the purposes of authors. As we will see, however, Rousseau is at least as guilty of this "fallacy" as Hobbes, because he imagines a state of nature where there are no relations among men at all, except fleeting encounters. This is far more of an anthropomorphic, even phobic, fantasy than Hobbes's, who always situates his individuals in constant interaction and relations with each other and sees this as always already a problem. Rousseau does include a historicization of human socialization, which was a great intellectual advance, but his original anthropology is quite idiosyncratic.

24. Thomas Hobbes, *The English Works of Thomas Hobbes*, edited by Sir William Molesworth, 11 vols. (London, 1839–45), I, 73–74.

25. Thomas Hobbes, *The English Works of Thomas Hobbes*, edited by Sir William Molesworth, 11 vols. (London, 1839–45), ii, xx, quoted in Tom Sorrell, "The Science in Hobbes's Politics," in Rogers and Ryan, *Perspectives on Thomas Hobbes*, 67–80, 70.

26. Hobbes, *Leviathan*, 38.

27. Tom Sorrell, "The Science in Hobbes's Politics," in Rogers and Ryan, *Perspectives on Thomas Hobbes*, 67–80; and idem, "Hobbes's Scheme of the Sciences," in Sorrell, *The Cambridge Companion to Hobbes*, 45–61. The quotation is from the former, 69.

28. Sorrell, "The Science in Hobbes's Politics," 71.

29. Hobbes, *Leviathan*, 29.

CHAPTER 4. THE STATE OF NATURE
AS AN EVER-PRESENT ORIGIN

1. Quentin Skinner, *Reason and Rhetoric in the Philosophy of Hobbes* (Cambridge: Cambridge University Press, 1996).

2. This ranked valuation of conceptual over poetic language becomes an explicit philosophical issue in Nietzsche and a foundation of his critique of the Western metaphysical tradition.

3. Hobbes, *Leviathan*, 80. See also Carole Pateman, *The Sexual Contract* (Stanford: Stanford University Press, 1988), for the most complete feminist analysis of social contract theory and its masculinist and classisist presuppositions. Pateman sees Hobbes as somewhat more open to female equality than the other contract theorists because he shows female independence and dominion over children in the state of nature. Perhaps, but it makes little difference to his overall argument.

4. Hobbes, *De Cive*, ch. 8.

5. Hobbes, *Leviathan*, 82.

6. Ibid., 85.

7. This point of view persisted, of course, beyond Hobbes's time, and had many reincarnations in other guises in modern philosophy. The closest historical proponent of a natural law explanation was John Locke. For the best exposition of the meaning of his philosophy in terms of the natural law and humanist traditions, see Kirstie M. McClure, *Judging Rights: Lockean Politics and the Limits of Consent* (Ithaca: Cornell University Press, 1996). I will look at Rousseau's version of natural law in history in the next chapter.

8. Hobbes, *Leviathan*, 83.

9. See Georgio Agemben, *Infancy and History*, translated by Liz Heron (New york: Verso, 1993), 91.

10. See especially Hannah Pitkin, *Fortune is a Woman* (Berkeley: University of California Press, 1984); and J. G. A. Pocock, *The Machiavellian Moment* (Princeton: Princeton University Press, 1975). The contemporary philosophical concept of historicity is largely Heideggerian.

11. Friedrich Nietzsche, *On the Genealogy of Morals*, translated by Walter Kaufmann (New York: Vintage, 1967); "Guilt, Bad Conscience and the Like," II, 1, 2, 57–59. Emphasis in the original. Nietzsche speaks of the "terror that formerly attended all promises." Hobbes would hardly disagree.

12. Hobbes, *Leviathan*, 91.

13. See Johnston, *The Rhetoric of Leviathan*, 144, for the best analysis of this aspect of Hobbes's science.

14. There is a huge literature by now on various aspects of this critique. See especially Carole Pateman, *The Sexual Contract* (Stanford: Stanford University Press, 1988); Seyla Benhabib, "The Generalized and the Concrete

Other," in *Feminism as Critique*, edited by Seyla Benhabib and Drucilla Cornell, (Minneapolis: University of Minnesota Press, 1978); Jean Bethke Elshtain, *Public Man, Private Woman* (Princeton: Princeton University Press, 1981); Kathleen Jones, *Compassionate Authority* (London: Routledge 1993); Alasdair MacIntyre, *After Virtue* (Notre Dame: University of Notre Dame Press, 1981); Michael Walzer, *Spheres of Justice* (New York: Basic Books, 1983); Michael Sandel, *Liberalism and the Limits of Justice* (Cambridge: Cambridge University Press, 1982). This general critique comes from many different schools and directions.

CHAPTER 5. COERCION IN THE SOCIAL CONTRACT

1. Friedrich Nietzsche, *On the Genealogy of Morals*, translated by Walter Kaufmann and R. J. Hollingdale (New York: Vintage, 1967).

2. Ibid., 3, 61.

3. Ibid., 1, 2, 58–59.

4. Hobbes, *Leviathan*, 82.

5. Nietzsche, *Genealogy*, 3,61.

6. Hobbes, *Leviathan*, 94.

7. Nietzsche, *Genealogy*, 5, 64.

8. Hobbes, *Leviathan*, 91.

9. Ibid., 115. I agree, at a minimum, with Alan Ryan's reply to recent critics who have attempted to liken Hobbes's state of nature to the rational decision-making model of the "prisoner's dilemma." "The essence of a prisoner's dilemma is that the parties to it are utility-maximizers, so that opponents in the game will always try to exploit each other and they know it. Hobbesian man will not. He is not a utility-maximizer, but a disaster-avoider. The proper response to my disarming myself is to disarm yourself, not to kill me; to seek peace, not to maximize advantage." See Alan Ryan, "Hobbes's Political Philosophy," in Sorrell, *The Cambridge Companion*, 208–45, 224. For the most complete presentation of the "prisoner's dilemma" in relation to Hobbes, see Jean Hampton, *Hobbes and the Social Contract Tradition* (Cambridge: Cambridge University Press, 1986); and David Gautier, *The Logic of Leviathan* (Oxford: Clarendon, 1969). It should be pretty clear that the state of nature is not about rational decision-making at all, but about fear and fantasy, passion and subjection, and the Herculean efforts of very confused and tormented subjects to try to reason their way clear to a properly submissive consent to be ordered around. Hobbes does not see reason as a very strong defense against the wilderness of men's natural treachery and chaos.

10. Sarah Kofman, *Nietzsche and Metaphor*, translated by Duncan Large (Stanford: Standford University Press, 1993), 29.

11. Carole Pateman's *The Sexual Contract* provides by far the most complete feminist analysis of this aspect of the social contract. She stresses that it is a pact of men, and that it depends on a hidden and denied "previous" or prior pact, the pact assigning the control of women to men and distributing women among men. She also analyzes the social contract in terms of contracts in general and wage labor in particular.

12. Hobbes, *Leviathan*, 83.

13. Sheldon Wolin, "The Idea of the State in America," in *The Problem of Authority in America*, edited by John P. Diggens and Mark E. Kann (Philadelphia: Temple University Press, 1981), 49.

14. Ian Shapiro, *The Evolution of Rights in Liberal Theory* (Cambridge: Cambridge University Press, 1986), 50.

CHAPTER 6. THE DEATH OF GOD

1. Friedrich Nietzsche, *Thus Spoke Zarathustra*, translated by Walter Kaufmann (New York: Viking Penguin 1954): "Retired," and "The Ugliest Man," 370–79, 371.

2. Nietzsche, *Zarathustra*, "The Ugliest Man," 376–79.

3. Ibid., 378–79.

4. Ernst Cassirer, *The Philosophy of the Enlightenment* (Princeton: Princeton University Press, 1951), especially 141–58. See also idem, *The Question of Jean-Jacques Rousseau*, translated and edited by Peter Gay (Bloomington: Indiana University Press, 1967).

5. B. Pascal, *Pensées*, edited by E. Havet, 5th ed. (Paris, 1897), vol. 1, art. VIII, 115. Quoted in Cassirer, *Philosophy*, 146.

6. Cassirer, *Philosophy*, 143.

7. Pascal, *Pensées*, I, 114. Quoted in Cassirer, *Philosophy*, 144.

8. Cassirer, *Philosophy*, 148.

9. I. Kant, *Werke* (*Critique of Judgment*, sec. 83), ed. Cassirer, vol. 11, 219f. Quoted in Cassirer, *Philosophy*, 151.

10. Cassirer, *Philosophy*, 152.

11. See Hannah Arendt, *On Revolution* (Harmondsworth: Penguin, 1990), ch. 2, 59–114. See also Bonnie Honig's excellent *Political Theory and the Displacement of Politics* (Ithaca: Cornell University Press, 1993) for the complex connections between Nietzsche and Arendt on this and many other questions. Luc Boltanski begins his fine sociological analysis, *Distant Suffering*, translated by Graham Burchell (Cambridge: Cambridge University Press, 1999), with a recapitulation of Arendt's argument and then takes it much further into a complex and subtle interpretation of the politics of pity and spectatorship in relation to suffering and the media in our time.

12. Kant, *Werke*, vol. VIII, 630. Quoted in Cassirer, *Philosophy*, 153–54.

13. Cassirer, *Philosophy*, 154.

14. Jean-Jacques Rousseau, *The Confessions of Jean-Jacques Rousseau* (Harmondsworth: Penguin Classics, 1954).

15. Cassirer, *Philosophy*, 154. As Nietzsche reminds us, it was Socrates who first made justice a rational standard against which to measure human life. Rousseau resurrects this philosophical move in a romantic key as a modern project of man.

CHAPTER 7. SUFFERING

1. Victor Gourevitch, in his introduction to Rousseau's *Discourses*, says: "The single most distinctive feature of Rousseau's original, natural man, and of men in the pre-political state of nature, is that they are 'good.' Rousseau always stressed that the doctrine of man's natural goodness was his central doctrine. It stands in clear opposition to the doctrine of original sin." See Gourevitch,"Introduction," Jean-Jacques Rousseau, *The Discourses and Other Early Political Writings*, edited and translated by Victor Gourevitch (Cambridge: Cambridge University Press, 1997), xx.

2. Jean-Jacques Rousseau, *The Confessions of Jean-Jacques Rousseau*, translated by J. M. Cohen (Harmondsworth: Penguin, 1954). Quoted in Tracy B. Strong, *Jean-Jacques Rousseau: The Politics of the Ordinary* (London: Sage, 1994), 13. I am indebted to Strong's quite courageous reading of Rousseau in *The Politics of the Ordinary*. Strong succeeds in countering some of the more thoughtless standard readings of Rousseau and in making positive sense of some of Rousseau's most difficult, even intractable, positions. He also, however, highlights how truly impossible some of those positions are.

3. Rousseau, *Confessions*, Bk. I, 1. Strong interprets this thus: "The only possible sense such a claim can make, even allowing for hyperbole, is to say that he is *homme* and no one else is (at least no one who will read his book)." This leads Strong to a complicated interpretation of what Rousseau means by *homme*, that is, the "human," which is not without its difficulties, as I will attempt to show.

4. Luc Boltanski, *Distant Suffering*, translated by Graham Burchell (Cambridge: Cambridge University Press, 1999), 91–93.

5. It is noteworthy that both Rousseau and Nietzsche are preoccupied with decadence, their own and others', and that they both understand decadence in contrast to natural health. Nietzsche does not think that a revolutionary social justice will cure this disease, however, and his concept of nihilism goes far beyond anything Rousseau imagined in relation to decadence.

6. Jean-Jacques Rousseau, *Discourse on the Arts and Sciences* (originally published in Geneva: Barillot and Son, 1750); reprinted in Jean-Jacques

Rousseau, *The Discourses and Other Early Political Writings* (Cambridge: Cambridge University Press, 1997), preface.

7. I'm not going to spend much time in this book on the relation between Rousseau and the French Revolution, but there are some excellent sources for inquiring into this relation. See especially Robert Darnton, *The Forbidden Best-Sellers of Pre-Revolutionary France* (New York: W. W. Norton, 1996); Roger Chartier, *The Cultural Origins of the French Revolution* (Durham, N.C.: Duke University Press, 1991); Lynn Hunt, *Politics, Culture and Class in the French Revolution* (Berkeley: University of California Press, 1984); and Keith Michael Baker, *Inventing the French Revolution* (Cambridge: Cambridge University Press, 1990.)

8. This is in contrast to Hobbes's scientific approach and Nietzsche's genealogical one. All of these approaches embody values, of course. It is morality, especially the morality of suffering and pity, which lies at the heart of the deadly argument between Nietzsche and Rousseau.

9. Strong, *Politics of the Ordinary,* especially ch. 2.

10. The continuing salience of the question of political legitimacy continues to distinguish the modern theorist from the postmodern one, who argues that there are no conceivable criteria for political legitimacy, nor any possible grounds for finding any. Nietzsche makes this argument most decisively.

11. Adam Smith, *The Theory of the Moral Sentiments*, edited by D. D. Raphael and A. L. Macfie (Oxford: Clarendon, 1976), 76. Quoted in Boltanski, *Distant Suffering*, 46–47.

12. Jean-Jacques Rousseau, *The Discourses and Other Early Political Writings*, edited by Victor Gourevitch (Cambridge: Cambridge University Press, 1997).

13. Rousseau, *Second Discourse*, 125.

14. Ibid., 132.

15. Strong, *Politics of the Ordinary*, 44. Strong's formulation shows, among other things, that development that is "not necessary but inevitable" is problematic; it involves what we mean by historical necessity, or temporal causation, and that is not at all clear, even in contemporary thought. This is a major focus for Nietzsche's work.

16. Asher Horowitz, in *Rousseau: Nature and History* (Toronto: University of Toronto Press, 1987), presents the most complete account of Rousseau's historical anthropology and of the importance of the development of his sense of history to the history of revolutionary philosophy. He argues that Rousseau "collapses" the concept of nature and that of culture, or artifice, "within a sophisticated concept of history" (51, 81). This is something of an overstatement; but he is correct that human nature, in Rousseau, is not abstract, fixed, or static, but is rather "constituted in historical activ-

ity, primarily in the social process of labour, as praxis" (81). Other critical sources for Rousseau include Robert Wokler's *Rousseau* (Oxford: Oxford University Press, 1995), T. Todorov's *Frêle bonheur, essai sur Rousseau* (Paris: Hachette, 1985), and the most influential study of Rousseau's complete system, Robert Derathé, *Jean-Jacques Rousseau et la science politique de son temps* (Paris: Vrin, 1970).

17. Rousseau, *Second Discourse*, 137–38.

18. Rousseau, Preface, *Second Discourse*, 127.

19. Rousseau, *Second Discourse*, 141.

20. Strong, *Politics of the Ordinary*, 33-34.

21. Rousseau, *Emile*. Quoted in Strong, *Politics of the Ordinary*, 52.

22. Rousseau, *Second Discourse*, 142.

23. Cassirer, *Philosophy*, 103, 97ff. Also quoted in Horowitz, Rousseau, 41–42.

24. Rousseau, *Second Discourse*, 142.

25. Ibid., 143, 157.

26. Strong, *Politics of the Ordinary*, 44.

27. Rousseau, *Lettre à Philopolis*. Quoted in Strong, *Politics of the Ordinary*, 45.

28. Strong, *Politics of the Ordinary*, 45.

29. Rousseau, *Second Discourse*, 150.

30. Ibid., 151, 152, 153.

31. Jean-Jacques Rousseau, *Essay on the Origin of Language*, quoted in Strong, *Politics of the Ordinary*, 42.

32. Luc Boltanski, *Distant Suffering*, translated by Graham Burchell (Cambridge: Cambridge University Press, 1999), 29.

33. Strong, *Politics of the Ordinary*, 42.

34. See especially Keith Ansell-Pearson, *Nietzsche Contra Rousseau* (Cambridge: Cambridge University Press, 1991), for a scholar who takes the opposite position from mine in Nietzsche's case against Rousseau. That is, he takes the side of Rousseau.

35. Ansell-Pearson, *Nietzsche*, 74.

36. Ansell-Pearson, in a note (note 43, ch. 2, 246) refers to L. Colletti's argument, in *From Rousseau to Lenin*, that Rousseau "confuses a critique of specific social relationships (civil society conceived as market capitalism) with a critique of social relationships *per se*, and thus a critique of a specific form of society becomes a critique of society in general" (164). This is correct, so far as it goes, but it does not get to the root of the issue. Traditional philosophical language uses definitions to universalize ahistorically. Without a critical methodological perspective, ruling philosophical usages present concepts as if they had no history. Western metaphysics seeks to legislate philosophically "once and for all," for all times and places, in a timeless

philosophical analysis. Rousseau, by adding history to the ingredients of such analysis, contributed greatly, although not clearly, to the problematization of such usages.

37. Nietzsche, *Twilight of the Idols* (*The Portable Nietzsche* edited by Walter Kaufman (New York: Viking, 1968)), "The Problem of Socrates," 2.

38. Nietzsche, *On the Genealogy of Morals* (. . .) II, sec. 13.

39. Rousseau, *Second Discourse*, 154.

40. Ibid., (note from 152), 218.

41. Horowitz, *Rousseau*, 128.

42. For the best discussion of Rousseau's psychology, see Jean Starobinsky, *Jean-Jacques Rousseau: La transparence and l'obstacle* (Paris: Presses Universitaires de France, 1957).

43. Rousseau, *Second Discourse*, 159.

44. Ibid., 161.

45. Rousseau, *Second Discourse*, as quoted in Strong, 32–33.

46. Strong, *Politics of the Ordinary*, 33.

47. Rousseau, *Second Discourse*, 167.

48. Ibid., 164. Feminists have made a meal of Rousseau on the grounds of his fetishism of self-sufficiency, his understanding of female sexuality, his notions of the family and the proper role of women, and many other issues. The best analyses include Jean Elshtain, *Public Man, Private Woman* (Princeton: Princeton University Press, 1981); Susan Moller Okin, *Women in Western Political Thought* (Princeton: Princeton University Press, 1979); and the most dazzling, Linda Zerilli's *Signifying Woman* (Ithaca: Cornell University Press, 1994).

49. Rousseau, *Second Discourse*, 166.

50. Ibid., 171.

51. Horowitz, *Rousseau*, 111.

52. Rousseau, *Second Discourse*, 170.

53. Ibid., 173.

54. Ibid., 173.

CHAPTER 8. SOCIAL JUSTICE AND THE GENERAL WILL

1. Jean-Jacques Rousseau, *The Social Contract*, (London: Penguin, 1968), 49.

2. Ibid., 52–53.

3. This reminds me of Ansell-Pearson's question, "If natural law is metaphorical, how does it oblige us?" How is obligation accomplished if not by metaphor, by language? Is covenanting or promising not metaphorical? As opposed to what? Promises are performatives, as they say now. They are metaphorical in the sense of linguistic, not causal. But then, obligations are meta-

phorical as well. As has been plain in this entire discussion of the state of nature and the social contract, the realm of human obligation and political legitimacy is metaphorical. Nietzsche makes the decisive contribution here, in what Sarah Kofman calls his "epistectomy." We'll get to that in the next chapter.

4. Rousseau, *Contract*, 53.

5. Ibid., 55.

6. Ibid., 55.

7. The best source for this background is Patrick Riley's *The General Will Before Rousseau: The Transformation of the Divine into the Civic* (Princeton: Princeton University Press, 1986).

8. Rousseau, *Contract*, 58.

9. Ibid., 59. Emphasis in the original.

10. Ibid., 59–60.

11. Strong, *Politics of the Ordinary*, 69.

12. Rousseau, *Contract*, 60.

13. Ibid.,

14. Ibid., 60–61.

15. Ibid., 61.

16. Ibid., 64.

17. Ibid., 65.

18. Ibid., 65, 55.

19. Ibid., 69.

20. Strong, *Politics of the Ordinary*, 76. Emphasis in the original.

21. Ibid., 77.

22. See ibid.,, 78, 79.

23. Rousseau, *Contract*, 75. Strong's translation.

24. Strong, *Politics of the Ordinary*, 82.

25. Ibid., 84.

26. Rousseau, *Contract*, 64.

27. Strong, *Politics of the Ordinary*, 85.

28. Rousseau, *Emile*. Quoted in Strong, 52.

29. Rousseau, *Contract*, 63.

30. Strong, *Politics of the Ordinary*, 90.

31. Roussseau, *Contract*. Quoted in Strong, *Politics of the Ordinary*, 91.

32. Strong, *Politics of the Ordinary*, 91.

33. Ibis., 100.

CHAPTER 9. NIETZSCHE

1. The serious work on Nietzsche first came here with Walter Kaufmann's rescue of him from his worst enemies, and with Martin Heidegger's

four volumes of lectures on Nietzsche, written during the Nazi period and only published in 1961. See Martin Heidegger, *Nietzsche*, translated by David Farrell Krell, 2 vols. (San Francisco: Harper and Row, 1969). Other serious analyses followed. I will mention only Karl Löwith's *Nietzsche's Philosophy of the Eternal Recurrence of the Same* (Berkeley: University of California Press, 1997), Gilles Deleuze's *Nietzsche and Philosophy* (New York: Columbia University Press, 1983), Sarah Kofman's *Nietzsche and Metaphor* (Stanford: Stanford University Press, 1993), Arthur Danto's *Nietzsche as Philosopher* (New York: Columbia University Press, 1965), Bernd Magnus's *Nietzsche's Existential Imperative* (Bloomington: Indiana University Press, 1978), Laurence Lampert's *Nietzsche's Teaching* (New Haven: Yale University Press, 1986), Tracy Strong's *Friedrich Nietzsche and the Politics of Transfiguration* (Berkeley: University of California Press, 1975), and Alexander Nehamas's *Nietzsche: Life as Literature* (Cambridge, Mass.: Harvard University Press, 1975). There are many other good commentaries on Nietzsche. Nietzsche scholarship is rich and varied; and it has always been a hornet's nest of controversy, or worse. There are several good places to get a rundown on the current state of contested interpretations; it is necessary to view these as well in the context of the great historical misappropriation of Nietzsche by the Nazis, a crime and an error that still lingers. See first Walter Kaufmann's commentaries on his brilliant translations of Nietzsche's works and his book, *Nietzsche: Philosopher, Psychologist, Antichrist* (Princeton: Princeton University Press, 1974). For more contemporary controversies, see especially the introductory chapters in Bernd Magnus, Stanley Stewart, and Jean-Pierre Mileur, *Nietzsche's Case* (New York: Routledge, 1993); Robert Solomon and Kathleen Higgens, eds., *Reading Nietzsche* (Oxford: Oxford University Press, 1988), and those in Bernd Magnus and Kathleeen Higgens, eds., *The Cambridge Companion to Nietzsche* (Cambridge: Cambridge University Press, 1996.) For especially the current European response to Nietzsche, see *The New Nietzsche*, Edited by David B. Allison (Cambridge, Mass.: MIT Press, 1995). Most Nietzsche scholars make some mention of how they see their own commentaries fitting into the very live struggle between analytical-philosophical approaches to Nietzsche and European, literary, deconstructive, or poststructuralist approaches. There is also a serious division among scholars about the use and importance of Nietzsche's unpublished notes, the *Nachlass*, or literary estate. The best discussion of this is Bernd Magnus's "The Use and Abuse of the *Will to Power*," in Solomon and Higgens, *Reading Nietzsche*. My tendency is to take with more than a grain of salt all analyses, however brilliant, which rely primarily on the unpublished sources.

2. Friedrich Nietzsche, *Thus Spoke Zarathustra* (Parts I–III, 1884; Parts I–IV, 1891), translated by Walter Kaufmann, in *The Portable Nietzsche*, edited by Walter Kaufmann. (New York: Viking, 1969) 439.

3. See Kathleen M. Higgens, "An Ad Hominen Introduction," *Nietzsche's Zarathustra* (Philadelphia: Temple University Press, 1987), 11. Good accounts of Nietzsche's life can be found in most works on Nietzsche. See also Ronald Hayman, *Nietzsche: A Critical Life* (New York: Oxford University Press, 1980).

4. Friedrich Nietzsche, *The Birth of Tragedy*, translated by Walter Kaufmann and R. J. Hollingdale (New York: Random House, 1957), and idem, *On the Genealogy of Morals*, translated by Walter Kaufmann and R. J. Hollingdale (New York: Random House, 1967).

5. Nietzsche, *The Birth of Tragedy*, 3, 19. See Kaufmann's introduction and notes.

6. Nietzsche, *Birth*, 20, 21. Emphasis in the original. All emphases will be in the original unless otherwise indicated.

7. Ibid., 21.

8. Ibid., 21–22.

9. Ibid., 22, 52.

10. Ibid., 22.

11. Letter to Heinrich von Stein, December 1882, in *Selected Letters of Friedrich Nietzsche*, edited and translated by Christopher Middleton (Chicago: University of Chicago Press, 1969), 197–98.

12. Sophocles, *Oedipus at Colonus*, lines 1224ff. Quoted in Nietzsche, *Birth*, 42.

13. Friedrich Nietzsche, *The Gay Science*, translated and with commentary by Walter Kaufmann (New York: Vintage, 1974), sec. 120, 176–77.

14. Nietzsche, *Birth*, 40.

15. Ibid., 39–41.

16. Ibid., 43.

17. Ibid., 44

18. Ibid., 45.

19. Ibid., 45.

20. I am not interpreting *The Birth of Tragedy* as a kind of Hegelian dialectical story of the opposition of suffering and life, Dionysus versus Apollo, the unity of culture versus individuation, all resolved in a tragic reconciliation of opposites that transforms both. Gilles Deleuze has given a fine critique of this dialectical interpretation in *Nietzsche and Philosophy* (New York: Columbia University Press, 1962) 8-14. While Nietzsche later expressed his opinion in *Ecce Homo*, translated by Walter Kaufmann (New York: Vintage, 1967), III, 270, that book was too Hegelian and Schopenhauerian, I am looking for a deeper interpretation that far exceeds those influences. The best understanding of Nietzsche as an artistic perspectivist is Alexander Nehamas's *Nietzsche: Life as Literature* (Cambridge: Cambridge University Press, 1975).

21. Nietzsche, *Birth*, 45–46.

22. Ibid., 55–56.

23. Ibid., 59. We will come back to the "Buddhistic" negation of the will in our discussion of the will to power and eternal recurrence. Nietzsche understanding of Buddhism is somewhat superficial.

24. Ibid., 65.

25. Ibid., 72.

26. See especially Friedrich Nietzsche, "The Problem of Socrates," in *Twilight of the Idols* (London: Penguin, 1968), 39–44. There is a large literature on Nietzsche's relationship to Socrates. See especially Werner Dannhauser, *Nietzsche's View of Socrates* (Ithaca: Cornell University Press, 1974); Walter Kaufmann, *Nietzsche: Philosopher, Psychologist, Antichrist* (New York: Vintage, 1950); Aryeh Botwinick, *Skepticism, Belief and the Modern* (Ithaca: Cornell University Press, 1997); and Alexander Nehamas, *Nietzsche: Life as Literature* (Cambridge, Mass.: Harvard University Press, 1985). Many major works on Nietzsche as philosopher relate him to Socrates. For an especially enjoyable view, see David Farrell Krell, *Infectious Nietzsche* (Bloomington: Indiana University Press, 1996), especially ch. 4.

27. Nietzsche, *Birth*, 84.

28. Ibid., 87.

29. One of the best philosophical discussions of Nietzsche's attack on Socratism is to be found in Randall Havas, *Nietzsche's Genealogy: Nihilism and the Will to Knowledge* (Ithaca: Cornell University Press, 1995). Havas wants to avoid a Schopenhauerian interpretation of suffering as the concern that human misery is somehow inevitable or unavoidable, for either tragedy or Nietzsche. I concur with this analysis. I am arguing that "making sense of our lives" does have to do with suffering, but not with its unavoidability. The pain of surgery is unavoidable, but it makes complete sense. The kind of suffering we are concerned with here is the kind that not only does not make sense but cannot, according to Nietzsche, make sense, at least in the Socratic sense. Havas argues that "making sense of our lives" does involve the authority of culture, although he interprets this very narrowly in terms of speaking and being intelligible.

30. Nietzsche, *Birth*, 87.

31. Ibid., 88.

32. Ibid., 89.

33. Ibid., 91.

34. Ibid., 93.

35. Ibid., 95–96.

36. Friedrich Nietzsche, *Thus Spoke Zarathustra*, translated by Walter Kaufmann (New York: Viking, 1968); *On the Genealogy of Morals*, translated by Walter Kaufmann and R. J. Hollingdale (New York: Vintage, Random House, 1989); *Beyond Good and Evil*, translated by Walter Kaufmann (New York: Random House, 1966).

CHAPTER 10. ON THE GENEALOGY OF MORALS

1. Anaximander, fragment 1, in Philip Wheelright, *The Pre-Socratics* (New York: Odyssey, 1966), 34.

2. I am especially indebted to Edith Wyschogrod's *An Ethics of Remembering: History, Heterology and the Nameless Others* (Chicago: University of Chicago Press, 1998) for helping me to unravel the intricacies of modern and postmodern notions of time and of Nietzsche's perspective in relation to those of other contemporary philosophers, from Kant to Derrida. I will make clear my agreements and disagreements with her account when we get there.

3. Nietzsche, *The Gay Science*, Bk. 5, sec. 357, 306.

4. Friedrich Nietzsche, *Human, All Too Human*, translated by R. J. Hollingdale (Cambridge: Cambridge University Press, 1986), sec. 25, 25. Emphasis in the original.

5. Nietzsche, *The Gay Science*, sec. 125, 183.

6. Ibid., sec. 125, 183; sec. 108, 167.

7. This version of God's death reminds us of Freud's famous tale of the primal horde and the killing of the Father, in *Totem and Taboo*. Freud famously denied that he had read Nietzsche, which no one believes. Nietzsche also gives us other interpretations of God's death, among them that God died of pity for man.

8. Nietzsche, *Genealogy*, 19.

9. Ibid., 20.

10. Some of the best thoughts on the question of the "ground" of geneaology are to be found in David Farrell Krell's wonderful book, *Infectious Nietzsche* (Bloomington: Indiana University Press, 1996), chs. 1–3.

11. Deleuze, in his brilliant *Nietzsche and Philosophy*, does much to explain the intricacies of active versus reactive forces and affirmative versus negative wills. He ends up absolutizing and typologizing these qualities of forces into what I think is too fixed a system of categories, very like a permanent metapsychology, the very spirit of what Nietzsche repudiates. Krell's critical questions about the grounds, or lack of them, the suspicion of all grounding in Nietzsche's genealogy applies here as well. Deleuze is at pains to separate high and low, active and reactive, affirmative and negative and to keep them apart, insisting that "geneaology . . . is attack, not vengeance." But genealogy is both active and reactive, as Nietzsche makes clear. Krell reminds us of the "*necessity of the necessarily illusory* supersensible world" (15). Deleuze acknowledges that "the spirit of vengeance is the genealogical element of *our* thought, the transcendental principle of *our* manner of thinking" (40), condemning all our history and philosophy and science to vengeful nihilism. This is one aspect of what Nietzsche is telling us, but not the whole of it, as we will see. And, with Krell, we still feel the need to ask, "Our

thought? our manner? but whose "ours?" (27). Genealogical critique always doubles back on itself, it always turns its reflective blade finally against itself. It has no stopping place, to way to go to ground. However much he condemns *ressentiment*, bad conscience, and the ascetic ideal, Nietzsche is fatally, profoundly interested in the deeper question of how and why this reversal of instinct serves life, and he demonstrates why we must be so also.

12. Nietzsche, *Genealogy*, 26.

13. Friedrich Nietzsche, *The Will to Power*, translated by Walter Kaufmann and R. J. Hollingdale (New York: Random House, Vintage, 1968), 76.

14. Nietzsche, *The Gay Science*, sec. 120, 176–77.

15. Nietzsche, *The Will to Power*, 29.

16. Ibid., 69.

17. See, for instance, Mark Warren, *Nietzsche and Political Thought* (Cambridge, Mass.: MIT Press, 1988).

18. Nietzsche, *The Will to Power*, 38–39.

19. Nietzsche, *Genealogy*, I, 7, 33.

20. Ibid., 6, 33. It is still fair to ask why Nietzsche calls this morality slavish, vile, and base. There are many levels to an answer to this question, but one that deserves to be mentioned has to do with the subjugation of instinct, the mastery of unruly, disruptive, murderous desires, the enforced command to cease, constrict, and constrain power, energy, force, a command that comes from without by the power of others, and then from within. It is a reactive response to what is done to one and what is required of one. It is an unconscious reaction; but then Nietzsche sees all important actions and reactions as unconscious. In the second and third essays of the *Genealogy*, Nietzsche will show how this discipline is created and will analyze its value. But he calls this impulse "slavish" to throw into relief the fear and rage that accompanies it, the cries stifled, the ferocity swallowed, the twisting of instinct and the cunning of intellect needed to compensate for the raw fact of domination and submission and the hatred it causes. The history that makes us moral beings is a cruel and slavish one because it necessitates self-mutilation, the torment and deformation of instinct and will that civilization requires. Nietzsche calls for a certain kind of recognition from us, pre-Freudian but still familiar, that we are all, after all, slaves and the descendants of slaves from childhood on. We all begin as children. We are psychologically, morally, owned. While we may come in time to liberate ourselves, it is a long struggle at which few entirely succeed. We feel like slaves, and for Nietzsche, affect is determinate.

21. Nietzsche, *Genealogy*, I, 13, 44–45.

22. Ibid., 7, 33. Nietzsche in many places asserts his personal knowledge of the instincts and motivations he is criticizing: "Need I say after all this that in questions of decadence I am experienced?" *Ecce Homo*, I, 1, 223.

23. Nietzsche, *Genealogy*, I, 9, 33–34.

24. Ibid., 8–9, 34–35.

25. Ibid., 10, 36.

26. Ibid., 19, 38.

27. Ibid., 11, 40.

28. Ibid., 11–12, 43–44. Nietzsche is not "ambivalent" toward morality, conscience, or ascetic ideals, as Peter Berkowitz argues in his Neo-Platonic rendition of Nietzsche in *Nietzsche: The Ethics of an Immoralist* (Cambridge, Mass.: Harvard University Press, 1995), 97. Philosophers, it seems, can't get over the lack of a straight argument. Nietzsche is not interested in straight, logical arguments; he is always interested in showing both sides of a phenomenon, its contradictory implications, both sides real.

29. Nietzsche, *Genealogy*, I, 13, 45.

30. Nietzsche, *The Gay Science*, 370, 328.

31. Nietzsche, *Genealogy*, II, 1, 57.

32. Ibid., 1, 58.

33. Ibid., 1, 58.

34. Ibid., 1, 58.

35. Ibid., 1, 61.

36. Ibid., 3, 61.

37. Ibid., 3, 61.

38. Ibid., 6, 65.

39. Ibid., I, 16, 53–54.

40. Ibid., II, 6, 66.

41. Ibid., 7, 67–68.

42. I thank Stephen Schenk for this connection, in a personal communication.

43. Nietzsche, *Genealogy*, III, 28, 163.

44. Ibid., II, 1, 2, 58–59.

45. Randall Havas, *Nietzsche's Genealogy* (Ithaca: Cornell University Press, 1995), 210.

46. Nietzsche, *Genealogy*, II, 3, 60.

47. Ibid., 8, 70.

48. The best explication of Nietzsche's critique of metaphysics and science belongs, I think, to Deleuze, *Nietzsche and Philosophy*. "His whole critique operates on three levels; against logical identity, against mathematical equality and against physical equilibrium" (45). Deleuze's chapter on critique is important for relating critique to will to power. But see also Babette E. Babich, *Nietzsche's Philosophy of Science: Reflecting Science on the Ground of Art and Life* (Albany: State University of New York Press, 1994) and Maudmarie Clark, *Nietzsche on Truth and Philosophy* (Cambridge: Cambridge University Press, 1990).

49. Nietzsche, *Genealogy*, II, 10, 72.

50. Ibid., 11, 74.

51. Ibid., 11, 76.

52. Ibid., 11, 76.

53. Ibid., 12–13, 77–78.

54. Ibid., 12–13, 77, 80.

55. Gilles Deleuze and Felix Guattari, *What Is Philosophy?* (New York: Columbia University Press, 1991), 8.

56. Nietzsche, *Genealogy*, II, 16, 84.

57. Ibid., 16, 84.

58. Ibid., 16, 84–85.

59. Nietzsche, *The Gay Science*, sec. 337, 268.

60. I agree with Havas that the argument sometimes made that his attack on pity is just a part of his attack on all the "unegoistic virtues" is false. Richard Schacht reads Nietzsche this way in *Nietzsche* (Boston: Routledge and Kegan Paul, 1983), 359–62. Havas is right to see that pity goes beyond a mere psychological error, and that Nietzsche's attack on it is central to his critique of morality itself; he thinks of pity as in some ways the essence of the moral point of view. Nevertheless, Havas himself develops a narrow reading of what Nietzsche's endorsement of suffering might mean.

61. Nietzsche, *Beyond Good and Evil*. Quoted in Havas, *Nietzsche's Genealogy*, 213.

62. Havas, *Nietzsche's Genealogy*, 214–17.

63. Nietzsche, *The Gay Science*, 338, 270.

64. Bernd Magnus, *Nietzsche's Case* (New York: Routledge, 1993), 30.

65. Nietzsche, *Genealogy*, III, 28, 162.

66. Ibid., 6, 106.

67. Ibid., 12, 119. Nietzsche's perspectivism and its relation to his theory of truth, if it can be argued that he has such a theory, is highly controversial. Some of his early unpublished writings on the subject can be found in Friedrich Nietzsche, *Philosophy and Truth*, edited and translated by Daniel Breazeale (Atlantic Highlands, N.J.: Humanities, 1979). Important passages on these questions are also to be found in *Beyond Good and Evil*. Many worthy commentators have argued about Nietzsche's philosophical conception of truth and his critique of traditional philosophical theories, as well as his perspectivism and the will to power as will to knowledge. See especially Alexander Nehamas, *Nietzsche: Life as Literature* (Cambridge, Mass.: Harvard University Press, 1985); Maudemarie Clark, *Nietzsche on Truth and Philosophy* (Cambridge: Cambridge University Press, 1990); Arthur C. Danto, *Nietzsche as Philosopher* (New York: Columbia University Press, 1965); Havas, *Nietzsche's Genealogy*, as well as Deleuze's chapter on critique. On the other hand, see Sarah Kofman's *Nietzsche and Metaphor* for a stunning analy-

sis that takes truth apart on the basis of the fundamental elements of impulse, metaphor, and style in Nietzsche.

68. Nietzsche, *Genealogy*, III, 13, 120; 15, 125–26.
69. Ibid., 14, 122.
70. Ibid., 14, 122.
71. Nietzsche, *The Will to Power*, 38.
72. Nietzsche, *Genealogy*, III, 15, 127.
73. Ibid., 17, 18, 130–35.
74. Ibid., 19, 136; 20, 140.
75. Ibid., 20, 140–41.
76. Ibid., 24, 151.
77. Ibid., 25, 152-53.
78. Ibid., 25, 155.
79. Ibid., 27, 160.
80. Ibid., 27, 161.
81. Ibid.

CHAPTER 11. THE WILL TO POWER
AND THE WILL TO NOTHINGNESS

1. Friedrich Nietzsche, *The Gay Science,* translated by Walter Kaufmann (New York: Vintage, 1974), V, 343, 279–80.
2. Friedrich Nietzsche, *The Will to Power*, translated by Walter Kaufmann and R. J. Hollingdale (New York: Vintage, 1968), III, 585B, 319.
3. Nietzsche, *The Will to Power,* 617, 331.
4. Ibid., I, 1.
5. Nietzsche, *Ecce Homo*, "Destiny," 4, 329.
6. Kaufmann, in Nietzsche, *Ecce Homo*, "Destiny," 4, 330, note 9.
7. Nietzsche, *Ecce Homo*, "Destiny," 7, 332.
8. Nietzsche, *The Will to Power*, I, 1–5.
9. Nietzsche, *The Gay Science*, V, 344, 383.
10. See Deleuze, *Nietzsche and Philosophy*, especially his second chapter, "Active and Reactive." It is a mark of how this fixed dualism leads Deleuze astray that he ends up misconstruing eternal recurrence as entirely positive, "the small, petty, reactive man will not recur" (71). As I hope to make clear in the following chapter, this is wishful thinking. Eternal recurrence is not selective, especially in that way. It is precisely the eternal return of the last man that Zarathustra finds so intolerable.
11. Nietzsche, *Zarathustra*, II, 111.
12. Deleuze, *Nietzsche and Philosophy*, 85.
13. Nietzsche, *The Will to Power*, 365.
14. Ibid., 635.

15. Nietzsche, *The Gay Science*, 317. Quoted in Strong, *Transfiguration*, 233.

16. Strong, *Transfiguration*, 233–34.

17. We might also reply with Nietzsche to Strong's interpretation of Rousseau that it is not our lot that we not age, that we not die. We do suffer time, in both these ways and many others. Time is both necessary and inevitable to us. Why would we wish that away?

18. Nietzsche, *The Will to Power*, 493.

19. Nietzsche, *Genealogy*, III, 25, 153.

20. Nietzsche, *The Will to Power*, III, 298.

21. Ibid., 299.

22. Krell, *Infectious Nietzsche*, 15.

23. Nietzsche, "On the Pathos of Truth." Quoted in Krell, *Infectious Nietzsche*, 32. This is not quite the version of that fable in that essay as published in Nietzsche, *Philosophy and Truth*, 61.

24. Friedrich Nietzsche, *Twilight of the Idols*, translated by R. J. Hollingdale (London: Penguin, 1990), 50–51.

25. Ibid., 50–51.

26. See especially Edith Wychogrod, *An Ethics of Remembering*, for what this reality portends for the "heterological historian." And see, of course, Jean Baudrillard, *The Ecstasy of Communication*, translated by Bernard and Caroline Schutz (New York: Semiotexte, Automedia, 1988).

27. Nietzsche, *The Will to Power*, III, 579, 310–11.

28. Ibid., 579, 311.

29. Ibid.

30. Krell, *Infectious Nietzsche*, 34–35, quoting Nietzsche, *Zarathustra*, II, 4, 146–49.

31. Nietzsche, *Zarathustra*, II, 4, 148.

32. Krell, *Infectious Nietzsche*, 68.

33. Nietzsche, *The Gay Science*. Quoted in Krell, *Infectious Nietzsche*, 17–18.

34. Krell, *Infectious Nietzsche*, 37.

35. Nietzsche, *The Will to Power*, III, 576–77, 309–10.

36. Ibid., 336.

37. Ibid., 482. In this section I will be following Sarah Kofman's *Nietzsche and Metaphor*, which I think is the best and clearest exposition of Nietzsche's theories of language. Eric Blondel's *Nietzsche: The Body and Culture*, translated by Seán Hand (Stanford: Stanford University Press, 1986) is also very suggestive and useful. On the other hand, D. Conway's *Nietzsche's Dangerous Game* (Cambridge: Cambridge University Press, 1997) goes too far in literalizing what he calls Nietzsche's "vitalism," which flows through "macro-capacitators" and "micro-capacitators." One can only shudder to imagine

Nietzsche's reaction to such felicities of language. Conway sometimes takes an edgy and contemptuous tone toward Nietzsche. Like too many academic philosophers, he searches for a linear logic in Nietzsche and then heaps scorn on him for lacking one, precisely missing the point.

38. Nietzsche, *Daybreak*. Quoted in Krell, *Infectious Nietzsche*, 44.

39. Nietzsche, *Twilight of the Idols*, 6, 48.

40. Kofman, *Nietzsche and Metaphor*, 8.

41. Nietzsche, *Twilight of the Idols*. Quoted in ibid., 11.

42. Nietzsche, *The Gay Science*, 84, 138–39.

43. Kofman, *Nietzsche and Metaphor*, 14–15.

44. Ibid., 24. We will return to this "return of the repressed" in the thought of eternal return in Nietzsche's work and its importance for theory thereafter.

45. See especially Nietzsche, *Zarathustra*, III, chs. 10–12, and Lampert's commentary on values, in Lampert, *Nietzsche's Teaching*, 192–94.

46. Nietzsche, *The Will to Power*. Quoted in Kofman, *Nietzsche and Metaphor*, 26.

47. Kofman, *Nietzsche and Metaphor*, 33.

48. Nietzsche, *Beyond Good and Evil*, 159–60.

49. See Nietzsche, *The Gay Science*, 354, 311, and also Kofman's note 16, ch. 3, 158–59, which distinguishes this origin of language from Rousseau's and situates it in Nietzsche's oeuvre.

50. Nietzsche, "The Philosopher" in Breazeale, *Philosophy and Truth*, 149.

51. Nietzsche, *The Will to Power*, 22, 32.

52. Nietzsche, "On Truth and Lies in a Nonmoral Sense," in Breazeale, *Truth and Philosophy*, 84.

53. Nietzsche, *The Will to Power*, III, 303.

54. Blondel, *Body and Culture*, 68.

55. Nietzsche, *Beyond Good and Evil*, 225.

56. Nietzsche's sister Elisabeth was his own worst enemy in this regard. On the other hand, Tracy Strong, in *Friedrich Nietzsche and the Politics of Transfiguration*, and Mark Warren, in *Nietzsche and Political Thought*, have done the most to rehabilitate Nietzsche in a progressive political direction by means of interpretations of the conditions of agency and eternal return. I have great sympathy with these efforts, but both authors seem to offer a tame Nietzsche, one without the cutting edge that the will to power has to have in any conception of Nietzsche's politics. Warren does a good job of severing Nietzsche's constructions of agency and responsibility from his "reactionary" political positions, but only at the cost of distorting the radicalness of Nietzsche's actual politics. Strong, in his article "Nietzsche's Political Aesthetics," in *Nietzsche's New Seas*, really reaches for an overtly political Nietzsche from

his last desperate days, without apparently recognizing the ubiquitously political Nietzsche of the will to power. See also Leslie Paul Thiele, *Friedrich Nietzsche and the Politics of the Soul* (Princeton: Princeton University Press, 1990) and Keith Ansell-Pearson, *Nietzsche Contra Rousseau* (Cambridge: Cambridge University Press, 1991) for valuable efforts to come to grips with Nietzsche's politics, neither entirely successful. I will attempt a more comprehensive coming to grips with Nietzsche's political commentators in my "Nietzsche's Antipolitics: The Will to Power and the Will to Nothingness," forthcoming.

57. Tracy Strong, in "Nietzsche's Political Misappropriation," in Magnus and Higgens, *The Cambridge Comapanion to Nietzsche*, 119–47, 125, presents a survey of various "misappropriations" of Nietzsche for nefarious political purposes. As I say above, I think that misses the point of Nietzsche—all interpretations are will to power, appropriations for political purposes, and which ones miss and which don't depends on the reader's own purposes. From what perspective one may draw the line against interpretations that are "beyond the pale" will be considered in the next chapter.

58. Nietzsche, *The Will to Power*, III, 643, 342.

59. Ibid., 617, 330.

60. Ibid., 616, 330.

61. Ibid., 675, 356.

62. Ibid., 717, 384.

63. Warren, *Nietzsche and Political Thought*, ch. 7.

64. For a more detailed and rigorous discussion of the relation among suffering, subject-formation, and power, see my "Suffering, Subjection, and Subject-Formation in Nietzsche, Foucault and Butler," forthcoming.

65. Nietzsche, *The Will to Power*, III, 7, 287.

66. For an important discussion of the place of rights in contemporary social theory, see Wendy Brown, *States of Injury: Power and Freedom in Late Modernity* (Princeton: Princeton University Press, 1995), ch. 2. See also the interesting critique of her position by Kenneth Baynes and Brown's effective response to it in Kennth Baynes, "Rights as Critique and the Critique of Rights: Karl Marx, Wendy Brown and the Social Function of Rights," and Wendy Brown, "Revaluing Critique: A Response to Kenneth Baynes," in *Political Theory*, vol. 28, no. 4 (August 2000): 451–80.

67. See, for instance, Ruth Abbey and Frederick Appel, "Nietzsche and the Will to Politics," *Review of Politics*, vol. 60, (1998): 83–114. The authors run down all the different commentators on Nietzsche as to whether they classify him as "political" or "antipolitical," using the most superficial understanding of what the political is. They pull quotations out of *Beyond Good and Evil* and *The Will to Power*, mostly, to argue for a Nietzsche who desires world domination by an elitist power aristocracy, forever ruling the herd. It's not that no such Nietzsche ever existed—that is surely one of the most

dramatic of his possible incarnations. But it trivializes the issues and doesn't settle anything of importance about Nietzsche or politics.

68. See especially Hannah Arendt, *On Revolution* (New York: Viking, 1965); Bonnie Honig, *Political Theory and the Displacement of Politics* (Ithaca: Cornell University Press, 1993); and Dana Villa, *Arendt, Heidegger and the Fate of the Political* (Princeton: Princeton University Press, 1996).

69. Nietzsche, *Genealogy,* II, 12.

70. But see my "Nietzsche's Politics: Theory and Practice in Postmodern Turmoil," forthcoming.

71. Nietzsche, *Beyond Good and Evil,* 242, 176–77.

72. Nietzsche, *The Will to Power,* I, 55, 38.

73. Nietzsche, *Beyond Good and Evil,* 188, 77.

74. See Nietzsche, *Zarathustra,* II, 18, 20; see also *Beyond Good and Evil* 285, *Twilight of the Idols,* "Morality," 3, and *Gay Science* 4.

75. Lampert, *Nietzsche's Teaching,* 134–35.

76. Nietzsche, *Beyond Good and Evil,* 262, 159–60.

77. I thank Simon Critchley for this reference to Laurence Sterne in a related context, "Metaphysics in the Dark," *Political Theory,* vol. 26, no. 6 (December 1998): 803–17.

CHAPTER 12. THE ETERNAL RECURRENCE OF THE SAME

1. Friedrich Nietzsche, *Twilight of the Idols,* translated by Walter Kaufmann (New York: Random House, 1968), 6, 96–97.

2. See Nietzsche, *Genealogy,* III, 20; *The Antichrist,* secs. 29–35; and *Twilight of the Idols,* sec. 6.

3. David Farrell Krell, *Infectious Nietzsche* (Bloomington: Indiana University Press, 1996), 75.

4. The difficulties of interpreting Nietzsche's doctrine of eternal recurrence are notorious and legion. Wyschogrod quotes a caveat expressed by Joan Stambaugh with respect to any discussion of eternal return. "Commenting on 'the intricacies, abysses and virtually insoluble problems,' that arise in pondering the eternal recurrence, she warns: 'Anyone who has tried long enough to grope his way around that philosophical terrain often returns from it as something far worse than the 'burnt child' [of the three metamorphoses in Zarathustra] and begins to fear that the element of recurrence is taking place precisely in his own desperate attempts to make sense of that doctrine.'" See Joan Stambaugh, *The Other Nietzsche* (Albany: State University of New York Press, 1994), 62. Quoted in Edith Wyschogrod, *Ethics of Remembering* (Chicago: University of Chicago Press, 1998), 265.

5. Friedrich Nietzsche, *Ecce Homo,* translated by Walter Kaufmann, (New York: Random House, 1967), "Zarathustra," 1, 295.

6. Nietzsche, *The Gay Science*, 341, 273–74. There is enormous scholarly controversy over how to interpret the doctrine of eternal recurrence of the same. Scholars tend to think of it either as a cosmological doctrine that recounts the literal recurrence of each moment of time over and over again in cosmic cycles, or as an ethical or existential imperative (understood in either a Kantian or poststructuralist way) that guides the life of the actor by the thought that everything he does should be considered in the light of its eternal recurrence and judged as to whether it should be enacted in that light. The best interpretation, and the best account of the nature of ongoing conflicting interpretations can be found in Bernd Magnus, Stanley Stewart, and Jean-Pierre Mileur, *Nietzsche's Case* (New York: Routledge, 1993). My interpretation derives from the perspective of suffering, and I think goes deeper than either mere cosmology or ethical imperatives. Eternal return has to answer to the historical and psychological demands of suffering and of nihilism for it to serve the purposes of Nietzsche or of our age.

7. Nietzsche, *Birth of Tragedy*, 3. Quoted in Krell, *Infectious Nietzsche*, 57.

8. Nietzsche, *Zarathustra*, "On Redemption," 251.

9. Ibid., 251–52.

10. Krell, *Infectious Nietzsche*, 61. I am in part following Krell's reading in this chapter, but not his conclusions.

11. Nietzsche, *Zarathustra*, "On Redemption," 251.

12. The formulation is Stambaugh's. Quoted in Krell, *Infectious Nietzsche*, 68.

13. Karl Löwith, *Nietzsche's Philosophy of the Eternal Recurrence of the Same*, translated by J. Harvey Lomax (Berkeley: University of California Press, 1997, first published 1935), 55.

14. Nietzsche. Quoted in ibid., 52.

15. Krell, *Infectious Nietzsche*, 68.

16. Ibid., 68.

17. Nietzsche, *Zarathustra*, "The Wanderer," III, 264.

18. Ibid., 265–66.

19. Nietzsche, *Zarathustra*, "On the Tree on the Mountainside," I, 154, paraphrased in Laurence Lampert, *Nietzsche's Teaching* (New Haven: Yale University Press, 1986), 47.

20. Nietzsche, *Beyond Good and Evil*, 225, 154.

21. Nietzsche, *Zarathustra*, " On The Vision and the Riddle," III, 268. It is the spirit of gravity that is Zarathustra's constant nemesis; it the spirit of gravity that has weighed down the human race with all its sanctity, prudity, and ponderousness, its self-importance. The spirit of gravity is the spirit of religion and morality, not to mention politics. Lampert's analysis of the spirit of gravity is quite fine.

22. Nietzsche, *Zarathustra*, "On the Vision and the Riddle," III, 269.

23. Nietzsche, *Beyond Good and Evil*, 225, 154.

24. Nietzsche, *Zarathustra*, "On the Vision and the Riddle," III, 269–70

25. Nietzsche, *Zarathustra*, "On the Vision and the Riddle," III, 271.

26. Nietzsche, *Ecce Homo*, 5, 6, 303–306.

27. Krell, *Infectious Nietzsche*, 62.

28. See Bernd Magnus, "The Deification of the Commonplace: Twilight of the Idols," in Solomon and Higgens, *Reading Nietzsche*, 152–81, for a splendid commentary on getting caught in trying get out of our finitude again and again.

29. Most commentators on Zarathustra are, intermittently, clear that there is a difference, one that Nietzsche intended, between Nietzsche himself and Zarathustra, at least in principle. They often also confound the two. The clearest unraveling of their complicated relationship can be found in Kathleen Marie Higgens', *Nietzsche's Zarathustra*. See also Gary Shapiro, *Nietzschean Narratives* (Bloomington: Indiana University Press, 1989.) The classic contemporary text on Zarathustra is Lampert's *Nietzsche's Teaching*, which is most valuable. Stanley Rosen's *The Mask of Enlightenment* (Cambridge: Cambridge University Press, 1995) is also very helpful. I try to sort out their respective interpretations in my "Nietzsche: Eternity and Responsibility," forthcoming.

30. Nietzsche, *Ecce Homo*, quoted in Krell, *Infectious Nietzsche*, 62.

31. Nietzsche, *Ecce Homo*, quoted in Krell, *Infectious Nietzsche*, 64, from an unpublished version.

32. Krell, *Infectious Nietzsche*, 64–65.

33. Nietzsche, *Ecce Homo*, quoted in Krell, *Infectious Nietzsche*, 65.

34. Nietzsche, *The Gay Science*, I, 7, 81. See also Blondel, *The Body and Culture*, ch. 6.

35. Nietzsche, *Ecce Homo*, quoted in Krell, 64–65.

36. Nietzsche, *The Will to Power*, III, 708, 378.

37. Krell, *Infectious Nietzsche*, 65.

38. Nietzsche, *The Will to Power*, III, 711, 378–79.

39. Krell, *Infectious Nietzsche*, 66.

40. Albert Camus, *Le mythe de Sisyphe*, quoted in Krell, 66.

41. Krell, *Infectious Nietzsche*, 67.

42. Nietzsche, *The Will to Power*, I, 55, 35–36.

43. Deleuze, *Nietzsche and Philosophy*, 35.

44. Magnus, "Deification of the Commonplace," in *Reading Nietzsche*, 171.

45. Nietzsche, *Ecce Homo*, "Why I am So Clever," 10. Quoted in Magnus, "Deification," 171.

46. Magnus, "Deification," 172.

47. Wyschogrod, *Ethics of Remembering*, 96.

48. Ibid., 68.

49. Maurice Blanchot, *The Writing of the Disaster*, translated by Ann Smock (Lincoln: University of Nebraska Press, 1986), 28. Quoted in Wyschogrod, *Ethics of Remembering*, 140.

50. Nietzsche, *Zarathustra*, III, 2, 234.

51. Deleuze, in *The New Nietzsche*, 86. Quoted in Wyschogrod, *Ethics of Remembering*, 157. But I recommend David Farrell Krell's exquisite working out of Nietzsche's ambivalences about the "sameness" of "the same," in chapter 8 of his *Infectious Nietzsche*.

52. See Wyschogrod, *Ethics of Remembering*, 159. I agree with her criticism of Heidegger's privileging of the future. Her discussion of various ways of theorizing the past, both as stretched and as punctiform, is quite illuminating.

Selected Bibliography

BOOKS

Agemben, Georgio. *Homo Sacer: Sovereign Power and Bare Life.* Translated by Daniel Heller-Roazen. Stanford: Stanford University Press, 1998.

Agemben, Georgio. *Infancy and History: Essays on the Destruction of Experience.* Translated by Liz Heron. New York: Verso, 1993.

Allison, David B., ed. *The New Nietzsche.* Cambridge, Mass.: MIT Press, 1995.

Althaus, Paul. *The Ethics of Martin Luther.* Philadelphia: Fortress, 1972.

Ansell-Pearson, Keith. *Nietzsche Contra Rousseau.* Cambridge: Cambridge University Press, 1991.

Arendt, Hannah. *On Revolution.* New York: Viking, 1965.

Arendt, Hannah. *The Human Condition.* Chicago: University of Chicago Press, 1958.

Aubrey, John. *Brief Lives, Chiefly of Contemporaries, Set Down by John Aubrey, Between the Years 1669 and 1696.* Edited by A. Clark. 2 vols. Oxford: Clarendon, 1898.

Babich, Babette. *Nietzsche's Philosophy of Science: Reflecting Science on the Ground of Art and Life.* Albany: State University of New York Press, 1994.

Baker, Keith Michael. *Inventing the French Revolution.* Cambridge: Cambridge University Press, 1990.

Baudrillard, Jean. *Simulacra and Simulation.* Translated by Sheila Faria Glaser. Ann Arbor: University of Michigan Press, 1994.

Baudrillard, Jean. *The Ecstasy of Communication.* Translated by Bernard and Caroline Schutz. New York: Semiotexte, Automedia, 1988.

Benhabib, Seyla, and Drucilla Cornell, eds. *Feminism as Critique.* Minneapolis, Minnesota: University of Minnesota Press, 1978.

Berkowitz, Peter. *Nietzsche: The Ethics of an Immoralist.* Cambridge, Mass.: Harvard University Press, 1995.

Blanchot, Maurice. *The Writing of the Disaster.* Translated by Ann Smock. Lincoln: University of Nebraska Press, 1986.

Blondel, Eric. *Nietzsche: The Body and Culture.* Translated by Seán Hand. Stanford: Stanford University Press, 1986.

Boltanski, Luc. *Distant Suffering: Morality, Media and Politics.* Translated by Graham Burchell. Stanford: Stanford University Press, 1999.

Botwinick, Aryeh. *Skepticism, Belief and the Modern.* Ithaca: Cornell University Press, 1997.

Botwinick, Aryeh. *Skepticism in Maimonides, Hobbes and Nietzsche.* Ithaca: Cornell University Press, 1997.

Boyle, Marjorie O'Rourke. *Rhetoric and Reform: Erasmus' Civil Dispute with Luther.* Cambridge, Mass.: Harvard University Press, 1983.

Burtt, E. A. *The Metaphysical Foundations of Modern Science.* New York: Doubleday Anchor, 1955.

Cassirer, Ernst. *The Philosophy of the Enlightenment.* Princeton: Princeton University Press, 1951.

Cassirer, Ernst. *The Question of Jean-Jacques Rousseau.* Translated and edited by Peter Gay. Bloomington: Indiana University Press, 1967.

Chartier, Roger. *The Cultural Origins of the French Revolution.* Durham, N.C.: Duke University Press, 1991.

Clark, Maudmarie. *Nietzsche on Truth and Philosophy.* Cambridge: Cambridge University Press, 1990.

Conway, Daniel. *Nietzsche's Dangerous Game.* Cambridge: Cambridge University Press, 1997.

Dannhauser, Werner. *Nietzsche's View of Socrates.* Ithaca: Cornell University Press, 1974.

Danto, Arthur. *Nietzsche as Philosopher.* New York: Columbia University Press, 1965.

Darnton, Robert. *The Forbidden Best-Sellers of Pre-Revolutionary France.* New York: W. W. Norton, 1996.

Deleuze, Gilles. *Nietzsche and Philosophy.* New York: Columbia University Press, 1983.

Deleuze, Gilles, and Felix Guattari. *What is Philosophy?* New York: Columbia University Press, 1991.

Derathé, Robert. *Jean-Jacques Rousseau et la science politique de son temps.* Paris: Vrin, 1970.

Diggens, John P., and Mark E. Kann, eds. *The Problem of Authority in America.* Philadelphia: Temple University Press, 1981.

Dillenberger, John, ed. *Martin Luther: Selections from His Writings.* New York: Doubleday Anchor, 1961.

Ehlstain, Jean Bethke. *Public Man, Private Woman.* Princeton: Princeton University Press, 1981.

Eisenstein, E. *The Printing Press as an Agent.* 2 vols. Cambridge: Cambridge University Press, 1979.

Erikson, Erik. *Young Man Luther.* New York: W. W. Norton, 1958.

Febvre, Lucien, and Henri-Jean Martin. *The Coming of the Book: The Impact of Printing, 1450–1800*. Translated by David Gerard. Edited by Geoffrey Nowell-Smith and David Wootton. London: NLB, 1976.

Foucault, Michel. *Madness and Civilization*. Translated by Richard Howard. New York: Vintage, 1965.

Foucault, Michel. *Power/Knowledge*. Translated and edited by Colin Gordon. New York: Pantheon, 1980.

Foucault, Michel. *The Birth of the Clinic*. Translated by A. M. Sheridan Smith. New York: Vintage, 1975.

Gauchet, Marcel. *The Disenchantment of the World*. Translated by Oscar Burge. Princeton: Princeton University Press, 1997.

Gautier, David. *The Logic of Leviathan*. Oxford: Clarendon, 1969.

Hampton, Jean. *Hobbes and the Social Contract Tradition*. Cambridge: Cambridge University Press, 1986.

Havas, Randall. *Nietzsche's Genealogy: Nihilism and the Will to Knowledge*. Ithaca: Cornell University Press, 1995.

Hayman, Ronald. *Nietzsche: A Critical Life*. New York: Oxford University Press, 1980.

Hazard, Paul. *The European Mind 1680–1715*. Harmondsworth: Penguin, 1964.

Heidegger, Martin. *Nietzsche*. 2 vols. Translated by David Farrell Krell. San Francisco: Harper and Row, 1969.

Higgens, Kathleen. *Nietzsche's Zarathustra*. Philadelphia: Temple University Press, 1987.

Hill, Christopher. *Intellectual Origins of the English Revolution*. Oxford: Clarendon, 1965.

Hill, Christopher. *Milton and the English Revolution*. Harmondsworth: Penguin, 1978.

Hill, Christopher. *The World Turned Upside Down*. Harmondsworth: Penguin, 1975.

Hobbes, Thomas. *Leviathan*. Introduction by Michael Oakeshott. Oxford: Basil Blackwell, 1651.

Hobbes, Thomas. *The English Works of Thomas Hobbes*. 11 vols. Edited by Sir William Molesworth. London: J. Bohn, 1839–45.

Honig, Bonnie. *Political Theory and the Displacement of Politics*. Ithaca: Cornell University Press, 1993.

Horowitz, Asher. *Rousseau: Nature and History*. Toronto: University of Toronto Press, 1987.

Hunt, Lynn. *Politics, Culture and Class in the French Revolution*. Berkeley: University of California Press, 1984.

Johnston, David. *The Rhetoric of Leviathan*. Princeton: Princeton University Press, 1986.

Jones, Kathleen. *Compassionate Authority*. London: Routledge, 1993.

Kaufmann, Walter. *Nietzsche: Philosopher, Psychologist, Antichrist*. Princeton: Princeton University Press, 1974.

Kaufmann, Walter, ed. *The Portable Nietzsche*. New York: Viking, 1969.

Keenan, Thomas. *Fables of Responsibility: Aberrations and Predicaments in Ethics and Politics*. Stanford: Stanford University Press, 1997.

Kellner, Douglas, ed. *Baudrillard: A Critical Reader*. Oxford: Basil Blackwell, 1994.

Koestler, Arthur. *The Sleepwalkers*. London: Hutchinson, 1959.

Kofman, Sarah. *Nietzsche and Metaphor*. Translated by Duncan Large. Stanford: Stanford University Press,1993.

Koyré, Alexander. *From the Closed World to the Infinite Universe*. Baltimore: Johns Hopkins University Press, 1973.

Koyré, Alexander. *The Astronomical Revolution*. Ithaca: Cornell University Press, 1973.

Krell, David Farrell. *Infectious Nietzsche*. Bloomington: Indiana University Press, 1996.

Kuhn, Thomas S. *The Copernican Revolution*. Cambridge, Mass.: Harvard University Press, 1957.

Lampert, Laurence. *Nietzsche's Teaching*. New Haven: Yale University Press, 1986.

Laqueur, Walter. *Making Sex*. Cambridge, Mass.: Harvard University Press, 1990.

Levinas, Emmanuel. *Basic Philosophical Writings*. Edited by Adrian T. Peperzak, Simon Critchley, and Robert Bernasconi. Bloomington and Indianapolis: Indiana University Press, 1996.

Levinas, Emmanuel. *Of God Who Comes to Mind*. Translated by Bettina Bergo. Stanford: Stanford University Press, 1998.

Levinas, Emmanuel. *The Levinas Reader*. Edited by Seán Hand. Oxford: Basil Blackwell, 1989.

Levine, Peter. *Living Without Philosophy: On Narrative, Rhetoric, and Morality*. Albany: State University of New York Press, 1998.

Locke, John. *A Letter on Toleration*. Indianapolis: Hacket, 1983.

Locke, John. *Two Treatises of Government*. Cambridge: Cambridge University Press, 1960.

Löwith, Karl. *Nietzsche's Philosophy of the Eternal Recurrence of the Same*. Translated by J. Harvey Lomax. Berkeley: University of California Press, 1997.

Luther, Martin. *Heidelberg Disputation*. Edited by E. Vogelsang in Luther's *Werke*, 5:338.

Luther, Martin. *Tischreden*. Weimar: Böhlaus Nachfolger, 1912–21.

MacIntyre, Alasdair. *After Virtue*. Notre Dame: University of Notre Dame Press, 1981.

Magnus, Bernd. *Nietzsche's Existential Imperative*. Bloomington: Indiana University Press, 1978.

Magnus, Bernd, and Kathleen Higgens, eds. *The Cambridge Companion to Nietzsche*. Cambridge: Cambridge University Press, 1996.

Magnus, Bernd, Stanley Stewart, and Jean-Pierre Mileur. *Nietzsche's Case: Philosophy as/and Literature*. New York: Routledge, 1993.

Mandrou, Robert. *From Humanism to Science 1480–1700*. Harmondsworth: Penguin, 1978.

McClure, Kirstie M. *Judging Rights: Lockean Politics and the Limits of Consent*. Ithaca: Cornell University Press, 1996.

McGrath, Alister. *Luther's Theology of the Cross*. Oxford: Basil Blackwell, 1985.

Middleton, Christopher, ed. and trans. *Selected Letters of Friedrich Nietzsche*. Chicago: University of Chicago Press, 1969.

Nehamas, Alexander. *Nietzsche: Life as Literature*. Cambridge, Mass.: Harvard University Press, 1975.

Nietzsche, Friedrich. *Beyond Good and Evil*. Translated by Walter Kaufmann. New York: Random House, 1966.

Nietzsche, Friedrich. *Ecce Homo*. Translated by Walter Kaufmann. New York: Vintage, 1967.

Nietzsche, Friedrich. *Human, All Too Human*. Translated by R. J. Hollingdale. Cambridge: Cambridge University Press, 1986.

Nietzsche, Friedrich. *On the Genealogy of Morals*. Translated by Walter Kaufmann and R. J. Hollingdale. New York: Vintage, 1967, 1989.

Nietzsche, Friedrich. *The Birth of Tragedy*. Translated by Walter Kaufmann. New York: Random House, 1957.

Nietzsche, Friedrich. *The Gay Science*. Translated by Walter Kaufmann. New York: Vintage, 1974.

Nietzsche, Friedrich. *The Twilight of the Idols*. Translated by R. J. Hollingdale. London: Penguin, 1990.

Nietzsche, Friedrich. *The Will to Power*. Translated by Walter Kaufmann and R. J. Hollingdale. New York: Random House, Vintage, 1968.

Nietzsche, Friedrich. *Thus Spoke Zarathustra*. Translated by Walter Kaufmann. New York: Viking, 1968.

Okin, Susan Moller. *Women in Western Political Thought*. Princeton: Princeton University Press, 1979.

Olin, John C., James D. Smart, and Robert E. McNally, eds. *Luther, Erasmus, and the Reformation: A Catholic-Protestant Reappraisal*. New York: Fordham University Press, 1969.

Pateman, Carole. *The Sexual Contract.* Stanford: Stanford University Press, 1988.

Pitkin, Hannah. *Fortune is a Woman.* Berkeley: University of California Press, 1984.

Pocock, J. G. A. *The Machiavellian Moment.* Princeton: Princeton University Press, 1975.

Pocock, J. G. A., ed. *Three British Revolutions: 1641, 1688, 1776.* Princeton: Princeton University Press, 1980.

Popkin, Richard. *The History of Scepticism from Erasmus to Spinoza.* Berkeley: University of California Press, 1979.

Porter, J. M. *Luther: Selected Political Writings.* Philadelphia: Fortress, 1974.

Riley, Patrick. *The General Will Before Rousseau: The Transformation of the Divine into the Civic.* Princeton: Princeton University Press, 1986.

Rogers, G. A. J. and Alan Ryan, eds. *Perspectives on Thomas Hobbes.* Oxford: Clarendon 1990.

Rosen, Stanley. *The Mask of Enlightenment.* Cambridge: Cambridge University Press, 1995.

Rossi, Paolo. *Francis Bacon: From Magic to Science.* Translated by Sacha Rabinowitz. Chicago: University of Chicago Press, 1968.

Rousseau, Jean-Jacques. *The Confessions of Jean-Jacques Rousseau.* Translated by J. M. Cohen. Harmondsworth: Penguin Classics, 1954.

Rousseau, Jean-Jacques. *The Discourses and Other Early Political Writings.* Edited and translated by Victor Gourevitch. Cambridge: Cambridge University Press, 1997.

Rousseau, Jean-Jacques. *The Social Contract.* Translated and introduced by Maurice Cranston. London: Penguin, 1968.

Sandel, Michael. *Liberalism and the Limits of Justice.* Cambridge: Cambridge University Press, 1982.

Sawday, Jonathan. *The Body Emblazoned: Dissection and the Human Body in Renaissance Culture.* London: Routledge, 1995.

Schacht, Richard. *Nietzsche.* Boston: Routledge and Kegan Paul, 1983.

Shapiro, Gary. *Nietzschean Narratives.* Bloomington: Indiana University Press, 1989.

Shapiro, Ian. *The Evolution of Rights in Liberal Theory.* Cambridge: Cambridge University Press, 1986.

Skinner, Quentin. *Reason and Rhetoric in the Philosophy of Hobbes.* Cambridge: Cambridge University Press, 1996.

Skinner, Quentin. *The Foundations of Modern Political Thought.* 2 vols. Cambridge: Cambridge University Press, 1978.

Solomon, Robert, and Kathleen Higgens, eds. *Reading Nietzsche.* Oxford: Oxford University Press, 1988.

Sommerville, Johann P. *Thomas Hobbes: Political Ideas in Historical Context*. New York: St. Martin's, 1992.

Sorrell, Tom. *Hobbes*. London: Routledge, 1986.

Sorrell, Tom, ed. *The Cambridge Companion to Hobbes*. Cambridge: Cambridge University Press, 1996.

Stafford, Barbara. *Body Criticism: Imaging the Unseen in Enlightenment Art and Medicine*. Cambridge, Mass.: MIT Press, 1994.

Stallybrass, Peter, and Allon White. *The Politics and Poetics of Transgression*. Ithaca: Cornell University Press, 1986.

Stambaugh, Joan. *The Other Nietzsche*. Albany: State University of New York Press, 1994.

Starobinsky, Jean. *Jean-Jacques Rousseau: La transparance and l'obstacle*. Paris: Presses Universitaires de France, 1957.

Stone, Lawrence. *The Crisis of the English Aristocracy 1558–1641*. Oxford: Oxford University Press, 1965.

Stone, Lawrence. *The Family, Sex, and Marriage in England 1500–1800*. New York: Harper and Row, 1977.

Strong, Tracy. *Friedrich Nietzsche and the Politics of Transfiguration*. Berkeley: University of California Press, 1975.

Strong, Tracy. *Jean-Jacques Rousseau: The Politics of the Ordinary*. London: Sage, 1994.

Thiele, Leslie Paul. *Friedrich Nietzsche and the Politics of the Soul*. Princeton: Princeton University Press, 1990.

Todorov, T. *Frêye bonheur, essai sur Rousseau*. Paris: Hachette, 1985.

Tuck, Richard. *Philosophy and Government 1572–1651*. Cambridge: Cambridge University Press, 1993.

Vesey, G., ed. *Idealism Past and Present*. Cambridge: Cambridge University Press, 1982.

Villa, Dana. *Arendt and Heidegger: The Fate of the Political*. Princeton: Princeton University Press, 1996.

Walzer, Michael. *Spheres of Justice*. New York: Basic Books, 1983.

Walzer, Michael. *The Revolution of the Saints*. New York: Athenian, 1970.

Warren, Mark. *Nietzsche and Political Thought*. Cambridge, Mass.: MIT Press, 1988.

Wheelright, Philip. *The Pre-Socraties*. New York: Odyssey, 1966.

Whitney, Charles. *Francis Bacon and Modernity*. New Haven: Yale University Press, 1986.

Wyschogrod, Edith. *An Ethics of Remembering: History, Heterology and the Nameless Others*. Chicago: University of Chicago Press, 1998.

Wokler, Robert. *Rousseau*. Oxford: Oxford University Press, 1995.

Wolin, Sheldon. *Politics and Vision*. Boston: Little, Brown, 1960.

Zerilli, Linda. *Signifying Women*. Ithaca: Cornell University Press, 1994.

PERIODICAL ARTICLES

Abbey, Ruth, and Frederick Appel. "Nietzsche and the Will to Politics." *Review of Politics,* vol. 60 (1998): 83–114.

Baumgold, Deborah. "Pacifying Politics: Resistance, Violence, and Accountability in Seventeenth-Century Contract Theory." *Political Theory,* vol. 21, no. 1 (February 1993): 6–27.

McClure, Kirshe M. "Difference, diversity and the Limits of Toleration." *Political Theory,* vol. 18, no. 3 (August 1990): 361–91.

Sterne, Laurence. "Metaphysics in the Dark." *Political Theory,* vol. 26, no. 6 (December 1998): 803–17.

Index

311

Revenge, 21, 134; in Christianity, 196; counterwill and, 257; death of God as, 122; imaginary, 196; justice and, 204; liberation from, 257; morality as, 195–199; politics of, 196; spirit of, 254; against the witness, 121, 122, 127

Revolution, 63, 131, 133, 135, 153, 243, 246

Right(s): absolute, 114, 160; of conscience, 116; divine, 45, 49, 239; equalizing, 116; to exist, 213; as force and will, 159; to make promises, 102, 105, 109, 199, 203, 204; meaning of, 159; natural, 159, 204; nature of, 157; political, 51, 105; private, 241; of private property, 116; proof of, 157; of resistance, 48; to self-defense, 114; social order as, 157

Robespierre, Maximilien, 47, 126

Rousseau, Jean-Jacques, 2, 8, 16, 17, 32, 201, 279n23, 283n1; on civil society, 105; as common man, 130; death of God and, 121–129; decadence and, 283n5; on desires, 82; on equality, 104; on the Festival of the Supreme Being, 47; General Will and, 46; on human nature, 61; idealization of original man, 142, 143; on inequality, 116, 129; justification of God by, 127; on morality, 83–84, 124, 131, 148; moral politics of, 123; on pity, 122; political theory of, 78, 122, 130, 131, 135, 157–166; politics of pity and, 12, 17; on revenge against the witness, 121, 122; social contract and, 105, 122; society and, 19, 143; on sovereignty, 49; theory of time, 101; on value of arts and sciences, 96; view on suffering, 18, 33, 129–155

Salvation, 12, 173, 196, 202, 256

Schopenhauer, Arthur, 185

Science, 12; birth of, 57; civil, 89; coherence in, 63; deductive system in, 70; dependence on language, 107; faith in, 222; faith in God and, 185; geometry, 90, 96; goal of, 63; increase in human power from, 64; knowledge and, 47; as knowledge of consequences, 90; modern, 61; moral, 89; natural, 57, 65, 88, 89; new, 65, 70; new knowledge and, 55; nihilism and, 222; opposition to religion, 216; of

politics, 57–73, 70–73, 86–91, 88, 105, 108; post-sceptical, 68; power of, 185; as practical knowledge, 91; rhetoric and, 98; as second nature, 88; as social use of language, 87; truth and, 107, 117; universal knowledge and, 70; will to truth in, 208

Secularism, 29, 30, 31, 35, 38

Sedition, 77, 79

Self: as agent of change, 76–80; appreciation, 86; art of, 184; common, 163; as constituted by social processes of history, 131; cultured, 131; deception, 221; denial, 180; development of, 58; dissociations of, 13, 14; divided, 40; "educated," 102; interest, 71; interiorization of, 40; as knower, 4, 76–80; memory and, 201; natural, 131; original, 102; perfecting, 138; personal, 40; preservation, 15, 16, 82, 100, 111; private, 112; recognition, 147; social, 40, 131; subjective, 40, 41, 132; as subject of language, 4; submission to society, 113; suffering, 99–108, 150–155; sufficiency, 160; unity of, 151

Shapiro, Ian, 116

Silenus, 176, 254

Simultaneity, 191–195

Sin: as bad conscience, 215; freedom and, 37; before God, 29; guilt and, 43; last, 208; original, 3, 28, 54, 135; pity as, 168, 208; predestined, 54; punishment for, 43, 124; suffering and, 56

Skepticism, 68, 216; Hobbesian version of, 69; in theology, 36

Skinner, Quentin, 35, 37, 42, 47, 48, 49, 50, 93, 97

Slavery, 153, 157, 158, 159, 189, 190, 195, 196, 245; *ressentiment* of, 21

Smith, Adam, 17, 133, 154

Social: actors, 131; classes, 132, 135, 190, 245; coexistence, 18; collectivity, 104; development, 93, 135, 140; dishonesty, 130; distress, 221; ego, 136; equality, 205; evolution, 144; existence, 38, 109, 200; humanity, 202; individuality, 151; inequality, 129, 130; injuries, 88; institutions, 63, 130, 140, 164; interdependence, 140; justice, 127, 155, 157–166, 283n5; labor, 151; morality, 149, 202; oppression, 132; order, 60, 157; pacts,